THE
BEST
OF
Gourmet

THE
BEST
OF
Gourmet
1990 EDITION

ALL OF THE BEAUTIFULLY
ILLUSTRATED MENUS FROM 1989
PLUS OVER 500 SELECTED RECIPES

FROM THE EDITORS OF GOURMET

CONDÉ NAST BOOKS

RANDOM HOUSE

NEW YORK

LIBRARY OF CONGRESS CATALOGING-IN-PUBLICATION DATA
(Revised for vol. 5)

Main entry under title:
The Best of Gourmet.
    Includes Indexes
    1. Cookery, International. I. Gourmet.
TX725.A1B4827   1986   641.5   87-640167
ISBN 0-394-55258-X (v.1)
ISBN 0-394-56039-6 (v.2)
ISBN 0-394-56955-5 (v.3)
ISBN 0-394-57529-6 (v.4)
ISBN 0-394-58321-3 (v.5)

ISSN 1046-1760
Most of the recipes in this work were previously published in *Gourmet* Magazine.

Manufactured in the United States of America

98765432   24689753   23456789

First Edition

Grateful acknowledgment is made to the following for permission to reprint recipes previously published in *Gourmet* Magazine.

Faye Levy: "Crab Meat and Couscous Salad with Mint Vinaigrette" (page 190); "Broiled Salmon with Leek and Dill Sauce" (page 121); "Snapper with Fresh Tomato Sauce and Basil Butter" (page 122); "Steamed Sole with Vegetables and Sage Vinaigrette" (page 124). Copyright © 1989 by Faye Levy. Reprinted by permission of the author.

Shirley Sarvis: "Compote Domaine Tempier" (page 244); "Dandelion Salad with Pine Nuts and Coppa" (page 195); "Fettuccine with Pine Nuts, Prosciutto, and Brown Butter" (page 166); "Pignoli Ice Cream" (page 239). Copyright © 1989 Shirley Sarvis. Reprinted by permission of the author.

Richard Sax: "Coffee Coffeecake with Espresso Glaze" (page 216); "Country Ham Patties with Red-eye Sour Cream Gravy" (page 147); "Lamb Brochettes with Savory Coffee Glaze" (page 148); "Rose's Legendary Honey Cake" (page 217). Copyright © 1989 Richard Sax. Reprinted by permission of the author.

The editors would like to thank the following illustrators for their contributions to *The Best of Gourmet—1990*: Barbara Fiore, Lauren Jarrett, Jeanne Meinke, Jenni Oliver, and Michael Rosen.

PROJECT STAFF

For Condé Nast Books

Jane J. Fisher, Director
Lorraine Davis, Editorial Director
Ellen Maria Bruzelius, Direct Marketing Manager
Kristine Smith-Cunningham, Advertising Promotion Manager
Mary Ellen Kelly, Fulfillment Manager
Katherine Ferrara, Assistant
Diane Pesce, Composition Production Manager
Serafino J. Cambareri, Quality Control Manager

For *Gourmet* Magazine

Jane Montant, Editor-in-Chief
Evie Righter, Senior Editor, Gourmet Books
Diane Keitt, Associate Editor
Romulo Yanes, Staff Photographer
Irwin Glusker, Design Consultant

Produced in association with
Media Projects, Incorporated

Carter Smith, Executive Editor
Toni Rachiele, Managing Editor
Judith Tropea, Project Editor
Martina D'Alton, Associate Project Editor
Petra Cogan, Indexer
Michael Shroyer, Art/Production Director

The editors would like to thank Georgia Chan Downard for her creative assistance in once again compiling "A Gourmet Addendum," and Blair Brown Hoyt.

Special thanks also is given to the food department and studio of *Gourmet* Magazine.

The text of this book was set in Times Roman by the Composition Department of Condé Nast Publications, Inc. and U.S. Lithograph Typographers. The four-color separations were done by The Color Company, Seiple Lithographers, and Applied Graphic Technologies—Kordet Division. The book was printed and bound at R. R. Donnelley and Sons. Text paper is 80-pound Mountie Gloss. Papermill: Northwest Paper Division of Potlatch Corporation. Paper merchant: Allan and Gray.

Front Jacket: "Risotto with Asparagus, Morels, and Peppers" (page 172).

Back Jacket: "Apple Strudel Tartlets with Hard Sauce" (page 230).

Frontispiece: "Chinese-style Steamed Shrimp with Garlic and Scallions" (page 132).

CONTENTS

INTRODUCTION

This year's edition of *The Best of Gourmet* marks the fifth anniversary of its publication, a very happy occasion for us, made more gratifying by the many positive responses we have received over the years from readers. We hope that we have, since the volume's inception, continued to refine it in the *Gourmet* tradition.

You will note in this year's *Best of Gourmet* that very little has changed in format. The Menu Collection, which features over 60 full-color photographs of the Gourmet's Menus and Cuisine Courante columns from 1989, sets the stage for the recipes that appear in Part Two, A Recipe Compendium. As in the previous volumes, these recipes have been organized into chapters and are arranged alphabetically with cross-references between recipes and photographs for maximum ease of use. Over 500 recipes from 1989 appear, ranging in simplicity from comforting old-fashioned meat loaf to stylish *aiguillettes de canard avec sauce Chambord* (sliced duck breast with Chambord sauce). Some combinations are markedly celebratory, those from the menu columns themselves. Recipes from the column Gastronomie sans Argent are seasonal; recipes from The Last Touch column tend toward the simple, while those from the magazine's In Short Order column are syncopated for today's fast-paced lifestyle.

Menus are also as varied as they have always been. We take you outdoors to the beach for *un pique-nique sur mer* where simple *pan bagnas* (Provençale sandwiches with tuna, basil, and tomato) are served; on a cross-country skiing weekend where three meals—a Saturday picnic lunch of pâté, cheese, and fruit, a Saturday dinner of braised rabbit Provençale, and a Sunday brunch with herbed scrambled eggs—are presented; or simply out to the garden for a luncheon among the rhododendrons, starring cold peppered tenderloin of beef with creamy tarragon caper sauce. We host you indoors with a gala New Year's open-house buffet that highlights stuffed breast of veal with paprika sauce; a pretty spring luncheon of shrimp, snow peas, and baby corn with coriander beurre blanc; or an all-purpose dinner for a special evening with four-peppercorn pork roast. We

surprise you with a Russian Easter Zakuska Party complete with blini with caviar and iced vodka; and a Cinco de Mayo Dinner of red snapper Veracruz. Last but not least, we honor you and your family in holiday fashion with a Thanksgiving turkey stuffed with mixed grains and chestnuts.

The recipes in this year's *The Best of Gourmet* reinforce a theme that began quietly in earlier editions: more and more of the recipes are simple to prepare and good for us. We know well that time is at a premium in most households. We are also very aware that certain foods are better for us than others. We know, too, that there need not be any sacrifice in taste or style if a dish is made with little cream and less butter. Indeed, we still serve some grand desserts here, to wit the marvelous tangerine and vanilla Bavarian on page 236. We believe in the main, however, that the recipes collected here from the last twelve issues of *Gourmet* reflect practical and healthful consideration, a timeliness befitting a need.

In this regard, A Gourmet Addendum this year features recipes of the seasons: thirty-six new combinations for starters, entrées, and desserts based on healthful, bountiful foods as they appear seasonally. Infinite menu potential for year-round dining results as a dividend.

In 1991, *Gourmet* magazine will celebrate its fiftieth anniversary. Over the years the magazine has chronicled an interest in food and style that peaked with all things French in the early 1970s, righted itself to applaud all things American and homegrown in the early 1980s, and now in the final years of this decade addresses the inescapable fact that what is sensible, and smart, is best. These two conditions are among the many that define style, something *Gourmet* has stood for since its beginning.

We welcome you, then, to our fifth anniversary of *The Best of Gourmet*. Let these pages inspire you to celebrate with us. Won't you stay with us for the next five years, and then some?

Jane Montant
Editor-in-Chief

THE MENU COLLECTION

Filled with over 70 pages of menus and exquisite full-color photographs, The Menu Collection invites you into a world where *Gourmet* dining and gracious entertaining are an integral part of living. This section captures each of *Gourmet* magazine's 1989 Menus and Cuisine Courante columns in a splendid album of seasonal menus and entertaining ideas. And, in keeping with *Gourmet* tradition, attention to detail makes each event and every dish unique. Designed to intrigue and inspire the cook, these pages, complete with menu page references for each dish, should compel the reader on to Part Two, A Recipe Compendium, where recipes for all of these dishes can be found.

The variety of menus and entertaining themes is outstanding; whatever look, feel, or taste you are searching for, it is sure to be found in these pages. During the year, several outdoor dining menus appropriate to seasonal themes or activities appear: for the summer months, a poolside Spanish luncheon of gazpacho and seafood *paella* salad makes a pretty and refreshing repast; on Labor Day, a clambake of lobsters and steamers and deep-dish blueberry pie salutes in grand fashion the end of the season; in the fall, a picnic under the apple tree reveals curried butternut squash soup and oatmeal trail mix cookies; and in winter, an ice-skating party features hearty cold-weather fare of oven-fried cornmeal chicken wings and chili con carne.

Then there are the more formal occasions. *Gourmet*'s Menus can be as elegant as a New Year's open-house buffet of spinach-stuffed breast of veal with paprika sauce; as sophisticated as a spring luncheon of shrimp, snow peas, and baby corn with coriander beurre blanc; as spirited as a Cinco de Mayo dinner of red snapper Veracruz; and as *continentale* as a dinner Italian style, featuring fettuccine with walnut sauce, and ocean perch with fennel, tomato, and fried basil leaves.

For people on the go who love to cook, Cuisine Courante menus are true time-savers. A Middle Eastern-style dinner boasts a manageable meal of grilled butterflied leg of lamb with cumin and grilled marinated eggplant and red onion, both dishes prepared on the bar-becue. These are served with bulgur and cucumber mint salad, each of which can be made in less than 45 minutes. Soothing apricot frozen yogurt ends the menu on an aromatic note.

Holidays are always specially celebrated at *Gourmet*, where traditions are preserved as culinary surprises abound. An Easter ham with mustard green stuffing and a lattice oat wheat crust, for example, gives the holiday table a spring-like festive look. The Thanksgiving turkey is stuffed, not with bread dressing, but with mixed grain and chestnut stuffing, while cranberry appears in the form of a delectable cranberry ginger pound cake. And what could be lovelier than a Christmas dinner goose redolent with sausage and fennel? Creamy eggnog ice cream with glacéed fruits or chopped almonds assures that culinary expectations never falter. The diner is delighted from start to finish!

Surprises continue with lesser-known but by no means less celebratory holidays. Why not host a Russian Easter Zakuska Party? The variety of intriguing canapés—or *zakuska*, meaning ''little bites''—include creamy mushroom croustades, blini with caviar, and herring in sour cream dill sauce. *Paskha*, an unusual cheese mold, and *kulich*, a domed sweet bread studded with raisins and almonds, serve as the traditional Russian Easter desserts.

As in previous years, Gerald Asher, *Gourmet*'s wine editor, has recommended complementary beverages for each of the menus. Libations range from iced vodka for the Russian Easter Zakuska party; to Logado, a red wine from Crete for our spiced lamb chops with ginger crisps tray meal; to an exceptional Château Lynch-Bages '66 to serve with the Bastille Day entrée.

Variety and choice make life compelling. In Part One we present you with so many beautiful choices it will be difficult to choose which menus to try first. Allow yourself time to enjoy the photographs; they are filled with subtle and unique ideas, fine details. Step into the pictures with your imagination, transfer the setting to your own home, borrowing and adapting as you will, to make the event your own. We present the ideas and recipes . . . the rest is up to you.

A NEW YEAR'S OPEN-HOUSE BUFFET

Cucumber Cups with Horseradish Cream and Salmon Roe, *p. 88*

Westphalian Ham Triangles, *p. 89*

Wild Mushroom Consommé, *p. 114*

Sonoma-Cutrer Chardonnay
Les Pierres Vineyard '86

Pumpernickel and Rye Breadsticks, *p. 108*

Stuffed Breast of Veal with Paprika Sauce, *p. 138*

Dilled Rice Pilaf, *p. 172*

Château Les Ormes-de-Pez
Saint Estèphe '84

Beet and Green Bean Salad
with Scallion Balsamic Vinaigrette, *p. 198*

Tangerine and Vanilla Bavarian, *p. 236*

Rigo Jancsi, *p. 212*

Pumpernickel and Rye Breadsticks, Wild Mushroom Consommé,
Cucumber Cups with Horseradish Cream and Salmon Roe, Westphalian Ham Triangles

Stuffed Breast of Veal with Paprika Sauce, Dilled Rice Pilaf

Tangerine and Vanilla Bavarian, Rigo Jancsi

Chile Con Carne, Cheddar Biscuits

AN ICE-SKATING PARTY

Oven-Fried Cornmeal Chicken Wings, p. 156

Chili Con Carne, p. 133

Heineken Beer   *Creamy Coleslaw, p. 200*

Cheddar Biscuits, p. 104

Lemon Sponge Pudding, p. 236

Oven-Fried Cornmeal Chicken
Wings, Creamy Coleslaw

A CROSS-COUNTRY SKIING WEEKEND

SATURDAY PICNIC LUNCH

Country Pâté, p. 87

Pepper-Coated Goat Cheese, p. 162

Boeger Winery
"Hangtown Red" '85

Dill-Coated Goat Cheese, p. 161

Marinated Mozzarella, p. 162

Fresh and Dried Fruit

SATURDAY DINNER

Creamy Polenta with Grilled Vegetables, p. 171

Braised Rabbit Provençale, p. 151

Rosso di
Montalcino '83

Garlic Bread, p. 105

Arugula Salad with Orange Vinaigrette, p. 194

Brandied Pear and Almond Cobbler, p. 244

SUNDAY BRUNCH

Glazed Canadian Bacon, p. 139

Herbed Scrambled Eggs, p. 164

Cranberry Sunrises, p. 246

Apple Rings with Orange and Maple Syrup, p. 243

Popovers, p. 106

Country Pâté, Pepper-Coated Goat Cheese, Dill-Coated Goat Cheese,
Marinated Mozzarella, Fresh and Dried Fruit

Creamy Polenta with Grilled Vegetables; Braised Rabbit Provençale;
Garlic Bread; Arugula Salad with Orange Vinaigrette

Scallop, Fennel, and Dill Gratins

CUISINE COURANTE

UPDATED CLASSICS

Scallop, Fennel, and Dill Gratins, p. 130

Clos du Val
Napa Valley
Sémillon '85

Coq au Vin with Shiitake Mushrooms
and Glazed Onions, p. 154

Chicory and Endive Salad with Roquefort
and Walnuts, p. 194

Mocha Meringue Mousses, p. 235

Hazelnut Sablés, p. 224

Scallop, Fennel, and Dill Gratins; Coq au Vin with Shiitake Mushrooms
and Glazed Onions; Chicory and Endive Salad with Roquefort and Walnuts

EASTER LUNCHEON

Shrimp, Chayote, and Coriander Tarts, *p. 94*

Ham with Mustard Green Stuffing
and Oat Wheat Crust, *p. 146*

Kreuznacher Brückes   Brown Rice and Wild Rice Timbales, *p. 172*
Riesling Kabinett '87

Sweet Potato Turnip Gratin, *p. 182*

Tosca Cake, *p. 222*

Candied Orange Ice Cream, *p. 222*

Shrimp, Chayote, and Coriander Tarts

Ham with Mustard Green Stuffing and Oat Wheat Crust,
Brown Rice and Wild Rice Timbales

Cappuccino Crème Brûlées

TRAY MEALS

Logado
Red Wine from Crete

Sautéed Spiced Lamb Chops with Ginger Crisps, p. 149

Minted Orzo with Currants, p. 168

Sautéed Mixed Vegetables, p. 185

Garlic Cumin Toasts, p. 107

Coconut Macaroon and Chocolate Sandwiches, p. 224

Château La Louvière
Graves Blanc '86

Monkfish Medallions with Tomato Lemon Coulis, p. 120

Pasta with Fennel and Olives, p. 168

Bibb Lettuce with Herb Vinaigrette, p. 194

Cappuccino Crème Brûlée, p. 234

Sautéed Spiced Lamb Chops with Ginger Crisps, Minted Orzo with Currants,
Sautéed Mixed Vegetables, Garlic Cumin Toasts

A SPRING LUNCHEON

Asparagus, Pea, and Tarragon Soup, p. 110

Whole-Wheat Salt Sticks, p. 103

Quivira
Dry Creek Valley
Sauvignon Blanc '87

Shrimp, Snow Peas,
and Baby Corn with
Coriander Beurre Blanc, p. 131

Mesclun and Radicchio Salad, p. 195

Toasted Coconut Cake with Lime Filling, p. 215

Sliced Oranges

Asparagus, Pea, and Tarragon Soup, Whole-Wheat Salt Sticks

Shrimp, Snow Peas, and Baby Corn
with Coriander Beurre Blanc

Toasted Coconut Cake
with Lime Filling,
Sliced Oranges

Paskha and Kulich

A RUSSIAN EASTER ZAKUSKA PARTY

Smoked Salmon Canapés, p. 97

Egg, Anchovy, and Caper Canapés, p. 96

Iced Vodka   *Radish Canapés, p. 97*

Creamy Mushroom Croustades, p. 89

Blini with Caviar, p. 85

Herring in Sour Cream Dill Sauce, p. 89

Paskha, p. 219

Kulich, p. 220

Smoked Salmon Canapés; Egg, Anchovy, and Caper Canapés; Radish Canapés; Creamy
Mushroom Croustades; Blini with Caviar; Herring in Sour Cream Dill Sauce

A
CINCO DE MAYO
DINNER

Guacamole Tostaditas, p. 88

Margaritas, p. 247   *Chicken and Bean Tostaditas, p. 86*

Chiles Rellenos, p. 180

Sterling Vineyards   *Red Snapper Veracruz, p. 124*
Napa Valley
Cabernet Blanc '88   *Flour Tortillas, p. 109*

Mixed Vegetable Salad
with Lime Vinaigrette, p. 201

Creamy Cinnamon Rice Pudding
with Fresh Fruit, p. 236

Mexican Tea Cakes, p. 225

Chiles Rellenos

Red Snapper Veracruz, Flour Tortillas,
Mixed Vegetable Salad with Lime Vinaigrette

Creamy Cinnamon Rice Pudding
with Fresh Fruit, Mexican Tea Cakes

Chocolate Caramel Walnut Tartlets

A BRIDAL SHOWER

Spinach and Feta Phyllo Rolls, p. 183

Trimbach Clos Ste-Hune
Riesling '82

Chicken Salmagundi, p. 152

Coarse Mustard Vinaigrette, p. 202   *Russian Dressing, p.153*

New Potatoes with Dill, p. 181

Chocolate Caramel Walnut Tartlets, p. 230

Spinach and Feta Phyllo Rolls, Chicken Salmagundi,
Coarse Mustard Vinaigrette, Russian Dressing, New Potatoes with Dill

LUNCHEON AMONG THE RHODODENDRONS

Pimm's Cups, p. 248   *Cheddar Twists*, p. 86

Asparagus with Pickled Ginger and Shallots, p. 174

*Cold Peppered Tenderloin of Beef with
Creamy Tarragon Caper Sauce*, p. 138

*Hanna Winery
Sonoma County
Chardonnay '87*

*Squash Cups with
Basil Vegetable Stuffing*, p. 184

Mixed Lettuces with Citrus Dressing, p. 196
Brie

Chocolate Raspberry Almond Torte, p. 213
Raspberries

Asparagus with Pickled Ginger and Shallots

Cold Peppered Tenderloin of Beef with Creamy Tarragon
Caper Sauce; Squash Cups with Basil Vegetable Stuffing

Chocolate Raspberry Almond Torte; Raspberries

Apricot Frozen Yogurt

A MIDDLE EASTERN-STYLE DINNER FROM THE GRILL

Grilled Butterflied Leg of Lamb with Cumin, p. 149

Grilled Marinated Eggplant and Red Onion, p. 150

Haut-Poitou
Cabernet Sauvignon '86   *Pistachio, Currant, and Scallion Bulgur*, p. 170

Cucumber Mint Salad, p. 195

Apricot Frozen Yogurt, p. 242

Grilled Butterflied Leg of Lamb with Cumin; Grilled Marinated
Eggplant and Red Onion; Pistachio, Currant, and Scallion Bulgur

BASTILLE DAY DINNERS

Muscadet de Sèvre-
et-Maine '88

Terrine de Deux Poissons, p. 122

Aiguillettes de Canard avec Sauce Chambord, p. 158

Confit d'Oignons et de Poivre Vert, p. 178

Château Lynch-Bages '66

Julienne de Courgettes et Carottes, p. 185

Salade de Laitues Variées avec Rissoles de Canard, p. 196

Gâteau de Mousse à la Nectarine, p. 218

Montagny '86

Rillettes de Saumon Fumé, p. 98

Steak au Poivre, p. 135

Beaune du Château
Premier Cru '85

Pommes Pailles, p. 181

Tomates Provençale, p. 184

Eclairs au Moka, p. 232

Terrine de Deux Poissons

Aiguillettes de Canard avec Sauce Chambord; Confit
d'Oignons et de Poivre Vert; Julienne de Courgettes et Carottes

Gâteau de Mousse à la Nectarine,
Eclairs au Moka

Lemon Almond Madeleines, Melons with Macerated Raspberries

UN PIQUE-NIQUE SUR MER

Marinated Black and Green Olives, p. 91

Crudités with Ravigote Mayonnaise, p. 87

Lirac Rouge   *Pan Bagnas, p. 125*

Assorted Cheeses   *French Bread*

Lemon Almond Madeleines, p. 224

Melons with Macerated Raspberries, p. 244

Pan Bagnas, Marinated Black and Green Olives

A POOLSIDE
SPANISH LUNCHEON

Gazpacho, p. 113

Seafood Paella Salad, p. 192

Bonny Doon Vineyard
Vin Gris de Cigare '88

Tomato-Garlic Mayonnaise, p. 192

Mixed Greens with Cumin Vinaigrette, p. 196

Cheese   Grapes   Bread

Almond Flan with Summer Fruit, p. 233

Gazpacho

Seafood Paella Salad

Almond Flan with Summer Fruit

Blueberry Lemonade Sorbet

CUISINE COURANTE

A SUMMER SUPPER

Iced Beet and Cucumber Soup, p. 111

Jekel Home Vineyard

Pinot Blanc '85

Shrimp and White Bean Salad, p. 193

Corn-Salad-Stuffed Tomatoes, p. 200

Italian Toasts, p. 107

Blueberry Lemonade Sorbet, p. 242

Shrimp and White Bean Salad,
Corn-Salad-Stuffed Tomatoes, Italian Toasts

LABOR DAY CLAMBAKE

Caramel
  Lemonade, *p. 253*

Clams on the Half Shell, *p. 126*

Tomato and Pepper Cocktail Sauce, *p. 126*

Caper, Shallot, and Parsley Sauce, *p. 126*

Shandies, *p. 252*

Summer Vegetables with Pesto Dip, *p. 94*

Clambake in a Pot, *p. 127*

———

Anchor Steam and
  Rolling Rock Beer

Lobsters   Steamers

Sage, Lemon, and Garlic Butter, *p. 127*

White Onions   Red Potatoes

Corn on the Cob   Tomato Butter, *p. 127*

The Firestone Vineyard
  Santa Ynez Valley
    Johannisberg Riesling '88

Parker House Rolls, *p. 102*

Deep-Dish Blueberry Pie, *p. 228*

Vanilla Ice Cream, *p. 241*

Peach Schnapps and Vodka Plugged Watermelon, *p. 245*

Deep-Dish Blueberry Pie, Vanilla Ice Cream,
Peach Schnapps and Vodka Plugged Watermelon

Lobsters; Steamers; Sage, Lemon, and Garlic Butter;
White Onions and Red Potatoes; Corn on the Cob,
Tomato Butter; Parker House Rolls; Caramel Lemonade

Tiramisù Ice-Cream Cake, Mocha Fudge Sauce

CUISINE COURANTE

DINNER ITALIAN STYLE

Arneis
Vietti '87

Fettuccine with Walnut Sauce, p. 166

Ocean Perch Fillets with Fennel, Tomato,
and Fried Basil Leaves, p. 120

Milanese Mixed Salad, p. 196

Tiramisù Ice-Cream Cake, p. 240   *Mocha Fudge Sauce, p. 240*

Vin Santo
Almond and Hazelnut Biscotti, p. 223

Ocean Perch Fillets with Fennel, Tomato, and Fried Basil Leaves

DINNER
FOR A
SPECIAL
OCCASION

Mercurey
  Clos de Tonnerre '85

Pumpkin Tortelloni with
Autumn Vegetables, p. 169

Four-Peppercorn Pork Roast, p. 142

Beaune
  Clos du Roi '78

Wild Rice with Currants and Scallions, p. 172

Crisp Braised Celery, p. 177

Beaulieu Vineyard
  Muscat de Frontignan

Deep Chocolate Torte
with Coffee Buttercream, p. 214

Pumpkin Tortelloni with Autumn Vegetables

Four-Peppercorn Pork Roast, Wild Rice with Currants
and Scallions, Crisp Braised Celery

Deep Chocolate Torte
with Coffee Buttercream

Oatmeal Trail Mix Cookies, Apple Cider

A PICNIC
UNDER THE APPLE TREE

Curried Butternut Squash Soup, p. 116

Assorted Sausages and Cheeses

Apple Cider

Pickled Red Onions, p. 206

Chutney   Olives   Mustard

McDowell Valley Vineyards   Assorted Breads
White Zinfandel '88

Oatmeal Trail Mix Cookies, p. 226

Apples

Curried Butternut Squash Soup, Assorted Sausages and
Cheeses, Pickled Red Onions, Chutney, Olives, Mustard,
Assorted Breads

THANKSGIVING DINNER

Oysters on the Half Shell, p. 129

*Roast Turkey with Five-Rice and Chestnut
Stuffing and Mushroom Giblet Gravy*, p. 158

*St. Clement
Napa Valley
Chardonnay '87*

Sweet Potato Purée with Walnuts, p. 182

*Cauliflower with Cheddar Sauce and
Rye Bread Crumbs*, p. 177

Lima Beans with Bacon, p. 174

Cranberry Citrus Relish, p. 205

*Heitz Wine Cellars
California Angelica*

Pumpkin Rum Raisin Tartlets, p. 231

Glazed Cranberry Ginger Pound Cake, p. 216

Oysters on the Half Shell

Roast Turkey with Five-Rice and Chestnut Stuffing and
Mushroom Giblet Gravy; Sweet Potato Purée with
Walnuts; Cauliflower with Cheddar Sauce and Rye Bread
Crumbs; Lima Beans with Bacon; Cranberry Citrus Re

Glazed Cinnamon Buns, Cranberry Applesauce

A HOLIDAY WEEKEND BREAKFAST

Freshly Squeezed Orange Juice

Glazed Cinnamon Buns, p. 100

Cranberry Applesauce, p. 203

*Turkey, Ham, and Vegetable Hash
with Fried Eggs, p. 164*

Sesame Maple Corn Sticks, p. 104

Coffee   Tea

Turkey, Ham, and Vegetable Hash
with Fried Eggs; Sesame Maple Corn Sticks

CHRISTMAS DINNER

Warm Shrimp and Scallop Salad with
Roasted Red Pepper Vinaigrette, p. 130

Meursault Clos   *Roast Goose with Sausage, Fennel, and Currant*
de la Barre   *Stuffing and Wild Mushroom Port Gravy, p. 156*
Domaine des
Comtes Lafon '83   *Sautéed Potatoes and Celery Root, p. 181*

Brussels Sprouts and Carrots with
Shallot Butter, p. 176

Quady's Essensia   *Black Forest Cake, p. 210*

Eggnog Ice Cream, p. 238

Roast Goose with Sausage, Fennel, and Currant Stuffing
and Wild Mushroom Port Gravy; Sautéed Potatoes and
Celery Root; Brussels Sprouts and Carrots with Shallot Butter

Black Forest Cake, Eggnog Ice Cream

Southern Coffee Parfaits, Praline Butter Cookies

A SOUTHERN TREE-TRIMMING PARTY

Lobster, Oyster, and Sausage Gumbo, p. 128

St. Chapelle
Idaho
Dry Johannisberg
Riesling '88

Rice with Red Beans and Peas, p. 128

Fried Cornmeal-Coated Okra, p. 128

Southern Coffee Parfaits, p. 234

Praline Butter Cookies, p. 227

Lobster, Oyster, and Sausage Gumbo
Rice with Red Beans and Peas; Fried Cornmeal-Coated Okra

PART TWO

A RECIPE COMPENDIUM

*P*art Two of *The Best of Gourmet*, A Recipe Compendium, is a collection of over 500 recipes selected from the pages of the 1989 issues of *Gourmet* magazine. Here you will find all of the recipes from the Gourmet's Menus and Cuisine Courante columns, the best recipes from Gastronomie sans Argent, In Short Order, and The Last Touch, and selected recipes from special feature articles that appeared throughout the year.

On a practical note, you will want to enjoy the recipes culled from Gastronomie sans Argent, which monthly features a seasonal food, then provides inventive economic recipes to use it to maximum delectable advantage. This year succulent ideas for pork tenderloin await: Chinese-style roast pork with chutney garlic sauce, pork rolls stuffed with rye bread, apple, and sage, braised pork with orange juice and coriander, and pork tenderloin cordon bleu, to name a few. Fruits and vegetables also get much-deserved attention. Full of nutritious produce, a variety of hearty soups are now at your fingertips. Cheddar vegetable soup; Hungarian-style mushroom barley; white bean and escarole; split pea, green pea, carrot, and turnip—each provides warmth whenever whim or cooler temperature dictates. A summer favorite, tomatoes, receives creative handling as well, in phyllo pizza, tomato vegetable Bloody Mary mix, fried cornmeal-coated green tomatoes, and ketchup! As for desserts, strawberries are transformed into strawberry-amaretto ice-cream cake roll, or strawberry coconut chiffon pie, or *coeurs à la crème* with strawberry sauce.

But the subject that received the most attention from Gastronomie sans Argent this past year was salad. Two separate columns featured salads exclusively—chicken salads appeared in the June issue and a variety of *salades françaises* in July. And it is no wonder! Today's lifestyle calls for meals short in preparation, long on nutritional goodness; salads fit that bill. Meals-in-one can be found among our chicken salads and range from a more basic chicken "club" salad, with its own quick basil mayonnaise, to an exotic curried chicken salad with mango and cashews, to a delicately refined Thai chicken salad with cellophane noodles. Creative entrées as well as side dishes appear among our *salades françaises* inclusions. Notable for its tarragon and chervil taste, *salade Du Barry au roquefort* (cauliflower, radish, watercress, and roquefort salad) makes a colorful side dish; *salade de pois chiche* (chick-pea salad), another accent dish, features Niçoise olives and fresh basil; while *salade de boeuf avec sauce vinaigrette aux anchois et au raifort* (roast beef salad with anchovy and horseradish vinaigrette) is a heartier ensemble that could serve as a light entrée.

From *Gourmet*'s In Short Order column come recipes that can be prepared in a limited amount of time with ingredients generally on hand in your kitchen. This collection ranges in sophistication from humble apple fool, to practical corn and potato chowder, to unique guacamole omelets with sour cream and chives, to elegant bay scallops with mustard thyme mayonnaise. There is something here that is appropriate for many a varied dining occasion. And, to repeat, each In Short Order recipe has been developed with a preparation time of 45 minutes or less.

Just as there are days when every minute counts, so are there times when you are able to attend to all the extras, the fine details that render a presentation special, a meal memorable long after the china has been put carefully back into the cabinet. The Last Touch column provides just such "detail" recipes. This year hors d'oeuvres, canapés, and crackers starred, with mush-

Grilled Pork Tenderloin with Mustard Cream Sauce (page 143)

rooms featured among the hors d'oeuvres: Consider pâté- and bacon-stuffed mushrooms, prosciutto- and Parmesan-stuffed mushrooms, and sherried mushrooms on toast. Canapés were also varied: clam, bacon, and onion; goat cheese and sun-dried tomato; even spicy peanut butter, bacon, and scallion. Making your own rye sunflower crackers, bacon mustard biscuit thins, and Parmesan garlic sticks has never been more straightforward. Not-to-be-missed dessert sauces should be mentioned here, too! A rich plum and Port sauce magically transforms a simple angel food cake or bowl of vanilla ice cream into a colorful, exceptional finale; while blueberry Chambord sauce, served over fresh melon and berries, would be the ideal light, yet elegant, way to bring dinner to a successful conclusion. And don't overlook the oatmeal cookie selection: oatmeal lace, Irish chewy oatmeal squares, and oatmeal date bars. Or, if a cool, refreshing dessert is more appropriate, try any one of several granitas. The flavors—pineapple, coconut caramel, mocha rum, and nectarine ginger—provide a rainbow of possibilities.

As in previous volumes, recipes from feature articles that appeared during 1989 have also been included in this year's *Best of Gourmet*. From an article by Faye Levy on *fruits de mer*—fruits of the sea—comes snapper with fresh tomato sauce and basil butter. Richard Sax investigates cooking with coffee and has contributed a compelling combination for lamb brochettes with savory coffee glaze. And Shirley Sarvis's pine nut exposé presents fettuccine with these extraordinary nuts, prosciutto, and brown butter, a recipe guaranteed to become one of *your* specialties as soon as you try it.

Whatever your tastes or culinary predilections, you will have ample recipes to choose from in this collection. There are updated classics such as *coq au vin* with shiitake mushrooms and glazed onions; many foreign specialties like *terrine de deux poissons* (salmon and sole terrine with watercress); *pissaladières* (small tomato, olive, and anchovy tarts), or *bacalao a la vizcaína* (salt cod Basque style with tomatoes and bacon); practical, friendly standbys like old-fashioned meat loaf; or, at the other end of the spectrum, the sublime spectacular—deep chocolate torte with coffee buttercream—a dessert that demands admiration, and gets it! There is literally something for everyone and every occasion.

This part, like The Menu Collection preceding it, should be perused at your leisure. This will allow you the time to discover recipes on your own and to build your own menus around dishes you already know or with other dishes from *The Best of Gourmet* library collection. Recipes are arranged by chapter from hors d'oeuvres to breads; soups; fish and shellfish; meat; poultry; cheese, eggs, and breakfast items; pasta and grains; vegetables; salads and salad dressings; sauces; desserts; and beverages. Within chapters, recipes are arranged alphabetically.

Here are the best recipes, over 500 of them, from 1989! When they are added to the four volumes of recipes from previous years, a truly outstanding library of entertaining ideas is at hand. Clear and concise instructions make A Recipe Compendium a usable, invaluable tool that we hope will become your source of cooking for years to come.

HORS D'OEUVRES AND CANAPÉS

HORS D'OEUVRES

Butter-Toasted Almonds and Hazelnuts
½ pound (about 1¾ cups) hazelnuts
5 tablespoons unsalted butter
½ pound (about 2 cups) blanched almonds,
    halved
coarse salt to taste

Toast the hazelnuts in one layer in a baking pan in a preheated 350° F. oven for 10 to 15 minutes, or until they are colored lightly and the skins blister. Wrap the hazelnuts in a kitchen towel and let them steam for 1 minute. Rub the hazelnuts in the towel to remove the skins and let them cool. In a large heavy skillet heat the butter over moderately high heat until the foam subsides and in it sauté the almonds, stirring constantly, for 3 to 4 minutes, or until they are lightly golden. Add the toasted hazelnuts and sauté the nuts, stirring constantly, for 3 minutes, or until they are all golden. Transfer the nuts with a slotted spoon to paper towels to drain and sprinkle them with the salt. Makes about 3¾ cups.

Blini with Caviar
(Buckwheat Yeast Pancakes with Caviar)
a ¼-ounce package (2½ teaspoons)
    active dry yeast
2½ tablespoons sugar
2 cups milk
2 tablespoons unsalted butter, melted, plus
    additional for brushing the griddle
1 cup buckwheat flour (available at natural
    foods stores and specialty foods shops)
1 cup all-purpose flour
1 teaspoon salt
2 large eggs, separated, the whites at
    room temperature
¾ cup well chilled heavy cream
caviar

sour cream as an accompaniment
melted butter as an accompaniment

In a large bowl proof the yeast with ½ tablespoon of the sugar in ⅓ cup lukewarm water for 10 minutes, or until it is foamy. Stir in 1 cup of the milk, heated to lukewarm, the remaining 2 tablespoons sugar, 2 tablespoons of the butter, and the buckwheat flour, beat the batter for 1 minute, and let it rise, covered with plastic wrap, in a warm place for 2 hours or chill it, covered tightly, overnight. (Chilling overnight produces a tangier flavor. Let the batter come to room temperature before continuing with the recipe.) Stir in the remaining 1 cup milk, heated to lukewarm, the all-purpose flour, the salt, and the yolks, beat the mixture for 1 minute, and let it rise, covered with the plastic wrap, in a warm place for 1 hour, or until it is double in bulk and bubbly. In a bowl beat the cream until it holds soft peaks and fold it into the batter. In a metal bowl beat the egg whites until they just hold stiff peaks and fold them into the batter.

Heat a griddle or large skillet over moderate heat until it is hot, brush it lightly with the additional melted butter, and spoon tablespoons of the batter onto the griddle, spreading them to form 3-inch rounds. Cook the *blini* for 1 minute, or until the undersides are golden, turn them, and cook them for 1 minute more, or until the undersides are golden. Transfer the *blini* as they are cooked to a heated platter and keep them warm, covered with a kitchen towel. Make *blini* with the remaining batter in the same manner, brushing the griddle lightly with the butter, and reheat them, covered with foil, in a preheated 300° F. oven for 5 to 10 minutes, or until they are warm. *The* blini *may be made 2 days in advance and kept covered and chilled. Reheat the* blini, *covered with foil, in a 350° F. oven for 10 to 15 minutes, or until they are warm, or microwave them on a microwave-safe platter, covered with microwave-safe plastic wrap, at high power (100%) for 2 minutes, or until they are warm.*

Arrange the *blini*, wrapped in a napkin, on a heated platter and serve them with the caviar, the sour cream, and the melted butter. Makes about 78 *blini*.

PHOTO ON PAGE 33

Cheddar Twists

quick puff paste (recipe follows)
an egg wash, made by beating
　1 egg with 2 teaspoons water
3 cups coarsely grated sharp Cheddar
coarse salt for sprinkling the dough

Halve the dough and reserve one half, wrapped and chilled. Roll out the remaining dough into an 18- by 12-inch rectangle on a lightly floured surface, brush it with some of the egg wash, and sprinkle it lightly with pepper. Sprinkle 1½ cups of the Cheddar over a crosswise half of the dough, fold the plain half of dough over the Cheddar, pressing it firmly to force out any air pockets, and roll the dough out slightly to make the layers adhere. Brush the dough with some of the remaining egg wash, sprinkle it lightly with the salt, and with a pastry wheel or knife cut it lengthwise into ½-inch strips. Twist the strips, arrange them on a greased baking sheet, pressing the ends onto the sheet, and bake them in the middle of a preheated 425° F. oven for 12 to 15 minutes, or until they are pale golden. Make more Cheddar twists with the remaining dough, pepper to taste, and the remaining egg wash, Cheddar, and salt in the same manner. *The twists may be made 3 days in advance and kept in an airtight container.* Makes about 36 twists.

Quick Puff Paste

2 cups all-purpose flour sifted with
　½ teaspoon salt
1¾ sticks (¾ cup plus 2 tablespoons) cold
　unsalted butter, cut into bits

In a large bowl blend the flour mixture and the butter until the mixture resembles meal. Add ⅓ to ½ cup ice water, or enough to just form a dough. Form the dough into a ball, dust it with flour, and chill it, wrapped in wax paper, for 1 hour. Roll the dough into a 12- by 6-inch rectangle on a floured surface, dusting it with flour if it sticks to the rolling pin. Fold the top third of the rectangle over the center and the bottom third over the top, forming a rectangle about 6 by 4 inches. Press down the top edge with the rolling pin so it adheres, turn the dough seam side down, and brush any excess flour from the dough. With an open side facing you roll the dough out again into a 12- by 6-inch rectangle and fold it into thirds as before. This completes 2 "turns." Make 2 more turns, always starting with the seam side down and an open end facing you. Chill the dough, wrapped in wax paper, for at least 30 minutes or for up to 1 week.

Chicken and Bean Tostaditas
(Tortilla Chips Topped with Shredded
Chicken and Bean Purée)

three 7-inch corn tortillas, each cut into
　4 wedges
vegetable oil for frying the tortillas
a 16-ounce can red kidney beans, rinsed
　and drained
⅓ cup finely chopped onion
1 teaspoon minced garlic
1 teaspoon ground cumin
2 tablespoons olive oil
1 tablespoon white-wine vinegar
¾ cup shredded cooked chicken
½ cup finely shredded romaine
sour cream to taste if desired
tomato strips and black olive slices for garnish

Arrange the tortilla wedges in one layer on a baking sheet, cover them with a kitchen towel, and let them stand for 1 hour. In a large heavy skillet heat ¾ inch of the vegetable oil to 375° F. and in it fry the wedges in batches for 30 seconds to 1 minute, or until they are crisp and most of the bubbling subsides. Transfer the chips with a slotted spoon to paper towels to drain and sprinkle them with salt. *The tortilla chips may be made 1 day in advance and kept in an airtight container.*

In a saucepan of boiling salted water blanch the beans for 2 minutes, drain them well, and in a blender or food processor purée them with ½ cup water. In a skillet cook the onion, the garlic, and the cumin in 1 tablespoon of the olive oil over moderately low heat, stirring, until the onion is soft, add the bean purée and salt and pepper to taste, and cook the mixture over moderate heat, stirring, for 5 minutes, or until it is very thick. Transfer the mixture to a bowl and let it cool.

In a small bowl whisk together the vinegar, the remaining 1 tablespoon olive oil, and salt and pepper to taste until the dressing is blended well and in 2 separate bowls toss the chicken and the romaine each with half the dressing. On each tortilla chip spread 1 heaping tablespoon of the bean purée and top it with some of the sour cream, some of the romaine, and a few strips of the chicken. Top the *tostaditas* with the tomato strips and the black olive slices. Makes 12 hors d'oeuvres.

Country Pâté

¼ pound chicken livers, trimmed
½ cup Sercial Madeira
¼ cup heavy cream
½ pound ground veal shoulder
½ pound ground pork shoulder
½ pound ground fresh pork fat
¼ pound cooked smoked ham, cut into
⅓-inch cubes
¼ pound skinless boneless chicken breast,
cut into ⅓-inch cubes
2 large eggs, beaten lightly
3 tablespoons all-purpose flour
5 garlic cloves, minced
1 tablespoon salt
2 teaspoons coarsely ground pepper
1½ teaspoons dried thyme,
crumbled
½ teaspoon mace
⅔ cup shelled natural pistachio nuts, blanched
and oven-dried (procedure follows)
¾ pound sliced lean bacon
Accompaniments
cornichons (French sour gherkins, available at
specialty foods shops and some supermarkets)
pickled onions
olives
assorted breads

In a bowl combine the chicken livers with the Madeira, let them marinate for 2 hours, and transfer the mixture to a blender. Add the cream and purée the mixture. In another bowl combine well the veal, the pork, and the pork fat, add the liver purée, and combine the mixture well. Add the ham, the chicken, the eggs, the flour, the garlic, the salt, the pepper, the thyme, the mace, and the pistachio nuts and combine the mixture well. (Test the seasoning by cooking a small amount of the mixture.) Line a 1½-quart pâté mold, measuring 11¼ by 4 inches across the top and 2⅜ inches deep, with some of the bacon, letting the ends hang over the sides. Fill the mold with the mixture, mounding the mixture slightly, fold the overhanging strips of bacon over the mixture, and cover the top with the remaining slices of bacon. Cover the mold with foil and a lid or with a triple thickness of foil, put it in a baking pan, and add enough hot water to the pan to come two thirds of the way up the sides of the mold. Bake the pâté in a preheated 350° F. oven for 1 hour and 15 minutes to 1½ hours, or until a meat ther-

mometer registers 150° F. Remove the mold from the pan, discard the water, and return the mold to the pan. Remove the lid, leaving the foil intact, let the pâté stand for 15 minutes, and weight it evenly with a 2-pound weight. Let the pâté cool and chill it, weighted, in the pan overnight. Remove the weight and the foil and unmold the pâté. The pâté keeps, wrapped well and chilled, for 1 week. Serve the pâté, sliced thin, with the *cornichons*, the pickled onions, the olives, and the breads.

PHOTO ON PAGE 17

To Blanch and Oven-Dry Pistachio Nuts

In a heatproof bowl pour boiling water to cover over the desired amount of pistachio nuts, shelled, let the nuts stand for 10 minutes, and drain them. Turn the nuts out onto a kitchen towel and rub off the skins. Bake the nuts on a baking sheet in a preheated 300° F. oven for 10 to 15 minutes, or until they are dry.

Crudités with Ravigote Mayonnaise

1 cup quick mayonnaise (page 202)
2 hard-boiled large egg yolks, sieved
¼ cup minced fresh parsley leaves
3 tablespoons snipped fresh chives
2 tablespoons minced drained bottled capers
1 teaspoon fresh lemon juice, or to taste
1 yellow bell pepper, cut into
½-inch strips
1 red bell pepper, cut into ½-inch strips
1 cucumber, seeded and cut into ½-inch
spears

In a bowl combine well the mayonnaise, the yolks, the parsley, the chives, the capers, the lemon juice, and salt and black pepper to taste. Serve the bell peppers and cucumber with the mayonnaise. Serves 6.

Cucumber Cups with Horseradish Cream and Salmon Roe

4 ounces (½ cup) cream cheese,
    softened
2 tablespoons drained bottled
    horseradish, or to taste
2 thin seedless cucumbers
3 ounces salmon roe

In a bowl beat the cream cheese until it is fluffy, add the horseradish, and beat the mixture well. Transfer the horseradish cream to a pastry bag fitted with a medium fluted tip. With a channel knife or vegetable peeler remove some of the peel decoratively in lengthwise strips from the cucumbers. Cut the cucumbers crosswise into 1¼-inch sections and halve each section decoratively. With a small melon-ball cutter cut out some of the core from each piece to form cups, being careful not to cut through the bottom. Pipe the horseradish cream into the cups and top it with the salmon roe. Makes about 30 hors d'oeuvres.

PHOTO ON PAGE 11

Oeufs Farcis au Caviar
(Stuffed Eggs with Caviar)

4 hard-boiled large eggs
2 tablespoons sour cream
1 teaspoon fresh lemon juice
2 tablespoons finely chopped red onion
2 tablespoons black or red lumpfish caviar

Halve the eggs lengthwise and remove the yolks. In a bowl mash the yolks with a fork, add the sour cream, the lemon juice, the onion, and salt and pepper to taste, and combine the mixture well. Divide 1 tablespoon of the caviar among the egg-white halves, fill the whites with the yolk mixture, and top each stuffed egg with some of the remaining caviar. Makes 8 stuffed eggs.

Eggplant, Garlic, and Yogurt Dip

1 large eggplant (about 1¼ pounds),
    halved lengthwise
1 unpeeled large garlic clove
3 tablespoons plain yogurt
¼ teaspoon ground cumin
a pinch of cayenne, or to taste
2 tablespoons minced fresh parsley leaves
crackers or *crudités* as an accompaniment

Arrange the eggplant, cut sides up, and the garlic in a microwave-safe plastic bag, tuck the opening under, and microwave the mixture at high power (100%) for 1 to 2 minutes, or until the garlic is softened slightly. Remove the garlic and continue to microwave the eggplant at high power (100%) for 10 to 12 minutes, or until it is soft. Peel the garlic and mince and mash it to a paste with a pinch of salt. In a small bowl combine the garlic paste, the yogurt, the cumin, the cayenne, and the parsley, scrape the eggplant into the mixture, discarding the skin, and with 2 knives blend the mixture well, cutting up the eggplant. Season the dip with salt and serve it with the crackers or *crudités*. Makes about 1½ cups.

Guacamole Tostaditas
(Tortilla Chips Topped with Avocado)

three 7-inch corn tortillas, each cut into 4
    rounds with a 2- to 2½-inch cutter
vegetable oil for frying the tortillas
1 firm-ripe avocado (preferably California)
1 tablespoon fresh lime juice, or to taste
2 tablespoons finely chopped onion
½ teaspoon minced garlic
½ teaspoon minced seeded Serrano or
    jalapeño pepper, or to taste
    (wear rubber gloves)
1½ tablespoons minced fresh coriander,
    or to taste, plus fresh coriander leaves
    for garnish
¼ cup finely chopped tomato

Arrange the tortilla rounds in one layer on a baking sheet, cover them with a kitchen towel, and let them stand for 1 hour. In a large heavy skillet heat ¾ inch of the oil to 375° F. and in it fry the rounds in batches for 30 seconds to 1 minute, or until they are crisp and most of the bubbling subsides. Transfer the chips with a slotted spoon to paper towels to drain and sprinkle them with salt. *The tortilla chips may be made 1 day in advance and kept in an airtight container.*

Peel and pit the avocado and in a large bowl mash the flesh coarse with a fork. Add the lime juice, the onion, the garlic, the pepper, the minced coriander, the tomato, and salt to taste and stir the mixture until it is combined well. Top each tortilla chip with about 1 tablespoon of the avocado mixture and garnish each *tostadita* with a coriander leaf. Makes 12 hors d'oeuvres.

Westphalian Ham Triangles

½ stick (¼ cup) unsalted butter, softened
2 tablespoons Dijon-style mustard
1 teaspoon honey, or to taste
8 thin (¼-inch-thick) slices of pumpernickel
    or rye bread (preferably cut from an
    unsliced loaf)
8 thin slices (about ¼ pound) of Westphalian
    ham or prosciutto
¼ cup minced fresh parsley leaves

In a small bowl whisk together well the butter, the mustard, the honey, and salt to taste. Spread some of the mustard butter on each bread slice and top it with a ham slice. Cut the sandwiches into triangles (about 4 or 5 from each bread slice), letting the sizes vary depending on where they are cut, cut away the crusts, and discard them. Spread one edge of each triangle with some of the mustard butter and dip it into the parsley to coat it. *The triangles may be made 6 hours in advance and kept on a tray covered with a dampened towel and plastic wrap and chilled.* Makes about 35 triangles.

PHOTO ON PAGE 11

Herring in Sour Cream Dill Sauce

two 13-ounce jars of herring in wine sauce,
    drained (1 pound drained weight)
⅓ cup sour cream
4 teaspoons Dijon-style mustard
2 tablespoons heavy cream
2 tablespoons snipped fresh dill plus dill
    sprigs for garnish if desired
1 small red onion, sliced into thin rings

If the herring is not already sliced, cut it into ¾-inch pieces. In a bowl whisk together the sour cream, the mustard, the heavy cream, and the snipped dill and fold in the herring and the onion rings. Chill the herring mixture, covered, for at least 1 hour and up to 24 hours. Transfer the herring mixture to a serving bowl, garnish it with the dill sprigs, and serve it at room temperature. Makes about 2 cups.

PHOTO ON PAGE 33

Creamy Mushroom Croustades

For the croustades
24 slices of very soft white bread, crusts
    discarded
½ stick (¼ cup) unsalted butter, melted
For the mushroom filling
3 tablespoons minced shallot
1½ tablespoons unsalted butter
¾ pound mushrooms, trimmed, halved,
    and sliced thin
⅛ teaspoon dried tarragon,
    crumbled
1 tablespoon all-purpose flour
½ cup chicken broth
3 tablespoons sour cream
½ teaspoon Worcestershire sauce
2 teaspoons fresh lemon juice
2 tablespoons minced fresh
    parsley leaves

parsley sprigs for garnish

Make the croustades: Roll each bread slice flat with a rolling pin and trim it to form a 2½-inch square. Brush both sides of the squares with the butter and fit each square gently into a ⅛-cup muffin tin (gem tin), pressing the bread against the sides of the tins. Bake the croustades in the middle of a preheated 350° F. oven for 20 minutes, or until the edges are golden. *The croustades may be made 1 day in advance and kept in an airtight container.*

Make the filling: In a skillet cook the shallot in the butter over moderate heat, stirring, until it is softened, add the mushrooms, the tarragon, and salt and freshly ground pepper to taste, and cook the mixture over moderately high heat, stirring, until the liquid the mushrooms give off is evaporated. Add the flour and cook the mixture over moderately low heat, stirring, for 2 minutes. Add the broth, bring the mixture to a boil, stirring, and stir in the sour cream and the Worcestershire sauce. Simmer the mixture for 2 minutes and stir in the lemon juice and the minced parsley. *The mushroom filling may be prepared 1 day in advance and kept covered and chilled.*

Divide the mushroom filling among the croustades, heat the croustades in a preheated 350° F. oven for 10 minutes, or until they are heated through, and garnish them with the parsley sprigs. Makes 24 croustades.

PHOTO ON PAGE 33

Pâté- and Bacon-Stuffed Mushrooms

5 slices of lean bacon
1 tablespoon unsalted butter
½ cup minced shallot
¼ teaspoon dried thyme
½ pound chicken livers, trimmed and halved
2 tablespoons Cognac or other brandy
⅓ cup heavy cream
freshly grated nutmeg to taste
½ lemon
36 small mushrooms (about 1 pound),
    stems discarded
snipped fresh chives or chopped fresh parsley
    leaves for garnish

In a heavy skillet cook the bacon over moderate heat until it is crisp, transfer it to paper towels to drain, and pour off all but 2 tablespoons of fat from the skillet. Add the butter to the skillet and in the fat cook the shallot and the thyme over moderately low heat, stirring, until the shallot is softened. Add the chicken livers and cook the mixture over moderately high heat, stirring, for 3 minutes, or until the livers are browned on the outside but still slightly pink within. Add the Cognac, cook the mixture until most of the liquid is evaporated, and transfer it to a food processor. Purée the mixture, add the cream, the nutmeg, and salt and pepper to taste, and blend the pâté until it is smooth. Transfer the pâté to a small bowl and chill it, covered, for at least 2 hours or overnight. Into a kettle of water squeeze the juice from the lemon, add the lemon shell, and bring the liquid to a boil. Add the mushrooms, boil them for 1 to 2 minutes, or until they are just tender, and transfer them with a slotted spoon to a bowl of ice and cold water. Put the mushrooms stemmed sides down on paper towels to drain and pat them dry. Stir the pâté until it is smooth, transfer it to a pastry bag fitted with a decorative tip, and pipe some of it into each mushroom cap. Chop the bacon fine and sprinkle the stuffed mushrooms with the chopped bacon and the chives or the parsley. Makes 36 hors d'oeuvres.

Prosciutto- and Parmesan-Stuffed Mushrooms

24 mushrooms (about 1 pound), stems
    removed and chopped fine
1 large garlic clove, minced
½ cup finely chopped onion
¼ cup olive oil

½ cup finely chopped prosciutto
    (about 3 ounces)
¼ cup dry bread crumbs
3 tablespoons minced flat-leafed parsley leaves
¾ cup freshly grated Parmesan
1 large egg, beaten lightly

In a skillet cook the chopped stems, the garlic, and the onion in 2 tablespoons of the oil over moderate heat, stirring, for 8 minutes, or until the stems are very tender, add the prosciutto, the bread crumbs, the parsley, ½ cup of the Parmesan, the egg, and salt and pepper to taste, and stir the mixture until it is combined well. Divide the mixture among the mushroom caps, mounding it slightly, and arrange the mushrooms in one layer in a lightly greased shallow baking dish. Sprinkle the mushrooms with the remaining ¼ cup Parmesan, drizzle them with the remaining 2 tablespoons oil, and bake them in the middle of a preheated 400° F. oven for 12 to 15 minutes, or until they are heated through. Makes 24 hors d'oeuvres.

Sherried Mushrooms on Toast

1 tablespoon unsalted butter
1 tablespoon vegetable oil
¼ pound mushrooms, sliced thin
1 shallot, minced
1 tablespoon all-purpose flour
½ cup chicken broth
2 tablespoons medium-dry Sherry,
    or to taste
½ teaspoon dried tarragon,
    crumbled
2 teaspoons minced fresh parsley leaves
2 tablespoons plain yogurt
toast points

In a skillet heat the butter and the oil over moderately high heat until the foam begins to subside and in the fat sauté the mushrooms and the shallot, stirring, until the mushrooms begin to give off their liquid. Sprinkle the flour over the mixture and cook the mixture, stirring, for 1 minute. Stir in the broth, the Sherry, the tarragon, the parsley, and salt and pepper to taste, bring the liquid to a boil, and simmer the mixture for 5 minutes, or until it is thickened. Stir in the yogurt, arrange the toast points on 2 plates, and spoon the mushroom mixture over them. Serves 2 as a first course.

Sour Cream- and Dill-Stuffed Mushrooms

½ lemon
36 mushrooms (about 1½ pounds), stems
    removed and chopped fine
2 tablespoons sour cream
2 tablespoons mayonnaise
2 teaspoons Dijon-style mustard
fresh lemon juice to taste
½ cup minced red onion
⅓ cup snipped fresh dill
dill sprigs for garnish

Into a kettle of water squeeze the juice from the lemon, add the lemon shell, and bring the liquid to a boil. Add the mushroom caps, boil them for 1 to 2 minutes, or until they are just tender, and transfer them with a slotted spoon to a bowl of ice and cold water. Put the caps stemmed sides down on paper towels to drain and pat them dry. In a bowl stir together the sour cream, the mayonnaise, the mustard, the lemon juice, and salt and pepper to taste and stir in the chopped stems, the onion, and the dill. Divide the mixture among the mushroom caps, mounding it slightly, and garnish each mushroom with a dill sprig. Makes 36 hors d'oeuvres.

Sugared Nuts

½ cup granulated sugar
½ cup firmly packed light brown sugar
1½ teaspoons cinnamon
1 teaspoon salt
1 large egg white
1 pound blanched whole almonds, walnuts, or
    a combination of both (about 3 cups)

Into a large bowl sift together the granulated sugar, the brown sugar, the cinnamon, and the salt. In a bowl whisk the egg white until it is foamy, add the nuts, and stir the mixture well. Add the nut mixture to the sugar mixture and toss the nuts until they are coated well. Spread the nuts in one layer on 2 buttered jelly-roll pans and bake them in the upper third and the lower third of a preheated 300° F. oven for 15 minutes. Switch the position of the pans and bake the nuts for 10 to 15 minutes more, or until the sugar coating is almost dry. Turn off the oven and let the nuts cool completely in the oven with the door propped open. The nuts keep in an airtight container for 2 weeks. Makes about 5 cups.

Marinated Black and Green Olives

2 cups small green olives (preferably
    picholine, available at specialty foods
    shops)
2 cups brine-cured black olives (preferably
    Niçoise, available at specialty foods shops)
2 small onions, sliced ½ inch thick
⅓ cup red-wine vinegar
2 bay leaves
12 thyme sprigs or 1½ teaspoons dried,
    crumbled
1 teaspoon fennel seeds, crushed lightly with
    the flat side of a knife
freshly ground pepper to taste
2 cups olive oil

In 2 saucepans of boiling water blanch the green olives and the black olives separately for 1 minute each and drain them in 2 sieves. Divide the onions between two 1-quart glass jars with tight-fitting lids, pack the green and black olives separately into the jars while they are still warm, and divide the vinegar, the bay leaves, the thyme, the fennel seeds, and the pepper between the jars, pushing the thyme into the mixture. Divide the oil between the jars, seal the jars with the lids, and let them stand in a cool, dark place, shaking them daily, for 3 days. The olives keep, covered and chilled, indefinitely. Makes 4 cups.

PHOTO ON PAGE 51

Marinated Olives, Nuts, and Pimiento

¾ cup Kalamata or other brine-cured
  black olives
½ cup small green olives, such as *picholine*
  (available at specialty foods shops)
½ cup small pimiento-stuffed olives
⅓ cup ¾-inch pieces drained bottled pimiento
¼ cup blanched whole almonds
⅓ cup unskinned hazelnuts, toasted lightly
¼ cup drained bottled cocktail onions
¼ cup thinly sliced onion
2 garlic cloves, sliced thin
½ lengthwise half of lemon, sliced
  thin crosswise
1½ teaspoons dried orégano
⅓ cup white-wine vinegar
1¼ cups olive oil

In a saucepan of boiling water blanch the Kalamata olives and the green olives for 1 minute, drain them, and in a bowl combine them well with the pimiento-stuffed olives, the pimiento, the almonds, the hazelnuts, and the cocktail onions. In a 1-quart jar with a tight-fitting lid pack decoratively the olive mixture, the sliced onion, the garlic, and the lemon and add the orégano, the vinegar, the oil, and pepper to taste. Seal the jar with the lid, shake the mixture, and chill it, shaking it daily, for 3 days. The marinated olive mixture keeps, covered and chilled, for 3 months. Makes about 3 cups.

Herbed Ricotta and Olive Toasts

½ cup whole-milk ricotta
2 tablespoons minced fresh basil leaves
1 tablespoon minced scallion greens
1 tablespoon minced fresh parsley leaves
2 rounded tablespoons minced Kalamata olives
1 teaspoon fresh lemon juice
six ½-inch-thick diagonally cut slices of
  Italian or French bread, each measuring
  about 4- by 2-inches, toasted lightly

In a bowl combine well the ricotta, the basil, the scallion greens, the parsley, the olives, the lemon juice, and salt and pepper to taste, divide the mixture among the toasts, and broil the toasts on a baking sheet under a preheated broiler about 4 inches from the heat for 1 to 1½ minutes, or until the topping is heated through. Serves 2 as an hors d'oeuvre.

Spicy Olive Salami Toasts

1 tablespoon minced drained bottled pickled
  hot peppers such as cherry peppers
  or *peperoncini*
1½ tablespoons minced Kalamata olives
3 slices of Genoa salami, minced
  (about 3 tablespoons)
1 tablespoon minced fresh parsley leaves
eight ½-inch-thick slices of Italian bread,
  toasted lightly
2 teaspoons Dijon-style mustard
3 tablespoons freshly grated Parmesan

In a bowl combine well the hot peppers, the olives, the salami, and the parsley. Spread one side of the toasts with the mustard, divide the hot pepper mixture among the toasts, spreading it evenly, and sprinkle the toasts with the Parmesan. On a baking sheet broil the toasts under a preheated broiler about 3 inches from the heat for 30 seconds to 1 minute, or until the Parmesan is golden. Serves 2 as an hors d'oeuvre.

Pecan Cornmeal Shortbread Rounds

1¾ sticks (14 tablespoons) salted butter,
  softened
1½ cups all-purpose flour
½ cup yellow cornmeal
2 teaspoons sugar
¾ teaspoon salt
1 large egg, beaten
¾ cup pecans, chopped fine and toasted
  lightly, plus additional pecan pieces
  for garnish

In a large bowl cream the butter until it is light and fluffy, stir in the flour, the cornmeal, the sugar, the salt, and the egg, and combine the mixture well. Stir in the chopped pecans, knead the dough until they are distributed, and chill it, wrapped in wax paper, for 1 hour. Roll out the dough ⅓ inch thick on a lightly floured surface and with a lightly floured 1½-inch scalloped cutter cut out rounds, rerolling the scraps as necessary. Garnish each round with an additional pecan piece, pressing the piece in gently. Bake the rounds on baking sheets in the middle of a preheated 350° F. oven for 22 to 25 minutes, or until they are pale golden, transfer them with a spatula to racks, and let them cool. Makes about 55 rounds.

Pistachio Twists

1 package (17¼ ounces) frozen puff pastry
    sheets (2 sheets), thawed
an egg wash made by beating 1 egg with
    2 teaspoons water
coarse salt for sprinkling the dough
1 cup shelled natural pistachio nuts, chopped
    fine and toasted lightly

Reserve 1 of the pastry sheets, wrapped and chilled. Roll out the remaining dough into an 18- by 12-inch rectangle on a lightly floured surface, brush it with some of the egg wash, and sprinkle it lightly with the salt and freshly ground pepper to taste. Sprinkle half the nuts over a crosswise half of the dough, with a rolling pin press them lightly into the dough, and fold the plain half of the dough over the nuts to form a 12- by 9-inch rectangle, pressing it firmly with the rolling pin to force out any air pockets. Roll the dough out lightly to make the layers adhere, brush it with some of the remaining egg wash, and sprinkle it lightly with more of the salt. Cut the dough crosswise into ½-inch strips with a pastry wheel or knife, twist the strips, and arrange them on greased baking sheets, pressing the ends onto the sheets. Bake the twists in the middle of a preheated 425° F. oven for 12 to 15 minutes, or until they are golden. Make more pistachio twists in the same manner. Makes 48 twists.

Scallion Biscuits with Ham

¾ cup all-purpose flour
1 teaspoon double-acting baking powder
¼ teaspoon baking soda
⅛ teaspoon salt, or to taste
¼ teaspoon sugar
1 tablespoon cold unsalted butter, cut into bits
¼ cup minced scallion including the
    green part
¼ cup small-curd cottage cheese, drained
    well in a sieve
2½ tablespoons milk
6 ounces thinly sliced smoked ham
coarse-grain mustard to taste

Into a bowl sift together the flour, the baking powder, the baking soda, the salt, the sugar, and freshly ground pepper to taste and blend in the butter until the mixture resembles coarse meal. Stir in the scallion and the cot-

tage cheese, add the milk, and combine the mixture until it just forms a soft, sticky dough. Turn the dough out onto a lightly floured surface and knead it gently about 5 times. Pat the dough or roll it lightly with a rolling pin into an 8- by 5-inch rectangle. Cut out 10 rounds with a 2-inch biscuit cutter, rerolling and cutting the scraps, and bake the biscuits on a buttered baking sheet in the middle of a preheated 425° F. oven for 12 to 15 minutes, or until they are golden. Split the biscuits in half horizontally, fill them with the ham slices, and top the ham with dollops of the mustard. Makes 10 hors d'oeuvres or an accompaniment to soup.

Shrimp, Chayote, and Coriander Tarts

1½ recipes *pâte brisée* (recipe follows)
3 small chayotes (about 1¼ pounds, available
    seasonally at specialty produce markets and
    some supermarkets)
⅓ cup finely chopped onion
⅓ cup finely chopped green bell pepper
⅓ cup finely chopped celery
1 tablespoon unsalted butter
6 Saltine crackers, crushed fine
    (about ½ cup)
10 ounces small shrimp, shelled, deveined,
    reserving 4 whole shrimp for garnish,
    and chopped
3 tablespoons minced fresh coriander leaves
    plus 8 coriander sprigs for garnish

Roll out the dough ⅛ inch thick on a floured surface, cut out eight 5-inch rounds, and fit them into 8 tart pans measuring 3 inches across the bottom. Chill the shells for 30 minutes, prick them with a fork, and bake them on a baking sheet in the middle of a preheated 450° F. oven for 6 to 8 minutes, or until they are pale golden. Let the shells cool in the pans on a rack for 1 minute, turn them out onto the rack, and let them cool completely. *The pastry shells may be made 1 day in advance and kept in an airtight container.*

In a large saucepan combine the chayotes and enough water to cover them by 2 inches, bring the water to a boil, and simmer the chayotes for 30 to 40 minutes, or until they are very tender. Drain the chayotes and let them cool until they can be handled. Halve and peel the chayotes, discarding the pits, and in a food processor purée them coarse. In a skillet cook the onion, the bell pepper, and the celery in the butter over moderately low heat, stirring occasionally, until the celery is softened, add the chayote purée, and cook the mixture, stirring occasionally, for 4 to 6 minutes, or until most of the liquid is evaporated. Stir in the crackers, the chopped shrimp, and salt and black pepper to taste, cook the mixture, stirring, for 1 minute, and stir in the minced coriander. In a small saucepan of boiling salted water cook the reserved whole shrimp for 1 minute, drain them, and halve them lengthwise.

Divide the filling among the shells, top each tart with a shrimp half, and heat the tarts on a baking sheet in a 450° F. oven for 5 minutes. Arrange the coriander sprigs on the tarts and serve the tarts hot. Serves 8.

PHOTO ON PAGE 23

Pâte Brisée

1¼ cups all-purpose flour
¾ stick (6 tablespoons) cold unsalted butter,
    cut into bits
2 tablespoons cold vegetable shortening
¼ teaspoon salt

In a large bowl blend the flour, the butter, the vegetable shortening, and the salt until the mixture resembles meal. Add 3 tablespoons ice water, toss the mixture until the water is incorporated, and form the dough into a ball. Knead the dough lightly with the heel of the hand against a smooth surface for a few seconds to distribute the fat evenly and re-form it into a ball. Dust the dough with flour and chill it, wrapped in wax paper, for 1 hour.

Summer Vegetables with Pesto Dip

1 cup bottled mayonnaise
2 cups firmly packed fresh basil leaves
½ cup pine nuts
1½ cups sour cream
2 large garlic cloves, minced and mashed to a
    paste with ½ teaspoon salt
assorted small vegetables

In a blender or food processor blend together the mayonnaise, the basil, and the pine nuts until the basil is puréed and the pine nuts are minced. Transfer the mixture to a bowl, stir in the sour cream and the garlic paste, and season the dip with salt and pepper. (*The dip will become more flavorful if it is made 2 days in advance and kept covered and chilled.*) Rinse the vegetables, trim them, and arrange them in a basket around the dip.

Walnut and Stilton Grapes

¼ pound Stilton, crumbled fine
3 ounces cream cheese, softened
¼ pound seedless green grapes
1 cup walnuts, toasted lightly and
    chopped fine
1 tablespoon minced fresh parsley leaves

In a bowl with an electric mixer cream together the cheeses until the mixture is smooth. Put ½ teaspoon of the mixture in the palm of one hand and in it roll a grape, rolling the mixture around the grape between both palms to coat it. Coat the remaining grapes in the same manner and chill them in a jelly-roll pan for 15 minutes. In a bowl combine the walnuts and the parsley. Roll the coated grapes in the walnut mixture to coat them completely and chill them in the jelly-roll pan until the coating is firm. Makes about 40 coated grapes.

CANAPÉS

Thai-Style Beef and Peanut Canapés

1 pound ground beef chuck
1½ tablespoons *naam pla* (fish sauce, available at some Asian markets)
3 tablespoons fresh lime juice
¼ teaspoon salt
¼ teaspoon chili powder
2 pickled *jalapeño* chilies, seeds and ribs discarded, minced (1½ tablespoons, wear rubber gloves)
2 tablespoons thinly sliced scallion
½ teaspoon sugar
1½ teaspoons soy sauce
3 teaspoons minced peeled fresh gingerroot
¼ cup finely chopped fresh coriander plus additional leaves for garnish
⅓ cup unsalted dry-roasted peanuts, chopped fine, plus additional peanut halves for garnish
sixty 2-inch rounds cut from slices of whole-wheat bread, toasted lightly

In a large bowl stir together the beef, the *naam pla*, the lime juice, the salt, the chili powder, the *jalapeño* chilies, the scallion, the sugar, the soy sauce, the gingerroot, the chopped coriander, and the chopped pea-

nuts. Spread 1 heaping teaspoon of the mixture on each bread round, garnish each round with an additional peanut half, and broil the rounds on a baking sheet under a preheated broiler about 6 inches from the heat for 3 to 4 minutes for medium-rare meat. (The soy sauce will prevent the meat from appearing pink.) Garnish the canapés with the additional coriander leaves and serve them warm. Makes 60 canapés.

Clam, Bacon, and Onion Canapés

a 6½-ounce can minced clams, drained
2 slices of lean bacon, cooked, drained, and chopped fine
2 tablespoons minced red onion
1 tablespoon minced fresh parsley leaves
2 tablespoons freshly grated Parmesan
2 tablespoons mayonnaise
eighteen 1½-inch toast rounds, cut from slices of white or whole-wheat bread, toasted lightly

In a small bowl stir together the clams, the bacon, the onion, the parsley, the Parmesan, and the mayonnaise until the mixture is combined well. Spread 1 teaspoon of the mixture on each toast round, mounding it, and broil the canapés in a jelly-roll pan under a preheated broiler about 4 inches from the heat for 3 to 4 minutes, or until they are bubbly and golden. Makes 18 canapés.

Deviled Ham and Caper Canapés

¼ pound Black Forest ham (available at specialty foods shops and some delicatessans), chopped fine
1 teaspoon dry mustard
1 teaspoon Dijon-style mustard
3 tablespoons mayonnaise
1 tablespoon drained bottled capers, chopped
a pinch of cayenne
twenty-four 1½-inch toast rounds

In a small bowl combine the ham, the mustards, the mayonnaise, the capers, and the cayenne and stir the mixture until it is combined well. Spread 1 teaspoon of the mixture on each toast round, mounding it, and broil the canapés in a jelly-roll pan under a preheated broiler about 4 inches from the heat for 2 to 4 minutes, or until they are puffed and golden. Makes 24 canapés.

Egg, Anchovy, and Caper Canapés

1½ tablespoons unsalted butter, softened
4 thin square slices of dense pumpernickel
    bread, crusts discarded
3 hard-boiled large eggs
3 to 4 flat anchovy fillets, cut lengthwise
    into very thin strips
16 drained bottled capers,
    or to taste

Spread the butter on the bread, season it with salt if desired, and with a 1½-inch round cutter cut out 4 rounds from each slice. Using an egg slicer or very sharp knife, cut the eggs crosswise into ¼-inch slices. Top each bread round with an egg slice, reserving the end egg slices for another use, and top the egg decoratively with some of the anchovy strips and some of the capers. *The canapés may be made 2 hours in advance and kept covered and chilled.* Makes 16 canapés.

PHOTO ON PAGE 33

Goat Cheese and Sun-Dried Tomato Canapés

¼ pound mild goat cheese, such as Montrachet
2 tablespoons drained and minced sun-dried
    tomatoes, reserving 1 tablespoon of the oil
2 tablespoons minced fresh parsley leaves
eighteen 1½-inch toast rounds, cut from
    slices of white or whole-wheat bread,
    toasted lightly

In a small bowl stir together the cheese, the sun-dried tomatoes with the reserved oil, and the parsley until the mixture is combined well. Spread 1 teaspoon of the mixture on each toast round, mounding it, and broil the canapés in a jelly-roll pan under a preheated broiler about 4 inches from the heat for 1 to 2 minutes, or until they are puffed and golden. Makes 18 canapés.

Jalapeño Cheddar Canapés

1 cup grated extra-sharp Cheddar
    (about ¼ pound)
1 large egg, beaten lightly
2½ teaspoons minced pickled *jalapeño* pepper
    (wear rubber gloves)
sixteen 1½-inch toast rounds, cut from
    slices of white or whole-wheat bread,
    toasted lightly

In a small bowl stir together the Cheddar, the egg, and the *jalapeño* pepper until the mixture is combined well. Spread 1 teaspoon of the mixture on each toast round, mounding it, and broil the canapés in a jelly-roll pan under a preheated broiler about 4 inches from the heat for 2 to 3 minutes, or until they are puffed and golden. Makes 16 canapés.

Spicy Peanut Butter, Bacon, and Scallion Canapés

½ cup peanut butter
¼ cup plus 1 tablespoon minced scallion
    including the green part
⅛ teaspoon cayenne
1½ teaspoons soy sauce
1 teaspoon fresh lemon juice
¼ teaspoon minced and mashed garlic
1 tablespoon mayonnaise
twenty-two 1½-inch toast rounds, cut from
    slices of white or whole wheat bread,
    toasted lightly
2 slices of lean bacon, cooked, drained, and
    chopped fine

In a small bowl stir together the peanut butter, ¼ cup of the scallion, the cayenne, the soy sauce, the lemon juice, the garlic, and the mayonnaise until the mixture is combined well. Spread 1 teaspoon of the mixture on each toast round, mounding it, and sprinkle the tops with the bacon. Broil the canapés in a jelly-roll pan under a preheated broiler about 4 inches from the heat for 1 to 2 minutes, or until they are puffed and golden. Sprinkle the canapés with the remaining 1 tablespoon scallion. Makes 22 canapés.

Pumpernickel Canapés with Cheese and Caraway Seeds

4 slices of pumpernickel bread, crusts
    discarded
1 tablespoon unsalted butter, melted
2 ounces cream cheese, softened
1 tablespoon dry white wine or vermouth
    if desired
1 large egg yolk
½ cup loosely packed grated Swiss cheese
2 teaspoons caraway seeds
parsley sprigs for garnish if desired

With a 2-inch scalloped round cutter cut out 2 rounds from each bread slice. Brush the rounds on both sides with the melted butter and bake them on a baking sheet in the middle of a preheated 350° F. oven, turning them once, for 15 minutes, or until they are toasted. In a bowl whisk together the cream cheese, the wine, and the egg yolk until the mixture is creamy, stir in the Swiss cheese and the caraway seeds, and season the mixture with salt and freshly ground pepper. Divide the mixture among the toasts, spreading it evenly, and broil the toasts under a preheated broiler about 4 inches from the heat for 1 minute, or until the tops are golden brown. Garnish the canapés with the parsley sprigs and serve them warm. Makes 8 canapés, serving 2.

Radish Canapés

1½ tablespoons unsalted butter, softened
4 thin square slices of dense pumpernickel
    bread, crusts discarded
8 to 10 radishes, sliced very thin using a
    mandoline or other hand-held slicer
small parsley sprigs for garnish

Spread the butter on the bread, season it with salt if desired, and cut each slice into 4 squares. Arrange the radish slices decoratively on the squares, reserving 16 slices for garnish. Cut through each reserved radish slice to the center, twist each slice gently, and set it on top of a canapé. Garnish the canapés with the parsley. Makes 16 canapés.

PHOTO ON PAGE 33

Shrimp and Dill Canapés

two 4¼-ounce cans tiny shrimp, drained
4 teaspoons minced onion
1 tablespoon snipped fresh dill
2 teaspoons fresh lemon juice
3 ounces cream cheese, softened

1 tablespoon mayonnaise
twenty-five 1½-inch toast rounds, cut from
    slices of white or whole-wheat bread,
    toasted lightly

In a saucepan of boiling water blanch the shrimp for 15 seconds and drain them in a colander. Refresh the shrimp under cold running water and drain them well. Reserve 25 of the smallest shrimp for garnish and chop the remaining shrimp. In a bowl combine the chopped shrimp, the onion, the dill, the lemon juice, the cream cheese, the mayonnaise, and pepper to taste and stir the mixture until it is combined well. Spread 1 teaspoon of the mixture on each toast round, mounding it, and top each canapé with 1 of the reserved whole shrimp. Broil the canapés in a jelly-roll pan under a preheated broiler about 4 inches from the heat for 3 to 4 minutes, or until they are pale golden. Makes 25 canapés.

Smoked Salmon Canapés

1½ tablespoons unsalted butter, softened
2 teaspoons well drained bottled horseradish
4 thin square slices of dense pumpernickel
    bread, crusts discarded
¼ pound sliced smoked salmon
dill sprigs for garnish

In a small bowl blend together well the butter and the horseradish and spread the mixture on the bread. Quarter each slice diagonally and cut the resulting triangles in half to form smaller triangles. Cut the salmon slices into 1½-inch squares, halve the squares diagonally to form triangles, and roll each triangle into a cone. Arrange the salmon cones on the bread triangles and insert a dill sprig in each cone. *The canapés may be made 4 hours in advance and kept covered loosely with a dampened paper towel and plastic wrap and chilled.* Makes 32 canapés.

PHOTO ON PAGE 33

Rillettes de Saumon Fumé
(*Smoked Salmon Spread*)

6 ounces smoked salmon
3 tablespoons *crème fraîche* (available at specialty foods shops and some supermarkets) or sour cream
1 tablespoon unsalted butter, softened
⅛ teaspoon freshly grated lemon zest
2 tablespoons finely chopped white part of scallion
2 teaspoons fresh lemon juice, or to taste
1 tablespoon snipped fresh dill plus dill sprigs for garnish
1 tablespoon salmon roe if desired

toast points or crackers as an accompaniment

In a food processor purée ¼ pound of the salmon with the *crème fraîche*, the butter, and the zest and transfer the purée to a bowl. Chop the remaining 2 ounces smoked salmon and stir it into the purée with the scallion, the lemon juice, and the snipped dill. With 2 teaspoons dipped in cold water form spoonfuls of the *rillettes* into oval mounds, arranging 3 mounds on each of 4 small plates. *The* rillettes *may be made 1 day in advance and kept covered and chilled. Let the* rillettes *come to room temperature before serving.* Garnish the *rillettes* with the dill sprig and the roe and serve them with the toast points. Serves 4 as a first course.

BREADS

YEAST BREADS

Apricot Cinnamon Bread

a ¼-ounce package (2½ teaspoons)
   active dry yeast
½ cup plus 1 teaspoon sugar
3 tablespoons unsalted butter
½ cup milk
3¼ to 3½ cups bread flour
2½ teaspoons salt
6 ounces dried apricots, chopped
2 teaspoons cinnamon
¼ teaspoon ground cloves
an egg wash made by beating 1 egg with
   1 teaspoon water

In a large bowl proof the yeast with 1 teaspoon of the sugar in ¾ cup lukewarm water for 5 minutes, or until the mixture is foamy. In a small saucepan melt the butter, add the milk, and heat the mixture to lukewarm. Add the milk mixture to the yeast mixture with 3¼ cups of the flour and the salt. Stir the dough until it forms a ball, turn it out onto a floured surface, and knead it, incorporating as much of the remaining ¼ cup flour as necessary to prevent the dough from sticking, for 10 minutes. Form the dough into a ball, put it in a well-buttered large bowl, and turn it to coat it with the butter. Let the dough rise, covered with plastic wrap, in a warm place for 1 hour, or until it is double in bulk. In a small bowl combine well the apricots and the remaining ½ cup sugar. Punch down the dough, turn it out onto a floured surface, and roll it into a 14- by 10-inch rectangle. Sprinkle the apricot mixture evenly over the dough, press it lightly into the dough, and sprinkle the dough with the cinnamon and the cloves. Beginning with a short end, roll the dough up tightly jelly-roll fashion, transfer the roll, seam side down, to a well-buttered loaf pan, 9 by 5 by 2¾ inches, tucking the ends under, and press the roll firmly so that it expands into the corners of the pan. Let the dough rise, covered with plastic wrap, in a warm place for 45 minutes, or until it reaches the top of the pan, brush the top gently with the egg wash, and bake the bread in the middle of a preheated 350° F. oven for 40 minutes, or until the top is golden brown. Let the bread cool in the pan for 10 minutes, turn it out onto a rack, and let it cool completely. *The bread may be made 1 day in advance and kept wrapped well in foil at room temperature.* Makes 1 loaf.

Chocolate and Vanilla Monkey Bread

For the chocolate dough
a ¼-ounce package (2½ teaspoons)
   active dry yeast
⅓ cup sugar
½ cup milk, heated to lukewarm
⅓ cup unsweetened cocoa powder
3 tablespoons unsalted butter, melted
½ teaspoon salt
3 cups all-purpose flour

For the vanilla dough
a ¼-ounce package (2½ teaspoons)
   active dry yeast
⅓ cup sugar
1 vanilla bean, cut into pieces
½ cup milk, heated to lukewarm
1 large egg
3 tablespoons unsalted butter, melted
3¾ to 4 cups all-purpose flour
½ teaspoon salt

¾ stick (6 tablespoons) unsalted butter,
   melted
1 cup sugar

Make the chocolate dough: In a large bowl proof the yeast with 1 teaspoon of the sugar in the milk and ½ cup lukewarm water for 5 minutes, or until the mixture is foamy. In a small bowl combine well the remaining sugar, the cocoa, the butter, and the salt, whisk the mixture into the yeast mixture, and stir in the flour. Knead the dough on a lightly floured surface for 10 minutes (the dough will be slightly sticky), put it in a well-buttered large bowl, and turn it to coat it with the butter. Let the dough rise, covered with plastic wrap, in a warm place for 1¼ hours, or until it is double in bulk.

Make the vanilla dough: In a large bowl proof the yeast with 1 teaspoon of the sugar in ½ cup lukewarm water for 5 minutes, or until the mixture is foamy. In a spice grinder or blender grind fine the vanilla bean with the remaining sugar, whisk the vanilla mixture into the yeast mixture with the milk, the egg, and the butter, and stir in 3¾ cups of the flour and the salt. Stir the dough until it forms a ball, turn it out onto a floured surface, and knead it, incorporating as much of the remaining ¼ cup flour as necessary to keep the dough from sticking, for 10 minutes. Transfer the dough to a well-buttered large bowl, turn it to coat it completely with the butter, and let it rise, covered with plastic wrap,

in a warm place for 1 hour, or until it is double in bulk.

Punch down the doughs, pinch off walnut-size pieces, and form them into balls. Have ready in separate small bowls the melted butter and the sugar. Butter generously a tube pan with a removable tube, 10 inches across the top and 4¼ inches deep. Dip each ball into the melted butter, letting the excess drip off, roll it in the sugar, and put it in the tube pan, alternating the doughs. Let the bread rise, covered with plastic wrap, in a warm place for 1 hour, or until it reaches the top of the pan, and bake it in the middle of a preheated 350° F. oven for 1 hour, or until the top is golden and crisp. Let the bread cool in the pan until it is warm and remove the tube from the rim. *The monkey bread may be made 1 day in advance and kept wrapped well in aluminum foil at room temperature. Reheat the bread, wrapped in foil, in a 250° F. oven for 30 minutes, or until it is heated through.*

Glazed Cinnamon Buns

For the dough
a ¼-ounce package (2½ teaspoons)
   active dry yeast
3 tablespoons sugar
2 tablespoons unsalted butter
½ cup milk
1¼ teaspoons salt
1 large egg
3 to 3¼ cups all-purpose flour

1½ tablespoons unsalted butter, melted
   and cooled
⅓ cup firmly packed light
   brown sugar
2 teaspoons cinnamon
½ cup raisins

For the glaze
1¼ cups confectioners' sugar
2 tablespoons unsalted butter, melted
   and cooled
2 to 3 tablespoons milk

Make the dough: In a large bowl proof the yeast with 1 tablespoon of the sugar in ½ cup warm water for 5 minutes, or until it is foamy. In a saucepan melt the butter, add the milk, the remaining 2 tablespoons sugar, and the salt, and heat the mixture to lukewarm. Stir into the yeast mixture, the milk mixture, the egg, and 3 cups of the flour and stir the mixture until it forms a dough. Turn the dough out onto a floured surface and knead it, incorporating as much of the remaining ¼ cup flour as necessary to prevent it from sticking, for 8 to 10 minutes, or until it is smooth and elastic. Form the dough into a ball, put it in a buttered bowl, and turn it to coat it with the butter. Let the dough rise, covered, in a warm place for 1 hour, or until it is double in bulk. *Alternatively, let the dough rise, covered and chilled, for at least 8 hours or overnight.*

Turn the dough out onto a lightly floured surface, roll it into a 12- by 9-inch rectangle, and brush it with the butter. In a small bowl stir together the brown sugar and the cinnamon, sprinkle the mixture evenly over the dough, pressing it in lightly, and sprinkle the raisins over the cinnamon mixture. Starting with a long side, roll up the dough tightly, jelly-roll fashion, cut it crosswise with a sharp knife into 12 equal pieces, and transfer each piece, cut side up, to a buttered ½-cup muffin tin. Let the buns rise, covered, in a warm place for 45 minutes, or until they are almost double in bulk, and bake them in the middle of a preheated 400° F. oven for 16 to 18 minutes, or until they are golden.

Make the glaze while the buns are baking: Into a bowl sift the sugar, whisk in the butter and 2 tablespoons of the milk, and whisk the mixture until it is combined well. Whisk in enough of the remaining 1 tablespoon milk to make a thick but pourable glaze.

Remove the buns from the oven, transfer them immediately to a rack, and pour about 1 tablespoon of the glaze over each bun. Makes 12 buns.

PHOTO ON PAGE 74

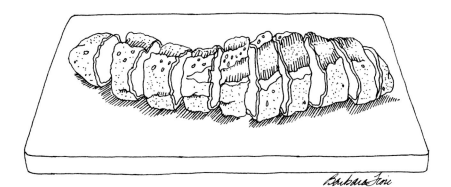

Italian Sweet Fruit and Nut Bread

For the sponge
2½ teaspoons (a ¼-ounce package)
   fast-acting yeast
½ cup all-purpose flour
a pinch of sugar

1 teaspoon fast-acting yeast
1½ tablespoons honey
1½ cups sugar
3 large eggs
3½ cups all-purpose flour
½ teaspoon salt
½ teaspoon fennel seeds, crushed
1 teaspoon vanilla
1½ tablespoons freshly grated orange zest
1½ tablespoons freshly grated lemon zest
1½ sticks (¾ cup) unsalted butter, cut into bits
   and softened

For the fruit and nut mixture
1 cup hazelnuts, toasted and skinned
   (procedure on page 224)
1 cup walnuts, toasted lightly
¾ cup unsalted dry-roasted peanuts
½ cup dried figs (preferably Mission),
   stemmed and chopped coarse
1 cup raisins
1 tablespoon firmly packed light brown sugar
1 teaspoon cinnamon
1 tablespoon all-purpose flour

Make the sponge: In a small bowl stir together the yeast, the flour, the sugar, and ½ cup very warm water and let the sponge rise, covered with plastic wrap, in a warm place for 30 minutes to 1 hour, or until it is double in bulk.

In the bowl of an electric mixer beat together the yeast, the honey, and ¼ cup very warm water, add the sugar, the eggs, and the sponge mixture, and beat the mixture well. Beat in 3 cups of the flour and the salt. With the electric mixer fitted with the dough hook beat in the fennel seeds, the vanilla, the orange zest, the lemon zest, and the butter and knead the dough at high speed for 5 minutes. Transfer the dough to a heavily floured surface and using a dough scraper knead in ¼ cup of the remaining flour. (The dough will be very soft and sticky and the consistency of a thick batter but it will be workable.) Put the dough in a buttered bowl, turning it to coat it with the butter, and let it rise, cov-

ered with plastic wrap and a kitchen towel, in a warm place for 3 hours, or until it is double in bulk.

Make the fruit and nut mixture: In a food processor pulse the hazelnuts, the walnuts, the peanuts, the figs, the raisins, the brown sugar, the cinnamon, and the flour until the fruit and nuts are chopped fine.

Knead the dough on a heavily floured surface and using the dough scraper knead in the remaining ¼ cup flour and the fruit and nut mixture in batches until the fruit and nuts are distributed evenly. (The dough will still be quite soft and sticky but workable.) Divide the dough in half, form each half into a ball, and put each ball in a well-buttered 1½-quart charlotte mold. Let the dough rise, covered with plastic wrap and a kitchen towel, in a warm place for 3 hours, or until it is almost double in bulk. Bake the breads in the middle of a preheated 400° F. oven for 10 minutes, reduce the heat to 350° F., and bake the breads for 50 to 60 minutes more, or until a skewer inserted in the center comes out clean and the bottoms, when unmolded, sound hollow when tapped. Unmold the breads carefully onto a rack and let them cool completely. The breads keep, wrapped well and frozen, for 1 month. Makes 2 small loaves.

Parker House Rolls

a ¼-ounce package (2½ teaspoons)
   active dry yeast
3 tablespoons sugar
2 tablespoons unsalted butter
½ cup milk
3¼ to 3½ cups bread flour
2½ teaspoons salt

In a large bowl proof the yeast with 1 tablespoon of the sugar in ¾ cup warm water for 5 minutes, or until the mixture is foamy. In a small saucepan melt the butter, add the milk, and heat the mixture to lukewarm. Add the milk mixture to the yeast mixture with the remaining 2 tablespoons sugar, 3¼ cups of the flour, and the salt. Stir the dough until it forms a ball, turn it out onto a floured surface, and knead it, incorporating as much of the remaining ¼ cup flour as necessary to prevent the dough from sticking, for 10 minutes, or until it is smooth and elastic. Form the dough into a ball, put it in a well buttered large bowl, and turn it to coat it with butter. Let the dough rise, covered with plastic wrap, in a warm place for 1 hour, or until it is double in bulk. Turn the dough out onto a floured surface, divide it into 20 pieces, and form each piece into a ball. Arrange the balls in rows in a buttered 13- by 9-inch baking pan and let them rise, covered with plastic wrap, in a warm place for 45 minutes, or until they are almost double in bulk. Using the length of a floured chopstick or the floured flat edge of a wooden spatula crease the balls down their centers until they are almost cut through, dust them with flour, and let them rise, covered, for 15 minutes. Bake the rolls in a preheated 400° F. oven for 15 minutes, or until they are golden. The rolls may be made 1 week in advance and kept wrapped well and frozen. Reheat the rolls, wrapped in foil, in a 400° F. oven for 25 minutes, or until they are heated through. Makes 20 rolls.

PHOTO ON PAGES 60 AND 61

Rye Sour-Cream Dinner Rolls

2½ teaspoons (a ¼-ounce package)
   active dry yeast
1 tablespoon sugar
½ cup sour cream
1 cup rye flour
2 to 2½ cups all-purpose flour
2 tablespoons caraway seeds
2 teaspoons salt

In a large bowl proof the yeast with the sugar in ¾ cup lukewarm water for 5 minutes, or until the mixture is foamy, add the sour cream and the rye flour, and combine the mixture well. Stir in 2 cups of the all-purpose flour, 1 tablespoon of the caraway seeds, and the salt, stirring until the dough forms a ball, and turn the dough out onto a floured surface. Knead the dough, incorporating as much of the remaining ½ cup all-purpose flour as necessary to form a smooth, slightly sticky dough, for 10 minutes, put it in a well-buttered large bowl, and turn it to coat it with the butter. Let the dough rise, covered with plastic wrap, in a warm place for 1 hour, or until it is double in bulk. Turn the dough out onto a floured surface, divide it into 12 pieces, and form each piece into a ball. Dip the top of each ball into the remaining 1 tablespoon caraway seeds, arrange the balls in rows in a buttered baking pan, 13 by 9 by 2 inches, and let them rise, covered with plastic wrap, in a warm place for 45 minutes, or until they are double in bulk. Bake the rolls in a preheated 400° F. oven for 18 minutes, or until they are golden. *The rolls may be made 1 week in advance and kept wrapped well and frozen. Reheat the rolls, wrapped in foil, in a 400° F. oven for 25 minutes, or until they are heated through.* Makes about 12 rolls.

Whole-Wheat Salt Sticks

2½ teaspoons (a ¼-ounce package)
   active dry yeast
1½ teaspoons sugar
1½ cups all-purpose flour
1 cup whole-wheat flour
½ cup cake flour (not self-rising)
1 teaspoon table salt
¼ cup vegetable oil
cornmeal for sprinkling the baking sheet
an egg wash, made by beating 1 large egg
   with 1 tablespoon water
coarse sea salt for sprinkling the breadsticks

In a small bowl proof the yeast with ½ teaspoon of the sugar in ½ cup lukewarm water for 10 minutes, or until it is foamy. In a food processor combine the flours, the table salt, and the remaining 1 teaspoon sugar and pulse the motor twice to combine the ingredients well. With the motor running, add the yeast mixture and the oil and blend the dough, adding up to 2 tablespoons water if necessary, 1 teaspoon at a time, to form a ball. Put the dough in an oiled bowl, turn it to coat it with the oil, and let it rise, covered, in a warm place for 1 hour, or until it is double in bulk. Punch down the dough and divide it into 20 pieces. Working with 1 piece of dough at a time and keeping the remaining pieces covered with an inverted bowl, roll the dough between the palms of the hands to form 8-inch-long sticks and arrange the sticks as they are formed 2 inches apart on a baking sheet sprinkled lightly with the cornmeal. Let the breadsticks rise, covered loosely, in a warm place for 20 minutes, brush them lightly with the egg wash, and sprinkle them with the sea salt. Bake the salt sticks in the middle of a preheated 450° F. oven for 15 minutes and let them cool on a rack for 30 minutes. The salt sticks keep in an airtight container for 1 week. Makes 20 salt sticks.

PHOTO ON PAGE 28

QUICK BREADS

Cheddar Biscuits

2 cups all-purpose flour
1 tablespoon double-acting baking powder
½ teaspoon salt
1½ cups coarsely grated extra-sharp Cheddar
(about 6 ounces)
1¼ cups heavy cream

Into a bowl sift together the flour, the baking powder, and the salt, add the Cheddar, and combine the mixture well. Add the cream and stir the mixture until it just forms a dough. Gather the dough into a ball, knead it gently 6 times on a lightly floured surface, and roll it or pat it out ½ inch thick. Cut out as many rounds as possible with a 2½-inch round cutter dipped in flour and transfer them to an ungreased baking sheet. Gather the scraps, reroll the dough, and cut out more rounds in the same manner. Bake the biscuits in the middle of a preheated 425° F. oven for 15 to 17 minutes, or until they are golden, transfer them to a rack, and let them cool for 5 minutes. Makes about 12 biscuits.

PHOTO ON PAGE 14

Cheddar, Scallion, and Bell Pepper Muffins

2 cups all-purpose flour
1½ teaspoons double-acting baking powder
½ teaspoon baking soda
¼ teaspoon cayenne
1 teaspoon salt
½ cup yellow cornmeal
2 cups coarsely grated extra-sharp Cheddar
½ cup thinly sliced scallion
1 cup finely chopped red bell pepper
¼ cup vegetable shortening
2 tablespoons sugar
2 large eggs at room temperature
1¼ cups buttermilk

Into a bowl sift together the flour, the baking powder, the baking soda, the cayenne, and the salt, add the cornmeal, the Cheddar, the scallion, and the bell pepper, and combine the mixture well. In a large bowl cream together the shortening and the sugar, add the eggs, and whisk the mixture until it is smooth. Whisk in the butter-

milk, add the flour mixture, and stir the batter until it is just combined. Divide the batter among 18 well-buttered ⅓-cup muffin tins and bake the muffins in the middle of a preheated 450° F. oven for 15 to 18 minutes, or until they are golden. Turn the muffins out onto racks and let them cool. Makes 18 muffins.

Corn Bread Gems

¼ cup yellow cornmeal
¼ cup all-purpose flour
1 teaspoon double-acting baking powder
1 teaspoon sugar
½ teaspoon salt
1 large egg, beaten lightly
5 tablespoons milk
1 tablespoon vegetable oil

In a bowl stir together the cornmeal, the flour, the baking powder, the sugar, and the salt, stir in the egg, the milk, and the oil, and stir the batter until it is just combined. Divide the batter among 12 well-buttered ⅛-cup gem tins, bake the muffins in the middle of a preheated 400° F. oven for 15 minutes, or until a tester comes out clean, and turn them out onto racks. *The muffins may be made 4 days in advance and kept in an airtight container.* Makes 12 muffins.

Sesame Maple Corn Sticks

¼ cup sesame seeds
vegetable shortening for greasing the molds
1¼ cups yellow cornmeal
¾ cup all-purpose flour
½ teaspoon baking soda
2 teaspoons double-acting baking powder
1 teaspoon salt
¾ cup sour cream
⅓ cup milk
⅓ cup maple syrup
1 large egg

In a skillet toast the sesame seeds in one layer over moderately low heat, shaking the skillet and stirring, until they are golden, transfer them to a small bowl, and let them cool. Grease 12 corn-stick molds, 5 inches long, generously with the shortening and heat them in a preheated 425° F. oven for 5 minutes. In a large bowl whisk together the cornmeal, the flour, the baking soda, the baking powder, the salt, and 3 tablespoons of the sesame seeds. In another small bowl whisk together the sour cream, the milk, the maple syrup, and the egg until the mixture is combined well, stir the sour cream mixture into the flour mixture, and stir the batter until it is just combined. Remove the molds from the oven, sprinkle the remaining 1 tablespoon sesame seeds evenly into the molds (about ¼ teaspoon in each mold), and spoon the batter over the seeds, spreading it evenly. Bake the corn sticks in the middle of the 425° F. oven for 13 to 15 minutes, or until they are golden, turn them out onto racks, and serve them warm. Makes 12 corn sticks.

PHOTO ON PAGE 75

Cranberry Chocolate-Chip Doughnut Holes

1 large egg
⅓ cup granulated sugar plus additional for
    sprinkling the doughnuts if desired
1 teaspoon vanilla
1 cup cranberries, picked over and chopped
½ cup semisweet chocolate chips
¾ cup all-purpose flour
2 teaspoons double-acting baking powder
¼ teaspoon salt
vegetable oil for deep-frying
⅓ cup sour cream
1½ tablespoons firmly packed brown sugar

In a bowl with an electric mixer beat the egg with ⅓ cup of the granulated sugar and the vanilla until it is thick and pale and stir in the cranberries and the chocolate chips. In a small bowl whisk together the flour, the baking powder, and the salt and fold the flour mixture into the egg mixture until the batter is combined well. Drop the batter by rounded teaspoons into 2 inches of 375° F. oil and fry the doughnut holes in batches for 1 minute on each side, transferring them as they are cooked to paper towels to drain. In a small bowl whisk together the sour cream and the brown sugar. Sprinkle

the doughnuts with the additional granulated sugar and serve them with the sweetened sour cream. The doughnut holes keep in an airtight container for 1 day. Makes about 24 doughnut holes.

Date, Nut, and Yogurt Scone

2 cups all-purpose flour
2 teaspoons double-acting baking powder
½ teaspoon baking soda
1 teaspoon salt
3 tablespoons sugar
5 tablespoons cold unsalted butter,
    cut into bits
1 cup chopped pitted dates (about 5 ounces)
1 cup chopped walnuts
an 8-ounce container of plain yogurt

Into a bowl sift together the flour, the baking powder, the baking soda, and the salt, add 2 tablespoons of the sugar and the butter, and blend the mixture until it resembles meal. Stir in the dates and the walnuts, add the yogurt, and combine the mixture well. Mound the dough in the middle of a buttered baking sheet, pat it into an 8-inch round, and sprinkle it with the remaining 1 tablespoon sugar. Bake the scone in the middle of a 425° F. oven for 15 to 20 minutes, or until it is cooked through, and cut it into 8 wedges. Let the wedges cool on a rack and serve them warm.

Garlic Bread

2 large garlic cloves
½ stick (¼ cup) unsalted butter, softened
1 tablespoon minced fresh parsley leaves
¼ teaspoon salt
a 14-inch loaf of Italian bread, cut diagonally
    into 1-inch slices leaving the slices attached
    on the bottom

In a small bowl combine well the garlic, forced through a garlic press, the butter, the parsley, the salt, and pepper to taste. Spread the mixture between the bread slices and wrap the bread in foil. *The bread may be prepared up to this point 1 day in advance and chilled.* Heat the bread in a preheated 350° F. oven for 10 minutes, open the foil slightly, and heat the bread for 5 minutes more. Serves 6.

PHOTO ON PAGES 18 AND 19

Popovers

4 large eggs, beaten lightly
1⅓ cups milk
5 tablespoons unsalted butter, melted
1⅓ cups all-purpose flour
¼ teaspoon salt
raspberry jam as an accompaniment

In a bowl beat together the eggs, the milk, and the butter until the mixture is combined well. Add the flour and the salt and beat the mixture until it is just combined. (The batter will be slightly lumpy.) Divide the batter among 9 very generously buttered ½-cup muffin tins or six ⅔-cup popover tins and bake the popovers in the middle of a preheated 375° F. oven for 1 hour. Cut a slit in the top of each popover with a small sharp knife and bake the popovers for 10 minutes more. Serve the popovers with the jam. Makes 6 or 9 popovers.

CRACKERS AND TOASTS

Bacon Mustard Biscuit Thins

6 slices of lean bacon
¼ cup Dijon-style mustard
2 cups all-purpose flour
1 tablespoon double-acting baking powder
½ teaspoon salt
1½ teaspoons freshly ground pepper
¾ stick (6 tablespoons) cold unsalted butter,
   cut into bits

In a large skillet cook the bacon over moderate heat, turning it, until it is crisp, transfer it to paper towels to drain, and chop it fine. In a small bowl combine well 2 tablespoons of the bacon drippings, the mustard, and ½ cup water. Into a bowl sift together the flour, the baking powder, the salt, and the pepper, add the butter, and blend the mixture until it resembles coarse meal. Toss the bacon with the flour mixture, add the mustard mixture, and stir it all together until it just forms a dough. Gather the dough into a ball, knead it gently 6 times on a lightly floured surface, and roll it out ⅛ inch thick. Cut out as many rounds as possible with a 2-inch cutter dipped in flour and arrange them on an ungreased baking sheet. Gather the scraps, reroll the dough, and cut out more rounds in the same manner. Bake the rounds in

2 batches in the middle of a preheated 450° F. oven for 10 to 12 minutes, or until they are golden, transfer the biscuit thins to racks, and let them cool. Makes about 80 crackers.

Cheddar Sesame Crisps

½ pound extra-sharp Cheddar, grated
1 stick (½ cup) cold unsalted butter,
   cut into bits
½ cup all-purpose flour
½ cup sesame seeds, toasted lightly and cooled
¼ cup minced shallot
½ teaspoon salt
white pepper to taste

In a food processor blend the Cheddar, the butter, the flour, the sesame seeds, the shallot, the salt, and the white pepper until the mixture forms a ball of dough. Halve the dough, on sheets of plastic wrap form each half into a log about 6 inches long and 1½ inches in diameter, and chill the dough, wrapped in the plastic wrap, for 1 to 2 hours, or until it is firm enough to slice. Cut the dough into ¼-inch slices, arrange the slices 2 inches apart on ungreased baking sheets, and bake them in batches in the middle of a preheated 400° F. oven for 5 to 7 minutes, or until the edges are golden brown. Transfer the crisps carefully with a metal spatula to racks, let them cool, and drain them on paper towels if desired. Makes about 56 crackers.

Oatmeal Dill Crackers

2½ cups old-fashioned rolled oats
2 teaspoons dill seed
1 tablespoon vegetable oil
coarse salt to taste

In a food processor grind coarse 1 cup of the oats. In a bowl combine well the ground oats, 1 cup of the remaining oats, and the dill seed, add the oil and ½ cup water, and stir the mixture until it forms a dough. On a work surface sprinkle ¼ cup of the remaining oats, on top of the oats pat out the dough slightly, and sprinkle the dough with the remaining ¼ cup oats. Sprinkle the dough with the salt, roll it out ⅛ inch thick, and with a 2-inch cutter cut out as many rounds as possible. Arrange the rounds on an ungreased baking sheet and bake them in the middle of a preheated 325° F. oven for

35 to 40 minutes, or until they are pale golden. Transfer the crackers to racks and let them cool. Makes about 40 crackers.

Rye Sunflower Crackers

⅓ cup shelled sunflower seeds, toasted
   lightly and cooled
1 cup unbleached all-purpose flour
⅓ cup wheat germ
½ cup rye flour (available at natural foods
   stores and some supermarkets)
2 teaspoons caraway seeds
⅓ cup extra-virgin olive oil
coarse salt to taste

In a food processor grind coarse the sunflower seeds with the unbleached flour, the wheat germ, the rye flour, and the caraway seeds, with the motor running add the oil and 6 tablespoons water, and blend the mixture until it just forms a ball of dough. Transfer the dough to a lightly floured surface and roll it out into a ⅛-inch-thick square. Cut the dough into 1½-inch squares with a knife, transfer the squares to an ungreased baking sheet, and prick each square several times with a fork. Sprinkle the squares with the salt and bake them in the middle of a preheated 400° F. oven for 10 to 12 minutes, or until they are golden. Transfer the crackers to racks and let them cool. Makes about 50 crackers.

Garlic Cumin Toasts

1 large garlic clove
½ teaspoon cuminseed
¼ teaspoon salt
3 tablespoons unsalted butter, softened
two 5-inch round hard rolls, cut into
   ⅓-inch-thick slices

Mince and mash the garlic and the cuminseed into a paste with the salt and in a small bowl combine the mixture with the butter. Spread some of the butter mixture on one side of each slice of roll and broil the slices, buttered sides up, on a baking sheet under a preheated broiler about 3 inches from the heat for 3 minutes, or until they are golden. Transfer the toasts to a serving dish. Makes about 16 toasts.

PHOTO ON PAGE 27

Italian Toasts

twelve ¼-inch-thick slices of Italian
   or French bread
1 large garlic clove if desired, halved
   crosswise
olive oil for brushing the toasts

In a ridged grill pan heated over moderately high heat until it is hot, or on a rack put over an electric burner set on low, grill the bread on both sides in batches for 1 minute, or until it is golden and crisp. Alternatively, toast the bread in a toaster. Rub 1 side of each toast with the garlic, cut side down, brush the toasts with the oil, and season them with salt. Makes 12 toasts.

PHOTO ON PAGE 57

JEANNE

Parmesan Garlic Sticks

½ stick (¼ cup) unsalted butter, cut into bits
½ cup all-purpose flour
2 to 3 large eggs
1 tablespoon minced garlic, mashed to a paste
   with ½ teaspoon salt
¾ cup freshly grated Parmesan

In a saucepan bring to a boil ½ cup water with the butter over high heat and reduce the heat to low. Add the flour all at once and beat the mixture with a wooden spoon until it leaves the side of the pan and forms a ball. Transfer the mixture to the bowl of an electric mixer and with the mixer at high speed beat in 2 of the eggs, 1 at a time, beating well after each addition. The dough should be thick enough to just fall from a spoon. If the dough is too stiff, break the remaining egg into a bowl, beat it lightly, and add enough of it to the dough to thin the dough to the desired consistency. Stir in the garlic paste and the Parmesan, transfer the dough to a pastry bag fitted with a ⅜-inch plain tip, and pipe 3-inch sticks 2 inches apart onto buttered baking sheets. Bake the sticks in batches in the middle of a preheated 425° F. oven for 18 to 20 minutes, or until they are puffed and crisp. Transfer the sticks to racks, let them cool, and serve them warm or at room temperature. Makes about 36 sticks.

Pumpernickel and Rye Breadsticks

1 loaf of pumpernickel or black bread
   (about 9 inches long)
1 loaf of seeded rye bread
   (about 9 inches long)
2 sticks (1 cup) unsalted butter, melted

With a long serrated knife cut the crusts from the loaves and cut each loaf lengthwise into ⅓-inch slices. Cut the slices lengthwise into ⅓-inch sticks and put the sticks on baking sheets. Brush the sticks with the butter, sprinkle them with salt to taste, and bake them in batches in the middle of a preheated 350° F. oven for 12 to 18 minutes, or until they are crisp. Transfer the sticks carefully to racks and let them cool. *The breadsticks may be made 3 days in advance and kept in an airtight container at room temperature.* Makes about 125 breadsticks.

PHOTO ON PAGE 11

PIZZAS AND OTHER BREADS

Pissaladières
(Small Tomato, Olive, and Anchovy Tarts)

½ pound frozen packaged puff pastry dough,
   thawed
4 thin onion slices
4 tomato slices
3 flat anchovy fillets, chopped
4 Niçoise, Kalamata, or other brine-cured
   black olives, pitted and quartered
2 tablespoons freshly grated Parmesan
½ teaspoon dried orégano, crumbled
½ teaspoon dried hot red pepper flakes
4 teaspoons extra-virgin olive oil

Roll out the dough to slightly less than ¼ inch thick on a lightly floured surface, cut out 4 rounds with a 4-inch cutter, and invert them onto a buttered baking sheet. Top each round with 1 onion slice, 1 tomato slice, one fourth of the anchovies, 1 olive, ½ tablespoon Parmesan, ⅛ teaspoon orégano, and ⅛ teaspoon red pepper flakes and drizzle each *pissaladière* with 1 teaspoon of the oil. Bake the *pissaladières* in the middle of a preheated 375° F. oven for 25 to 30 minutes, or until they are puffed and golden brown around the edges. Makes 4 *pissaladières*, serving 2.

Tomato Phyllo Pizza

5 tablespoons unsalted butter, melted and
   kept warm
seven 17- by 12-inch sheets of *phyllo*, stacked
   between 2 sheets of wax paper and covered
   with a dampened kitchen towel
7 tablespoons freshly grated Parmesan
1 cup coarsely grated mozzarella
1 cup very thinly sliced onion
2 pounds tomatoes (about 5), cut into ¼-inch-
   thick slices
½ teaspoon dried orégano, crumbled
1 teaspoon fresh thyme leaves, or ¼ teaspoon
   crumbled dried, plus fresh thyme sprigs for
   garnish

Brush a baking sheet lightly with some of the butter, lay 1 sheet of the *phyllo* on the butter, and brush it lightly with some of the remaining butter. Sprinkle the *phyllo* with 1 tablespoon of the Parmesan, lay another sheet of the *phyllo* on top, and press it firmly so that it adheres to the bottom layer. Butter, sprinkle, and layer the remaining *phyllo* in the same manner, ending with a sheet of phyllo and reserving the remaining 1 tablespoon Parmesan. Sprinkle the top sheet of *phyllo* with the mozzarella, scatter the onion evenly on top, and arrange the tomatoes in one layer over the onion. Sprinkle the pizza with the reserved 1 tablespoon Parmesan, the orégano, the thyme leaves, and salt and pepper to taste and bake it in the middle of a preheated 375° F. oven for 30 to 35 minutes, or until the edges are golden. Arrange the thyme sprigs along the pizza's perimeter and with a pizza wheel or sharp knife cut the pizza into squares. Serves 8 to 10 as a first course.

White Bean, Tomato, and Basil Pita Pizzas

two 5- to 6-inch *pita* loaves
2 tablespoons olive oil plus additional for
   brushing the *pita* loaves
½ cup finely chopped onion
1½ teaspoons minced garlic
1 cup drained canned white beans,
   rinsed and drained
⅓ cup dry white wine
1 tablespoon minced fresh basil or
   parsley leaves
2 tomatoes, sliced
⅔ cup grated mozzarella

Halve the *pita* loaves horizontally to form 4 rounds, arrange the rounds, rough sides up, on a baking sheet, and brush the tops lightly with the additional oil. Sprinkle the *pita* rounds with salt to taste and toast them in the middle of a preheated 350° F. oven for 10 minutes, or until they are pale golden and crisp. While the *pitas* are toasting, in a skillet cook the onion and the garlic in the remaining 2 tablespoons oil over moderately low heat, stirring, until the onion is very soft, add the beans, the wine, and salt and pepper to taste, and simmer the mixture, stirring occasionally, for 5 minutes, or until the beans are very soft and about half the liquid has evaporated. In a blender or food processor purée the mixture and season it with salt and pepper. Divide the bean purée among the *pita* toasts and sprinkle the *pita* toasts with the basil. Divide the tomato slices and the mozzarella among the *pita* toasts and broil the pizzas under a preheated broiler about 4 inches from the heat for 3 to 4 minutes, or until the cheese is melted and golden. Serves 2.

Flour Tortillas

2 cups all-purpose flour
¼ cup cold vegetable shortening, cut into pieces
1 teaspoon salt

In a bowl blend the flour and the shortening until the mixture resembles fine meal. In a small bowl stir together the salt and ⅔ cup warm water, add the salted water to the flour mixture, and toss the mixture until the liquid is incorporated. Form the dough into a ball and knead it on a lightly floured surface for 2 to 3 minutes, or until it is smooth. Divide the dough into 12 equal pieces, form each piece into a ball, and let the dough stand, covered with plastic wrap, for at least 30 minutes and up to 1 hour. Heat a griddle over moderately high heat until it is hot, on a lightly floured surface roll 1 of the balls of dough into a 7-inch round, and on the griddle cook the tortilla, turning it once, for 1 to 1½ minutes, or until it is puffy and golden on both sides. Wrap the tortilla in a kitchen towel and make tortillas with the remaining dough in the same manner, stacking and enclosing them in the towel as they are done. Wrap the tortillas in the towel and then in foil and keep them warm in a very low oven for 1 hour if necessary.

The tortillas may be made 1 day in advance and kept chilled in the refrigerator in a plastic bag. To reheat the tortillas divide them into 2 stacks and wrap each stack in foil. Heat the tortillas in a preheated 325° F. oven for 15 to 20 minutes, or until they are heated through. Makes 12 tortillas.

PHOTO ON PAGE 36

JEANNE

SOUPS

Asparagus, Pea, and Tarragon Soup

1¾ pounds asparagus, trimmed and
    cut into ¼-inch slices
a 10-ounce package frozen peas, thawed
5 cups chicken broth
1 tablespoon chopped fresh tarragon or
    1 teaspoon dried, crumbled, plus tarragon
    sprigs for garnish

In a large saucepan combine the asparagus, the peas, the broth, the chopped tarragon, and 1 cup water, bring the liquid to a boil, and simmer the mixture, uncovered, for 10 minutes, or until the asparagus is very tender. In a blender or food processor purée the mixture in batches until it is smooth and pour the soup into the pan. Season the soup with salt and pepper, heat it until it is heated through, and divide it among heated bowls. Garnish the soup with the tarragon sprigs. Makes about 8 cups, serving 4.

PHOTO ON PAGE 28

Southwestern Black Bean Soup with Jalapeño Cream

1 pound dried black beans (turtle beans),
    picked over
6 cups beef broth
two 14- to 16-ounce cans tomatoes including
    the juice, chopped
2 teaspoons ground cumin
⅔ cup sour cream or plain yogurt
2 to 4 fresh or pickled *jalapeño* peppers,
    minced (wear rubber gloves)
3 tablespoons minced fresh coriander leaves
    plus whole coriander leaves for garnish
½ cup chopped red onion for garnish

In a large bowl let the beans soak in enough cold water to cover them by 2 inches for 1 hour and drain them. In a heavy kettle combine the beans with 8 cups water and the broth, bring the liquid to a boil, stirring occa-sionally, and simmer the beans, uncovered, for 1 hour. Stir in the tomatoes with the juice and the cumin and simmer the mixture, uncovered, for 1½ hours, or until the beans are soft. Let the mixture cool for 15 minutes and in a blender or food processor purée it in batches un-til it is smooth, transferring it to a clean kettle as it is pu-réed. If a completely smooth texture is desired, force the purée through a sieve into a clean kettle. Bring the soup to a simmer and season it with salt and pepper. *The soup may be made 4 days in advance, cooled complete-ly, and kept covered and chilled.*

In a small bowl whisk together the sour cream, the *ja-lapeño* peppers, and the minced coriander. Ladle the soup into heated bowls and garnish each serving with some of the *jalapeño* cream, the onion, and the whole coriander leaves. Makes about 8 cups, serving 4 to 6.

Red Bean Soup with Cayenne Toast Points

a 19-ounce can kidney beans including the
    liquid
½ pound *kielbasa* or other smoked sausage,
    cut into ¼-inch-thick rounds
¼ cup chopped white part of scallion plus ¼
    cup thinly sliced scallion greens
1 cup chicken broth
1 teaspoon ground cumin
2 tablespoons unsalted butter
cayenne to taste
5 slices of homemade-type white bread, crusts
    discarded and the bread cut into 10 triangles

In a food processor purée the beans with the liquid and transfer the purée to a large saucepan. In a large skillet brown the *kielbasa* over moderate heat and trans-fer it with a slotted spoon to paper towels, and let it drain. In the fat remaining in the skillet cook the white part of scallion, stirring, until it is golden and transfer it with a slotted spoon to the saucepan. Into the pan stir the *kielbasa*, the broth, and the cumin, bring the mixture to a boil, and simmer it, stirring occasionally, for 15 minutes. Stir in the scallion greens and simmer the soup for 1 minute.

In a small saucepan melt the butter with the cayenne over moderately low heat, brush the cayenne butter on one side of the bread triangles, and toast the triangles on a rack set in a jelly-roll pan in the upper third of a preheated 400° F. oven for 5 to 8 minutes, or until they are golden. Serve the soup with the cayenne toast points. Makes about 3 cups, serving 2.

Beet Soup with Dill

a 1-pound jar beets
1 cup beef broth
1 tablespoon red-wine vinegar
1 teaspoon dried dill
¼ cup plain yogurt
1 tablespoon drained bottled horseradish

Drain the beets, reserving the juice, and cut half of them into julienne strips. In a blender purée the remaining beets with ⅓ cup of the reserved juice, the broth, the vinegar, and the dill, transfer the mixture to a saucepan, and simmer it for 10 minutes. Stir in the julienne beets, continue to simmer the soup until the beets are heated through, and divide it between 2 heated bowls. In a small bowl whisk together the yogurt and the horseradish and put a dollop of the mixture in each bowl. Serves 2.

Iced Beet and Cucumber Soup

a 1-pound jar of whole beets, drained,
    reserving ½ cup of the liquid, and sliced
    (about 1½ cups)
1½ cups peeled, seeded, and finely chopped
    cucumber plus, if desired, thin decorative
    slices of unpeeled cucumber for garnish
1 cup buttermilk
1 tablespoon red-wine vinegar
1½ teaspoons fresh lemon juice, or to taste
¾ cup cracked ice
3 tablespoons snipped fresh dill plus dill
    sprigs for garnish if desired

In a blender purée the beets with the reserved beet liquid, ¾ cup of the chopped cucumber, the buttermilk, the vinegar, the lemon juice, the ice, and salt and pepper to taste. Transfer the soup to a bowl, stir in the remaining ¾ cup chopped cucumber and the snipped dill, and divide the soup among 4 chilled bowls. Garnish the iced beet and cucumber soup with the cucumber slices and the dill sprigs. Makes about 4 cups, serving 4.

JEANNE

Carrot Soup with Chutney

1 small onion, chopped
1 tablespoon unsalted butter
1½ cups thinly sliced carrot (about 3 large)
1 rib of celery, sliced
1½ tablespoons rice (not converted)
¼ cup dry white wine
2 cups chicken broth plus additional to thin
    the soup if desired
¼ cup bottled mango chutney plus
    additional for garnish
2 tablespoons heavy cream

In a saucepan cook the onion in the butter over moderately low heat, stirring, until it is softened, add the carrot, the celery, and the rice, and cook the mixture, stirring, for 1 minute. Add the wine and cook the mixture for 1 minute. Add 2 cups of the broth, bring the liquid to a boil over moderately high heat, and simmer the mixture for 15 to 20 minutes, or until the rice is tender. In a blender or food processor purée the mixture with ¼ cup of the chutney and return the mixture to the pan. Stir in the cream, the additional broth, and salt and pepper to taste and heat the mixture until it is hot. Divide the soup between heated bowls and garnish it with the additional chutney. Serves 2.

Cold Carrot Soup with Scallion Swirl

1½ cups thinly sliced carrot
⅛ teaspoon crumbled dried rosemary
1 cup chopped scallion
2 slices of homemade-type white bread, crusts
   discarded and the bread cut into
   ½-inch cubes
1 tablespoon unsalted butter, melted
½ cup half-and-half

In a saucepan combine the carrot, the rosemary, and 2 cups water, bring the water to a boil, and boil the mixture gently for 10 to 12 minutes, or until the carrot is very tender. In a small saucepan combine the scallion and 1 cup water, bring the water to a boil, and boil the mixture gently for 10 to 12 minutes, or until the scallion is very tender.

While the vegetables are cooking, in a bowl toss the bread cubes with the butter and salt to taste, toast them on a baking sheet in the upper third of a preheated 400° F. oven for 3 to 5 minutes, or until they are golden, and reserve the croutons. In a blender purée the carrot mixture with the half-and-half until the mixture is smooth, transfer the soup to a metal bowl set in a larger bowl of ice and cold water, and chill it, stirring occasionally, for 5 minutes. In a clean blender purée the scallion mixture until it is smooth, force the purée through a fine sieve into the small saucepan, and boil it until it is reduced to about ¼ cup. Season the scallion purée with salt and pepper, transfer it to a small metal bowl set in the larger bowl of ice and cold water, and chill it, stirring occasionally, for 5 minutes. Divide the carrot soup between 2 bowls, spoon the scallion purée decoratively over it, and sprinkle the soup with the reserved croutons. Makes about 2 cups, serving 2.

Cheddar Vegetable Soup

1 large onion, chopped
¼ cup vegetable oil
1 large red bell pepper, cut into
   ¼-inch strips
2 boiling potatoes (about 1 pound)
2 zucchini (about 1 pound), scrubbed, halved
   lengthwise, and cut crosswise into
   ½-inch slices
a 10-ounce package frozen corn, thawed
⅓ cup all-purpose flour
4 cups chicken broth

2 cups milk
⅛ teaspoon cayenne, or to taste
10 ounces extra-sharp Cheddar, grated
   (about 3½ cups)

In a heavy kettle cook the onion in the oil over moderately low heat, stirring, until it is softened, stir in the bell pepper, the potatoes, peeled and cut into ½-inch cubes, the zucchini, and the corn, and cook the mixture, stirring, for 3 minutes. Add the flour and cook the mixture, stirring, for 3 minutes. Add the broth in a stream, stirring, and stir in the milk, the cayenne, and salt and black pepper to taste. Bring the mixture to a boil and simmer it, uncovered, stirring occasionally, until it is thickened. Add the Cheddar in 5 batches, stirring after each addition until it is melted, but do not let the soup come to a boil or the cheese will separate. Makes about 11 cups, serving 6 to 8.

Chicken Noodle Soup

the wings and backs from 2 chickens, cut into
   1-inch pieces with a cleaver
2 ribs of celery, sliced
1 carrot, sliced
1 onion, cut into 8 pieces
1 cup small egg noodles
1 tablespoon minced fresh parsley leaves

In a kettle combine the wings and backs, 6 cups water, the celery, the carrot, and the onion, bring the water to a boil, skimming the froth and fat, and boil the mixture for 20 minutes. Strain the mixture through a sieve set over a saucepan. Bring the stock to a boil, add the noodles, and boil them for 5 to 8 minutes, or until they are tender. While the noodles are cooking, discard the skin and bones from the chicken, reserving the meat, discard the remaining solids except the carrots, and mash the carrots lightly with a fork. Add the chicken and the carrots to the soup, bring the soup to a boil, and add the parsley and salt and pepper to taste. Makes about 3½ cups, serving 2.

Corn and Potato Chowder

2 slices of lean bacon, cut into
   ½-inch pieces
⅓ cup finely chopped onion
1 carrot, sliced thin

1 rib of celery, sliced thin
1 bay leaf
a ½-pound russet (baking) potato
1 cup chicken broth
1 cup milk
1 cup fresh corn kernels
    (cut from about 2 ears)
cayenne to taste
sour cream as an accompaniment
    if desired

In a large heavy saucepan cook the bacon over moderate heat, stirring, until it is crisp, transfer it to paper towels to drain, and reserve it. To the fat add the onion, the carrot, the celery, the bay leaf, and salt and black pepper to taste and cook the mixture, stirring, for 5 to 10 minutes, or until the vegetables are crisp-tender. Add the potato, peeled and cut into ⅓-inch dice, and the broth, bring the mixture to a boil, and simmer it, covered, for 10 to 15 minutes, or until the potato is tender. Add the milk and the corn and simmer the mixture for 3 minutes, or until the corn is tender. Discard the bay leaf, transfer about 1 cup of the mixture to a blender or food processor, and purée it. Add the purée to the pan with the cayenne and stir the chowder until it is combined well. Divide the chowder between 2 bowls and top it with the sour cream and the reserved bacon. Makes about 3 cups, serving 2.

Potage Froid aux Concombres
(Cold Cucumber Soup)

1 leek, slit lengthwise, washed well, and
    sliced thin crosswise
2 garlic cloves, minced
2 tablespoons olive oil
1¼ pounds cucumbers (about 2), peeled,
    seeded, and chopped
1 cup buttermilk or plain yogurt
1 cup chicken broth
2 tablespoons chopped fresh basil leaves

In a large baking dish combine well the leek, the garlic, and the oil and microwave the mixture at high power (100%), stirring once, for 6 to 8 minutes, or until the vegetables are softened. Stir in the cucumbers and salt to taste and microwave the mixture at high power (100%) for 5 to 7 minutes, or until the cucumber is just tender. In a blender purée the mixture with the butter-

milk and the broth until the mixture is smooth, transfer the soup to a metal bowl set in a larger bowl of ice and cold water, and stir the soup until it is cold. Stir in the basil and salt and pepper to taste. Makes about 3 cups, serving 2.

Gazpacho

2½ pounds tomatoes, peeled, seeded, and
    chopped fine
½ pound seedless cucumber, cut into ½-inch
    dice, plus thin slices for garnish
1 cup finely chopped red onion
1 red bell pepper, chopped fine, plus julienne
    strips for garnish
1 yellow bell pepper, chopped fine, plus
    julienne strips for garnish
¾ teaspoon minced garlic
¼ cup extra-virgin olive oil
¼ cup red-wine vinegar
1 cup tomato juice
1 cup beef broth
1 tablespoon tomato paste
1 teaspoon ground cumin
1 teaspoon salt
1 tablespoon Worcestershire sauce

In a bowl combine the tomatoes, the diced cucumber, the onion, the chopped bell peppers, the garlic, the oil, the vinegar, the tomato juice, the broth, the tomato paste, the cumin, the salt, the Worcestershire sauce, and black pepper to taste, stir in ½ cup ice cubes, and chill the soup, covered, for at least 4 hours or overnight. Ladle the soup into chilled bowls and garnish it with the sliced cucumber and the bell pepper strips. Makes about 8 cups, serving 6.

PHOTO ON PAGE 53

Chilled Cream of Green Tomato Soup

1½ cups sliced onion
2 garlic cloves, minced
2 tablespoons olive oil
2¼ pounds green (unripe) tomatoes (about 5),
    cored and cut into large pieces
a ½-pound boiling potato
2 cups chicken broth
1 teaspoon sugar
½ teaspoon dried thyme
1 cup heavy cream
⅛ teaspoon cayenne,
    or to taste

In a kettle cook the onion and the garlic in the oil over moderately low heat, stirring occasionally, until they are softened, add the tomatoes, the potato, peeled and cut into ½-inch pieces, the broth, the sugar, the thyme, and 1½ cups water, and bring the mixture to a boil. Boil the mixture, covered, stirring occasionally, for 45 minutes. In a blender purée the mixture in batches, transferring it to a large bowl as it is puréed, and let it cool. Stir in the cream, the cayenne, and salt to taste and chill the soup, covered, until it is cold. Makes about 9 cups, serving 6 to 8.

Kale and Salt Cod Soup

1 pound thick-cut (½ to 1½ inches) skinless
    boneless salt cod, cut into 1-inch pieces
    and rinsed
1 large onion, halved lengthwise and sliced
    thin crosswise
¼ cup plus 1 tablespoon olive oil (preferably
    extra-virgin)
1 pound boiling potatoes
½ pound kale, coarse stems discarded and the
    leaves washed well and chopped coarse

In a large ceramic or glass bowl let the salt cod soak in cold water to cover by 2 inches, changing the water several times, for 24 hours. Drain the salt cod and reserve it in a bowl.

In a kettle cook the onion in 1 tablespoon of the oil over moderately low heat, stirring occasionally, until it is softened. Add the potatoes, peeled and cut into ½-inch pieces, and 10 cups water, bring the liquid to a boil, and boil the mixture for 15 to 20 minutes, or until the potatoes are very tender. Break up the potatoes in the

mixture, add the reserved salt cod, and cook the mixture at a bare simmer, stirring occasionally, for 15 minutes. Stir in the kale, the remaining ¼ cup oil, and salt to taste and simmer the soup, stirring occasionally, for 4 minutes. Makes about 12 cups, serving 6.

Hungarian-Style Mushroom Barley Soup

2 onions, chopped
⅓ cup olive oil
3 carrots, chopped
1 green bell pepper, chopped
1 tablespoon paprika (preferably Hungarian)
1½ pounds fresh mushrooms, sliced
½ ounce dried sliced mushrooms
½ teaspoon dried thyme, crumbled
½ cup pearl barley
5 cups chicken broth
2 teaspoons cornstarch
¼ cup fresh lemon juice
3 tablespoons snipped fresh dill

In a heavy kettle cook the onions in the oil over moderately low heat, stirring, until they are softened, add the carrots, the bell pepper, and the paprika, and cook the mixture, stirring, for 1 minute. Stir in the fresh mushrooms, the dried mushrooms, the thyme, the barley, the broth, and 4 cups water, bring the liquid to a boil, stirring, and simmer the mixture, uncovered, for 50 minutes, or until the barley is tender. In a small bowl dissolve the cornstarch in the lemon juice and stir the mixture into the mushroom barley mixture with the dill. Bring the soup to a boil, stirring, and boil it until it is thickened slightly. Makes about 9½ cups, serving 4 to 6.

Wild Mushroom Consommé

4 pounds fresh mushrooms, minced
    (preferably in a food processor)
1½ ounces dried morels (available at specialty
    foods shops)
2 cups chopped onion
1½ tablespoons salt
⅓ cup fresh lemon juice, or to taste
¾ cup Sercial Madeira, or to taste

In a stockpot or kettle combine the fresh mushrooms, the dried morels, the onion, the salt, and 4 quarts water, bring the water to a boil, and simmer the mixture for 2 hours. Add the lemon juice, strain the mixture through a fine sieve lined with a double thickness of rinsed and squeezed cheesecloth into a large bowl, and stir in the Madeira and salt and pepper to taste. *The consommé may be made 3 days in advance, cooled uncovered, and kept covered and chilled. Reheat the consommé, but do not let it boil.* Ladle the consommé into a heated tureen. Makes about 12 to 14 cups, serving 12.

PHOTO ON PAGE 11

Onion and Beer Soup

1 pound (about 4) onions, sliced thin
1 bay leaf
3 tablespoons unsalted butter
a 12-ounce beer (not dark)
2 cups chicken broth
½ teaspoon Angostura bitters
coarsely grated Cheddar as an accompaniment
    if desired

In a kettle cook the onions with the bay leaf in the butter over moderate heat, stirring occasionally, for 20 minutes, or until they are golden. Add the beer, bring the mixture to a boil, and boil it, stirring, for 5 minutes. Add the broth, the bitters, and salt and pepper to taste, bring the soup to a boil, and simmer it for 2 minutes. Discard the bay leaf, divide the soup between 2 heated bowls, and sprinkle the Cheddar over it. Makes about 3 cups, serving 2.

Onion and Lentil Soup Gratiné

⅓ cup lentils, picked over and rinsed
½ bay leaf
2 onions (about ¾ pound), halved lengthwise
    and sliced crosswise

2 tablespoons unsalted butter
2 tablespoons gin
2 cups beef broth
1 teaspoon Worcestershire sauce
two ½-inch slices of Italian bread, toasted
    lightly
⅔ cup coarsely grated Gruyère or
    Swiss cheese
paprika for sprinkling the soup

In a saucepan combine the lentils and the bay leaf with enough water to cover the lentils by 3 inches, bring the water to a boil, and boil the lentils for 25 minutes, or until they are tender. While the lentils are boiling, in a kettle cook the onions in the butter over moderate heat, stirring occasionally, for 20 minutes, or until they are softened and golden. Add the gin, cook the mixture, stirring, until the gin is almost evaporated, and stir in the broth and the Worcestershire sauce. Drain the lentils in a sieve, discarding the bay leaf, rinse them briefly, and drain them well. Add the lentils to the kettle, bring the soup to a boil, stirring, and simmer it for 3 minutes. Divide the soup between 2 flameproof soup bowls, float the toasts in it, and sprinkle them with the Gruyère. Broil the soups under a preheated broiler about 2 inches from the heat until the Gruyère is melted and bubbly and sprinkle them with the paprika. Serves 2.

Lemon Tomato Broth

a 14- to 16-ounce can tomatoes, drained,
    reserving ½ cup of the juice
1 tablespoon unsalted butter
1½ cups chicken broth
½ teaspoon freshly grated lemon rind
2 tablespoons fresh lemon juice
1 teaspoon minced fresh parsley leaves
2 thin lemon slices for garnish if desired

In a saucepan cook the tomatoes in the butter over moderately low heat, stirring and breaking them up, for 5 minutes. Add the reserved juice, the broth, the rind, and the lemon juice, bring the liquid to a boil, and simmer the soup for 15 minutes. Stir in the parsley, simmer the soup for 2 minutes, and force it through a sieve into a bowl. Divide the soup between 2 heated bowls and garnish each serving with a lemon slice. Makes about 2½ cups, serving 2.

Split Pea, Green Pea, Carrot, and Turnip Soup

1 pound green split peas, picked over
1 large onion, chopped
1 large turnip, peeled and cut into ½-inch dice
2 carrots, cut into ½-inch dice
two 10-ounce packages frozen green peas,
    thawed
¼ teaspoon dried thyme, crumbled
2 cups chicken broth
1 cup diced cooked smoked ham
3 tablespoons olive oil
3 slices of day-old rye bread, crusts discarded
    and the bread cut into ½-inch cubes

In a heavy kettle combine the split peas, the onion, the turnip, the carrots, the green peas, the thyme, and 8 cups water, bring the water to a boil, stirring, and simmer the mixture, uncovered, stirring occasionally, for 1½ hours. Stir in the broth and salt and pepper to taste and simmer the soup, uncovered, for 5 minutes. In a skillet sauté the ham in the oil over moderately high heat, stirring, for 2 minutes, transfer it with a slotted spoon to a plate, and keep it warm. In the fat remaining in the skillet sauté the bread cubes, stirring, until they are crisp. Ladle the soup into heated bowls and top each serving with some of the ham and some of the croutons. Makes about 10 cups, serving 4 to 6.

Curried Butternut Squash Soup

2½ pounds butternut squash, peeled and
    halved lengthwise
1 cup chopped onion
2 tablespoons vegetable oil
4 garlic cloves, chopped fine
1 tablespoon curry powder
1 teaspoon ground cumin
a pinch of cayenne
3 cups chicken broth
1 pound tart apples
⅓ to ⅔ cup toasted squash seeds (recipe
    follows), or to taste, as an accompaniment
    if desired

Scoop out the seeds and strings from the squash, reserving the seeds to toast, and slice the squash thin. In a large heavy saucepan cook the onion in the oil over moderate heat, stirring, until it is golden, add the garlic, the curry powder, the cumin, and the cayenne, and cook the mixture, stirring, for 30 seconds. Add the squash, the broth, 3 cups water, and the apples, peeled, cored, and chopped, bring the liquid to a boil, and simmer the mixture, covered, for 25 minutes, or until the squash is tender. Purée the mixture in a blender or food processor in batches and transfer the soup to the pan. Season the soup with salt and pepper and heat it over moderately low heat, stirring, until it is hot. *The soup may be made 2 days in advance, kept covered and chilled, and reheated.* Transfer the soup to thermos containers. Pour the soup into mugs and sprinkle it with the toasted squash seeds. Makes about 10 cups, serving 6.

PHOTO ON PAGE 69

Toasted Squash Seeds

squash seeds from 2½ pounds
    butternut squash
1 tablespoon unsalted butter

Spread the seeds on a double thickness of microwave-safe paper towels, set the towels on the floor of a microwave oven, and microwave the seeds at high power (100%) for 3 to 5 minutes, or until they are dry. (Alternatively the seeds may be spread on a double thickness of paper towels and allowed to stand at room temperature for 1 to 2 days, or until they are dry.) Let the seeds cool, peel them from the paper towels, and in a skillet sauté them in the butter over moderately high heat, stirring, for 1 to 2 minutes, or until they are golden. Transfer the seeds with a slotted spoon to paper towels to drain, season them with salt, and let them cool. Makes ⅓ to ⅔ cup.

Vegetable, Beef, and Alphabet Soup

2½ pounds beef shanks
5 cups beef broth
5 cups chicken broth
a 14- to 16-ounce can tomatoes including the
    juice, chopped
2 large turnips, peeled and cut into
    ¼-inch dice
4 carrots, cut diagonally into ⅛-inch slices
½ pound green beans, cut into 1½-inch pieces
¾ cup alphabet noodles
⅔ cup minced fresh parsley leaves

In a heavy kettle combine the beef shanks, the beef

broth, the chicken broth, and 3 cups water, bring the liquid to a boil, and simmer the mixture, uncovered, skimming the froth occasionally, for 1½ hours, or until the meat is tender. Transfer the beef shanks to a cutting board and cut the meat into ½-inch pieces, discarding the fat and bones. Return the meat to the kettle and add the tomatoes with the juice, the turnips, and the carrots. Bring the liquid to a boil and simmer the mixture, uncovered, for 10 minutes. Stir in the green beans, the noodles, and salt and pepper to taste and boil the soup, stirring, for 10 minutes, or until the vegetables and the noodles are tender. Stir in the parsley and simmer the soup for 1 minute. Makes about 10 cups, serving 4 to 6.

White Bean and Escarole Soup

1 pound dried white beans, such as Great
  Northern or navy, picked over
4 cloves
2 onions
1 bay leaf
2 large garlic cloves, chopped
½ cup olive oil
1 pound escarole, trimmed, washed well,
  and spun dry
4 cups chicken broth
1 large tomato, seeded and chopped

In a heavy kettle combine the beans with enough cold water to cover them by 2 inches, bring the water to a boil, and boil the beans for 2 minutes. Remove the kettle from the heat, let the mixture stand, covered, for 1 hour, and drain the beans. Press the cloves into 1 of the onions. In the kettle combine the clove-studded onion, the beans, the bay leaf, and enough water to cover the onion by 2 inches, bring the water to a boil, and simmer the mixture, uncovered, for 1½ hours, or until the beans are tender. In a large skillet cook the remaining onion, chopped, and the garlic in ⅓ cup of the oil over moderate heat, stirring, until the onion is golden, add the escarole, and sauté the mixture over moderately high heat, stirring, until the escarole is wilted and bright green.

Stir the broth into the bean mixture, let the mixture cool for 15 minutes, and in a blender or food processor purée it with the escarole mixture in batches until the mixture is smooth, transferring the mixture to a clean kettle as it is puréed. Heat the soup over moderate heat until it is heated through. In a small skillet sauté the tomato in the remaining 2 tablespoons oil over moderately high heat, stirring, for 1 minute. Ladle the soup into heated bowls and top each serving with some of the tomato. Makes about 10 cups, serving 4 to 6.

STOCKS

Chicken Stock

3 pounds chicken backs, wings, necks,
  and bones, or a combination
2 onions, peeled and halved
2 whole cloves
4 unpeeled garlic cloves
1 rib of celery, halved
2 carrots, halved
1 teaspoon salt
6 long parsley sprigs
12 black peppercorns
½ teaspoon dried thyme, crumbled
1 bay leaf

If using wings, cut each wing at the joints into 3 pieces. In a stockpot or kettle combine the chicken parts with 14 cups cold water. Bring the water to a boil, skimming the froth, add ½ cup cold water, and bring the mixture to a simmer, skimming the froth. Add the onions, stuck with the cloves, the garlic, the celery, the carrots, the salt, the parsley, the peppercorns, the thyme, and the bay leaf and simmer the mixture, skimming the froth, for 3 hours. Strain the stock through a fine sieve into a bowl and let it cool to warm. If a more concentrated flavor is desired boil the stock until it is reduced to the desired concentration. Chill the stock and remove the fat. Makes about 10 cups.

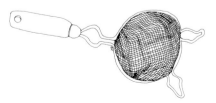

Brown Stock

3 pounds veal or beef bones, sawed into
   2-inch pieces
2 pounds stew beef, cut into 1½-inch cubes
2 unpeeled onions, quartered
2 carrots, halved
2 ribs of celery, halved
4 unpeeled garlic cloves
6 long parsley sprigs
1 teaspoon salt
½ teaspoon dried thyme, crumbled
1 bay leaf

Spread the bones and the beef in a flameproof roasting pan and roast them in a preheated 400° F. oven for 25 minutes. Add the onions and the carrots, roast the mixture, stirring once or twice, for 30 minutes more, or until it is browned well, and transfer it with a slotted spoon to a stockpot or kettle. Pour off any fat from the pan, add 2 cups water, and deglaze the pan over high heat, scraping up the brown bits. Add the liquid to the pot with 14 cups cold water and bring the liquid to a boil, skimming the froth. Add ½ cup cold water and bring the mixture to a simmer, skimming the froth. Add the celery, the garlic, the parsley, the salt, the thyme, and the bay leaf and simmer the mixture for 4 hours. If a more concentrated flavor is desired, boil the stock until it is reduced to the desired concentration. Strain the stock through a fine sieve into a bowl and let it cool to warm. Chill the brown stock and remove the fat. Makes about 8 cups.

White Fish Stock

1 pound bones and trimmings of any white
   fish such as sole, flounder, or whiting,
   chopped
1 cup sliced onion
12 long parsley sprigs
2 tablespoons fresh lemon juice
½ teaspoon salt
½ cup dry white wine

In a well buttered heavy saucepan combine the fish bones and trimmings, the onion, the parsley, the lemon juice, and the salt and steam the mixture, covered, over moderately high heat for 5 minutes. Add 3½ cups cold water and the wine, bring the liquid to a boil, skimming the froth, and simmer the stock for 20 minutes. Strain the stock through a fine sieve into a bowl, let it cool to warm, and chill it, covered. Makes about 3 cups.

Vegetable Stock

3 onions, chopped
3 tablespoons unsalted butter
the white and pale green part of 2 leeks,
   washed well and chopped
2 carrots, chopped
2 ribs of celery, chopped
¼ pound mushrooms (preferably ones
   with opened caps), chopped
1 cup potato peelings
¼ cup lentils
6 unpeeled garlic cloves
½ teaspoon black peppercorns
½ teaspoon dried thyme, crumbled
1 bay leaf
12 long parsley sprigs
1 teaspoon salt

In a stockpot or kettle cook the onions in the butter over moderate heat, stirring, until they are golden, add the leeks, the carrots, the celery, the mushrooms, the potato peelings, and ⅓ cup water, and simmer the mixture, covered, stirring occasionally, for 5 minutes. Add 12 cups cold water, the lentils, the garlic, the peppercorns, the thyme, the bay leaf, the parsley, and the salt, bring the mixture to a boil, and simmer it, uncovered, for 2 hours. Strain the stock through a fine sieve into a bowl and let it cool. Chill the stock and remove the fat. Makes about 9 cups.

FISH AND SHELLFISH

FISH

Cod Steaks in Spicy Yogurt Sauce

four ¾-inch-thick cod or scrod steaks
(about 2 pounds)
flour seasoned with salt and pepper for
dredging the cod
½ cup vegetable oil
2 large onions, sliced thin
3 garlic cloves, minced
¼ teaspoon turmeric
¼ teaspoon ground ginger
⅛ teaspoon cinnamon
⅛ teaspoon ground cloves
¼ teaspoon dried hot red pepper flakes
1 cup plain yogurt
¼ cup minced fresh coriander

Dredge the cod in the flour, shaking off the excess. In a large heavy skillet heat ¼ cup of the oil over moderately high heat until it is hot but not smoking, and in it sauté the cod, turning it once, for 1 minute, or until it is browned. Transfer the cod with a slotted spatula to a platter, add the remaining ¼ cup oil to the skillet, and in it cook the onions over moderate heat, stirring occasionally, until they are golden. Stir in the garlic, the turmeric, the ginger, the cinnamon, the cloves, and the red pepper flakes and cook the mixture, stirring, for 1 minute. Remove the skillet from the heat, stir in the yogurt, and in a blender purée the mixture until it is smooth. Return the mixture to the skillet, add the cod, and cook the mixture, covered, at a bare simmer (do not let it boil), turning the cod once, for 6 minutes, or until it just flakes. Transfer the mixture to a platter and sprinkle it with the coriander. Serves 4.

Baked Cod Steaks with Spinach and Feta

1 pound spinach, coarse stems discarded and
the leaves washed well
¼ cup chopped white part of scallion
1 tablespoon olive oil
1 garlic clove, minced
2 tablespoons chopped Kalamata olives
½ teaspoon orégano, crumbled
½ cup crumbled Feta
1 tablespoon fresh lemon juice
four ¾-inch-thick cod or scrod steaks
(about 2 pounds)

In a large saucepan cook the spinach with the water clinging to its leaves, covered, over moderate heat for 1 minute, or until it is wilted, and drain it well. Squeeze the spinach to remove most of the water and chop it coarse. In a small skillet cook the scallion in the oil over moderate heat, stirring occasionally, until it is softened, stir in the garlic, and cook the mixture, stirring, for 1 minute. Stir in the spinach, the olives, the orégano, the Feta, and the lemon juice and combine the mixture well. Arrange the cod steaks in a lightly oiled baking dish large enough to hold them in one layer, top them with the spinach mixture, and bake them in the middle of a preheated 450° F. oven for 8 to 10 minutes, or until they just flake. Serves 4.

Norwegian-Style Cod Steaks with Lemon Butter

four ¾-inch-thick cod or scrod steaks
    (about 2 pounds)
2 tablespoons fresh lemon juice
½ stick (¼ cup) cold unsalted butter,
    cut into bits
2 hard-boiled large eggs, sliced thin
    lengthwise
2 plum tomatoes, seeded and chopped
2 tablespoons minced fresh parsley leaves

In a deep heavy skillet large enough to hold the cod in one layer combine the cod with enough salted cold water to cover it by 1 inch, bring the water to a simmer, and poach the cod, covered, at a bare simmer for 5 to 6 minutes, or until it just flakes. Transfer the cod with a slotted spatula to heated plates. In a small saucepan combine the lemon juice, the butter, and salt and pepper to taste, heat the mixture, swirling the pan, until the butter is just melted, and remove the pan from the heat. Arrange 2 of the egg slices on each cod steak and sprinkle the cod with the tomatoes. Spoon the butter sauce over the cod and sprinkle it with the parsley. Serves 4.

Bacalao a la Vizcaína
(Salt Cod Basque Style
with Tomatoes and Bacon)

1 pound thick-cut (½ to 1½ inches) skinless
    boneless salt cod, cut into 1½-inch pieces
    and rinsed
¾ cup chopped drained pimiento
a 28-ounce can Italian plum tomatoes
    including the juice
¼ teaspoon cayenne
⅓ cup all-purpose flour
4 slices of lean bacon, cut into 1-inch pieces
2 tablespoons olive oil
1 large onion, chopped
1 large garlic clove, minced
sliced steamed potatoes as an accompaniment

In a large ceramic or glass bowl let the salt cod soak in cold water to cover by 2 inches, changing the water several times, for 24 hours. In a blender purée the pimiento with ¼ cup of the juice from the tomatoes and the cayenne and reserve the mixture. Drain the salt cod well and in a bowl toss it with the flour.

In a large heavy skillet cook the bacon over moderate heat, turning it, until it is crisp and transfer it with a slotted spoon to a bowl. Add 1 tablespoon of the oil to the skillet, heat the fat over moderately high heat until it is hot but not smoking, and in it brown the salt cod in batches, transferring it with the slotted spoon to the bowl with the bacon as it is browned. To the skillet add the remaining 1 tablespoon oil and in it sauté the onion, stirring occasionally, until it is golden. Add the garlic, sauté the mixture for 30 seconds, and stir in the reserved pimiento mixture, the tomatoes with the remaining juice, and the salt cod and bacon mixture. Simmer the mixture, covered, stirring occasionally and breaking up the tomatoes, for 1 hour. Add salt to taste and serve the mixture with the potatoes. Serves 4 to 6.

Grilled Halibut Steaks with Tomato, Cucumber,
and Lemon Dressing

¼ teaspoon freshly grated lemon zest
1½ tablespoons fresh lemon juice
½ teaspoon dried orégano, crumbled
¼ cup olive oil
¾ cup cherry tomatoes, halved, seeded, and
    sliced thin
½ cup seeded and thinly sliced cucumber
vegetable oil for brushing the pan
two 1-inch-thick halibut steaks (about 1 pound)

In a bowl whisk together the zest, the lemon juice, the orégano, and salt and pepper to taste, whisk in the oil, whisking until the dressing is emulsified, and stir in the tomatoes and the cucumber. Heat a ridged grill pan or cast-iron skillet over high heat until it is smoking, brush it with the oil, and in it grill the halibut, patted dry, over moderate heat, turning it once and covering it for the last 4 minutes of cooking, for 8 minutes. Transfer the halibut to plates and spoon the tomato mixture over it. Serves 2.

Monkfish Medallions with Tomato Lemon Coulis

2 small monkfish fillets (about 1 pound total),
    cut crosswise into 1-inch-thick medallions
¾ teaspoon dried thyme, crumbled
2 tablespoons unsalted butter
1 teaspoon minced garlic
1 cup coarsely chopped tomato
1 tablespoon fresh lemon juice, or to taste
1 tablespoon minced fresh parsley leaves

Season the monkfish with ½ teaspoon of the thyme and salt and pepper. In a heavy skillet heat 1 tablespoon of the butter over moderately high heat until the foam subsides and in it sauté the monkfish, turning it once, for 10 minutes, or until it is cooked through. Divide the monkfish between 2 heated plates and keep it warm, covered. In the skillet cook the garlic in the remaining 1 tablespoon butter over moderately low heat, stirring, until it is golden, add the tomato, the lemon juice, and the remaining ¼ teaspoon thyme, and cook the *coulis*, stirring, for 5 minutes. Stir in any juices that have accumulated on the plates, the parsley, and salt and pepper to taste and spoon the *coulis* over the monkfish. Serves 2.

Ocean Perch Fillets with Fennel, Tomato, and Fried Basil Leaves

For the fried basil leaves
whole basil leaves, rinsed and patted dry
vegetable oil for deep-frying

¼ cup plus 6 tablespoons olive oil
1 onion, chopped fine
1 fennel bulb, trimmed and chopped fine
   (about 2 cups)
3 garlic cloves, minced
¼ teaspoon fennel seeds, crushed lightly
⅓ cup shredded fresh basil leaves
2 tablespoons finely chopped fresh parsley
   leaves, preferably flat-leafed
3 tomatoes, chopped fine
¼ cup chopped pitted brine-cured
   black olives
⅛ teaspoon cayenne
½ teaspoon salt
freshly ground white pepper to taste

4 ocean perch fillets (about 1½ pounds)
1 tablespoon minced shallot
½ cup dry white wine
2 tablespoons fresh lemon juice
thinly sliced lemon for garnish if desired

Make the fried basil leaves: In a skillet fry the basil leaves in batches in 1 inch of 300° F. oil for 20 to 30 seconds, or until the bubbling noise of the oil dissipates and the leaves are crisp. Transfer the basil leaves with a slotted spoon to paper towels to drain and while they are still warm sprinkle them with salt if desired.

In a skillet heat 6 tablespoons of the oil over moderate heat until it is hot but not smoking and in it cook the onion, the fennel, and one third of the garlic, stirring occasionally, for 13 to 15 minutes, or until the vegetables are tender. Add the fennel seeds, the shredded basil, the parsley, the tomatoes, the olives, the cayenne, the salt, and the white pepper and cook the vegetable mixture until it is just heated through. Reserve the vegetable mixture.

While the vegetables are cooking, season the fillets with salt and white pepper. In a saucepan cook the shallot and the remaining garlic in the remaining ¼ cup oil over moderately low heat for 1 minute. Add the wine and the lemon juice, bring the liquid to a boil, and boil the mixture until it is reduced by half. Pour the mixture into a baking pan large enough to hold the fillets in one layer. Put the fillets, skin sides down, on top of the mixture in the pan and bake them in the middle of a preheated 425° F. oven for 12 minutes, or until they just flake.

Divide the reserved vegetable mixture among 4 heated dinner plates, put a fillet on each bed of vegetables, and garnish the plates with the fried basil leaves and the lemon slices. Serves 4.

PHOTO ON PAGE 63

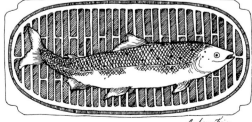

Broiled Salmon with Leek and Dill Sauce

For the sauce

1¼ pounds (about 3 large) leeks, split
    lengthwise, washed well, and the white and
    pale green parts sliced thin
2 tablespoons unsalted butter
⅓ cup dry white wine
1 cup white fish stock (page 118) or ¾ cup
    bottled clam juice
1 cup heavy cream
2 tablespoons snipped fresh dill

four 1-inch-thick salmon steaks
2 tablespoons vegetable oil
2 teaspoons fresh lemon juice
½ teaspoon snipped fresh dill
dill sprigs for garnish

Make the sauce: In a large skillet cook the leeks in the butter with salt and pepper to taste, covered, over moderately low heat, stirring occasionally, for 10 minutes, or until they are very tender. Add the wine and the stock and bring the mixture to a boil. Add the cream, boil the mixture, uncovered, until it is thick enough to coat a spoon, and season it with salt and pepper. *The sauce may be made up to this point 1 day in advance and kept covered and chilled. Reheat the sauce in a saucepan over low heat, stirring.* Stir in the dill and keep the sauce warm, covered.

Put the salmon steaks on a plate and drizzle them with the oil and the lemon juice. Sprinkle the steaks with the snipped dill and turn them to coat them on both sides with the mixture. Transfer the steaks to the lightly oiled rack of a broiler pan and sprinkle them with salt and pepper to taste. Broil the steaks under a preheated broiler about 4 inches from the heat for 4 minutes on each side, or until they are just cooked through. Divide the sauce among 4 heated plates, arrange a salmon steak on each plate, and garnish it with the dill sprigs. Serves 4.

Terrine de Deux Poissons
(*Salmon and Sole Terrine with Watercress*)

For the salmon mousseline

6 ounces skinless salmon fillet, any bones
    discarded
¼ pound sea scallops, rinsed and patted dry
1 tablespoon tomato paste
½ teaspoon salt

a pinch of freshly grated nutmeg
¼ teaspoon white pepper
1⅓ cups well chilled heavy cream

For the sole and watercress mousseline

2 cups loosely packed watercress leaves,
    rinsed well and drained
¼ pound sole fillet
¼ pound sea scallops, rinsed and patted dry
½ teaspoon salt
a pinch of freshly grated nutmeg
¼ teaspoon white pepper
1 cup well chilled heavy cream

watercress sprigs for garnish
vinaigrette de moutarde aux herbes (mustard
    herb vinaigrette, recipe follows) as an
    accompaniment

Make the salmon *mousseline*: In a food processor purée the salmon with the scallops, the tomato paste, the salt, the nutmeg, and the white pepper until the mixture is smooth, with the motor running add the cream in a stream, and blend the mixture just until it is combined. (Be careful not to over-blend the mixture or it will curdle.) Transfer the *mousseline* to a bowl and chill it, covered.

Make the sole and watercress *mousseline*: In a saucepan of boiling salted water blanch the watercress leaves for 15 seconds, drain them in a sieve, and refresh them under cold water. Squeeze the watercress dry between paper towels. In a food processor purée the watercress, add the sole, the scallops, the salt, the nutmeg, and the white pepper, and purée the mixture until it is smooth.

With the motor running add the cream in a stream and blend the mixture just until it is combined. (Be careful not to over-blend the mixture or it will curdle.) Transfer the *mousseline* to a bowl.

Assemble the terrine: For a checkerboard effect, transfer each *mousseline* to a pastry bag fitted with a ¾-inch plain tip and pipe alternating rows of the *mousselines* lengthwise in a well-buttered 1¼-quart terrine, rapping the terrine on a hard surface several times to expel any air bubbles and smoothing the layers with a rubber spatula. (Alternatively, the mousselines may be spread in layers in the terrine.) Cover the terrine with buttered wax paper and seal it tightly with foil.

Put the terrine in a baking pan, add enough water to the pan to come halfway up the sides of the terrine, and bake the terrine in the middle of a preheated 350° F.

oven for 45 minutes, or until it is firm to the touch and has shrunk slightly from the sides of the mold. Let the terrine cool on a rack for 10 minutes, discard the foil and paper, and pour off the excess liquid. Invert a platter over the terrine and invert the terrine onto it. Blot up the excess liquid with paper towels and let the terrine cool to room temperature. *The terrine may be made 1 day in advance and kept covered and chilled. Let the terrine come to room temperature before serving.*

Arrange the watercress sprigs along the top and around the edges of the terrine and serve the mustard herb vinaigrette separately. Serves 4 to 8 as a first course.

PHOTO ON PAGE 48

Vinaigrette de Moutarde aux Herbes
(Mustard Herb Vinaigrette)

2½ tablespoons white-wine vinegar,
    or to taste
1 tablespoon Dijon-style mustard
⅓ cup vegetable oil
3 tablespoons minced scallion
3 tablespoons minced fresh parsley leaves or a
    combination of other fresh herb leaves such
    as basil, thyme, and chervil

In a bowl whisk together the vinegar, the mustard, and salt and pepper to taste, add the oil in a stream, whisking, and whisk the dressing until it is emulsified. Stir in the scallion and the parsley. Makes about ⅔ cup.

Snapper with Fresh Tomato Sauce and Basil Butter
For the basil butter
1 cup packed fresh basil leaves
¼ cup packed fresh parsley sprigs
3 tablespoons unsalted butter, softened
For the tomato sauce
1 tablespoon olive oil
2 pounds tomatoes, peeled, seeded, and
    chopped fine
½ teaspoon dried thyme, crumbled

1 tablespoon minced shallot
1½ pounds snapper or scrod fillets
    (½ to ¾ inch thick)
2 tablespoons dry white wine

⅓ cup white fish stock (page 118) or bottled
    clam juice
3 large garlic cloves, minced
1 tablespoon minced fresh basil leaves

Make the basil butter: In a food processor chop coarse the basil and the parsley, add the butter and salt and pepper to taste, and process the mixture until the basil is chopped fine and the mixture is combined well. Transfer the butter to a small bowl. *The basil butter may be made 1 day in advance and kept covered and chilled. Bring the butter to room temperature before using.*

Make the tomato sauce: In a large skillet heat the oil over moderate heat until it is hot but not smoking and in it cook the tomatoes with the thyme and salt and pepper to taste, stirring, for 10 minutes, or until the tomatoes are softened and the sauce is thickened. *The tomato sauce may be made 1 day in advance and kept covered and chilled.*

Sprinkle the shallot over the bottom of a buttered shallow baking dish just large enough to hold the snapper fillets in one layer and arrange the snapper, skin sides down, on it. Pour the wine and the stock over the snapper, sprinkle the snapper with salt and pepper to taste, and bake it, its surface covered with a buttered piece of wax paper, in the middle of a preheated 425° F. oven for 10 minutes, or until it is just cooked through. Transfer the snapper with a slotted spatula to a platter and keep it warm, covered. Strain the cooking liquid through a fine sieve into the tomato sauce, add the garlic, and bring the sauce to a boil. Simmer the sauce, stirring, for 3 to 5 minutes, or until it is thickened, and stir in the basil and salt and pepper to taste. Pour off any liquid from the snapper, divide the sauce among 4 heated plates, and arrange a fillet on each plate. Top the snapper with the basil butter to taste. Serves 4.

Red Snapper Veracruz
(Red Snapper Baked in Spicy Tomato Sauce
with Olives and Capers)

2 garlic cloves
½ teaspoon salt
½ cup fresh lime juice
a 3½- to 4-pound whole red snapper, cleaned
For the sauce
1½ cups chopped onion
1½ tablespoons minced garlic
3 bay leaves
1½ teaspoons dried orégano, crumbled
1 teaspoon dried thyme, crumbled
⅓ cup olive oil
two 28-ounce cans Italian plum tomatoes
    including the juice, chopped
3 pickled *jalapeño* peppers, seeded and cut
    into thin strips (¼ cup; wear rubber gloves)
1 cup coarsely chopped pimiento-stuffed
    green olives
3 tablespoons capers
¼ cup chopped fresh flat-leafed parsley leaves
    if desired
For the garnish
flat-leafed parsley sprigs plus chopped flat-
    leafed parsley leaves
pimiento-stuffed green olives
chili flowers (procedure follows) if desired

flour tortillas (page 109) as an
    accompaniment

Mince the garlic, mash it with the salt, forming a paste, and in a bowl stir together well the garlic paste and the lime juice. With a sharp fork poke several holes in each side of the red snapper, put the snapper in a large shallow dish, and pour the lime juice mixture inside the cavity and over the snapper. Let the snapper marinate, covered and chilled, turning it once, for 2 hours.

Make the sauce while the snapper is marinating: In a heavy kettle cook the onion, the garlic, the bay leaves, the orégano, the thyme, and salt and black pepper to taste in the oil over moderate heat, stirring, for 10 to 15 minutes, or until the onion is very soft and pale golden. Stir in the tomatoes with the juice, the *jalapeño* peppers, the olives, and the capers, bring the mixture to a boil, and simmer it, stirring occasionally, for 1 to 1½ hours, or until it is very thick and reduced to about 5 cups. Stir in the parsley and discard the bay leaves.

Transfer the snapper with spatulas to a lightly oiled baking dish, spoon about half the sauce over the fish, keeping the remaining sauce warm, covered, and bake the snapper, covered, in the middle of a preheated 350° F. oven for 50 to 60 minutes, or until it just flakes. Transfer the snapper carefully to a large platter and spoon some of the sauce around the fish.

Garnish the snapper with the parsley sprigs, the chopped parsley, the olives, and the chili flowers and serve it with the remaining sauce and the tortillas. Serves 6.

PHOTO ON PAGE 36

To Make Chili Flowers for Garnish
fresh green or red chili peppers (available at
    specialty produce markets and many
    supermarkets)

Wearing rubber gloves, with a very sharp knife slit the peppers lengthwise from the tip end at 6 equal intervals, leaving at least 1 inch of the stem end intact, and scrape out the seeds and ribs gently. Let the peppers stand in a bowl of ice and cold water overnight, or until they are curled.

Steamed Sole with Vegetables and Sage Vinaigrette
For the vinaigrette
3 tablespoons extra-virgin olive oil
1 teaspoon white-wine vinegar
2 tablespoons minced fresh sage leaves

3 tablespoons olive oil
6 ounces small mushrooms, stems discarded
    and the caps sliced thin
1 red bell pepper, cut into ½-inch dice
1 green bell pepper, cut into ½-inch dice
1 yellow bell pepper, cut into ½-inch dice
4 sole or flounder fillets (about 1¼ pounds)
1 tablespoon minced fresh sage leaves
¼ cup chopped scallion
2 large garlic cloves, minced

Make the vinaigrette: In a small bowl whisk together the oil, the vinegar, the sage, and salt and pepper to taste until the vinaigrette is combined well.

In a large heavy skillet heat the oil over moderately high heat until it is hot but not smoking and in it sauté the mushrooms and the bell peppers with salt and black pepper to taste, stirring, for 5 to 7 minutes, or until the vegetables are just tender and the excess liquid is evaporated. Sprinkle the sole fillets on both sides with salt and black pepper to taste, sprinkle the fillets on the skinned sides with half the sage, and fold each fillet in half to enclose the sage. Sprinkle the fillets with the remaining sage, arrange them in a steamer set over boiling water, and steam them, covered, for 2 minutes, or until they are opaque. Transfer the fillets to a platter and keep them warm, covered. Reheat the vegetable mixture over moderate heat, stir in the scallion and the garlic, and cook the mixture for 1 minute, or until it is heated through. Transfer a fillet to each of 4 plates, divide the vegetable mixture among the plates, and drizzle the sole and vegetables with the vinaigrette. Serves 4.

Crispy Fried Squid

¾ pound cleaned squid
⅓ cup all-purpose flour
1 large egg
1½ cups fine Ritz cracker crumbs
vegetable oil for deep-frying
lemon wedges and/or a quick mayonnaise
   (page 202) as accompaniments if desired

Cut the squid body sacs crosswise into ⅓-inch rings, slice the flaps thin, and halve the tenticles lengthwise. Have ready in 3 separate shallow bowls for the flour, the egg, beaten with 1 tablespoon water, and the crumbs. Working in small batches dredge the squid in the flour, shaking off the excess, dip it in the egg mixture, letting the excess drip off, and coat it with the crumbs, transferring it as it is coated to a baking sheet lined with wax paper. In a deep skillet fry the squid in batches in 1 inch of 380° F. oil for 30 seconds, or until it is golden brown, transferring it with a slotted spoon as it is fried to paper towels to drain and making sure the oil returns to 380° F. before adding each new batch. Serve the fried squid with the lemon wedges and/or the mayonnaise. Serves 2.

Swordfish with Lemon, Olives, and Sun-Dried Tomatoes

1 lemon, sliced thin
a ¾-pound swordfish steak, about ¾ inch thick
6 Kalamata olives, pitted and cut into slivers
3 tablespoons chopped sun-dried tomatoes
1 tablespoon thinly sliced scallion
1 tablespoon olive oil

Arrange the lemon slices, overlapping slightly, in a microwave-safe shallow baking dish, put the swordfish on top of them, and sprinkle it with the olives, the tomatoes, and the scallion. Drizzle the fish with the oil, cover the dish tightly with microwave-safe plastic wrap, and microwave it at high power (100%) for 4 minutes. Remove the dish from the oven, cut a 2-inch slit in the plastic wrap, and let the dish stand for 2 minutes. Serves 2.

Pan Bagnas
(Provençal Sandwiches with Tuna, Basil, and Tomato)

½ cup red-wine vinegar
6 flat anchovy fillets, rinsed, patted dry,
   and minced
2 garlic cloves, minced
1 cup extra-virgin olive oil
two 8-inch round loaves of crusty bread
2 cups thinly sliced radish
2 cups loosely packed fresh basil leaves
1 cup minced onion, soaked in cold water
   for 10 minutes and drained well
two 6½-ounce cans tuna in oil, drained and flaked
4 tomatoes (about 1½ pounds), sliced thin

In a bowl whisk together the vinegar, the anchovies, the garlic, and salt and pepper to taste, add the oil in a stream, whisking, and whisk the dressing until it is emulsified. Halve the breads horizontally, hollow out the halves, leaving ½-inch-thick shells, and spoon one fourth of the dressing evenly into each half.

Working with one loaf at a time, arrange half the radish in the bottom shell, top it with one third of the basil, and sprinkle half the onion over the basil. Arrange half the tuna on the onion, top it with one third of the remaining basil, and arrange half the tomatoes on the basil. Fit the top shell over the tomatoes. Assemble another *pan bagna* with the remaining bread, radish, basil, onion, tuna, and tomatoes in the same manner. Wrap the *pan bagnas* in plastic wrap and put them in a jelly-roll pan. Top the *pan bagnas* with a baking sheet and a large bowl filled with several 2-pound weights and chill them for 1 hour. *The pan bagnas may be made 4 hours in advance and kept covered and chilled.* Serve the *pan bagnas* cut into wedges. Serves 6.

PHOTO ON PAGE 51

SHELLFISH

Clams on the Half Shell

36 small hard-shelled clams, scrubbed
    and covered with crushed ice
tomato and pepper cocktail sauce (recipe
    follows) as an accompaniment
caper, shallot, and parsley sauce (recipe on
    this page) as an accompaniment
lemon wedges as an accompaniment

Hold each clam in the palm of the hand with the hinge against the heel of the palm. Force a clam knife between the shells, cut around the inside edges to sever the connecting muscles, and twist the knife slightly to open the shells. Cut the muscles attaching the clam to the shells, leaving the clam in the bottom shell, and twist off the top shell, discarding it. Arrange the clams on the half shell on a bed of crushed ice and serve them with the sauces and the lemon wedges. Serves 12.

Tomato and Pepper Cocktail Sauce

⅓ cup drained bottled roasted red peppers
½ cup ketchup
2 tablespoons fresh lemon juice
1 tablespoon bottled horseradish, or to taste
a dash of Tabasco, or to taste
½ teaspoon Worcestershire sauce

In a blender purée the roasted peppers with the ketchup and the lemon juice, transfer the purée to a bowl, and stir in the horseradish, the Tabasco, the Worcestershire sauce, and salt and black pepper to taste. Makes about 1 cup.

Caper, Shallot, and Parsley Sauce

½ cup white-wine tarragon vinegar
2 teaspoons fresh lemon juice
½ teaspoon sugar
2 tablespoons olive oil
¼ cup finely chopped shallot
3 tablespoons minced fresh parsley leaves
2 tablespoons chopped capers

In a small bowl combine well the vinegar, the lemon juice, 2 tablespoons water, the sugar, the oil, the shallot, the parsley, the capers, and salt and pepper to taste. Makes about 1 cup.

Clams Casino with Coriander

3 slices of lean bacon, each cut
    crosswise into fourths
3 tablespoons unsalted butter, softened
2 tablespoons minced scallion
1 tablespoon minced bottled roasted
    red pepper
2 tablespoons minced fresh coriander
Tabasco to taste
12 medium hard-shelled clams, shucked
    (procedure follows), reserving the
    bottom shells
lemon juice to taste

In a skillet cook the bacon over moderate heat, turning it once, until it is golden but still soft, transfer it to paper towels to drain, and reserve it. In a small bowl stir together the butter, the scallion, the roasted pepper, the coriander, the Tabasco, and salt and black pepper to taste. Arrange the reserved clam shells in a baking pan just large enough to hold them in one layer and divide the butter mixture among them. Top the butter mixture with the clams, sprinkle the clams with the lemon juice, and top each clam with a piece of the reserved bacon. Bake the clams in the middle of a preheated 450° F. oven for 10 minutes. Serves 2.

To Shuck Hard-Shelled Clams

Scrub the clams thoroughly with a stiff brush under cold water, discarding any that have cracked shells or that are not shut tightly.

Working over a bowl to reserve the liquor, hold each clam in the palm of the hand with the hinge against the heel of the palm. Force a clam knife between the shells, cut around the inside edges to sever the connecting muscles, and twist the knife slightly to open the shells.

If the clams are not to be served raw, they may be opened in the oven: Arrange the clams in one layer in a baking pan and put the pan in a preheated 450° F. oven for 3 to 5 minutes, or until the shells have opened. Reserve the liquor and discard any unopened clams.

Clambake in a Pot
(Lobsters and Steamers with Sage, Lemon, and Garlic Butter; White Onions and Red Potatoes; Corn on the Cob with Tomato Butter)

12 ears of corn in their husks
twelve 1¼-pound live lobsters
4 pounds small white onions, outer
    skins discarded
4 pounds small red potatoes, scrubbed
6 pounds steamers (soft-shelled clams), scrubbed
sage, lemon, and garlic butter (recipe follows)
tomato butter (recipe on this page)

Remove the outer husks of each ear of corn until the innermost layer is reached. Peel back the pale green layers without breaking them off, discard the silk, and fold the husks back into place. In a very large (30- to 40-quart) stockpot containing 1 inch water layer in order the lobsters, the onions, the corn, the potatoes, and the steamers. Cover the stockpot and set it on a rack set over glowing and lightly flaming coals (procedure follows). Steam the mixture for 30 minutes from the time the water boils. Check a clam for doneness: If it is cooked the rest of the "clambake" will also be done. Transfer the steamers, the potatoes, the corn, the onions, and the lobsters with tongs to bowls or platters and serve the seafood with the sage, lemon, and garlic butter and the corn with the tomato butter. Serves 12.

PHOTO ON PAGES 60 AND 61

Clambake Fire Procedure

In a pit dug in sand or dirt or in a large grill ignite enough charcoal to measure 6 to 8 inches deep. Let the charcoal burn for 30 minutes, or until the coals are glowing (white and still flaming lightly), and set a rack no more than 2 inches from the coals. (The stockpot can be put directly on the coals if desired.)

Sage, Lemon, and Garlic Butter

4 sticks (2 cups) unsalted butter
4 large garlic cloves, halved
¼ cup finely chopped fresh sage leaves
¼ cup fresh lemon juice

In a saucepan melt the butter with the garlic, the sage, the lemon juice, and salt and pepper to taste, stirring occasionally. Makes about 2¼ cups.

Tomato Butter

1 stick (½ cup) unsalted butter, softened
1 tablespoon tomato paste
¼ teaspoon salt
½ teaspoon pepper

In a small bowl combine well the butter, the tomato paste, the salt, and the pepper. Makes ½ cup.

Homard à l'Américaine
(Lobster in Spicy Tomato Sauce)

1 cup coarsely grated carrot
½ cup thinly sliced shallot
2 tablespoons unsalted butter
2 tablespoons olive oil
a 2- to 2½-pound live lobster
1½ pounds tomatoes, chopped coarse
¼ cup dry white wine
¼ teaspoon dried tarragon, crumbled
1 teaspoon dried hot red pepper flakes
2 tablespoons Cognac
¼ cup minced fresh parsley leaves

In a large deep skillet cook the carrot and the shallot in the butter and the oil over moderate heat, stirring occasionally, until they are softened. While the vegetables are cooking, plunge the lobster into a kettle of boiling salted water and boil it, covered, for 8 minutes. Transfer the lobster to a work surface and let it cool until it can be handled. To the skillet add the tomatoes, the wine, the tarragon, the red pepper flakes, and salt and black pepper to taste, bring the mixture to a boil, stirring, and boil it for 10 minutes, or until it is thickened. While the sauce is cooking, pull the lobster tail apart from the body and stir 2 tablespoons of the tomalley and any roe from the tail and body sections into the sauce. Cut the tail section crosswise through the shell into medallions with a cleaver, separate the claws and joints, and crack the shells of the claws and joints with the back of the cleaver. Add the lobster to the skillet, discarding the body section. In a ladle or small saucepan heat the Cognac, ignite it carefully, and pour it over the lobster, shaking the skillet gently until the flames go out. Simmer the mixture, stirring, for 1 minute and sprinkle the parsley over it. Serves 2.

Lobster, Oyster, and Sausage Gumbo

2 pounds hot smoked sausage, mild smoked
    sausage, or *kielbasa*, cut into ½-inch slices
1 tablespoon vegetable oil
½ cup all-purpose flour
2 red bell peppers, chopped
1 pound onions, sliced thin
2 bay leaves
two 2-pound live lobsters
36 shucked oysters, reserving the liquor
a 28-ounce can plum tomatoes including
    the juice
1 teaspoon dried thyme, crumbled
1 teaspoon dried orégano, crumbled
1 teaspoon cayenne, or to taste
¾ cup thinly sliced scallion
rice with red beans and peas (recipe follows)
    as an accompaniment
fried cornmeal-coated okra (recipe on this
    page) as an accompaniment

In a large heavy skillet brown the sausage in batches in the oil over moderate heat, transferring it as it is browned with a slotted spoon to a bowl. Pour off all but ¼ cup of the fat, add the flour to the skillet, and cook the *roux* over moderately low heat, stirring constantly, for 45 minutes to 1 hour, or until it is the color of milk chocolate. *If desired, the* roux *may be made 1 day in advance, transferred to a bowl, and kept covered and chilled. Return the* roux *to the skillet and proceed.* Add the bell peppers and the onions and cook the mixture over low heat, stirring occasionally, until the vegetables are softened.

While the *roux* mixture is cooking, in a large kettle bring 12 cups water with the bay leaves to a boil, plunge the lobsters headfirst into the water, and boil them, covered, for 10 minutes. Transfer the lobsters with tongs to a colander set over a large bowl, reserving the cooking liquid in the kettle, and let them cool until they can be handled. Break apart and crack the lobster shells, remove and reserve the meat from the claws, tails, joints, and bodies, and add the shells, tomalley, juices, and any roe to the reserved cooking liquid. Bring the reserved liquid in the kettle to a boil, skimming the froth, and simmer the mixture, uncovered, for 15 minutes. Strain the stock through a fine sieve set over a large bowl, discarding the solids, and return it to the kettle, cleaned.

Bring the stock to a boil, stir in the *roux* mixture, the sausage, the oyster liquor, the tomatoes with the juice, the thyme, the orégano, and the cayenne, and simmer the gumbo, stirring occasionally and breaking up the tomatoes, for 2 hours. Stir in the reserved lobster meat, cut into pieces, and the oysters, cook the gumbo for 2 minutes, or until the edges of the oysters begin to curl, and stir in the scallion. *The gumbo may be made 2 days in advance, allowed to cool completely, and kept covered and chilled. Reheat the gumbo over moderately low heat.* Transfer the gumbo to a tureen, serve it over the rice, and sprinkle it with the fried cornmeal-coated okra. Makes about 15 cups, serving 12.
PHOTO ON PAGE 81

Rice with Red Beans and Peas

2½ cups long-grain rice (not converted)
1½ teaspoons salt
a 19-ounce can kidney beans, rinsed and
    drained
a 10-ounce package frozen peas, blanched in
    boiling water for 1 minute and drained

In a large heavy saucepan combine the rice, the salt, and 5 cups water, bring the water to a boil, and boil the rice, uncovered, stirring occasionally, until the water is level with it. Reduce the heat to low, cook the rice, covered, for 15 minutes, or until it is tender and the water is absorbed, and stir in the beans and the peas. Serves 12.
PHOTO ON PAGE 81

Fried Cornmeal-Coated Okra

2 pounds okra, cut crosswise into ¼-inch
    slices, discarding the stems and tips
½ cup yellow cornmeal
vegetable oil for deep-frying
coarse salt for sprinkling the okra

In a bowl toss the okra with the cornmeal to coat it thoroughly and in a coarse sieve shake off the excess cornmeal. In a large deep skillet heat 1 inch of the oil to 375° F. on a deep-fat thermometer, in it fry the okra in batches, stirring occasionally, for 2 to 3 minutes, or until it is golden, and transfer it with a slotted spoon to paper towels to drain. Sprinkle the okra with the salt to taste. Makes about 4 cups.
PHOTO ON PAGE 81

Oysters on the Half Shell

40 oysters
8 parsley sprigs for garnish
16 lemon wedges as an accompaniment

Scrub the oysters thoroughly with a stiff brush under running cold water. Hold each oyster in a kitchen towel in the palm of the hand with the hinged end away from you, force an oyster knife between the shells at the hinged end, pressing down on the knife to pop open the shell, and slide the blade against the flat upper shell to cut the large muscle and free the upper shell. If the shell crumbles and cannot be opened at the hinge, insert the knife between the shells at the curved end of the oyster, pry the shells open, and sever the large muscle. Break off and discard the upper shell and slide the knife under the oyster to release it from the bottom shell.

Rinse and dry the oyster shells, reserving the oysters, and arrange 5 of them on each of 8 oyster plates. Spoon the reserved oysters into the shells and arrange the parsley and the lemon wedges decoratively on the plates. Serves 8.

PHOTO ON PAGE 71

Bay Scallops in Garlic Butter Sauce

⅛ teaspoon freshly grated lemon zest
2 tablespoons minced fresh
    parsley leaves
1 garlic clove, minced
2 tablespoons unsalted butter
¾ pound bay scallops
¼ cup dry white wine
Italian bread as an accompaniment

In a small bowl toss together the zest and the parsley and reserve the mixture. In a heavy skillet cook the garlic in the butter over moderately low heat, stirring occasionally, for 1 minute, increase the heat to high, and cook the garlic, stirring, until it is pale golden. Add the scallops, patted dry, cook them, stirring occasionally, for 1½ to 2 minutes, or until they are just firm, and transfer them with a slotted spoon to a platter. Add the wine to the pan juices, boil the mixture, stirring, until it is reduced to about ¼ cup, and season the sauce with salt and pepper. Spoon the sauce over the scallops, sprinkle the scallops with the reserved parsley mixture, and serve them with the bread. Serves 2.

Bay Scallops with Mustard Thyme Mayonnaise

½ cup mayonnaise
1 teaspoon chopped fresh thyme leaves or
    ¼ teaspoon crumbled dried
4 teaspoons coarse-grained mustard
½ teaspoon fresh lemon juice, or to taste
10 ounces bay scallops
flour for dredging the scallops
1 tablespoon unsalted butter
¼ cup vegetable oil

In a small bowl whisk together the mayonnaise, the thyme, the mustard, and the lemon juice and chill the sauce, covered, for 30 minutes. In a large colander dredge the scallops in the flour, shaking off the excess. In a large heavy skillet heat the butter and the oil over moderately high heat until the fat is hot but not smoking and in the fat sauté the scallops, shaking the skillet, for 2 minutes, or until they are golden. Serve the scallops with the sauce. Serves 2.

Scallop, Fennel, and Dill Gratins

1 cup finely chopped white part of leek,
    washed well and drained
1 cup thinly sliced fennel bulb
1½ tablespoons olive oil
½ cup dry white wine
1 pound bay scallops, rinsed and patted dry
1½ tablespoons unsalted butter, softened
1½ tablespoons all-purpose flour
¼ cup plain yogurt
2 tablespoons snipped fresh dill
½ cup grated Gruyère (about 2 ounces)
dill sprigs and lemon wedges for garnish
    if desired

In a skillet cook the leek and the fennel with salt and pepper to taste in the oil over moderately low heat, stirring, until the fennel is tender, add the wine and ¼ cup water, and bring the liquid to a boil. Boil the liquid until it is reduced by half, add the scallops, and cook them over moderately high heat, stirring, for 2 to 3 minutes, or until they are opaque. In a small bowl knead together the butter and the flour until the *beurre manié* is combined well, add the *beurre manié*, a little at a time, to the scallop mixture, stirring, and bring the mixture to a boil. Simmer the mixture, stirring, for 2 minutes, stir in the yogurt and salt and pepper to taste, and simmer the mixture, stirring, for 1 minute. *The mixture may be prepared up to this point 1 day in advance, cooled completely, and chilled in an airtight container. Reheat the mixture over low heat until it is heated through.* Stir in the dill, divide the mixture among 6 large scallop shells or small gratin dishes, and top each gratin with some of the Gruyère. Arrange the gratins on a jelly-roll pan, broil them under a preheated broiler about 4 inches from the heat for 3 to 5 minutes, or until the Gruyère is melted and golden, and garnish each gratin with a dill sprig and a lemon wedge. Serves 6 as a first course.

PHOTO ON PAGE 20

Warm Shrimp and Scallop Salad with Roasted Red Pepper Vinaigrette

For the vinaigrette
1 red bell pepper, roasted (procedure on
    page 188) and chopped
1 large garlic clove, chopped coarse
½ large cucumber, peeled, seeded, and
    chopped coarse (about ½ cup)
1 tomato, peeled, seeded, and chopped coarse
    (about ¾ cup)
1 large egg
3 tablespoons wine vinegar
3 tablespoons fresh lemon juice
¾ cup olive oil

For the salad
6 tablespoons olive oil
40 shrimp (about 1½ pounds), shelled and
    deveined
16 sea scallops (about ½ pound), halved
    horizontally
2 tablespoons snipped fresh chives, or to taste
3 avocados (preferably California), pitted and
    the flesh scooped into balls with a small
    melon-ball cutter (about 1 cup)
6 cups packed *mesclun* (mixed baby greens
    such as dandelion, baby romaine, and baby
    oak leaf, available at specialty produce
    markets)

Make the vinaigrette: In a blender blend together the bell pepper, the garlic, the cucumber, the tomato, the egg, the vinegar, the lemon juice, and salt and black pepper to taste until the mixture is very smooth, with the motor running add the oil in a stream, and blend the dressing until it is emulsified. *The dressing may be made 8 hours in advance and kept covered and chilled.*

Make the salad: In a large skillet, preferably nonstick, heat 1½ tablespoons of the oil over moderately high heat until it is hot but not smoking and in it sauté half the shrimp for 1 to 2 minutes, or until they are just firm to the touch. Transfer the shrimp to a bowl and keep them warm, covered. Sauté the remaining shrimp in 1½ tablespoons of the remaining oil in the same manner and transfer them to the bowl. Wipe out the skillet and in it heat 1½ tablespoons of the remaining oil over moderately high heat until it is hot but not smoking. Sauté half the scallops, patted dry, in the oil for 30 seconds to 1 minute, or until they are golden and just cooked through, and transfer them to the bowl. Sauté the remaining scallops in the remaining 1½ tablespoons oil in the same manner, transfer them to the bowl, and toss the mixture gently with the chives, the avocados, and salt and pepper to taste. Onto each of 8 plates pour ⅓ cup of the dressing, divide the *mesclun* among the plates, and top each serving with some of the seafood mixture. Serves 8.

Shrimp, Snow Peas, and Baby Corn with Coriander Beurre Blanc

24 large shrimp (about 2 pounds), shelled
   and, if desired, deveined
½ cup vegetable oil
1 bunch of fresh coriander sprigs (1 cup)
3 garlic cloves, crushed lightly
½ teaspoon salt
2 tablespoons fresh lemon juice
For the beurre blanc
¼ cup dry white wine
¼ cup white tequila
2 tablespoons white-wine vinegar
1 tablespoon minced shallot
1 stick (½ cup) cold unsalted butter,
   cut into 8 pieces
lemon juice to taste

½ pound snow peas, trimmed and
   strings discarded
a 14- to 15-ounce can water-packed whole
   baby corn (available at Oriental markets,
   specialty foods shops, and some
   supermarkets), drained
1 tablespoon unsalted butter
½ cup minced fresh coriander

In a large bowl combine the shrimp with the oil, the coriander sprigs, the garlic, the salt, and the lemon juice and let them marinate, covered and chilled, stirring occasionally, for at least 4 hours or overnight.

Make the *beurre blanc*: In a small heavy saucepan combine the wine, the tequila, the vinegar, and the shallot, bring the liquid to a boil, and boil it until it is reduced to about 3 tablespoons. Reduce the heat to moderately low and whisk in the butter, 1 piece at a time, lifting the pan from the heat occasionally to cool the mixture and adding each new piece of butter before the previous one has melted completely. (The sauce must not get hot enough to liquefy. It should be the consistency of hollandaise.) Season the *beurre blanc* with the lemon juice, salt, and pepper and keep it warm, set over a pan of hot water.

Drain the shrimp and discard the coriander sprigs and the garlic. Heat a large heavy skillet over moderately high heat until it is hot and in it sauté the shrimp in the oil clinging to them for 1½ to 2 minutes, or until they are just firm. Season the shrimp with salt and pepper and keep them warm. In a large saucepan of boiling salted water blanch the snow peas and the corn for 1 minute, drain the vegetables, and in a bowl toss them with the butter and salt and pepper to taste. Stir the minced coriander into the *beurre blanc* and spoon the sauce onto 4 plates. Arrange 6 shrimp around the edges of each plate and divide the vegetables among the plates, mounding them in the center. Serves 4.

PHOTO ON PAGE 30

Louisiana-Style Baked Shrimp

¾ pound shrimp (about 20), shelled
3 tablespoons unsalted butter
1 teaspoon chili powder
1 teaspoon freshly ground black pepper
⅛ teaspoon cayenne
1 teaspoon minced garlic
2 teaspoons Worcestershire sauce
2 tablespoons dry red wine
¼ teaspoon salt
crusty Italian bread as an accompaniment

Arrange the shrimp in a baking dish just large enough to hold them in one layer. In a small saucepan combine the butter, the chili powder, the black pepper, the cayenne, the garlic, the Worcestershire sauce, the wine, and the salt, bring the mixture to a boil, and pour it over the shrimp. Bake the shrimp in a preheated 400° F. oven for 8 to 10 minutes, or until they are just firm, and serve them with the bread. Serves 2.

*Chinese-Style Steamed Shrimp with Garlic
and Scallions*

3 scallions
1½ tablespoons soy sauce
1 tablespoon white-wine vinegar
1 tablespoon minced garlic
2 teaspoons finely grated peeled fresh
    gingerroot
2 teaspoons Oriental sesame oil
1 teaspoon sugar
½ teaspoon dried hot red pepper flakes
¼ teaspoon salt
1 pound (about 24) large shrimp, shelled,
    leaving the tail and the first joint of the
    shell intact, and deveined
rice as an accompaniment
    if desired

Mince the white part of the scallions, reserving the green tops, and in a large bowl stir together the minced scallions, the soy sauce, the vinegar, the garlic, the gingerroot, the oil, the sugar, the red pepper flakes, and the salt. Add the shrimp, rinsed and patted dry, toss them to coat them with the marinade, and let them marinate at room temperature, stirring occasionally, for 15 minutes.

If using a bamboo steamer to steam the shrimp mixture, bring enough water to a boil in a wok so that the bottom rim of the steamer sits in the water but the lattice tray sits above it. To approximate a bamboo steamer, use a vegetable steamer rack set in a wide, deep kettle, add enough water to the kettle to come just below the steamer rack, and bring it to a boil, covered.

Spread the shrimp mixture evenly in a wide, heat-proof dish (such as a glass pie plate) large enough to fit inside the bamboo steamer or kettle with at least 1 inch around the side, put the dish on the bamboo steamer or steamer rack over boiling water (wear oven mitts), and steam the shrimp, covered, for 4 to 8 minutes, or until they are just firm to the touch. Wearing oven mitts remove the bamboo steamer with the dish from the wok or remove the dish from the kettle and sprinkle the shrimp with the reserved scallion greens, sliced thin.

Serve the shrimp with the rice. Serves 2.

PHOTO ON FRONTISPIECE

MEAT

BEEF AND VEAL

Chili Con Carne

3 cups chopped onion
¼ cup vegetable oil
1 tablespoon minced garlic
3 pounds boneless beef chuck, ground coarse
   in a food processor or by the butcher
¼ cup chili powder
1 tablespoon ground cumin
1½ tablespoons unsweetened cocoa powder
2 tablespoons paprika
1 tablespoon dried orégano, crumbled
1½ tablespoons dried hot red pepper flakes,
   or to taste
1 bay leaf
two 8-ounce cans tomato sauce
1 cup chicken broth
3 tablespoons cider vinegar
a 19-ounce can kidney beans, rinsed and drained
3 green bell peppers, cut into ½-inch pieces
6 scallions, trimmed
6 tablespoons sour cream

In a kettle cook the onion in the oil, covered, over moderately low heat, stirring occasionally, until it is softened, add the garlic, and cook the mixture, stirring, for 1 minute. Add the chuck and cook it over moderate heat, stirring and breaking up the lumps, for 10 minutes, or until it is no longer pink. Add the chili powder, the cumin, the cocoa powder, the paprika, the orégano, the red pepper flakes, and the bay leaf and cook the mixture, stirring, for 1 minute. Add the tomato sauce, the broth, and the vinegar, bring the mixture to a boil, and simmer it, covered, stirring occasionally, for 1 hour and 15 minutes, or until the meat is tender. Add the kidney beans, the bell peppers, and salt and freshly ground black pepper to taste, simmer the mixture, uncovered, stirring occasionally, for 15 minutes, or until the peppers are tender, and discard the bay leaf. (The chili will improve in flavor if cooled completely, uncovered, and chilled, covered, overnight. Add more water if necessary when reheating the chili.) *The chili may be made 3 days in advance and reheated.* Ladle the chili into mugs and garnish each serving with a scallion and a tablespoon of the sour cream. Serves 6.

PHOTO ON PAGE 14

Meatball Stroganov

For the meatballs

½ cup finely chopped shallot
1 tablespoon unsalted butter
½ cup milk
1 cup fresh bread crumbs
1 pound ground chuck
½ pound ground pork
1 large egg, beaten lightly
freshly grated nutmeg to taste
flour for dredging the meatballs
2 tablespoons vegetable oil

¾ cup finely chopped onion
4 cups thinly sliced mushrooms
    (about ¾ pound)
⅓ cup dry white wine
¼ cup dry Sherry
2 cups beef broth
2 teaspoons Worcestershire sauce, or to taste
2 tablespoons unsalted butter, softened
2 tablespoons all-purpose flour
½ cup sour cream
¼ cup snipped fresh dill
buttered noodles as an accompaniment

Make the meatballs: In a skillet cook the shallot in the butter over moderately low heat, stirring, until it is soft. In a small bowl pour the milk over the bread crumbs and let the bread crumbs soak for 5 minutes. In a bowl stir together the chuck, the pork, the egg, the bread crumb mixture, the shallot, the nutmeg, and salt and pepper to taste. Form the mixture into meatballs about the size of a walnut (there should be about 50 meatballs) and dredge the meatballs lightly in the flour. In a large heavy skillet heat the oil over moderately high heat until it is hot but not smoking, in it brown the meatballs in 2 batches, and transfer them with a slotted spoon to a bowl.

To the fat remaining in the skillet add the onion and cook it over moderately low heat, stirring, until it is soft. Add the mushrooms and cook the mixture over moderate heat, stirring, for 10 minutes, or until the liquid the mushrooms give off is evaporated. Add the wine and the Sherry, bring the liquid to a boil, and boil the mixture until the liquid is reduced by half. Add the broth and the Worcestershire sauce and bring the liquid to a boil. In a small bowl knead together the butter and the flour until the mixture is combined well, add the butter

mixture, a little at a time, to the liquid, stirring, and boil the sauce for 2 minutes. Return the meatballs to the skillet and simmer the mixture, covered, for 8 to 10 minutes, or until the meatballs are cooked through. Stir in the sour cream and the dill, season the mixture with salt and pepper, and serve it over the noodles. Serves 4 to 6.

Meat Loaf with Onions and Horseradish

1 large egg
¼ cup finely chopped onion
4 teaspoons drained bottled horseradish
2 tablespoons old-fashioned rolled oats
¾ pound ground chuck
1 tablespoon ketchup

In a bowl stir together the egg, the onion, the horseradish, the oats, and salt and pepper to taste, add the chuck, and combine the mixture well. Form the mixture into a 5½- by 3½-inch loaf in a shallow baking pan, spread the ketchup over it, and bake the meat loaf in the middle of a preheated 400° F. oven for 30 minutes. Let the meat loaf stand for 3 minutes before slicing it. Serves 2.

Old-Fashioned Meat Loaf

1½ cups finely chopped onion
½ cup finely chopped celery
2 garlic cloves, minced
1½ teaspoons dried thyme, crumbled
2 tablespoons unsalted butter
2 teaspoons salt
1½ teaspoons freshly ground pepper
2 cups finely chopped mushrooms
    (preferably chopped in a food processor)
1½ pounds ground chuck
¾ pound ground pork
1 cup fresh bread crumbs
2 large eggs, beaten lightly
⅔ cup bottled chili sauce or ketchup
a 14- to 16-ounce can stewed tomatoes,
    drained and chopped
⅓ cup minced fresh parsley leaves
3 slices of lean bacon, halved crosswise

In a skillet cook the onion, the celery, the garlic, and the thyme in the butter over moderately low heat, stirring, until the onion is soft, add the salt, the pepper, and the mushrooms, and cook the mixture over moderate heat, stirring, for 5 to 10 minutes, or until the mushrooms are tender and the liquid they give off is evaporated. Transfer the mixture to a large bowl and let it cool. To the bowl add the chuck, the pork, the bread crumbs, the eggs, ⅓ cup of the chili sauce, the tomatoes, and the parsley and stir the mixture until it is combined well. Form the mixture into a 10- by 7-inch oval loaf in a shallow baking pan, spread the remaining ⅓ cup chili sauce over it, and drape the bacon pieces across the meat loaf. Bake the meat loaf in the middle of a preheated 350° F. oven for 1 hour, or until a meat thermometer inserted in the center registers 155° F. Serves 6 to 8.

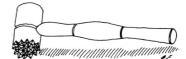

Steak au Poivre
(Steak with Peppercorns)

3 tablespoons black peppercorns
four ½-pound boneless shell steaks,
    each about ¾ inch thick
1½ tablespoons vegetable oil
1½ tablespoons unsalted butter
¼ cup minced shallot
½ cup Cognac
1 cup beef broth
⅔ cup heavy cream
watercress sprigs for garnish

With the bottom of a heavy skillet crush the peppercorns coarse in a heavy-duty sealable plastic bag or between 2 sheets of wax paper and press the pepper into both sides of the steaks, patted dry. Let the steaks stand at room temperature, covered loosely with wax paper, for 1 hour. In a large heavy skillet heat the oil and the butter over moderately high heat until the foam subsides and in the fat sauté the steaks, seasoning them with salt, for 2 to 2½ minutes on each side, or until they are just springy to the touch, for medium-rare meat. Transfer the steaks with a slotted spatula to a platter and keep them warm, covered loosely. Pour off almost all the fat remaining in the skillet, add the shallot, and cook it over moderate heat, stirring, until it is softened. Add the Cognac and boil it until it is reduced to a glaze. Add the broth and boil the mixture until it is reduced by half. Add the cream and boil the mixture, stirring occasionally, until it is thickened slightly. Season the sauce with salt and pour it into a heated sauceboat. Garnish the steaks with the watercress and serve the sauce separately. Serves 4.

Steak Diane
(Steak with Cognac Shallot Sauce)

⅓ cup beef broth
2 teaspoons Worcestershire sauce
1 teaspoon fresh lemon juice
1 teaspoon Dijon-style mustard
1½ teaspoons Cognac
1½ teaspoons Sherry
½ teaspoon cornstarch
1 tablespoon unsalted butter
1 tablespoon olive oil
two 6-ounce boneless rib-eye or blade steaks,
    flattened ¼ inch thick between sheets of
    dampened wax paper
½ cup thinly sliced shallot
2 teaspoons minced fresh parsley leaves

In a small bowl combine well the broth, the Worcestershire sauce, the lemon juice, the mustard, the Cognac, the Sherry, and the cornstarch. In a large heavy skillet heat the butter and the oil over moderately high heat until the foam subsides, in the fat sauté the steaks for 45 seconds on each side for medium-rare meat, and transfer them to a plate. In the fat remaining in the skillet cook the shallot over moderately low heat, stirring, until it is softened, stir the broth mixture, and add it to the skillet with any juices that have accumulated on the plate. Boil the Cognac shallot sauce, stirring, for 1 minute, or until it is thickened, pour it over the steaks, and sprinkle the steaks with the parsley. Serves 2.

Filets Mignons with Pearl Onions and Artichokes

3 tablespoons unsalted butter, softened
1 tablespoon minced red bell pepper
a pinch of dried thyme, crumbled
2 teaspoons minced watercress leaves plus
    watercress sprigs for garnish
1 cup pearl onions, blanched in boiling water
    for 5 minutes and peeled
3 canned artichoke bottoms, drained and cut
    crosswise into ¼-inch slices
1 tablespoon vegetable oil
2 filets mignons, each 1½ inches thick

In a small bowl stir together 2 tablespoons of the butter, the bell pepper, the thyme, and 1 teaspoon of the watercress leaves and chill the butter mixture. In a small heavy skillet cook the onions, the artichoke bottoms, and the remaining 1 teaspoon minced watercress in the remaining 1 tablespoon butter with salt and pepper to taste over moderate heat, stirring, until the mixture is heated through, transfer the mixture to a bowl, and keep it warm. In the skillet heat the oil over moderately high heat until it is hot but not smoking, add the filets, patted dry and seasoned with salt and pepper, and sauté them for 6 to 7 minutes on each side for rare meat. Transfer the filets to heated plates and top each filet with half the butter mixture. Spoon half the onion mixture onto each plate and garnish the plates with the watercress sprigs. Serves 2.

Sautéed Steaks with Bell Pepper and Horseradish

two 1-inch rib-eye or strip steaks
1 teaspoon Worcestershire sauce
1 tablespoon vegetable oil
1½ tablespoons unsalted butter
1 small red bell pepper, chopped fine
1 tablespoon drained bottled horseradish,
    or to taste

Rub the steaks with the Worcestershire sauce. In a large heavy skillet heat the oil over moderately high heat until it is hot but not smoking and in it sauté the steaks, patted dry and seasoned with salt and pepper, turning them once, for 10 minutes for medium-rare meat. Transfer the steaks to plates and pour off the oil remaining in the skillet. In the skillet heat the butter over moderately high heat, swirling the skillet occasionally, until the foam subsides, add the bell pepper and the

horseradish, and cook the mixture, stirring, for 1 minute. Spoon the bell pepper mixture over the steaks. Serves 2.

Meatball Chili Stew

1 cup dried kidney beans, picked over
1 pound ground chuck
1 pound ground pork
1½ cups fresh bread crumbs
½ cup minced fresh parsley leaves
¾ cup half-and-half
1 teaspoon ground cumin
1 teaspoon paprika
½ teaspoon cayenne
⅛ teaspoon allspice
⅛ teaspoon cinnamon
⅛ teaspoon turmeric
⅛ teaspoon ground coriander
⅛ teaspoon cardamom
¼ cup vegetable oil
2 cups chopped onion
4 garlic cloves, minced
an 8-ounce can tomato sauce
a 14- to 16-ounce can plum tomatoes
    including the juice
2 cups beef broth
¼ cup chili powder
Accompaniments
1 cup thinly sliced scallion greens
sour cream
rice

In a saucepan combine the beans with enough cold water to cover them by 2 inches, bring the water to a boil, and boil the beans for 2 minutes. Remove the pan from the heat and let the beans soak for 1 hour. While the beans are soaking, in a bowl combine well the chuck, the pork, the bread crumbs, the parsley, the half-and-half, the cumin, the paprika, the cayenne, the allspice, the cinnamon, the turmeric, the coriander, the cardamom, and salt to taste. Form the mixture into walnut-size meatballs, transferring them as they are formed to a jelly-roll pan.

Drain the beans in a colander, rinse them, and reserve them. In a kettle heat the oil over moderately high heat until it is hot but not smoking and in it brown the meatballs in batches, transferring them as they are browned to a bowl. Add the onion and cook it over moderate heat, stirring, until it is golden. Add the garlic, cook the mixture, stirring, for 30 seconds, and stir in the tomato sauce, the tomatoes with the juice, the broth, the chili powder, the meatballs with any juices that have accumulated in the bowl, and the reserved beans. Bring the liquid to a boil and braise the mixture, covered, in a preheated 350° F. oven for 50 minutes to 1 hour, or until the beans are tender. *The stew improves in flavor if cooled to room temperature, uncovered, and chilled, covered, overnight.*

Serve the stew with the scallion greens, the sour cream, and the rice. Serves 8.

Greek Beef and Onion Stew

½ cup vegetable oil
4 pounds beef chuck, cut into 1½-inch pieces
1½ cups chopped onion
4 garlic cloves, minced
2 cups dry red wine
1 cup beef broth
an 8-ounce can tomato sauce
½ cup red-wine vinegar
2½ tablespoons firmly packed brown sugar
a 3½-inch cinnamon stick
1½ teaspoons ground cumin
1 bay leaf
2 pounds small white onions, blanched in
    boiling water for 1 minute, drained,
    and peeled
½ cup minced fresh parsley leaves
rice or mashed potatoes as an accompaniment

In a kettle heat the oil over moderately high heat until it is hot but not smoking and in it brown the chuck, patted dry, in batches, transferring it as it is browned to a bowl. Pour off all but 1 tablespoon fat from the kettle, add the chopped onion, and cook it over moderate heat, stirring occasionally, until it is golden. Add the garlic and cook the mixture, stirring, for 30 seconds. Add the wine, the broth, the tomato sauce, the vinegar, the brown sugar, the cinnamon stick, the cumin, the bay leaf, 1 cup water, and the chuck with any juices that have accumulated in the bowl, bring the liquid to a boil, and braise the mixture, covered, in a preheated 350° F. oven for 2 hours. Stir in the small onions and braise the mixture, covered, for 1 to 1½ hours more, or until the onions are tender. *The stew improves in flavor if cooled to room temperature, uncovered, and chilled, covered, overnight.* Discard the bay leaf and the cinnamon stick, sprinkle the stew with the parsley, and serve it with the rice. Serves 8.

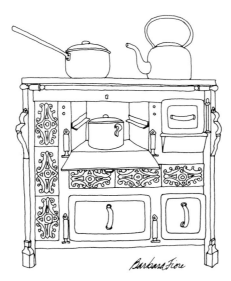

Barbara Fiore

Mediterranean Beef Stew with Olives and Pimientos

 6 slices of lean bacon
 4 pounds beef chuck,
   cut into 1½-inch pieces
 ¼ cup all-purpose flour seasoned
   with salt and pepper
 1 tablespoon vegetable oil
 1 cup chopped onion
 2 cups chopped celery
 2 tablespoons brandy
 2 cups dry red wine
 two 14- to 16-ounce cans plum tomatoes
   including the juice
 ¼ cup tomato paste
 1 bay leaf
 two 3-inch strips of orange zest
 6 carrots, halved lengthwise and cut crosswise
   into 2-inch pieces
 ½ pound small mushrooms, halved lengthwise
 ¾ cup pitted black olives, quartered
 ¾ cup drained bottled pimiento, cut
   into ¾-inch pieces
 ½ cup minced fresh parsley leaves
 mashed potatoes as an accompaniment

In a kettle cook the bacon over moderate heat, turning it, until it is crisp, transfer it to paper towels to drain, and crumble it. Heat the fat remaining in the kettle over moderately high heat until it is hot but not smoking and in it brown the chuck, tossed with the flour, in batches, transferring it as it is browned to a bowl. Add the oil to the kettle and in the fat cook the onion and the celery over moderate heat, stirring occasionally, until the vegetables are golden. Add the brandy and cook the mixture, stirring, until the brandy is almost evaporated. Stir in the wine, the tomatoes with the juice, the tomato paste, 1 cup water, the bay leaf, the orange zest, and the chuck with any juices that have accumulated in the bowl, bring the liquid to a boil, and braise the mixture, covered, in a preheated 350° F. oven for 1½ hours. Stir in the carrots and the mushrooms and braise the mixture, covered, for 1 hour. Stir in the olives and the pimientos and braise the mixture, covered, for 15 minutes, or until the vegetables are tender. *The stew improves in flavor if cooled to room temperature, uncovered, and chilled, covered, overnight.* Discard the bay leaf, season the stew with salt and pepper, and sprinkle it with the parsley. Serve the stew with the mashed potatoes. Serves 8.

*Cold Peppered Tenderloin of Beef with Creamy
Tarragon Caper Sauce*

 a trimmed 1½- to 2-pound tenderloin of beef,
   tied, at room temperature
 1 tablespoon coarsely ground black pepper
 1 teaspoon coarse salt
 2 tablespoons vegetable oil
 For the sauce
 1 teaspoon egg yolk
 2 tablespoons heavy cream
 2 tablespoons white-wine vinegar
 1 teaspoon Worcestershire sauce
 1½ teaspoons Dijon-style mustard
 ½ cup olive oil
 1½ teaspoons minced fresh tarragon
 1 tablespoon drained capers
 2 tablespoons minced scallion
 2 tablespoons minced fresh parsley leaves

Pat dry the tenderloin and coat it on all sides with the pepper and the salt. In an ovenproof skillet just large enough to hold the tenderloin heat the oil over high heat until it is hot but not smoking and in it brown the tenderloin on all sides. Roast the tenderloin in the skillet in a preheated 500° F. oven for 15 to 20 minutes, or until a meat thermometer registers 130° F. for medium-rare meat, and let it cool to room temperature. *The tenderloin may be roasted 2 days in advance and kept wrapped and chilled. Bring the tenderloin to room temperature before slicing it.*

Make the sauce: In a blender or food processor blend the yolk, the cream, the vinegar, the Worcestershire sauce, and the mustard, with the motor running add the oil in a stream, and blend the mixture until it is emulsified. Transfer the mixture to a small bowl and stir in the tarragon, the capers, the scallion, the parsley, and salt to taste. *The sauce may be made 1 day in advance and kept covered and chilled.*

Slice the tenderloin crosswise ⅓ inch thick, arrange it on a platter, and spoon some of the sauce over it. Serve the remaining sauce separately. Serves 4.

PHOTO ON PAGE 42

Stuffed Breast of Veal with Paprika Sauce

For the stuffing
 ½ pound veal sweetbreads
 ½ pound ground veal
 ¼ cup finely chopped shallot

3 garlic cloves, minced

a 10-ounce package frozen chopped spinach,
  thawed, drained, and squeezed dry

1 large egg white

2 teaspoons salt

¾ teaspoon freshly ground black pepper

⅓ cup heavy cream

1 yellow bell pepper, diced

1 red bell pepper, diced

1 tablespoon vegetable oil

a 5- to 6-pound boned lean breast of veal,
  trimmed of as much fat as possible on the
  boned side

½ pound sliced bacon, halved crosswise

3 cups chicken broth

1 cup chopped onion

2 tablespoons vegetable oil

½ cup paprika (preferably Hungarian sweet)

2 tablespoons tomato paste

1 cup sour cream

3 tablespoons all-purpose flour

Make the stuffing: In a bowl let the sweetbreads soak in ice water to cover for 30 minutes and drain them. In a large saucepan of boiling salted water simmer the sweetbreads for 10 minutes. Drain the sweetbreads and let them cool. Separate the sweetbreads into small pieces, discarding the membranes. In a food processor purée the sweetbreads with the ground veal, the shallot, the garlic, the spinach, the egg white, the salt, and the black pepper, with the motor running add the cream, and blend the mixture well. Transfer the sweetbread mixture to a bowl. In a large skillet cook the bell peppers in the oil over moderate heat, stirring, until they are softened, let the bell pepper mixture cool, and stir it into the sweetbread mixture. *The sweetbread mixture may be made 1 day in advance and kept covered and chilled.*

Put the veal breast, boned side up, on a work surface with a long side facing you. Season the veal with salt and pepper and spread the stuffing evenly over it, leaving a 1-inch border on all sides. Beginning with the long side facing you, roll up the veal jelly-roll fashion and tie it at 1-inch intervals with kitchen string. Transfer the veal breast carefully to an oiled large roasting pan, arranging it in the pan diagonally if necessary, and drape the bacon slices over it. Roast the veal in the middle of a preheated 450° F. oven for 30 minutes, reduce the heat to 375° F., and roast the veal for 40 to 50 min-

utes more, or until it is tender and a meat thermometer inserted in the center registers 160° F. Transfer the veal carefully to a cutting board and let it stand for 20 minutes.

While the veal is standing, skim the fat from the roasting pan, add 1 cup water, and deglaze the pan over high heat, scraping up the brown bits. Boil the mixture until it is reduced by half, strain it through a fine sieve over a bowl, and add the broth. In a large saucepan cook the onion in the oil over moderately low heat, stirring, until it is softened, remove the saucepan from the heat, and stir in the paprika and 1 cup of the broth mixture. Return the saucepan to the heat and cook the mixture, stirring, for 2 minutes. Stir in the tomato paste and the remaining broth mixture, bring the mixture to a boil, stirring, and simmer it for 3 minutes. In a heatproof bowl whisk together the sour cream and the flour, add 1 cup of the paprika broth in a slow stream, whisking, and whisk the sour cream mixture into the paprika broth. Bring the sauce to a boil, whisking, and simmer it for 5 minutes. Strain the sauce through a fine sieve into another saucepan and keep it warm.

Remove the strings from the veal, discarding them, and cut the veal crosswise into ½-inch-thick slices. Spoon some of the sauce onto a heated large platter, arrange the slices decoratively on it, and serve the remaining sauce separately. Serves 12.

PHOTO ON PAGE 12

PORK

Glazed Canadian Bacon

a 2½-pound piece of Canadian bacon, rind
  removed (if attached) with a sharp knife

2 tablespoons cloves

½ cup firmly packed dark brown sugar

3 tablespoons Dijon-style mustard

Score the top and sides of the bacon lightly into diamonds, stud the center of each diamond with a clove, and put the bacon in a shallow roasting pan. In a small bowl combine well the brown sugar and the mustard and pour the mixture over the bacon. Bake the bacon in a preheated 350° F. oven, basting it several times with the glaze, for 30 minutes and let it stand, covered with foil, for at least 10 minutes and up to 1 hour before slicing. Serves 6 with plenty of leftovers.

Pork and Pear Deep-Dish Pie

2 pounds smoked pork butt, cut into
   ½-inch pieces
3 tablespoons unsalted butter
1 tablespoon vegetable oil
1 garlic clove, minced
1½ cups thinly sliced onion
¾ teaspoon dried sage, crumbled
¼ teaspoon salt
¼ teaspoon black pepper
¼ teaspoon ground mace
¼ teaspoon ground cloves
1½ tablespoons all-purpose flour
3 firm-ripe Anjou pears (about 1½ pounds),
   peeled, cored, halved lengthwise, and cut
   crosswise into thin slices
1 tablespoon firmly packed light brown sugar
1 large russet (baking) potato, peeled and
   sliced thin
¼ cup finely chopped fresh parsley leaves
1½ recipes *pâte brisée* (page 94)
an egg wash made by beating 1 large egg with
   1 tablespoon water

In a large skillet combine the pork with enough water to just cover it, bring the water to a boil, and simmer the pork, stirring occasionally, for 30 minutes. Transfer the pork with a slotted spoon to a colander, discarding the liquid, and season it with salt and freshly ground black pepper.

While the pork is simmering, in a skillet heat the butter and the oil over moderate heat until the foam subsides and in the fat cook the garlic and the onion, stirring, until they are golden. Reduce the heat to moderately low, stir in the sage, the salt, the pepper, the mace, and the cloves, and cook the mixture for 1 minute. Stir in the flour and cook the mixture, stirring constantly, for 3 minutes. Stir in the pears and the brown sugar and cook the mixture, stirring, for 1 minute.

In a large bowl combine the pork, the pear mixture, the potato, and the parsley and spoon the mixture into a well-buttered 2-quart deep-dish pie plate. Roll out the *pâte brisée* ⅛ inch thick on a lightly floured surface, reserving some for decorative cut-outs if desired, and fit it over the pie plate. Trim the excess dough and crimp the edge onto the rim of the plate. Arrange the cut-outs on top if desired, brush the top with the egg wash, and bake the pie in the bottom third of a preheated 375° F. oven for 45 minutes, or until the crust is golden. Serves 6 to 8.

Pork, Sweet Potato, and Black Bean Stew

1 pound boneless pork shoulder,
   cut into 1-inch cubes
2 teaspoons chili powder
1 teaspoon honey
½ teaspoon salt
1 onion, chopped
2 pounds sweet potatoes, peeled and
   cut into 1-inch cubes
¼ cup fresh orange juice
a 10-ounce can black beans, drained
   and rinsed
a *beurre manié* made by kneading together
   1 teaspoon softened butter and
   1 teaspoon flour
1 tablespoon minced fresh coriander leaves
   if desired

In a 2½-quart glass casserole combine the pork, the chili powder, the honey, the salt, the onion, the sweet potatoes, the orange juice, and ¼ cup water, cover the surface of the pork mixture with wax paper, and microwave the pork mixture at high power (100%) for 8 minutes. Stir the pork mixture and microwave it, covered with wax paper, at medium power (50%) for 15 minutes, or until the pork is just tender. Stir in the black beans and the *beurre manié* and microwave the stew, covered with wax paper, at medium power (50%) for 2 minutes. Stir in the minced coriander and salt and pepper to taste. Serves 2.

Pork Chops with Cabbage and Dill Seed

1 tablespoon vegetable oil
1 tablespoon unsalted butter
four 3-ounce boneless loin pork chops
   (each about ½-inch thick)
1 onion, chopped
2 cups coarsely grated cabbage
1 teaspoon dill seed
½ cup dry white wine
1 to 2 teaspoons wine vinegar, or to taste

In a heavy skillet heat the oil and the butter over moderately high heat until the foam begins to subside and in the fat sauté the chops, patted dry and seasoned with salt and pepper, turning them once, for 7 minutes, or until they are cooked through and barely pink within. Transfer the chops to a plate and keep them warm, covered. Pour off all but 1 tablespoon of the fat, in the fat remaining in the skillet cook the onion and the cabbage over moderate heat, stirring, until the vegetables are softened, and add the dill seed and the wine. Bring the liquid to a boil and simmer the mixture, covered partially, for 15 minutes, or until the cabbage is crisp-tender. Stir in the vinegar and salt to taste and divide the cabbage mixture and the chops between 2 plates. Serves 2.

Pork Rolls Rellenos
(Pork Rolls Filled with Cheese and Jalapeño Peppers)

For the sauce
1 onion, minced
2 tablespoons vegetable oil
2 garlic cloves, minced
a 14½-ounce can plum tomatoes including the juice
½ cup chicken broth
2 canned peeled mild green chilies, minced

1½ pounds pork tenderloin, trimmed of any membrane, cut crosswise into 12 slices, and pounded thin, cut sides down, between 2 sheets of moistened wax paper
¾ pound Monterey Jack, cut into twelve 3- by 1- by ½-inch pieces
2 pickled whole *jalapeño* peppers, seeds and ribs discarded and the flesh cut lengthwise into 12 strips total (wear rubber gloves)

⅔ cup milk
2 large eggs, beaten until frothy
flour seasoned with salt and black pepper for dredging the pork
1½ cups yellow cornmeal
vegetable oil for frying the pork

Make the sauce: In a heavy saucepan cook the onion in the oil over moderately low heat until it is softened, add the garlic, and cook the mixture for 2 minutes. Add the tomatoes with the juice and the broth, bring the liquid to a boil, breaking up the tomatoes, and simmer the mixture for 10 minutes. Add the mild green chilies and salt and black pepper to taste.

In the center of each pork slice arrange 1 piece of the Monterey Jack and 1 strip of the *jalapeño* pepper, fold the ends over the filling, and roll the pork up tightly. Chill the pork rolls for 15 minutes. In a bowl whisk together the milk and the eggs. Working with 1 pork roll at a time, dredge the rolls in the seasoned flour, shaking off the excess, and dip them in the egg mixture, letting the excess drip off. Dredge the pork rolls in the cornmeal.

In a large heavy skillet heat 1 inch of the oil over moderately high heat until it is hot but not smoking and in it fry the pork rolls in batches, turning them once, adding more oil as necessary, and transferring the rolls with a slotted spoon to paper towels to drain, for 8 minutes. In a shallow baking dish bake the pork rolls in one layer, uncovered, in the middle of a preheated 350° F. oven for 10 minutes. Serve the pork rolls with the sauce, heated. Serves 6.

JEANNE

Chinese-Style Roast Pork with Chutney Garlic Sauce

1½ pounds pork tenderloin, trimmed of
    any membrane
⅓ cup soy sauce
2 tablespoons medium-dry Sherry
2 tablespoons ketchup
1 tablespoon light brown sugar
2 tablespoons fresh lemon juice
3 garlic cloves, minced
3 tablespoons minced peeled fresh gingerroot
For the sauce
3 garlic cloves, minced
6 tablespoons soy sauce
2 tablespoons red-wine vinegar
½ cup bottled mango chutney
2 tablespoons honey
1 teaspoon Oriental sesame oil (available at
    Oriental markets and many supermarkets)

In a small deep dish just large enough to hold the pork combine the soy sauce, the Sherry, the ketchup, the brown sugar, the lemon juice, the garlic, the ginger-root, and pepper to taste, add the pork, turning it to coat it thoroughly, and let it marinate, covered and chilled, for at least 3 hours or, preferably, overnight.

Arrange the pork on a rack in a roasting pan, reserving the marinade in a small bowl, add ½ inch hot water to the pan, and roast the pork in a preheated 350° F. oven, basting it occasionally only during the first hour with the reserved marinade, for 1 hour and 15 minutes, or until a meat thermometer registers 155° F. for meat that is just cooked through but still juicy. Transfer the pork to a cutting board and let it stand for 5 minutes.

Make the sauce while the pork is standing: In a small saucepan combine the garlic, the soy sauce, and the vinegar, bring the mixture to a boil, and simmer it for 3 minutes. Stir in the chutney, the honey, the oil, and ¼ cup water and bring the mixture to a boil, stirring.

Carve the pork diagonally into thin slices, arrange the slices on a heated platter, and spoon the sauce over the slices. Serves 4 to 6.

Four-Peppercorn Pork Roast

a 4½-pound boneless pork loin, tied
3 tablespoons unsalted butter, softened
2 tablespoons all-purpose flour
¼ cup mixed black, white, pink, and green
    peppercorns (available at specialty foods
    shops), crushed coarse
For the sauce
¼ cup all-purpose flour
1¾ cups chicken broth
2 tablespoons red-wine vinegar,
    or to taste

rosemary sprigs for garnish if desired

Pat the pork dry and season it with salt. In a small bowl combine the butter and the flour to make a paste, coat the top of the pork loin with the paste, and sprinkle the paste with the peppercorns, pressing them in lightly. In a roasting pan roast the pork on a rack in the middle of a preheated 475° F. oven for 30 minutes, reduce the heat

to 325° F., and roast the pork for 1½ to 1⅔ hours more, or until a meat thermometer registers 155° F. Transfer the pork roast to a cutting board and let it stand for 10 minutes.

Make the sauce while the roast is standing: Pour off all but ¼ cup of the fat from the roasting pan, whisk in the flour, and cook the *roux* over moderate heat, stirring, for 3 minutes. Add the broth and 1 cup water in a stream, whisking, and bring the liquid to a boil. Stir in the vinegar and salt to taste and simmer the sauce until it is thickened to the desired consistency.

Discard the strings from the roast and cut the roast into ½-inch slices. Arrange the slices on a platter and garnish the platter with the rosemary. Pour the sauce into a sauceboat and serve it with the pork. Serves 10.

PHOTO ON PAGE 66

Braised Pork Tenderloin with Orange Juice and Coriander

1½ pounds pork tenderloin,
    trimmed of any membrane
6 garlic cloves, peeled and halved
2 tablespoons vegetable oil
1½ cups thinly sliced onion
¼ teaspoon freshly ground pepper
¼ teaspoon freshly grated nutmeg
a 2-inch piece of cinnamon stick
½ teaspoon dry mustard
1½ cups fresh-squeezed orange juice
1 cup chicken broth
⅓ cup chopped fresh coriander
    plus additional for garnish
1 scallion, sliced thin, for garnish

Cut 12 incisions in the pork with a sharp paring knife, insert the garlic, and season the pork with pepper. In a heavy kettle sear the pork, patted dry, in the oil over moderately high heat for 8 minutes, or until it is browned, and transfer it with tongs to a plate. To the kettle add the onion and cook it over moderately low heat, stirring occasionally and scraping up the brown bits, until it is softened and browned lightly. Add the pepper, the nutmeg, the cinnamon stick, and the mustard and cook the mixture, stirring, for 1 minute. Add the orange juice, the broth, and ⅓ cup of the coriander and bring the mixture to a boil. Add the pork, braise it, covered, in the middle of a preheated 350° F. oven, turning it occasionally, for 45 minutes to 1 hour, or until

a meat thermometer registers 155° F., for meat that is just cooked through but still juicy, and transfer it to a heated platter. Boil the sauce over moderately high heat, stirring, until it is thickened, spoon it over the pork, discarding the cinnamon stick, and sprinkle the meat with the additional coriander and the scallion. Serves 4 to 6.

Grilled Pork Tenderloin with Mustard Cream Sauce

1½ pounds pork tenderloin, trimmed of any
    membrane
¾ cup vegetable oil
¼ cup dry white wine
3 garlic cloves, crushed lightly
For the mustard cream sauce
¾ cup dry white wine
1 tablespoon minced shallot
1 cup heavy cream
3 tablespoons Dijon-style mustard
freshly ground white pepper to taste

steamed baby carrots or steamed carrots, cut
    into sticks, as an accompaniment if desired
deep-fried carrot tops as an accompaniment if
    desired

In a small deep dish just large enough to hold the pork combine the oil, the wine, and the garlic, add the pork, turning it to coat it thoroughly, and let it marinate, covered and chilled, overnight. Drain the pork, discarding the marinade, and grill it on an oiled rack set about 6 inches over glowing coals, turning it, for 25 minutes, or until a meat thermometer registers 155° F., for meat that is just cooked through but still juicy. Transfer the pork to a cutting board and let it stand while making the mustard cream sauce.

Make the sauce: In a small heavy saucepan boil the wine with the shallot until it is reduced to about 2 tablespoons. Add the cream, bring the mixture just to a boil, and simmer it for 2 minutes, or until it is thickened slightly. Strain the sauce through a fine sieve into a bowl and whisk in the mustard, the white pepper, and salt to taste.

Cut the pork diagonally into ½-inch slices and serve it with the mustard cream sauce, the carrots, and the carrot tops. Serves 4 to 6.

PHOTO ON PAGE 82

Pork Tenderloin Cordon Bleu
(Pork with Ham,
Gruyère, and Cream Sauce)

6 slices (4½ ounces) of cooked smoked ham
6 ounces Gruyère cheese, sliced paper-thin
   with a cheese slicer
1½ pounds pork tenderloin, trimmed of any
   membrane, cut crosswise into 12 slices,
   and pounded ½ inch thick, cut sides down,
   between 2 sheets of moistened wax paper
3 large eggs, beaten until frothy
2 tablespoons fresh lemon juice
flour seasoned with salt and pepper for
   dredging the pork
½ stick (¼ cup) unsalted butter
2 tablespoons vegetable oil
2 tablespoons medium-dry Sherry
½ cup chicken broth
¼ cup heavy cream

Divide the ham, folding it if necessary, and the Gruyère among half the pork slices, top the Gruyère with the remaining pork slices, and gently flatten the pork "packets" ¼ inch thick between 2 sheets of moistened wax paper. Working with 1 packet at a time, dip the packets in the eggs combined with the lemon juice, letting the excess drip off, and dredge them lightly in the flour, shaking off the excess.

In each of 2 large skillets heat 2 tablespoons of the butter with 1 tablespoon of the oil until the foam subsides, divide the pork packets between the skillets, and sauté them over moderately high heat, turning them once, for 8 minutes, or until they are deep golden. Transfer the packets with a slotted spatula to a large plate. Combine all the pan juices and the brown bits in one of the skillets, add the Sherry, and deglaze the skillet over moderately high heat, scraping up the brown bits, for 1 minute. Add the broth and the pork packets with any juices that have accumulated on the plate and simmer the mixture, covered, turning the packets once, for 10 minutes. Transfer the pork packets with the slotted spatula to a platter and keep them warm, covered. Whisk the cream into the broth mixture, cook the mixture over high heat, stirring, until it is thickened slightly, and pour the sauce over the pork. Serves 6.

Pork Tenderloin Parmigiana

For the sauce
½ cup minced onion
2 tablespoons olive oil
2 garlic cloves, minced
½ teaspoon dried basil, crumbled
½ teaspoon dried orégano, crumbled
a 28-ounce can Italian plum tomatoes
   including the juice

1½ cups fine dry bread crumbs
   (page 145)
1¼ cups (5 ounces) freshly grated Parmesan
¼ cup finely chopped fresh parsley leaves
1½ pounds pork tenderloin, trimmed of any
   membrane, cut crosswise into 12 slices,
   and pounded thin, cut sides down, between
   2 sheets of moistened wax paper
flour seasoned with salt and pepper for
   dredging the pork
3 large eggs, beaten until frothy
about ½ cup olive oil for sautéing the pork
½ pound mozzarella, sliced ¼ inch thick

Make the sauce: In a heavy saucepan cook the onion in the oil over moderately low heat until it is softened, add the garlic, and cook the mixture for 1 minute. Stir in

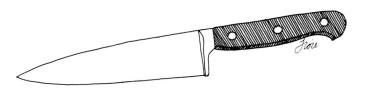

the basil, the orégano, the tomatoes with the juice, and salt and pepper to taste, bring the mixture to a boil, and simmer it, stirring occasionally, for 30 minutes. Purée the mixture through a food mill fitted with the coarse disk into a bowl and keep the sauce warm, covered.

In a large bowl combine well the bread crumbs, ¾ cup of the Parmesan, the parsley, and salt and pepper to taste. Working with 1 slice of the pork at a time, dredge the pork lightly in the flour, shaking off the excess, dip it in the eggs, and dredge it in the bread crumb mixture. In a large heavy skillet heat 2 tablespoons of the oil over moderately high heat until it is hot but not smoking, in it sauté one fourth of the pork slices, turning them once, for 4 minutes, and transfer them in one layer to a large flameproof baking dish. Sauté the remaining pork in the remaining oil in the same manner and transfer it to the dish. (*The pork may be prepared up to this point 4 hours in advance and kept covered and chilled. Bring the pork to room temperature before proceeding with the recipe.*)

Top each pork slice with 2 tablespoons of the sauce, divide the mozzarella among the slices, and sprinkle the tops with the remaining ½ cup Parmesan. Bake the cheese-topped pork in a preheated 450° F. oven for 2 minutes, or until the cheeses are melted. (For a more golden topping put the pork under a preheated broiler about 4 inches from the heat for 1 minute, or until the cheeses are browned and bubbling.) Serve the pork with the remaining sauce. Serves 6 to 8.

To Make Fine Dry Bread Crumbs

a 1-pound loaf of homemade-type white
　　bread, sliced

Put the bread slices on a rack to dry overnight or dry them on a baking sheet in a preheated 250° F. oven, turning them, for 25 to 30 minutes, or until they are crisp but not colored. Break the bread into 1-inch pieces and grind it fine in batches in a food processor or blender. Store the crumbs in a cool, dry place. Makes about 3½ cups.

Pork Tenderloin Rolls with Rye Bread, Apple, and Sage Stuffing

For the stuffing
½ cup finely chopped onion
1 rib of celery, chopped
3 tablespoons unsalted butter

1 Granny Smith or other tart green apple,
　　peeled, cored, and cut into ¼-inch dice
6 pitted prunes, diced
⅓ cup pecans, minced
3 tablespoons finely chopped
　　fresh parsley leaves
¾ teaspoon ground sage
¼ teaspoon dried thyme, crumbled
a pinch of nutmeg
2 cups ⅓-inch cubes of rye bread
　　(about 4 slices)

1½ pounds pork tenderloin, trimmed of any
　　membrane, cut crosswise into 12 slices,
　　and pounded thin between 2 sheets of
　　moistened wax paper
flour seasoned with salt and pepper for
　　dredging the pork
½ stick (¼ cup) unsalted butter
½ cup dry white wine
1 cup chicken broth
1 tablespoon red currant jelly

Make the stuffing: In a skillet cook the onion and the celery in the butter over moderately low heat, stirring occasionally, until the vegetables are softened. Add the apple and cook the mixture, stirring, for 3 minutes. Stir in the prunes, the pecans, the parsley, the sage, the thyme, the nutmeg, and the bread cubes and toss the mixture until it is combined well. Season the stuffing with salt and pepper.

Spoon about 1½ tablespoons of the stuffing onto the center of each pork slice, roll the pork up, tucking in the ends, and secure the rolls with wooden picks. Dredge the pork lightly in the flour, shaking off the excess. In a large heavy skillet heat the butter over moderately high heat until the foam subsides, in it sauté the pork rolls, turning them, for 6 minutes, or until they are browned, and transfer them with a slotted spoon to a plate.

Add the wine to the large skillet and cook the mixture over moderately high heat, scraping up the brown bits, for 1 minute. Stir in the broth and the jelly, bring the mixture to a boil, stirring, and boil it, stirring, until the jelly is dissolved. Add the pork rolls in one layer and simmer them, covered, for 15 minutes. Transfer the rolls with the slotted spoon to a platter and keep them warm, covered. Boil the sauce over high heat, stirring, until it is thickened slightly, season it with salt and pepper, and pour it over the pork. Serves 6.

Italian Sausage, Pepper, and Red Onion Sandwiches

¾ pound hot or sweet Italian sausage
2 tablespoons olive oil
1 small red onion, halved and sliced thin
2 garlic cloves, minced
3 Italian peppers or 1 green bell pepper
    (about ⅔ pound), cut into ¼-inch strips
1 small red bell pepper, cut into ¼-inch strips
1 cup thinly sliced mushrooms
a pinch of dried hot red pepper flakes
a pinch of fennel seeds if desired
⅛ teaspoon dried orégano, crumbled
⅛ teaspoon dried rosemary, crumbled
⅓ cup canned tomato sauce
2 long Italian rolls, halved horizontally
    and toasted lightly

In a large skillet cook the sausage, covered, over moderately low heat for 15 minutes, or until it is no longer pink, and transfer it with a slotted spoon to paper towels to drain. Pour off the fat, wipe the skillet, and in it cook the onion in the oil over moderately low heat until it is softened. Add the garlic and the peppers and cook the mixture, covered, over moderate heat for 10 minutes, or until the peppers are softened. Add the mushrooms, the red pepper flakes, the fennel seeds, the orégano, and the rosemary and cook the mixture, covered, for 3 minutes. Stir in the tomato sauce and the sausage, sliced ½ inch thick, add salt and freshly ground black pepper to taste, and divide the mixture between the bottom halves of the rolls. Serves 2.

Ham with Mustard Green Stuffing and Oat Wheat Crust

For the stuffing
¾ cup finely chopped celery
2 tablespoons olive oil
1 pound mustard or turnip greens, washed
    well, coarse stems discarded, and chopped
    coarse (about 12 cups)
¾ cup finely chopped scallion
½ cup finely chopped fresh parsley leaves

a 10- to 12-pound fully cooked whole
    (bone-in) cured smoked ham (not with
    water added), the skin and fat trimmed and
    discarded
1 onion, chopped

1 rib of celery, chopped
2 tablespoons olive oil
2 cups Sercial Madeira
3 cups beef broth
1 bay leaf
10 parsley sprigs
For the crust
1¾ teaspoons active dry yeast
3½ cups unbleached all-purpose flour
½ cup oat bran (available at natural foods
    stores and some supermarkets)
1 teaspoon salt
2 tablespoons olive oil
1 large egg, beaten lightly

Make the stuffing: In a kettle cook the celery in the oil over moderately low heat until it is softened, add the greens, the scallion, and ½ cup water, and cook the mixture, covered partially, over moderate heat, stirring occasionally, for 8 to 10 minutes, or until the greens are tender and the liquid is almost evaporated. Stir in the parsley and salt and pepper to taste. Let the stuffing cool.

Make deep slits with a long-bladed knife in the top of the ham to form 6 to 8 pockets and divide the stuffing among the pockets, packing it firmly. In a roasting pan large enough to hold the ham cook the onion and the celery in the oil over moderately high heat, stirring occasionally, until the vegetables are browned, deglaze the pan with the Madeira, and add the broth, the bay leaf, and the parsley. Arrange the ham in the pan, baste it with the cooking liquid, and braise it, covered tightly with foil, in a preheated 325° F. oven, basting it every 20 minutes, for 2 hours. *The ham may be prepared up to this point 1 day in advance, cooled, and kept covered and chilled in the pan. Bring the ham to room temperature before proceeding with the recipe.* Transfer the ham to a jelly-roll pan and discard the cooking liquid and vegetables.

Make the crust: In a small bowl proof the yeast in ¼ cup lukewarm water for 10 minutes, or until it is foamy. In a food processor process 3 cups of the flour with the bran to combine the mixture, with the motor running add 1 cup room-temperature water, the salt, the oil, and the yeast mixture, and process the dough for 45 seconds. Knead the dough on a floured surface, kneading in the remaining ½ cup flour, for 2 to 3 minutes, or until it is smooth and elastic. Form the dough into a ball, put it in an oiled bowl, turning it to coat it with the oil, and let it rise, covered with plastic wrap, in a warm place for 50 minutes to 1 hour, or until it is double in bulk. Roll out the dough ¼ inch thick on a lightly floured surface, forming an oval large enough to cover the ham. Cut slits decoratively in the dough with a fluted pastry wheel, leaving a 2-inch border, drape the dough over the ham, separating the slits to form designs, and trim the dough where necessary, folding the ends under the ham to secure them. Brush the dough with the egg and bake the ham in a preheated 375° F. oven for 40 to 45 minutes, or until the crust is golden. Loosen the crust from the pan, transfer the ham to a platter, and let it stand, covered loosely, for 20 minutes. Serves 8 to 12.

PHOTO ON PAGE 24

Country Ham Patties with Red-eye Sour Cream Gravy

For the patties
1 onion, chopped fine
½ stick (¼ cup) unsalted butter
1½ pounds cooked ham
    (preferably Smithfield or other country-
    style ham), chopped fine
freshly ground pepper to taste
8 *cornichons* (French sour gherkins, available
    at specialty foods shops and some
    supermarkets), chopped fine
2 tablespoons fresh bread crumbs
1 large whole egg
1 large egg yolk
⅓ cup mayonnaise
2 tablespoons sour cream
1 tablespoon plus 2 teaspoons
    Dijon-style mustard
¼ teaspoon Worcestershire sauce
¼ teaspoon Tabasco, or to taste
flour for dredging the patties

For the gravy
3 tablespoons bourbon
1 tablespoon firmly packed light brown sugar
1 tablespoon red-wine vinegar
⅓ cup brewed coffee
½ cup sour cream at room temperature

Make the patties: In a skillet cook the onion in 1 tablespoon of the butter over moderately low heat, stirring, until it is very soft and let the mixture cool slightly. In a bowl toss together the onion mixture, the ham, the pepper, the *cornichons*, and the bread crumbs. In another bowl whisk together the whole egg, the yolk, the mayonnaise, the sour cream, the mustard, the Worcestershire, and the Tabasco until the mixture is smooth and stir the egg mixture into the ham mixture until the mixture is combined well. Form the mixture into 8 patties, each about 3 inches in diameter, and chill the patties, covered, on a tray lined with wax paper for at least 30 minutes and up to 2 hours. Dredge the patties gently in the flour, shaking off any excess carefully. In a large heavy skillet heat the remaining 3 tablespoons butter over moderately high heat until the foam subsides and in it sauté the patties, in 2 batches if necessary, shaking the skillet gently to prevent them from sticking, for 4 to 5 minutes on each side, or until they are golden brown. Transfer the patties to a platter and keep them warm.

Make the gravy: Pour off any fat from the skillet and to the skillet add the bourbon carefully. Add the brown sugar and the vinegar, bring the mixture to a boil, scraping up the brown bits, and boil it for 1 minute. Add the coffee, ¼ cup water, and salt to taste, bring the mixture to a boil, and boil it for 2 minutes. In a small bowl whisk the coffee mixture into the sour cream until the gravy is smooth and serve the gravy with the patties. Serves 4 as a light entrée or 8 for breakfast.

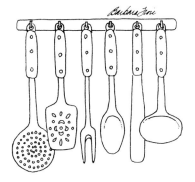

Black-Eyed Pea and Ham Stew

1 pound dried black-eyed peas, picked over
1 smoked ham hock, blanched in boiling
 water for 2 minutes and drained
1 cup chopped onion
1 cup chopped green bell pepper
1 cup chopped celery
1½ pounds cooked ham,
 cut into 1½-inch pieces
1 bay leaf
1 tablespoon Worcestershire sauce
2 tablespoons ketchup
2½ tablespoons arrowroot
Tabasco to taste
½ cup minced fresh parsley leaves
½ cup thinly sliced scallion greens
rice as an accompaniment

In a kettle combine the peas with enough cold water to cover them by 2 inches, bring the water to a boil, and boil the peas for 2 minutes. Remove the kettle from the heat and let the peas soak for 1 hour. Drain the peas in a colander, rinse them, and in the kettle combine them with the ham hock, 8 cups cold water, the onion, the bell pepper, the celery, the ham, and the bay leaf. Bring the water to a boil and simmer the mixture, stirring occasionally, for 30 minutes. Stir in the Worcestershire sauce and the ketchup, simmer the mixture for 15 to 20 minutes, or until the peas are tender, and remove the kettle from the heat. In a small bowl stir together ½ cup of the hot cooking liquid and the arrowroot until the arrowroot is dissolved, stir the arrowroot mixture into the stew, and cook the stew over moderately low heat, stirring, for 1 minute, or until it is thickened. Do not let the stew boil. *The stew improves in flavor if cooled to room temperature, uncovered, and chilled, covered, overnight. Heat the stew over moderately low heat until it is hot, but do not let it boil.* Season the stew with salt and the Tabasco and stir in the parsley and the scallion greens. Discard the bay leaf and serve the stew with the rice. Serves 8.

LAMB

Lamb Brochettes with Savory Coffee Glaze

For the glaze
⅓ cup finely chopped onion
2 garlic cloves, crushed
2 tablespoons olive oil
¼ cup firmly packed dark brown sugar
¾ cup strong brewed coffee
½ cup canned beef broth or chicken broth
⅓ cup heavy cream
a 3-inch strip of orange rind removed with
 a vegetable peeler
For the brochettes
8 small white onions (about ¾ pound),
 blanched in boiling water for 2 minutes,
 drained, and peeled
1 pound boneless leg of lamb, trimmed and
 cut into thirty-two 1-inch cubes
8 mushrooms (about ½ pound), stems
 trimmed flush with the caps, blanched in
 boiling water for 1 minute, and drained
1 red bell pepper, cut into 1½-inch pieces,
 blanched in boiling water for 1 minute,
 and drained

rice pilaf as an accompaniment

Make the glaze: In a large skillet cook the onion and the garlic in the oil over moderately low heat, stirring, until the mixture is very soft, add the brown sugar, the coffee, the broth, the cream, the rind, and salt and pepper to taste, and bring the mixture to a boil. Simmer the mixture until it is reduced to about 1 cup and has the consistency of a light syrup, strain it through a fine sieve into a bowl, and discard the solids.

Make the brochettes: In a kettle of boiling water cook the onions for 8 to 10 minutes, or until they are just tender, and drain them. Season the lamb with salt and black pepper and thread 8 skewers with the lamb, the onions, the mushrooms, and the bell pepper, alternating the ingredients in a decorative pattern. Transfer the brochettes to the rack of a broiler pan and pour half the glaze over them. Broil the brochettes under a preheated broiler about 4 inches from the heat, turning them and basting them often with the remaining glaze, for 10 to 15 minutes for medium-rare meat. Spoon the pan juices over the brochettes and serve the brochettes with the rice. Serves 4.

Sautéed Spiced Lamb Chops with Ginger Crisps

4 large or 6 small rib lamb chops (about
   1¼ pounds total)
2 teaspoons ground coriander seeds
1 teaspoon firmly packed dark brown sugar
½ teaspoon freshly ground pepper
½ teaspoon salt
½ cup fine julienne peeled fresh gingerroot
vegetable oil for frying the gingerroot
2 tablespoons unsalted butter

Pat the chops dry, prick them all over with a fork, and arrange them on a plate. In a small bowl combine well the coriander seeds, the brown sugar, the pepper, and the salt, rub the mixture onto both sides of each chop, and let the chops stand at room temperature for 15 minutes. While the chops are standing, in a small saucepan fry the gingerroot in 2 batches in ½ inch of 375° F. oil for 30 seconds, or until it turns pale golden, and transfer it with a slotted spoon to paper towels to drain. In a large heavy skillet heat the butter over moderately high heat until the foam subsides and in it sauté the chops, turning them once, for 7 minutes for medium-rare meat. Divide the chops between 2 plates and top them with the ginger crisps. Serves 2.

PHOTO ON PAGE 27

Grilled Butterflied Leg of Lamb with Cumin

2 tablespoons ground cumin
¼ cup fresh lemon juice
¼ cup vegetable oil
a 16-ounce container plain yogurt
a 6½- to 7½-pound whole leg of lamb,
   trimmed, boned, and butterflied
   (4½ to 5½ pounds boneless)
grilled marinated eggplant and red onion
   (page 150) as an accompaniment
mint sprigs for garnish

In a large shallow dish whisk together the cumin, the lemon juice, the oil, and the yogurt. Arrange the lamb, fat side down, on a cutting board and with a sharp knife make ½-inch-deep slashes every 1½ to 2 inches down the length of the thicker parts of the meat. Transfer the lamb to the dish, turning it to coat it with the marinade, and let it marinate, fat side up, covered and chilled, overnight. Let the lamb come to room temperature, fit it flat into an oiled grill basket, and close the top of the basket. Grill the lamb, fat side down, on a rack set 5 to 6 inches over glowing coals for 15 minutes. Turn the lamb and grill it for 10 to 12 minutes more, or until a meat thermometer inserted into one of the thickest parts registers 140° F., for medium-rare meat. (Alternatively, the lamb may be broiled on the rack of a broiler pan under a preheated broiler about 4 inches from the heat for 10 to 12 minutes on each side for medium-rare meat.) Transfer the lamb to a carving board and let it stand for 10 minutes. Slice the lamb across the grain, arrange it with the grilled eggplant and red onion on a platter, and garnish the platter with the mint sprigs. Serves 8 with generous leftovers.

PHOTO ON PAGE 45

Grilled Marinated Eggplant and Red Onion

⅓ cup fresh lemon juice
3 large garlic cloves
1½ cups vegetable oil or olive oil
two 1-pound eggplants
three 1-pound red onions
½ cup vinegar

In a blender or food processor blend together the lemon juice, the garlic, and salt to taste and with the motor running add the oil in a stream. Cut the eggplants crosswise into ¾-inch-thick slices and score the cut sides of each slice ¼ inch deep. In a shallow dish large enough to hold the eggplant slices in one layer or in a large sealable plastic bag combine the eggplant and the marinade, turning the slices to coat them well, and let the slices marinate, covered and chilled, for at least 4 hours or overnight. Drain the eggplant in a colander set over a shallow dish and reserve the marinade in the dish.

Cut the onions crosswise into ¾-inch-thick slices and fasten each slice horizontally with 2 wooden picks to hold the rings together. In a large saucepan combine 2 quarts water and the vinegar and bring the liquid to a boil. Add the onions, simmer them for 5 to 7 minutes, or until they are just tender, and drain them. While the onions are still hot, put them in the dish with the reserved marinade, turning them to coat them well, let them marinate for 30 minutes, and drain them.

Grill the eggplant and onion slices around the periphery of an oiled rack set 5 to 6 inches over glowing coals for 5 minutes on each side, or until they are tender. (Alternatively, the eggplant and onion slices may be broiled on the rack of a broiler pan under a preheated broiler about 4 inches from the heat for 3 to 5 minutes on each side, or until they are tender.) Serves 8.

PHOTO ON PAGE 45

Lamb Patties with Minted Onion Marmalade

¾ pound onion, sliced thin
2 tablespoons unsalted butter
1 tablespoon sugar
2 tablespoons white-wine vinegar
¼ teaspoon dried mint, crumbled
1 pound ground lamb (use ¾ pound if very lean)
vegetable oil for brushing the grill pan or skillet

In a heavy skillet cook the onion in the butter with salt and pepper to taste over moderate heat, stirring, until it is softened, add the sugar, and cook the mixture, stirring, until the onion is golden. Add the vinegar and the mint and simmer the mixture, stirring occasionally, until almost all the liquid is evaporated. Add ¼ cup water, simmer the mixture until it is thickened slightly but still moist, and keep the marmalade warm, covered.

Shape the lamb into four 1-inch-thick patties. Brush a well seasoned ridged grill pan or cast-iron skillet with the oil and heat it over moderately high heat until the oil just begins to smoke. Add the patties, seasoned with salt and pepper, cook them, covered, turning them once, for 6 minutes for medium-rare meat, and serve them with the onion marmalade. Serves 2.

Lamb and Eggplant Stew

½ cup vegetable oil
4 pounds boneless lamb shoulder, cut
    into 1½-inch pieces
2 onions, halved lengthwise and sliced
    thin crosswise
2 garlic cloves, minced
2 pounds eggplant (about 2 large)
1¼ teaspoons ground cumin
½ teaspoon cinnamon
⅛ teaspoon allspice
2 tablespoons red-wine vinegar
2 cups chicken broth
2 red bell peppers, cut lengthwise into
    ¼-inch strips
rice as an accompaniment

In a kettle heat the oil over moderately high heat until it is hot but not smoking and in it brown the lamb in batches, transferring it as it is browned to a bowl. Add the onions and cook them over moderate heat, stirring occasionally, until they are just golden. Add the garlic, half the eggplant, cut into 1-inch pieces, the cumin, the cinnamon, the allspice, the vinegar, the broth, and the lamb with any juices that have accumulated in the bowl, bring the liquid to a boil, and braise the mixture, covered, in a preheated 350° F. oven for 1 hour. Stir in the remaining eggplant, cut into 1-inch pieces, and the bell peppers, braise the mixture, covered, for 30 to 40 minutes more, or until the eggplant is very tender, and season the stew with salt and black pepper. *The stew improves in flavor if cooled to room temperature, uncovered, and chilled, covered, overnight.* Serve the stew with the rice. Serves 8.

OTHER MEATS

Braised Rabbit Provençale

4 slices of lean bacon, chopped coarse
two 2½- to 3-pound rabbits, thawed if frozen
 and cut into, 8 serving pieces, reserving the
 livers, hearts, and kidneys for another use
2 onions, sliced
2 teaspoons minced garlic
¾ cup dry red wine
a 28-ounce can plum tomatoes
2 red bell peppers, cut into ½-inch
 julienne strips
2 green bell peppers, cut into ½-inch
 julienne strips
the rind of ½ orange, removed with a
 vegetable peeler
¾ teaspoon dried thyme
¾ teaspoon dried rosemary, crumbled
½ teaspoon dried hot red pepper flakes
1 teaspoon fennel seeds
1 cup pitted Kalamata or other brine-cured
 black olives
⅓ cup minced fresh parsley leaves plus
 parsley sprigs for garnish

In a large heavy ovenproof kettle cook the bacon over moderate heat, stirring, until it is crisp, transfer it with a slotted spoon to paper towels to drain, and reserve it. Pour off all but ¼ cup of the fat from the kettle and in the remaining fat brown the rabbit, patted dry and seasoned with salt and pepper, in batches over moderately high heat, transferring it as it is browned to a plate. Remove the kettle from the heat, stir in the onions and the garlic, and cook the mixture over moderately low heat, stirring, until the garlic is golden. Stir in the wine, the tomatoes, the red and green bell peppers, the rind, the thyme, the rosemary, the red pepper flakes, the fennel seeds, and the reserved bacon, add the rabbit and any juices that have accumulated on the plate, and bring the mixture to a boil, stirring. Braise the rabbit, covered, in the middle of a preheated 325° F. oven for 1 hour to 1½ hours, or until it is tender. Transfer the rabbit to a serving dish, keep it warm, covered, and skim the fat from the tomato mixture. Add to the tomato mixture the olives and ¼ cup of the minced parsley, boil the mixture, stirring, for 5 minutes, or until it is thickened slightly, and season it with salt and black pepper. Spoon the mixture over the rabbit, sprinkle the rabbit with the remaining minced parsley, and garnish it with the parsley sprigs. Serves 6.

PHOTO ON PAGES 18 AND 19

POULTRY

CHICKEN

Chicken and Mushrooms in Sherry Cream Sauce

1 whole skinless boneless chicken breast
   (about ¾ pound), cut into ½-inch strips
1 tablespoon all-purpose flour
2 tablespoons vegetable oil
1 onion, halved lengthwise and sliced
   thin crosswise
½ pound mushrooms, sliced thin
3 tablespoons medium-dry Sherry
⅓ cup heavy cream
½ cup chicken broth
cooked noodles as an accompaniment
1 tablespoon minced fresh parsley leaves

Pat the chicken dry and in a bowl toss it with the flour and salt and pepper to taste. In a large heavy skillet heat 1 tablespoon of the oil over high heat until it is hot but not smoking, in it brown the chicken, and transfer the chicken to a bowl. Heat the remaining 1 tablespoon oil in the skillet until it is hot but not smoking and in it sauté the onion and the mushrooms, stirring, for 2 to 3 minutes, or until the vegetables are golden. Add the Sherry, deglaze the skillet, stirring and scraping up the brown bits, and stir in the chicken, the cream, and the broth. Bring the liquid to a boil and boil it until it is thickened. Arrange the noodles on a platter, spoon the chicken mixture over them, and sprinkle it with the parsley. Serves 2.

Chicken Salmagundi

4½ pounds skinless boneless chicken breasts
3 pounds green beans, trimmed
2 heads of romaine, rinsed, coarse ribs
   discarded, spun dry, and shredded
2 cups thinly sliced celery
½ cup minced shallot

2 tablespoons white-wine vinegar
¼ cup olive oil
6 flat anchovy fillets, quartered lengthwise
6 hard-boiled large eggs, sliced thin
12 lemon wedges
coarse mustard vinaigrette (recipe follows)
   as an accompaniment
Russian dressing (page 153) as an
   accompaniment

In a kettle large enough to hold the chicken in one layer combine the chicken and enough salted cold water to cover it by 1 inch, bring the water to a boil, skimming the froth, and simmer the chicken for 10 minutes. Let the chicken cool in the liquid for 20 minutes, cut it into ½-inch strips, and reserve the strips in the cooking liquid. In a kettle of boiling salted water cook the green beans for 6 to 8 minutes, or until they are crisp-tender, drain them, and plunge them into a bowl of ice and cold water to stop the cooking. Drain the beans and reserve them. *The chicken and beans may be prepared up to this point 1 day in advance and kept covered and chilled.*

In a bowl toss together the romaine, the celery, and the shallot and divide the mixture between 2 platters. Arrange the chicken, drained, and the reserved green beans decoratively on the romaine mixture. In a bowl whisk together the vinegar, the oil, and salt and pepper to taste and drizzle the chicken and the green beans with the mixture. Top the green beans with the anchovy fillets and fan out the eggs decoratively on top of the salad. Divide the lemon wedges between the platters and serve the salad with the coarse mustard vinaigrette and the Russian dressing. Serves 12.

PHOTO ON PAGE 39

Coarse Mustard Vinaigrette

6 tablespoons white-wine vinegar
½ cup coarse-grained mustard
1¼ cups olive oil

In a bowl whisk together the vinegar, the mustard, and salt and pepper to taste, add the oil in a stream, whisking, and whisk the vinaigrette until it is emulsified. Makes about 1½ cups.

PHOTO ON PAGE 39

Russian Dressing

1½ cups quick mayonnaise
   (page 202) or bottled mayonnaise
5 tablespoons bottled chili sauce
1 tablespoon minced bottled pimiento
1 tablespoon minced fresh chives or
   scallion greens

In a bowl whisk together the mayonnaise, the chili sauce, the pimiento, the chives, and salt and pepper to taste and whisk in 2 tablespoons water if necessary to thin the dressing. Makes about 1½ cups.

PHOTO ON PAGE 39

Chicken Cutlets with Artichokes, Tomato, and Mozzarella

1 skinless boneless whole chicken breast,
   halved, the fillets separated, and the pieces
   pounded ¼ inch thick to form 4 cutlets
¼ cup all-purpose flour seasoned with salt
   and pepper for dredging the cutlets
2 tablespoons unsalted butter
1 tablespoon olive oil
½ teaspoon minced garlic, or to taste
2 tablespoons dry white wine
2 tablespoons fresh lemon juice
four ¼-inch-thick slices of tomato
½ cup sliced drained marinated
   artichoke hearts
four ¼-inch-thick slices of mozzarella
1 tablespoon minced fresh parsley leaves

Sprinkle the chicken cutlets with salt and pepper to taste and dredge them in the flour, coating them thoroughly and shaking off the excess. In a heavy skillet heat 1 tablespoon of the butter and the oil over moderately high heat until the foam subsides and in the fat sauté the cutlets in 2 batches for 1 minute on each side, or until they are just cooked through, transferring them as they are cooked to a heated flameproof platter. Remove the skillet from the heat, add the garlic, and cook it over moderately low heat, stirring, until it just begins to color. Add the wine and the lemon juice and simmer the mixture until it is reduced by half. Remove the skillet from the heat, add the remaining 1 tablespoon butter, and swirl the skillet until it is incorporated. Pour the sauce over the cutlets and top the cutlets with the tomato, the artichoke hearts, and the mozzarella. Broil the cutlets under a preheated broiler about 3 inches from the heat until the mozzarella is melted and sprinkle the cutlets with the parsley. Serves 2.

Fesenjan
(Persian-Style Chicken with Walnut, Onion, and Pomegranate Sauce)

½ stick (¼ cup) unsalted butter
a 2½- to 3-pound chicken, cut into serving
   pieces
2 onions, sliced thin
1 teaspoon ground cinnamon
2 cups coarsely ground toasted walnuts
1 pomegranate (about 8 to 10 ounces), halved
   and squeezed gently to yield enough seeds
   and juice to measure about ⅔ cup
½ cup tomato sauce
1½ cups chicken broth
1 tablespoon plus 1 teaspoon fresh lemon
   juice
¼ teaspoon salt
¼ teaspoon pepper
1 tablespoon unsulfured molasses

In a large heavy skillet heat the butter over moderately high heat until the foam subsides, in it sauté the chicken, patted dry, turning it once, for 15 minutes, or until it is browned on all sides, and transfer it to a plate. Add the onion to the skillet and cook it over moderately low heat, scraping up the brown bits, for 10 minutes, or until it is golden and softened. Stir in the cinnamon and cook the mixture, stirring, for 1 minute. Stir in the walnuts and cook the mixture, stirring, for 1 minute. Stir in the pomegranate seeds and juice, the tomato sauce, the broth, the lemon juice, the salt, the pepper, and the molasses, bring the mixture to a boil, and simmer it for 3 minutes. Add the chicken and any juices that have accumulated on the plate and simmer the mixture, covered, for 15 to 20 minutes, or until the chicken is cooked through. Serves 4 to 6.

Grilled Chicken with Caponata

2 tablespoons olive oil plus additional for
    brushing the chicken breasts
2 cups ½-inch dice unpeeled eggplant
⅓ cup finely chopped onion
¾ cup thinly sliced celery
2 tablespoons tomato paste mixed with
    ½ cup water
⅓ cup chopped pitted green olives
1½ tablespoons finely chopped drained
    bottled capers
3 tablespoons red-wine vinegar
1 tablespoon sugar, or to taste
2 tablespoons golden raisins
2 tablespoons lightly toasted pine nuts
2 tablespoons finely chopped fresh parsley
    leaves, preferably flat-leafed
1 boneless whole chicken breast (about
    1 pound), halved

In a heavy skillet heat 1 tablespoon of the oil over moderately high heat until it is hot but not smoking and in it cook the eggplant, stirring, for 5 minutes, or until it is tender. Transfer the eggplant to a bowl and reserve it. To the skillet add 1 tablespoon of the remaining oil and in it cook the onion and the celery over moderate heat, stirring, for 5 minutes. Add the tomato paste mixture, the olives, the capers, and salt and pepper to taste and cook the mixture, stirring, for 2 minutes. Add the vinegar, the sugar, the raisins, the pine nuts, and the reserved eggplant, cook the mixture, stirring, until it is thickened, and cook it, covered, for 5 minutes, or until the celery is tender. Remove the skillet from the heat, stir in the parsley, and let the *caponata* cool. While the *caponata* is cooling, grill the chicken breasts, brushed with the additional oil and seasoned with salt and pepper, on a rack set over glowing coals or, covered, in a well seasoned ridged grill pan heated over moderately high heat until it is hot, turning them once, for 8 to 10 minutes, or until they are just cooked through. Divide the chicken breasts and the *caponata* between 2 plates. Serves 2.

Grilled Chicken Breasts with Indonesian-Style Peanut Sauce

¼ cup creamy peanut butter
1 tablespoon medium-dry Sherry or Scotch
4 teaspoons soy sauce
4 teaspoons fresh lemon juice
2 teaspoons firmly packed brown sugar
1½ teaspoons minced garlic
¼ teaspoon Tabasco, or to taste
vegetable oil for brushing the grill pan
    or skillet
1 whole chicken breast, boned, leaving the
    skin on, and halved (about ¾ pound)

In a small heavy saucepan combine the peanut butter, the Sherry, the soy sauce, the lemon juice, the brown sugar, the garlic, the Tabasco, and ⅓ cup water and bring the mixture just to a boil over moderate heat, stirring until it is smooth. Remove the pan from the heat and keep the sauce warm, covered. Brush a well seasoned ridged grill pan or cast-iron skillet with the oil and heat it over moderately high heat until the oil just begins to smoke. Add the chicken, patted dry and seasoned with salt and pepper, skin side down and grill it, covered, turning it once, for 10 minutes, or until it is just cooked through. Transfer the chicken to a cutting board, let it stand for 5 minutes, and cut it lengthwise into thin slices. Divide the chicken between 2 heated plates and drizzle it with the sauce. Serves 2.

Coq au Vin with Shiitake Mushrooms and Glazed Onions

¼ cup olive oil
4½ pounds chicken pieces, rinsed and
    patted dry
½ cup finely chopped shallot
½ cup finely chopped onion
3 carrots, quartered lengthwise and cut
    crosswise into ¼-inch pieces (about ¾ cup)
1 bay leaf
¾ teaspoon dried thyme, crumbled
¼ cup Cognac or other brandy
¼ cup all-purpose flour
2 cups dry white wine
2⅔ cups chicken broth
½ pound *shiitake* mushrooms, stems
    discarded and the caps sliced thin
¾ pound pearl onions, blanched in boiling
    water for 3 minutes, drained, and peeled
1½ tablespoons sugar
freshly grated nutmeg to taste
baked spaghetti squash (page 155) as an
    accompaniment

3 tablespoons finely chopped fresh parsley
　　leaves
fresh thyme sprigs for garnish if desired

In a heavy kettle heat 2 tablespoons of the oil over moderately high heat until it is hot but not smoking and in it sauté the chicken pieces, seasoned with salt and pepper, in batches, turning them once, for 8 to 10 minutes, or until they are browned. Transfer the chicken pieces as they are browned to a plate and keep them warm, covered. Pour off all but 2 tablespoons of the fat from the kettle and in the remaining fat cook the shallot, the chopped onion, the carrots, the bay leaf, and the dried thyme over moderately low heat, stirring, for 10 minutes, or until the carrots are just tender. Add the Cognac and boil it until it is nearly evaporated. Stir in the flour, cook the mixture over moderately low heat, stirring, for 3 minutes, and whisk in the wine and 2 cups of the broth. Bring the mixture to a boil, add the chicken, and simmer the mixture, covered, for 15 to 20 minutes, or until the chicken is tender.

　While the mixture is simmering, in a heavy skillet cook the mushrooms in 1 tablespoon of the remaining oil over moderate heat, stirring, for 5 minutes, or until all the liquid they give off is evaporated and they are tender, and reserve them. In the skillet, cleaned, combine the pearl onions, the remaining 1 tablespoon oil, ½ tablespoon of the sugar, and the remaining ⅔ cup broth, bring the mixture to a boil, and simmer it, covered, for 12 to 15 minutes, or until the onions are tender. Simmer the mixture, uncovered, until the liquid is reduced to a syrup, add the remaining 1 tablespoon sugar and 3 tablespoons water, and cook the mixture over moderately high heat, swirling the skillet, until the sugar is melted and the onions are golden and glazed evenly. Season the onions with salt and pepper.

　Transfer the chicken with a slotted spoon to a plate, keep it warm, covered, and discard the bay leaf from the sauce. Boil the sauce for 5 minutes, or until it is reduced to about 3 cups, season it with the nutmeg and salt and pepper, and stir in the reserved mushrooms and the chicken. Transfer the spaghetti squash to a heated platter, arrange the chicken on it, and spoon some of the sauce and the onions over the chicken. Sprinkle the chicken with the parsley, garnish it with the thyme sprigs, and serve it with the remaining sauce. Serves 6.

PHOTO ON PAGE 21

Baked Spaghetti Squash

a 3- to 3½-pound spaghetti squash
3 tablespoons unsalted butter if desired

Prick the squash a few times with a sharp knife to prevent bursting, bake it on a jelly-roll pan in the middle of a preheated 350° F. oven for 1 to 1¼ hours, or until it feels slightly soft when pressed, and let it stand for 5 minutes. To microwave: Prick the squash a few times with a sharp knife to prevent bursting, place it on a paper towel, and microwave it at high power (100%), turning it once, for 12 to 15 minutes, or until it feels slightly soft when pressed. Let the squash stand for 5 minutes.

　Halve the squash lengthwise, discard the seeds, and scrape the flesh with a fork into a bowl. Toss the squash with the butter and salt and pepper to taste. Serves 6.

Oven-Fried Cornmeal Chicken Wings

⅓ cup fresh lime juice
⅓ cup vegetable oil
1½ teaspoons Tabasco
¾ teaspoon cayenne
¾ teaspoon dried orégano
¾ teaspoon ground cumin
3 garlic cloves, minced
½ onion, minced
18 chicken wings (about 3 pounds), wing tips
   cut off and reserved for making stock
   if desired
1 cup yellow cornmeal
½ cup (2½ ounces) finely grated dry
   Asiago or Parmesan
½ teaspoon paprika
½ teaspoon salt
¼ teaspoon freshly ground black pepper
1 tablespoon minced fresh parsley leaves
an egg wash, made by beating 2 large eggs
   with 2 tablespoons cold water and
   2 tablespoons fresh lemon juice
2 tablespoons unsalted butter, melted

In a large bowl whisk together the lime juice, the oil, the Tabasco, the cayenne, the orégano, the cumin, the garlic, and the onion, add the chicken wings, stirring to coat them with the marinade, and let them marinate, covered and chilled, stirring occasionally, for 3 hours or overnight.

In another large bowl combine the cornmeal, the Asiago, the paprika, the salt, the black pepper, and the parsley. Remove the wings from the marinade with a slotted spoon, letting the excess marinade drip off, dip them in the egg wash, and coat them with the cornmeal mixture, shaking off the excess. Arrange the chicken wings in one layer on a rack and let them dry for 30 minutes. Arrange the wings, skin sides up, in one layer in lightly oiled jelly-roll pans, drizzle the butter over them, and bake the wings in a preheated 425° F. oven for 35 minutes, or until they are crisp and golden. Transfer the wings to paper towels to drain. Serve the wings warm or at room temperature. Makes 18 wings, serving 6.

PHOTO ON PAGE 15

Spiced Chicken Wings

10 chicken wings (about 2 pounds), wing tips
   cut off (and reserved for making stock if
   desired) and the wings halved at the joint
1½ teaspoons ground cumin
1 teaspoon curry powder
½ teaspoon salt
½ cup distilled white vinegar
1 tablespoon Worcestershire sauce

In a bowl toss the wings with the cumin, the curry powder, and the salt until they are coated well, bake them in an oiled baking pan in a preheated 475° F. oven, turning them once, for 15 minutes, and drizzle them with ¼ cup of the vinegar. Bake the wings for 5 minutes more, combine the remaining ¼ cup vinegar and the Worcestershire sauce, and drizzle the wings with the vinegar mixture. Bake the wings, turning them once, for 10 minutes more, or until they are browned. Serves 2.

ASSORTED FOWL

Roast Goose with Sausage, Fennel, and Currant Stuffing and Wild Mushroom Port Gravy

For the stuffing
enough Italian bread cut into ¾-inch
   cubes to measure 6 cups (about 1 loaf)
1 pound sweet Italian sausage, casings
   discarded and the meat chopped
¼ cup olive oil
1½ teaspoons minced garlic
1½ cups finely chopped onion
2 cups thinly sliced fennel (about 1 bulb)
1 teaspoon dried sage, crumbled
1 teaspoon dried thyme, crumbled
3 cups chopped mushrooms (about ¾ pound)
½ pound fresh chestnuts, shelled and peeled
   (procedure on page 274), cooked
   (procedure on page 157), and chopped
   coarse, or 6 ounces vacuum-packed
   chestnuts, chopped coarse (about 1 cup)
⅔ cup currants, soaked in boiling water to
   cover for 5 minutes and drained well
½ cup minced fresh parsley leaves (preferably
   flat-leafed)

a 12-pound goose, the loose fat removed, the neck and liver reserved for another use, and the remaining giblets chopped coarse
1 carrot, chopped
1 rib of celery, chopped
1 onion, chopped
½ cup chicken broth
For the gravy
¾ ounce dried *porcini* (available at specialty foods shops)
3 cups chicken broth
1 cup dry white wine
¼ cup Tawny Port
⅓ cup all-purpose flour

sautéed potatoes and celery root (page 181) as an accompaniment
fresh flat-leafed parsley sprigs for garnish

Make the stuffing: Toast the bread cubes in one layer in jelly-roll pans in a preheated 350° F. oven, tossing them occasionally, for 10 minutes, or until they are dry, transfer them to a large bowl, and let them cool. In a large heavy skillet cook the sausage over moderate heat, stirring and breaking up any lumps, until it is no longer pink, transfer it with a slotted spoon to the bowl, and pour off all but 1 tablespoon of the fat remaining in the skillet. To the skillet add 2 tablespoons of the oil, in it cook the garlic, the onion, the fennel, the sage, the thyme, and salt and pepper to taste over moderate heat, stirring, for 10 minutes, or until the vegetables are soft, and transfer the mixture to the bowl. In the skillet cook the mushrooms with salt and pepper to taste in the remaining 2 tablespoons oil over moderate heat, stirring, until almost all the liquid they give off is evaporated, transfer them to the bowl, and stir in the chestnuts, the currants, the parsley, and salt and pepper to taste. *The stuffing may be made 1 day in advance and kept covered and chilled. (Do not stuff the goose in advance.)*

Rinse the goose, pat it dry, and season it inside and out with salt and pepper. Pack the neck cavity loosely with some of the stuffing, fold the neck skin under the body, and fasten it with a skewer. Pack the body cavity loosely with some of the remaining stuffing and truss the goose. Transfer the remaining stuffing to a buttered 2-quart baking dish and reserve it, covered and chilled. Put the goose, breast side up, on a rack in a roasting pan, scatter the carrot, the celery, the onion, and the chopped giblets on the bottom of the pan, and roast the goose in the middle of a preheated 425° F. oven for 30 minutes. Reduce the heat to 325° F., pour 1 cup boiling water carefully over the goose (the juices will splatter), and roast the goose, basting it with the pan juices and skimming off the fat, reserving it for another use such as sautéed potatoes and celery root, for 2 to 2½ hours more, or until the juices run clear when the fleshy part of a thigh is pricked with a skewer and a meat thermometer inserted in the fleshy part of a thigh registers 175° F. During the last hour of roasting bake the reserved stuffing, drizzled with the ½ cup broth and covered, in the 325° F. oven. Transfer the goose to a platter, remove the skewer and the trussing strings, and keep the goose warm, covered loosely with foil.

Make the gravy: In a bowl let the *porcini* soak in 1 cup of the broth, heated, for 30 minutes, or until they are softened. Strain the liquid through a fine sieve lined with a coffee filter or a double thickness of rinsed and squeezed cheesecloth and reserve it. Rinse the *porcini*, drain them well, and chop them fine. Remove the vegetables and the giblets from the roasting pan with a slotted spoon and discard them. Pour off the fat from the pan juices and reserve it. Add the wine and the Port to the pan, deglaze the pan over moderately high heat, scraping up the brown bits clinging to the bottom and sides, and boil the mixture until it is reduced by half. In a saucepan combine ¼ cup of the reserved fat and the flour and cook the *roux* over moderately low heat, whisking, for 3 minutes. Add the remaining 2 cups broth, the wine mixture, and the reserved *porcini* liquid in a stream, whisking, bring the mixture to a boil, whisking, and simmer the gravy, whisking occasionally, for 3 minutes, or until it is thickened. Stir in the *porcini* and salt and pepper to taste, simmer the gravy for 2 minutes, and transfer it to a heated sauceboat.

Spoon the sautéed potatoes and celery root around the goose and garnish the platter with the parsley sprigs. Serves 8.

PHOTO ON PAGE 78

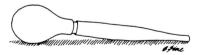

To Cook Chestnuts

In a deep skillet arrange shelled and peeled chestnuts in one layer, add water to cover, and simmer the chestnuts for 45 minutes, or until they are tender. Drain the chestnuts and pat them dry.

Aiguillettes de Canard avec Sauce Chambord
(Sliced Duck Breast with Chambord Sauce)

2 tablespoons rendered duck fat (reserved
    from making duck cracklings, procedure
    follows) or vegetable oil
four 6-ounce boneless duck breasts (cut from
    two 4½- to 5-pound ducks), skinned,
    reserving the skin for making duck
    cracklings
2 teaspoons sugar
½ cup red-wine vinegar
¾ cup dry red wine
2 teaspoons cornstarch
1 cup chicken broth
⅓ cup Chambord (black-raspberry–flavored
    liqueur) or *crème de cassis*
2 tablespoons unsalted butter if desired

In a large heavy skillet heat the duck fat over moderate heat until it is hot but not smoking and in it cook the duck breasts, patted dry and seasoned with salt and pepper, turning them once, for 6 to 8 minutes, or until they are just springy to the touch for medium meat. Transfer the duck with tongs to a cutting board and let it stand for 5 minutes.

While the duck is standing, pour off the fat remaining in the skillet, add the sugar and the vinegar, and boil the mixture, stirring occasionally, until it is reduced to a glaze. Add the wine and boil the mixture until it is reduced by half. Dissolve the cornstarch in the broth, stirring, add the mixture to the skillet with the Chambord, and bring the mixture to a boil, stirring. Boil the sauce for 1 minute, remove the skillet from the heat, and whisk in the butter, cut into pieces, until it is incorporated and salt to taste. Cut the duck breasts lengthwise into thin slices, spoon some of the sauce onto 4 heated plates, and arrange the duck slices over it. Serve the remaining sauce separately. Serves 4.

PHOTO ON PAGE 48

To Make Duck Cracklings
uncooked duck skin, chopped

In a heavy saucepan or heavy skillet large enough to hold the skin in one layer combine the chopped skin with enough water to cover it, bring the water to a boil, and cook the mixture at a slow boil, stirring occasionally, until the water is evaporated (the bubbling noise will subside) and the fat is rendered. (As the water evaporates the liquid will become clear.) Continue to cook the cracklings in the rendered fat over moderate heat, stirring, until they are golden. Transfer the cracklings with a slotted spatula to paper towels to drain and sprinkle them with salt to taste. Strain the duck fat through a fine sieve into a small heatproof bowl and reserve it. The duck fat keeps, covered and chilled, indefinitely. The cracklings keep, covered and chilled, for 1 week.

Roast Turkey with Five-Rice and Chestnut Stuffing
and Mushroom Giblet Gravy

For the stuffing
2 teaspoons salt
2½ cups (1 pound) rice blend (a mixture of
    wild rice, sweet brown rice, long-grain
    brown rice, Wehani, and Black Japonica,
    available at natural foods stores and some
    specialty foods shops) or a combination of
    wild rice and brown rice
2 cups chopped onion
2 cups thinly sliced celery
1 stick (½ cup) unsalted butter
1 pound fresh chestnuts, shelled and peeled
    (procedure on page 274), cooked
    (procedure on page 157), and chopped
    coarse, or ¾ pound vacuum-packed
    chestnuts, chopped coarse (about 2 cups)
4 teaspoons minced fresh rosemary or
    1 teaspoon dried, crumbled
1 tablespoon minced fresh thyme leaves or
    1 teaspoon dried, crumbled
1 cup thinly sliced scallion greens
½ cup minced fresh parsley leaves
1 cup fine fresh bread crumbs

a 12- to 14-pound turkey, the neck and giblets
    (excluding the liver) reserved for making
    turkey giblet stock
1½ sticks (¾ cup) unsalted butter, softened
1 cup chicken broth
For the gravy
½ pound mushrooms, chopped fine
4 cups turkey giblet stock (page 159) and the
    reserved cooked neck and giblets
1 cup dry white wine
⅓ cup all-purpose flour

fresh rosemary sprigs for garnish

Make the stuffing: In a kettle bring 5 quarts water to a boil with the salt. Sprinkle in the rice, stirring until the water returns to a boil, and boil it for 10 minutes. Drain the rice in a large colander and rinse it under running water. Set the colander over a kettle of boiling water, steam the rice, covered with a kitchen towel and the lid, for 40 to 45 minutes, or until it is tender, and transfer it to a bowl. In a large skillet cook the onion and the celery with salt and pepper to taste in ½ stick of the butter over moderately low heat, stirring occasionally, until the vegetables are softened and transfer the mixture to the bowl of rice. Add the remaining ½ stick butter, melted, the chestnuts, the rosemary, the thyme, the scallion greens, the parsley, and the bread crumbs. *The stuffing may be made 1 day in advance and kept covered and chilled. (Do not stuff the turkey in advance.)*

Rinse the turkey, pat it dry, and season it inside and out with salt and pepper. Pack the neck cavity loosely with some of the stuffing, fold the neck skin under the body, and fasten it with a skewer. Pack the body cavity loosely with some of the remaining stuffing, transfer the remaining stuffing to a buttered 2-quart baking dish, and reserve it, covered and chilled. Truss the turkey, spread it with ½ stick of the butter, and roast it on the rack of a roasting pan in a preheated 425° F. oven for 30 minutes. Reduce the heat to 325° F., baste the turkey with the pan juices, and drape it with a piece of cheesecloth soaked in the remaining 1 stick butter, melted and cooled. Roast the turkey, basting it every 20 minutes, for 2½ to 3 hours more, or until the juices run clear when the fleshy part of a thigh is pricked with a skewer and a meat thermometer inserted in the fleshy part of a thigh registers 180° F. During the last half hour of roasting bake the reserved stuffing, drizzled with the broth and covered, in the 325° F. oven. Discard the cheesecloth and trussing string, transfer the turkey to a heated platter, and keep it warm, covered loosely with foil.

Make the gravy: In a small saucepan combine the mushrooms and 1 cup of the stock, bring the stock to a boil, and simmer the mixture for 10 to 12 minutes, or until the stock is almost evaporated. Skim the fat from the turkey pan juices, reserving ¼ cup fat, add the wine to the pan, and deglaze the pan over moderately high heat, scraping up the brown bits clinging to the bottom and sides. Boil the wine mixture until it is reduced by half and reserve it. In a saucepan combine the reserved fat and the flour and cook the *roux* over moderately low

heat, whisking, for 3 minutes. Add the remaining 3 cups stock and the reserved wine mixture in a stream, whisking, bring the mixture to a boil, whisking, and simmer the gravy, whisking occasionally, for 10 minutes. Add the reserved cooked giblets and the neck meat, chopped fine, the mushrooms, and salt and pepper to taste, simmer the gravy for 2 minutes, and transfer it to a heated pitcher or sauceboat.

Garnish the turkey with the rosemary sprigs. Serves 8.

PHOTO ON PAGES 72 AND 73

Turkey Giblet Stock

the neck and giblets (excluding the liver) of a
    12- to 14-pound turkey
4 cups chicken broth
1 rib of celery, chopped
1 carrot, chopped
1 onion, quartered
1 bay leaf
½ teaspoon dried thyme, crumbled
1 teaspoon black peppercorns

In a large saucepan combine the neck and the giblets, the broth, the celery, the carrot, the onion, and 4 cups water and bring the liquid to a boil, skimming the froth. Add the bay leaf, the thyme, and the peppercorns and cook the mixture at a bare simmer for 2 hours, or until it is reduced to about 4 cups. Strain the stock through a fine sieve into a bowl, reserving the neck and giblets for the gravy. *The stock may be made 2 days in advance, cooled completely, uncovered, and kept chilled or frozen in an airtight container.* Makes about 4 cups giblet stock.

Sautéed Turkey Cutlets with
Balsamic Vinegar and Honey Glaze

3 tablespoons balsamic vinegar
1½ teaspoons honey
¾ pound turkey cutlets, each about ¼ inch thick
½ cup fine dry bread crumbs seasoned
   with salt and pepper
¼ cup olive oil
2 garlic cloves, minced
1 tablespoon unsalted butter
¼ cup dry white wine
minced fresh parsley leaves for garnish

In a small bowl stir together the vinegar and the honey until the honey is dissolved and reserve the mixture. Dredge the turkey in the bread crumbs, pressing the crumbs to make them adhere. In a large heavy skillet heat the oil over moderately high heat until it is hot but not smoking, in it sauté the turkey in batches, turning it once, for 1 minute, and transfer it to a platter. Wipe out the skillet, in it cook the garlic in the butter over moderately low heat, stirring, for 1 minute, or until it is pale golden, and stir in the wine. Boil the mixture until the liquid is reduced to about 2 tablespoons, stir in the reserved vinegar mixture, and boil the mixture until it is syrupy. Spoon the glaze over the cutlets and sprinkle the cutlets with the parsley. Serves 2.

Souffléed Turkey and Swiss Cheese Sandwiches

3 tablespoons mayonnaise
¼ teaspoon dried dill
1 scallion, sliced thin
2 slices of whole-wheat or multi-grain bread,
   toasted
2 dill pickles, sliced thin crosswise
¼ pound sliced cooked turkey breast
1 large egg white at room temperature
⅓ cup finely grated Swiss cheese
⅛ teaspoon paprika

In a small bowl whisk together the mayonnaise, the dill, the scallion, and freshly ground pepper to taste. Spread one side of each slice of toast with the mayonnaise mixture, top the mayonnaise mixture with half the pickles, and top the pickles with the turkey. In another small bowl beat the egg white until it holds stiff peaks, fold in the Swiss cheese, the paprika, and salt and pepper to taste, and divide the cheese mixture between the sandwiches, spreading it evenly on top of the turkey. On a baking sheet broil the sandwiches under a preheated broiler about 4 inches from the heat for 30 seconds to 1 minute, or until the topping is puffed and golden. Transfer the sandwiches to 2 heated plates, and garnish the plates with the remaining pickles. Serves 2.

CHEESE, EGGS, AND BREAKFAST ITEMS

CHEESE

Grilled Cheddar and Chutney Sandwiches

2 garlic cloves, unpeeled
1½ tablespoons unsalted butter
3 tablespoons bottled mango chutney, minced
4 slices of homemade-type white bread
3 ounces sharp Cheddar, sliced thin

In a small saucepan of boiling water boil the garlic for 5 minutes, discard the peel, and mash the garlic to a paste. In the pan melt the butter and stir in the garlic paste. Spread the chutney on 2 of the bread slices, divide the Cheddar between the chutney-topped slices, and top it with the remaining 2 bread slices. Brush both sides of the sandwiches with the garlic butter. In a ridged grill pan or heavy skillet cook the sandwiches over moderately high heat, turning them once, for 4 minutes, or until they are golden. Serves 2.

Goat Cheese Marinated in Peppercorns and Thyme

a 12-ounce log of mild goat cheese, cut
   crosswise into 4 pieces
1½ tablespoons mixed dried black, white,
   pink, and green peppercorns (available at
   specialty foods shops and some
   supermarkets), crushed
6 to 8 fresh thyme sprigs
1¼ to 1½ cups olive oil

In a 1-pint jar with a tight-fitting lid combine the cheese with the peppercorns and the thyme, pour enough of the oil over the mixture to cover the cheese completely, and let the cheese marinate, covered and chilled, for 1 week and up to 3 weeks. Let the mixture come to room temperature before serving.

Goat Cheese Marinated in Rosemary, Fennel,
and Hot Red Pepper

a 12-ounce log of mild goat cheese, cut
   crosswise into 4 pieces
1 tablespoon fennel seeds, crushed
1 teaspoon crushed dried hot red pepper flakes
6 to 8 fresh rosemary sprigs
the zest of 1 lemon removed with a
   vegetable peeler
1 to 1½ cups olive oil

In a 1-pint jar with a tight-fitting lid combine the cheese with the fennel seeds, the red pepper flakes, the rosemary, and the lemon zest, pour enough of the oil over the mixture to cover the cheese completely, and let the cheese marinate, covered and chilled, for 1 week and up to 3 weeks. Let the mixture come to room temperature before serving.

Dill-Coated Goat Cheese

about 8 fresh dill sprigs
a 3-ounce *crottin* of soft mild goat cheese
assorted breads as an accompaniment

Press the dill lightly onto the top, bottom, and side of the cheese, wrap the cheese in plastic wrap, and press the dill firmly onto it. Chill the cheese, wrapped well, for at least 1 day and up to 4 days. Serve the cheese at room temperature with the breads.

PHOTO ON PAGE 17

Pepper-Coated Goat Cheese

a 3-ounce *crottin* of soft mild goat cheese
1½ tablespoons black peppercorns,
    crushed coarse
assorted breads as an accompaniment

Roll the cheese in the pepper, coating it well on the top, bottom, and side. Chill the cheese, wrapped well, for at least 1 day and up to 4 days. Serve the cheese at room temperature with the breads.

PHOTO ON PAGE 17

Marinated Mozzarella

1¾ cups olive oil
2 tablespoons dried rosemary, crumbled
2 large garlic cloves, sliced thin
1 pound whole-milk mozzarella,
    cut into ¾-inch cubes
4 large fresh rosemary sprigs
assorted breads as an accompaniment

In a saucepan combine the oil, the dried rosemary, and half the garlic, simmer the mixture for 2 minutes, and let it cool to room temperature. Put the mozzarella and the remaining garlic into a 1-quart jar with a tight-fitting lid, strain the flavored oil through a fine sieve over the mixture, discarding the solids, and push the rosemary sprigs down into the jar. Let the mozzarella marinate, covered and chilled, for at least 1 hour and up to 2 days. Serve the marinated mozzarella at room temperature with the breads.

PHOTO ON PAGE 17

EGGS

Zucchini and Bell Pepper Frittata

⅓ cup finely chopped onion
1 cup thinly sliced zucchini
½ cup finely chopped red bell pepper
½ cup finely chopped green bell pepper
1½ tablespoons olive oil
4 large eggs
⅔ cup freshly grated Parmesan
2 tablespoons minced fresh parsley leaves

In a 9-inch non-stick skillet cook the onion, the zucchini, and the peppers with salt and black pepper to taste

in 1 tablespoon of the oil over moderate heat, stirring, for 10 minutes, or until the vegetables are tender. In a bowl whisk together the eggs, ⅓ cup of the Parmesan, and the parsley, add the vegetable mixture, and stir the mixture until it is combined well. In the skillet heat the remaining ½ tablespoon oil over moderate heat until it is hot but not smoking, pour in the egg mixture, distributing the vegetables evenly, and cook the *frittata*, without stirring, for 8 to 10 minutes, or until the edge is set but the center is still soft. Sprinkle the remaining ⅓ cup Parmesan over the top, and place the frittata, still in the skillet, in the broiler. (If the skillet handle is plastic, wrap it in a double thickness of foil.) Broil the *frittata* under a preheated broiler about 4 inches from the heat for 3 to 4 minutes, or until the cheese is golden, and let it cool in the skillet for 5 minutes. Run a knife around the edge and slide the *frittata* onto a serving plate. Cut the *frittata* into wedges and serve it warm or at room temperature. Serves 2.

Bacon, Cheddar, and Scallion Omelet

1 tablespoon unsalted butter
4 large eggs, beaten lightly with
    1 tablespoon cold water
2 slices of lean bacon, cooked and crumbled
3 tablespoons grated sharp Cheddar
1 scallion including the green part, sliced

In an 8-inch non-stick skillet heat the butter over moderately high heat until the foam subsides and in it cook the eggs with salt and pepper to taste, undisturbed, for 5 seconds. Reduce the heat to moderate and cook the eggs, shaking the skillet and lifting the cooked portion to let the uncooked egg flow underneath it, until the omelet is just set but still soft and moist. Sprinkle the omelet with the bacon, the Cheddar, and the scallion, fold it over, and slide it onto a plate. Halve the omelet and put each half on a plate. Serves 2.

Tortilla Española
(Spanish Potato Omelet)

2 large russet (baking) potatoes
    (about 1 pound)
½ large onion, sliced thin
½ teaspoon coarse salt
⅓ cup olive oil
2 large eggs

Peel the potatoes, cut them crosswise into ⅛-inch-thick slices, and in a bowl combine them with the onion and the salt. In an 8-inch skillet heat the oil until it is hot but not smoking and add the potato mixture gradually, turning the mixture with a thin spatula to coat the vegetables with the oil (to prevent them from sticking together). Cook the mixture, lifting and turning it frequently with the spatula, for 12 to 15 minutes, or until the potatoes are almost tender but not browned. (The potato slices should remain separated.) In a large bowl whisk together the eggs until they are foamy and season them with salt and freshly ground pepper. In a colander set over a bowl drain the potato mixture, reserving 1½ tablespoons of the oil, add the potato mixture to the eggs, combining the mixture gently, and let the mixture stand for 10 minutes. In the skillet, cleaned, heat 1 tablespoon of the reserved oil over moderately high heat until it is hot but not smoking, pour in the potato and egg mixture, spreading it out immediately with the spatula, and cook it, shaking the skillet frequently to prevent the omelet from sticking, for 2 minutes, or until the underside is golden brown. Invert a plate over the skillet and invert the omelet onto it. Add the remaining ½ tablespoon reserved oil to the skillet, slide the omelet back into the skillet, and brown the other side. (If pieces of the omelet stick to the plate, scrape them off and fit them back into the omelet.) Cook the omelet for 2 minutes more. Reduce the heat to moderate and cook the omelet for 2 minutes more on each side, inverting the omelet in the same manner, or until the potatoes are tender. Transfer the omelet to a serving plate, sprinkle it with salt, and serve it warm or at room temperature. Serves 2.

Guacamole Omelets with Sour Cream and Chives

1 avocado (preferably California)
⅓ cup chopped seeded tomato
2 tablespoons minced red onion
cayenne to taste
1 tablespoon fresh lemon juice
4 large eggs
1½ tablespoons unsalted butter, cut into bits
sour cream as an accompaniment
snipped fresh chives for garnish

Peel, pit, and chop the avocado. In a bowl toss together the avocado, the tomato, the onion, the cay-enne, the lemon juice, and salt to taste. In another bowl whisk together lightly the eggs, 2 tablespoons water, and salt to taste.

Heat an 8-inch skillet, preferably non-stick, over moderately high heat until it is hot, add half the butter, and heat it, tilting and rotating the skillet to coat it with the butter, until the foam subsides. Pour in half the egg mixture, tilting and rotating the skillet to spread the mixture evenly, and cook it for 1 to 2 minutes, or until it is just set. Spoon half the *guacamole* over half the omelet, fold the omelet over the filling, and transfer it to a plate. Make another omelet in the same manner using the remaining butter, egg mixture, and *guacamole*. Top the omelets with the sour cream and sprinkle them with the chives. Serves 2.

Pork Egg Foo Yong

¾ cup beef broth
2 teaspoons soy sauce
2 teaspoons cornstarch
1 cup frozen peas
4 large eggs
2 cups chopped iceberg lettuce, rinsed and
    spun dry
¼ cup thinly sliced scallion
½ cup chopped cooked pork or 1 rib pork
    chop, cooked and the meat chopped
2 tablespoons vegetable oil

In a small saucepan combine the broth and the soy sauce and bring the mixture to a boil. In a small bowl dissolve the cornstarch in 2 tablespoons cold water, add the cornstarch mixture to the broth mixture, and boil the mixture, stirring, for 1 minute. Stir in the peas and keep the sauce warm over low heat. In a bowl whisk together the eggs and stir in the lettuce, the scallion, and the pork. In an 8-inch heavy skillet heat 1 tablespoon of the oil over moderate heat until it is hot but not smoking and spoon half the egg mixture into it, spreading it evenly. Cook the mixture, without stirring, for 1 to 2 minutes, or until the eggs are almost set and the underside is golden, turn the omelet carefully with a spatula, and cook it for 30 seconds to 1 minute more, or until the eggs are just set. Transfer the omelet to a plate, cook the remaining egg mixture in the same manner in the remaining 1 tablespoon oil, and transfer the omelet to another plate. Spoon the sauce around the egg foo yong. Serves 2.

Herbed Scrambled Eggs

12 large eggs
3 tablespoons unsalted butter
1 tablespoon snipped fresh chives or
    minced scallion greens
1 tablespoon minced fresh parsley leaves
1 tablespoon snipped fresh dill

In a bowl whisk together lightly the eggs, ¼ cup water, and pepper to taste. In a large heavy skillet heat the butter over moderate heat until the foam begins to subside, add the egg mixture, and reduce the heat to moderately low. Cook the egg mixture, stirring, for 8 to 10 minutes, or until it is just set, and add salt to taste. (The scrambled eggs will have large curds and appear very creamy.) Serve the eggs sprinkled with the chives, the parsley, and the dill. Serves 6.

BREAKFAST ITEMS

Banana Walnut French Toast

1 large banana, halved lengthwise and
    cut into ⅛-inch slices, reserving some slices
    for garnish
3 tablespoons finely chopped walnuts, toasted
    lightly
1 teaspoon fresh lemon juice
four 1-inch-thick diagonal slices of day-old
    French or Italian bread
2 large eggs, beaten lightly
½ cup milk
¼ cup heavy cream
2 tablespoons light brown sugar
2 teaspoons light rum
¼ teaspoon cinnamon
¼ teaspoon freshly grated nutmeg
2 tablespoons unsalted butter
confectioners' sugar for sifting over the toast
maple syrup as an accompaniment

In a small bowl combine the banana slices, the walnuts, and the lemon juice. Cut through the bread slices horizontally to within ¼ inch of the crust, forming a pocket, into each pocket stuff one fourth of the banana mixture, and press the pockets closed. In a shallow bowl or pie plate large enough to hold the 4 slices of bread in one layer whisk together the eggs, the milk, the cream, the brown sugar, the rum, the cinnamon, the nutmeg, and a pinch of salt, add the filled bread slices, and let them soak, chilled, turning them once, for 25 minutes, or until they absorb the egg mixture. In a heavy skillet heat the butter over moderate heat until the foam subsides and in it cook the soaked bread slices, turning them occasionally with a spatula, for 12 to 15 minutes, or until they are crisp and golden. Transfer the toast with the spatula to heated plates and over it sift the confectioners' sugar. Garnish the toast with the reserved banana slices and serve it with the syrup. Serves 2.

Turkey, Ham, and Vegetable Hash with Fried Eggs

3 pounds russet (baking) potatoes
    (about 5 large)
¾ cup finely chopped onion
¾ cup well washed finely chopped white part
    of leek
¾ cup finely chopped red bell pepper
½ stick (¼ cup) unsalted butter
2 cups shredded cooked turkey
1 cup finely chopped cooked ham
½ cup heavy cream
½ cup finely chopped fresh parsley leaves
2 tablespoons vegetable oil
fried eggs as an accompaniment

In a kettle combine the potatoes with enough cold water to cover them by 1 inch, bring the water to a boil, and simmer the potatoes, covered, for 15 to 20 minutes, or until they are tender. Drain the potatoes and let them cool until they can be handled. While the potatoes are cooling, in a 12-inch non-stick skillet cook the onion, the leek, and the bell pepper with salt and black pepper to taste in 2 tablespoons of the butter over moderately low heat, stirring, for 10 minutes, or until the vegetables are softened. Peel the potatoes and cut them into ⅓-inch dice (there should be about 5 cups). In a large bowl stir together the vegetable mixture, the turkey, the ham, the potatoes, the cream, the parsley, and salt and black pepper to taste until the mixture is combined well. In the skillet melt the remaining 2 tablespoons butter with the oil over moderate heat, transfer the hash to the skillet, and cook it, tamping it down firmly with a spatula occasionally, for 25 minutes. If the skillet handle is plastic, wrap it in a double thickness of foil. Bake the hash in the middle of a preheated 375° F. oven for 15 minutes, invert it onto a serving plate, and serve it with the fried eggs. Serves 6.

PHOTO ON PAGE 75

Spiced Raisin Pancakes
with Chocolate Maple Syrup

¼ cup maple syrup
1 tablespoon unsweetened cocoa powder
½ stick (¼ cup) unsalted butter plus additional
    butter, melted, for brushing the griddle
1 cup all-purpose flour
2 teaspoons double-acting baking powder
½ teaspoon salt
1 teaspoon cinnamon
⅛ teaspoon ground cloves
¼ cup raisins
2 tablespoons firmly packed brown sugar
¾ cup milk
1 large egg, beaten lightly

To make the syrup: In a small saucepan heat the syrup until it is hot, remove the pan from the heat, and whisk in the cocoa powder and 1 tablespoon of the butter until the mixture is smooth.

To make the pancakes: Into a bowl sift together the flour, the baking powder, the salt, the cinnamon, and the cloves and stir in the raisins and the brown sugar. Add the milk, the egg, and 3 tablespoons of the remaining butter, melted, and stir the batter until it is just combined. (The batter will be slightly lumpy). Heat a griddle over moderately high heat until it is hot but not smoking and brush it with some of the additional melted butter. Drop the batter by scant ¼ cups onto the griddle and cook the pancakes for 1 minute, or until the undersides are golden brown. Turn the pancakes and cook them for 1 minute more, or until the undersides are golden brown. Serve the pancakes on heated plates with the chocolate maple syrup. Makes about sixteen 3-inch pancakes, serving 2.

Corn Waffles with Peppercorn Syrup

½ cup maple syrup
1½ teaspoons drained green peppercorns,
    crushed lightly, or ½ teaspoon freshly
    ground black pepper
½ cup all-purpose flour
½ cup yellow cornmeal
1 tablespoon sugar
2 teaspoons double-acting baking powder
¼ teaspoon salt
1 large egg
2 tablespoons unsalted butter, melted and
    cooled, plus additional as an accompaniment
    if desired
⅔ cup cooked fresh corn kernels or thawed
    frozen plus additional for garnish
vegetable oil for brushing the waffle iron
cooked breakfast sausage links as an
    accompaniment

In a small saucepan combine the syrup and the peppercorns, bring the syrup just to boil, and let it stand off the heat while making the waffles. In a bowl whisk together the flour, the cornmeal, the sugar, the baking powder, and the salt. In another bowl whisk together the egg, the melted butter, ½ cup water, and ⅔ cup of the corn, add the egg mixture to the flour mixture, and stir the batter until it is just combined. Heat a waffle iron until it is hot, brush it with the oil, and pour half the batter onto it. Cook the waffle according to the manufacturer's instructions, transfer it to a baking sheet, and keep it warm, uncovered, in a warm oven. Make another waffle with the remaining batter in the same manner. Serve the waffles on heated plates with the syrup, the additional butter and corn, and the sausages. Serves 2.

JEANNE

PASTA AND GRAINS

PASTA

*Fettuccine with Pine Nuts, Prosciutto,
and Brown Butter*

¾ pound fresh or dried fettuccine
1 stick (½ cup) unsalted butter
2 teaspoons fresh lemon juice, or to taste
2 ounces thinly sliced prosciutto, torn into
    2-inch-long strips
1 cup finely chopped fresh parsley leaves
⅓ cup pine nuts, toasted lightly
thin lemon wedges as an accompaniment

In a kettle of boiling salted water cook the fettuccine until it is *al dente* and drain it. While the fettuccine is cooking, in a skillet heat the butter over moderately high heat, swirling it, until it is golden brown, remove the skillet from the heat, and stir in the lemon juice, the prosciutto, the parsley, and the pine nuts. In a bowl toss the fettuccine with the butter sauce and salt and pepper to taste and serve it with the lemon wedges. Serves 6 as a first course and 3 as an entrée.

Fettuccine with Tomato Basil Cream

½ cup heavy cream
½ cup chicken broth
¼ cup olive oil
½ pound tomatoes, seeded and chopped
⅓ cup fresh basil leaves, cut into
    julienne strips
½ pound dried fettuccine
2 tablespoons freshly grated Parmesan

In a large skillet combine the cream, the broth, ⅓ cup water, and the oil, bring the liquid to a boil, and cook the mixture at a vigorous simmer for 5 minutes. Add the tomatoes and the basil and simmer the mixture for 1 minute. While the sauce is cooking, in a kettle of boiling salted water cook the fettuccine until it is *al dente* and drain it well. Toss the fettuccine in the skillet with the Parmesan and the sauce to coat it well. Serves 2.

Fettuccine with Walnut Sauce

¾ cup walnuts (3 ounces), toasted until
    golden and cooled
1 garlic clove
½ teaspoon salt
¼ teaspoon freshly ground white pepper
½ tablespoon unsalted butter
1 tablespoon olive oil
¼ cup heavy cream
1 tablespoon freshly grated Parmesan plus
    additional to taste
¼ cup finely minced fresh parsley leaves,
    preferably flat-leafed
⅛ teaspoon dried basil, crumbled
⅛ teaspoon dried marjoram, crumbled
½ tablespoon fresh lemon juice, or to taste
½ pound dried fettuccine

In a food processor blend the walnuts, the garlic, the salt, the pepper, and the butter until the mixture forms a smooth paste. With the motor running add the oil slowly and blend the mixture until it is combined well. Transfer the mixture to a large bowl and whisk in the cream, 1 tablespoon of the Parmesan, the parsley, the basil, the marjoram, and the lemon juice.

In a large kettle of boiling salted water cook the fettuccine until it is *al dente* and ladle out about 2 cups of the cooking liquid. Drain the fettuccine and transfer it to a large bowl. To the walnut mixture add ½ cup of the reserved cooking liquid and whisk the mixture until it is smooth and creamy, adding more of the cooking liquid as necessary to make a sauce that will just coat the fettuccine. (The sauce will thicken as it stands and may require up to an additional ¾ cup of the reserved cooking liquid to maintain the desired consistency.) Toss the fettuccine with the sauce, sprinkle the dish with the additional Parmesan, and serve it immediately. Serves 4 as a first course.

Linguine with Asparagus, Garlic, and Lemon

1 onion, chopped
1½ teaspoons minced garlic
2 tablespoons olive oil
1 tablespoon unsalted butter
6 ounces dried *linguine*
½ pound asparagus, trimmed, peeled, and
    sliced thin diagonally
2 tablespoons dry white wine
1 tablespoon fresh lemon juice, or to taste
2 tablespoons freshly grated Parmesan

In a heavy skillet cook the onion and the garlic in the oil and the butter over moderate heat, stirring, until the mixture is golden and season it with salt and pepper. While the vegetables are cooking, in a kettle of boiling salted water cook the *linguine* for 10 minutes, or until it is *al dente*, and drain it. To the skillet add the asparagus and cook the mixture over moderate heat, stirring, for 2 minutes. Add the wine and cook the mixture, stirring, for 2 minutes. Remove the skillet from the heat, add 1 tablespoon water, the lemon juice, the *linguine*, the Parmesan, and salt and pepper to taste, and toss the mixture well. Serves 2.

Baked Macaroni and Cheese with Cauliflower and Ham

2 cups (about ½ pound) 1-inch cauliflower
    flowerets
1 cup (¼ pound) elbow macaroni
2 tablespoons minced onion
1 tablespoon plus 2 teaspoons unsalted butter
1 tablespoon all-purpose flour
1 cup milk
¼ cup heavy cream
a pinch of freshly grated nutmeg
1½ cups (about 5 ounces) coarsely grated
    extra-sharp Cheddar
1 cup (about 5 ounces) ½-inch cubes
    of cooked ham
½ cup dry bread crumbs

In a large saucepan of boiling salted water blanch the cauliflower for 5 minutes, refresh it under cold water, and drain it well. Or microwave the cauliflower in a glass dish, covered with microwave-safe plastic wrap, at high power (100%) for 5 minutes. In another large saucepan of boiling salted water cook the macaroni for 7 minutes, or until it is *al dente*, refresh it under cold water, and drain it well.

In a large saucepan cook the onion in 1 tablespoon of the butter over moderately low heat until it is softened, stir in the flour, and cook the mixture, stirring, for 2 minutes. Whisk in the milk, the cream, and the nutmeg, bring the mixture just to a boil, stirring, and simmer it, stirring, for 3 minutes. Add 1 cup of the Cheddar, stirring until it is melted completely, stir in the macaroni, the cauliflower, and the ham, and season the mixture with salt and freshly ground pepper. Mound the mixture into a buttered 1½-quart flameproof shallow baking dish and top it with the remaining ½ cup Cheddar. Toss the bread crumbs with the remaining 2 teaspoons butter, melted, and sprinkle the crumb mixture over the cheese. Bake the gratin in the middle of a preheated 375° F. oven for 25 minutes, or until the topping is golden. Or in a microwave-safe shallow baking dish microwave the gratin at high power (100%) for 10 minutes. (For a crisper topping, put the gratin under the broiler for 30 seconds.) Serves 2.

Macaroni with Hot Sausage, Mushrooms, and Zucchini

2 cups thinly sliced onion
2 tablespoons olive oil
½ pound hot Italian sausage,
    casings discarded
¼ pound mushrooms, sliced thin
a ½-pound zucchini, scrubbed and sliced thin
½ teaspoon dried orégano
1¼ cups macaroni
½ cup freshly grated Parmesan

In a skillet cook the onion in the oil over moderate heat, stirring, for 5 minutes, add the sausage, and cook it over moderately high heat, breaking up the lumps, until it is cooked through. Add the mushrooms, the zucchini, and the orégano and cook the mixture, stirring, until the vegetables are tender. While the mixture is cooking, in a kettle of boiling salted water boil the macaroni until it is *al dente*, drain it well, and transfer it to a bowl. Add the sausage mixture, the Parmesan, and salt to taste and toss the mixture well. Serves 2.

Minted Orzo with Currants

½ cup *orzo* (rice-shaped pasta)
2 tablespoons olive oil
¼ cup dried currants
1 teaspoon minced fresh mint leaves or
    ¼ teaspoon dried, or to taste
2 teaspoons white-wine vinegar

In a large saucepan of boiling salted water cook the *orzo* with 1 tablespoon of the oil for 5 minutes, add the currants, and boil the mixture for 4 minutes, or until the *orzo* is *al dente*. Drain the mixture in a sieve and in a bowl combine it well with the mint, the vinegar, the remaining 1 tablespoon oil, and salt and pepper to taste. Serves 2.

PHOTO ON PAGE 27

Cauliflower and Red Bell Pepper Pasta

2 garlic cloves, minced
1 red bell pepper, chopped
2 tablespoons olive oil
3 cups ½-inch cauliflower flowerets
a pinch of dried hot red pepper flakes
1 teaspoon white-wine vinegar
3 ounces *fusilli* or other corkscrew-
    shaped pasta
1 tablespoon unsalted butter
2 tablespoons freshly grated Parmesan

In a skillet cook the garlic and the bell pepper in the oil over moderately low heat, stirring, until the pepper is softened. Add the cauliflower, increase the heat to moderately high, and sauté the mixture, stirring, for 1 minute. Add ⅓ cup water, the red pepper flakes, the vinegar, and salt and pepper to taste and bring the liquid to a boil. Simmer the mixture, covered, for 5 minutes, or until the cauliflower is tender, and boil it, uncovered, until the liquid is reduced to about ¼ cup. While the cauliflower is cooking, cook the *fusilli* in a saucepan of boiling salted water until it is *al dente*, drain it, and in a large bowl toss it with the butter. Add the cauliflower mixture and the Parmesan and toss the mixture well. Serves 2.

Pasta with Fennel and Olives

1 cup coarsely chopped fennel bulb
2 tablespoons olive oil
1 cup small bow-shaped pasta or other
    small pasta
1 teaspoon fennel seeds
⅓ cup chopped pitted Kalamata or other brine-
    cured black olives
¼ teaspoon dried hot red pepper flakes,
    or to taste
1 teaspoon white-wine vinegar
2 tablespoons minced fresh parsley leaves

In a large heavy skillet cook the fennel bulb in the oil over moderately low heat, stirring, until it is crisp-tender. In a large saucepan of boiling salted water cook the pasta with the fennel seeds for 5 to 7 minutes, or until the pasta is *al dente*, drain the mixture well, and transfer it to the skillet. Stir in the olives, the red pepper flakes, the vinegar, the parsley, and salt to taste. Serves 2.

Pasta with Uncooked Tomato, Basil, and Mozzarella Sauce

1½ pounds tomatoes (about 3), seeded
    and chopped
3 garlic cloves, minced
½ cup packed fresh basil leaves,
    chopped coarse
1 cup diced mozzarella
    (about ¼ pound)
½ cup olive oil (preferably extra-virgin)
2 tablespoons red-wine vinegar
1 pound dried pasta

In a large bowl combine well the tomatoes, the garlic, the basil, the mozzarella, the oil, the vinegar, and salt and pepper to taste and let the sauce stand, covered, at room temperature for at least 1 hour and up to 4 hours. Just before serving, in a kettle of boiling salted water cook the pasta until it is *al dente*, drain it well, and add it to the sauce. Toss the pasta well with the sauce and serve immediately. Serves 4 to 6.

Baked Penne with Gorgonzola and Radicchio

¼ pound *penne* (quill-shaped macaroni)
¼ pound mushrooms, sliced (about 1½ cups)
1 garlic clove, minced
1 tablespoon unsalted butter
⅛ teaspoon dried sage, crumbled

1 small head of *radicchio*, cored and shredded
  (about 2 cups)
½ cup heavy cream
¼ cup freshly grated Parmesan
⅓ cup crumbled Gorgonzola or other
  blue cheese

In a kettle of boiling salted water cook the *penne* for 8 minutes, or until it is just *al dente*, and drain it well. While the *penne* is cooking, in a skillet cook the mushrooms and the garlic in the butter over moderately low heat, stirring, until they are softened and the mushrooms give off their liquid, stir in the sage and the *radicchio*, and remove the skillet from the heat. In a large bowl whisk together the cream and the Parmesan and stir in the Gorgonzola, the mushroom mixture, the *penne*, and salt and freshly ground pepper to taste. Transfer the mixture to a buttered shallow 1½-quart baking dish and bake it in the middle of a preheated 450°F. oven for 12 to 15 minutes, or until the top is browned and bubbly. Serves 2 as an entrée.

Pumpkin Tortelloni with Autumn Vegetables
For the tortelloni
¼ pound shallots, minced
  (about 1 cup)
3 garlic cloves, minced
3 tablespoons unsalted butter
½ cup fresh bread crumbs
1 teaspoon dried sage, crumbled
½ teaspoon salt
1 cup solid pack canned pumpkin
¼ teaspoon freshly grated lemon zest
½ cup freshly grated Parmesan
40 won ton wrappers (available at Oriental
  markets and many supermarkets), thawed
  if frozen
For the vegetables
4 carrots
1 pound broccoli, the stems removed and
  reserved for another use and the flowerets
  cut into ½-inch pieces (about 4 cups)
3 tablespoons unsalted butter
⅔ cup olive oil
2½ cups chicken broth
½ pound green beans, trimmed and cut
  diagonally into ½-inch lengths

½ pound plum tomatoes, halved, the seeds and
  core discarded, and cut into ⅓-inch dice
½ cup solid pack canned pumpkin

about ¼ cup freshly grated Parmesan

Make the *tortelloni*: In a heavy saucepan cook the shallots and the garlic in the butter over moderately low heat, stirring, until the vegetables are softened, stir in the bread crumbs, the sage, and the salt, and cook the mixture, stirring, for 1 minute. Stir in the pumpkin, the zest, and pepper to taste and cook the mixture, stirring, until it is heated through. Remove the pan from the heat, stir in the Parmesan, and let the filling cool. Put 1 won ton wrapper on a work surface with a corner pointing toward you. Put 1 slightly rounded teaspoon of the filling in the center of the wrapper, brush 2 adjacent sides lightly with water, and fold the opposite corner over the filling to form a triangle, pressing out the air. Press the edges together firmly, sealing them well. Pick up the pasta, bring together the points at the ends of the long side, and press them together firmly, moistening them if necessary. Make *tortelloni* with the remaining wrappers and filling in the same manner, arranging them as they are formed in one layer on a floured dish towel. *The tortelloni may be cooked immediately or dried on the towel, turning them occasionally, for 3 hours. The dried tortelloni may be made 1 week in advance and kept covered and chilled. They may also be frozen in one layer on a tray overnight, transferred to an airtight container, and kept frozen for 1 month.*
Prepare the vegetables: Cut 4 or 5 lengthwise grooves in each carrot with a channel knife and cut the carrots crosswise into ¼-inch slices. In a large skillet combine the carrots, the broccoli, the butter, the oil, and the broth, bring the liquid to a boil, and simmer the mixture, covered, for 3 minutes, or until the vegetables are barely tender. Stir in the green beans, the tomatoes, the pumpkin, and salt and pepper to taste, return the liquid to a simmer, and simmer the mixture for 7 minutes, or until the vegetables are tender.
While the vegetables are cooking, in a kettle of boiling salted water cook the *tortelloni*, stirring, for 2 to 3 minutes, or until they are *al dente*, and remove the kettle from the heat. Transfer 4 *tortelloni* with a slotted spoon to each of 10 plates and spoon the vegetables and broth over them. Sprinkle each serving with some of the Parmesan. Serves 10.

PHOTO ON PAGE 64

GRAINS AND WILD RICE

Barley with Cabbage and Ham in Sour Cream Tomato Sauce

⅓ cup pearl barley
1 teaspoon all-purpose flour
½ cup canned tomato sauce
¼ cup sour cream
⅔ cup chopped cooked ham
3 cups chopped cabbage
1 onion, sliced thin
2 tablespoons vegetable oil

In an 8-inch-square glass baking dish combine the barley and 1⅓ cups water and microwave the mixture, covered tightly with microwave-safe plastic wrap, at high power (100%) for 20 minutes. In a bowl whisk together the flour and 1 tablespoon of the tomato sauce and whisk in the remaining tomato sauce and the sour cream. Remove the plastic wrap carefully from the baking dish and stir in the ham, the tomato sauce mixture, and salt and pepper to taste. In a shallow glass baking dish combine well the cabbage, the onion, and the oil and microwave the mixture, covered tightly with microwave-safe plastic wrap, at high power (100%) for 6 minutes, or until the cabbage is crisp-tender. Remove the plastic wrap carefully, stir the cabbage mixture into the barley mixture, and microwave the mixture, covered tightly with the plastic wrap, at high power (100%) for 3 minutes. Serves 2.

Pistachio, Currant, and Scallion Bulgur

1½ cups chicken broth
2 cups *bulgur* (available at natural foods stores and most supermarkets)
⅓ cup dried currants
5 to 6 tablespoons fresh lemon juice, or to taste
¼ teaspoon cinnamon
½ cup vegetable oil
½ cup shelled natural pistachio nuts, chopped coarse
½ cup chopped scallion

In a large saucepan bring the broth and 1½ cups water to a boil, add the *bulgur* gradually, stirring, and cook it,

covered, over very low heat for 10 to 15 minutes, or until the liquid is absorbed. Fluff the *bulgur* with a fork and add the currants. Remove the pan from the heat and let the mixture stand, covered, for 5 minutes. In a small bowl whisk together the lemon juice, the cinnamon, the oil, and salt and pepper to taste. Transfer the *bulgur* mixture to a large bowl, drizzle the dressing over it, tossing the mixture to distribute the dressing evenly, and stir in the pistachios and the scallion. Serve the *bulgur* at room temperature. Serves 8.

PHOTO ON PAGE 45

Bulgur Pilaf with Scallions and Cumin

3 scallions
½ teaspoon ground cumin
1 tablespoon vegetable oil
½ cup *bulgur*
½ teaspoon salt

Slice thin the white part of the scallions and slice thin enough of the green part to measure 3 tablespoons, keeping the white and green parts separate. In a small heavy saucepan cook the white part of the scallions with the cumin in the oil over moderately low heat, stirring, until it is softened, add the *bulgur*, and cook the mixture, stirring, for 1 minute. Add ¾ cup water and the salt, bring the liquid to a boil, and cook the mixture, covered, over low heat for 10 to 15 minutes, or until the liquid is absorbed. Stir in the scallion greens, remove the pan from the heat, and let the pilaf stand, covered, for 5 minutes. Serves 2.

Bulgur and Pea Pilaf with Lemon and Parsley

1 small onion, chopped
1 tablespoon unsalted butter
½ cup *bulgur*
¾ cup chicken broth
½ teaspoon lemon zest
1 cup frozen peas, thawed
1 tablespoon minced fresh parsley leaves

In a small heavy saucepan cook the onion in the butter over moderately low heat, stirring, until it is softened, stir in the *bulgur*, and cook the mixture, stirring, for 1 minute. Add the broth and the lemon zest, bring the liquid to a boil, and cook the mixture, covered, over low heat for 8 minutes, or until most of the liquid is absorbed. Stir in the peas and the parsley, cook the pilaf for 2 minutes, or until all of the liquid is absorbed, and fluff it with a fork. Serves 2.

Couscous aux Aubergines et aux Courgettes
(Couscous with Eggplant and Zucchini)

1 teaspoon Dijon-style mustard
2 teaspoons red-wine vinegar
1 teaspoon fresh thyme leaves or ¼ teaspoon
   dried, crumbled
¼ cup extra-virgin olive oil
¼ teaspoon salt
½ cup couscous
2 small zucchini (about ¼ pound each),
   scrubbed, quartered lengthwise, and cut
   crosswise into ¼-inch slices
2 small eggplants (about 3 ounces each), cut
   crosswise into ¼-inch slices
2 tablespoons chopped pitted black olives

In a small bowl whisk together the mustard, the vinegar, the thyme, and salt and pepper to taste, add 3 tablespoons of the oil in a stream, whisking, and whisk the dressing until it is emulsified. In a small saucepan bring to a boil ¾ cup water with the remaining 1 tablespoon oil and the salt, stir in the couscous, and remove the pan from the heat. Let the mixture stand, covered, while cooking the vegetables. In a large bowl toss the zucchini and the eggplant with 2 tablespoons of the dressing, heat a well seasoned cast-iron skillet over moderately high heat until it is hot, and in it sauté the vegetables, stirring, for 8 minutes, or until they are charred lightly and tender. Return the vegetables to the bowl, add the olives, the remaining dressing, and salt and pepper to taste, and toss the mixture until it is combined well. Divide the couscous between 2 plates and top it with the vegetable mixture, dividing it equally. Serves 2 as a side dish or luncheon entrée.

Creamy Polenta with Grilled Vegetables

4 cups chicken broth
¾ teaspoon salt
1 cup yellow cornmeal
3 tablespoons unsalted butter, cut into pieces
⅓ cup freshly grated Parmesan
12 baby carrots, blanched for
   2 minutes, drained, and patted dry
12 baby eggplants, halved lengthwise
18 scallions, trimmed
olive oil for brushing the vegetables and
   the grill pan

In a large heavy saucepan bring the broth and 2 cups water to a boil, add the salt and the cornmeal in a slow stream, whisking constantly, and cook the mixture over moderately low heat, whisking constantly, for 15 minutes. Stir in the butter, the Parmesan, and salt and pepper to taste and if necessary whisk in enough water to thin the polenta so that it will just fall from a spoon in a continuous stream. Keep the polenta warm, its surface covered with a round of wax paper. Brush the carrots, the eggplants, and the scallions with the oil and season the vegetables with salt and pepper. Heat a well seasoned large ridged grill pan or cast-iron skillet over moderately high heat, brush it with the oil, and in it grill the vegetables, covered, in batches for 5 to 7 minutes, or until they are crisp-tender, transferring them as they are grilled to a plate. Divide the polenta among 6 plates and arrange the vegetables on top of it. Serves 6.

PHOTO ON PAGES 18 AND 19

Oriental-Style Rice with Pickled Ginger and Soy

¾ cup unconverted long-grain rice
4 teaspoons soy sauce
2 teaspoons minced drained pickled ginger
¼ cup minced scallion
1 teaspoon white-wine vinegar

In a 2-quart glass bowl combine the rice, the soy sauce, and 1½ cups water, microwave the mixture, covered tightly with microwave-safe plastic wrap, at high power (100%) for 5 minutes, and microwave it at medium power (50%) for 15 minutes, or until most of the liquid is absorbed. Let the rice stand, covered, for 5 minutes and stir in the ginger, the scallion, the vinegar, and salt and pepper to taste. Serves 2.

Curried Rice Pilaf with Peanuts

1 small onion, chopped
1 garlic clove, minced
1 tablespoon vegetable oil
⅔ cup converted long-grain rice
½ teaspoon curry powder
⅛ teaspoon dried hot red pepper flakes
⅔ cup chicken broth
2 teaspoons bottled mango chutney
½ teaspoon salt
2 scallions, chopped
¼ cup peanuts, chopped

In a heavy saucepan cook the onion and the garlic in the oil over moderately low heat, stirring, until the onion is softened, add the rice, the curry powder, and the red pepper flakes, and cook the mixture, stirring, for 1 minute. Stir in the broth, ⅔ cup water, the chutney, and the salt, bring the liquid to a boil, and cook the mixture, covered, over low heat for 18 to 20 minutes, or until the liquid is absorbed. Fluff the pilaf with a fork, add the scallions and the peanuts, and let the pilaf stand, covered, off the heat for 5 minutes before serving. Serves 2 as a side dish.

Dilled Rice Pilaf

2 tablespoons unsalted butter
2 cups converted rice
2 cups chicken broth
⅓ cup snipped fresh dill, or to taste

In a large heavy saucepan melt the butter over moderately low heat, add the rice, and cook the mixture, stirring, for 1 minute, or until the rice is coated well with the butter. Add the broth and 1¾ cups water, bring the liquid to a boil, and cook the rice, covered, over low heat for 20 minutes. Fluff the rice with a fork and let it stand, covered, for 5 minutes. Stir in the dill and transfer the rice to a heated serving dish. Makes about 6 cups, serving 12.

PHOTO ON PAGE 12

Brown Rice and Wild Rice Timbales

½ cup finely chopped onion
3 tablespoons unsalted butter
1 cup long-grain brown rice
1 cup wild rice

1 small firm yellow or red bell pepper, peeled
   with a vegetable peeler and cut into 1-inch
   julienne strips
½ cup minced fresh parsley leaves

In a large heavy saucepan cook the onion in the butter over moderately low heat, stirring occasionally, until it is softened, stir in the brown rice and the wild rice, and cook the mixture, stirring, for 1 minute. Add 4 cups water, bring the liquid to a boil, and simmer the mixture, covered, for 45 minutes. Remove the pan from the heat and let the mixture stand for 15 minutes. Fluff the rice with a fork and transfer it to a bowl. Add the bell pepper, the parsley, and salt and black pepper to taste, combine the mixture well, and divide it among eight ½-cup timbale molds, pressing it into the molds gently. Invert the molds onto the ham platter. Serves 8.

PHOTO ON PAGE 24

Wild Rice with Currants and Scallions

1 large onion, chopped
2 tablespoons vegetable oil
2 cups wild rice, rinsed and drained
½ cup currants
1 bunch of scallions, sliced diagonally
   (about 1 cup)

In a large saucepan cook the onion in the oil over moderately low heat, stirring, until it is softened, stir in the rice, and stir the mixture to coat the rice with the oil. Add 5 cups water and bring the liquid to a boil. Stir in the currants and salt to taste and simmer the mixture, covered, for 20 minutes, or until the rice is tender. Drain the rice mixture, transfer it to a bowl, and stir in the scallions. Pack the rice mixture into a 7-cup ring mold and invert the mold onto a platter. Serves 10.

PHOTO ON PAGE 66

Risotto with Asparagus, Morels, and Peppers

1½ ounces dried morels (available at specialty
   foods shops)
5 cups chicken broth or chicken stock
   (page 117)
½ pound asparagus, cut diagonally into
   ¼-inch slices, reserving the tips separately
⅔ cup chopped red bell pepper
⅔ cup yellow bell pepper

1 onion, chopped
3 tablespoons unsalted butter
2 cups Arborio rice (available at specialty
    foods stores)
⅔ cup dry white wine
1 cup freshly grated Parmesan

In a small bowl let the morels soak in 1½ cups hot water for 30 minutes, or until they are softened. Drain the morels in a fine sieve set over a bowl, reserving the liquid, and chop any large ones coarse. In a large saucepan combine the broth, the reserved mushroom liquid, and 1 cup water, and bring the liquid to a boil. Add the sliced asparagus and simmer the mixture for 2 minutes. Add the reserved asparagus tips and the peppers, simmer the vegetables for 2 minutes, and transfer them with a slotted spoon to a bowl. Keep the liquid at a bare simmer. In a large heavy saucepan cook the onion in the butter over moderately low heat, stirring, until it is soft. Add the rice and cook the mixture over moderate heat, stirring with a wooden spatula, for 2 minutes, or until the rice is well coated with the butter. Add the white wine and cook the mixture over moderately high heat, stirring, for 1 to 3 minutes, or until the wine is absorbed. Add ⅔ cup of the broth mixture and cook the mixture over moderately high heat, stirring, for 3 minutes, or until the liquid is absorbed. Add more of the broth mixture, ⅔ cup at a time, stirring and cooking the mixture for 3 minutes, or until the liquid is absorbed, after each addition, until the rice begins to soften. (By now, about 4½ cups of the broth mixture will have been absorbed.) Add more of the broth, ½ cup at a time, stirring and simmering the mixture for 3 minutes, or until the liquid is absorbed, after each addition, until the rice is barely *al dente*. (About 5½ cups of the broth will have been absorbed.) Stir in the asparagus and peppers, the morels, and ½ cup of the broth mixture and simmer the mixture, stirring, for 3 minutes, or until the liquid is absorbed. (The mixture should be creamy, but the rice should be *al dente*. If necessary, add more broth and cook the mixture in the same manner until the rice is *al dente*.) Remove the pan from the heat, stir in the Parmesan and pepper to taste, and transfer the risotto to a heated serving bowl. Serves 4 as a main course or 6 to 8 as a first course or side dish.

PHOTO ON FRONT JACKET

Risotto with Pomegranate Seeds

1 onion, minced
2 tablespoons unsalted butter
2 tablespoons olive oil
2½ cups Arborio rice (available at specialty
    foods shops and some supermarkets)
½ cup dry white wine
5 cups chicken broth plus additional
    if necessary
6 ounces Gorgonzola cheese, cut into
    small cubes
1 pomegranate (about 8 to 10 ounces), halved
    and squeezed gently to yield enough seeds
    to measure about ⅔ cup

In a large saucepan cook the onion in the butter and the oil over moderately low heat until it is softened, add the rice, and cook the mixture over moderately low heat, stirring, for 2 minutes. (Do not let the rice brown.) Add the wine and cook the mixture over moderately high heat for 1 minute. Add about ½ cup of the broth, heated, stirring constantly, and cook the mixture over moderate heat, stirring, until the broth is absorbed. Continue adding the broth, about ½ cup at a time, stirring constantly and letting each portion be absorbed before adding the next. The cooking time will be about 18 minutes for creamy *al dente* rice.) Remove the pan from the heat and add the Gorgonzola, stirring until it is melted completely. Stir in the pomegranate seeds and season the risotto with salt and pepper. Serves 6 to 8.

VEGETABLES

Artichokes with Walnut Garlic Parsley Sauce

2 large artichokes
½ lemon
½ cup packed flat-leafed parsley leaves
1 small garlic clove, chopped
¼ cup walnuts
2 tablespoons fresh lemon juice
½ cup olive oil

Break off and discard the stems and tough outer leaves of the artichokes. Cut off the top quarter of each artichoke with a very sharp stainless-steel knife, snip off the sharp tips of the leaves with scissors, and rub the cut surfaces with the lemon half. Trim the bases and wrap each artichoke in a sheet of microwave-safe plastic wrap, enclosing it completely. Microwave the artichokes at high power (100%) for 12 minutes, or until the stem ends are tender, and let them cool, wrapped, until they are lukewarm.

While the artichokes are cooling, in a blender or food processor blend the parsley, the garlic, the walnuts, the lemon juice, and salt to taste until the mixture forms a paste. With the motor running add the oil in a stream, blend the sauce until it is emulsified, and divide it between 2 small bowls. Unwrap the artichokes and serve them with the sauce. Serves 2.

Asparagus with Pickled Ginger and Shallots

2½ pounds asparagus, trimmed and peeled
2 tablespoons white-wine vinegar
1 teaspoon Dijon-style mustard
1½ tablespoons drained pickled ginger slices
    plus 4 teaspoons fine julienne strips
¼ cup vegetable oil
2 tablespoons finely chopped shallot
2 teaspoons snipped fresh chives

In a large deep skillet of boiling salted water cook the asparagus for 3 to 7 minutes, or until the stalks are tender but not limp. Transfer the asparagus to a bowl of ice and cold water to stop the cooking, drain them, and pat them dry. In a blender blend together the vinegar, the mustard, the 1½ tablespoons ginger slices, and salt and pepper to taste and with the motor running add the oil in a slow stream, blending the dressing until it is emulsified. Divide the dressing among 4 plates, spreading it evenly, and sprinkle it with the shallot and the chives. Divide the asparagus among the plates and garnish them with the julienne ginger. Serves 4.

PHOTO ON PAGE 41

Green Beans with Walnuts and Brown Butter

½ pound green beans, trimmed
1 tablespoon unsalted butter
2 tablespoons finely chopped walnuts

In a large saucepan of boiling salted water cook the green beans, uncovered, for 4 to 6 minutes, or until they are crisp-tender, drain them, and plunge them into a bowl of ice and cold water to stop the cooking. In a skillet cook the butter and the walnuts over moderate heat, swirling the skillet occasionally, until the foam subsides and the butter is nut-brown. Add the beans, drained well, toss them with the butter mixture, and season them with salt and freshly ground pepper. Serves 2.

Lima Beans with Bacon

two 10-ounce packages frozen baby lima
    beans
4 slices of lean bacon
½ cup thinly sliced white part of scallion
½ cup thinly sliced scallion greens

In a saucepan combine the lima beans and 1 cup water, bring the water to a boil, and simmer the beans, covered, for 14 to 16 minutes, or until they are tender. In a skillet cook the bacon over moderate heat, turning it, until it is crisp, transfer it to paper towels to drain, and crumble it. Pour off all but 1 tablespoon of the fat from the skillet. Add the white part of scallion and cook it, stirring occasionally, until it is softened. Add the white part of scallion and the scallion greens to the beans, season the mixture with salt and pepper, and transfer it to a serving dish. Sprinkle the beans with the bacon. Serves 8.

PHOTO ON PAGES 72 AND 73

Beets with Lime Butter

¾ pound beets, peeled and grated coarse
   (about 1¾ cups)
⅛ teaspoon freshly grated lime zest
2 tablespoons unsalted butter, cut into bits
1½ teaspoons fresh lime juice, or to taste
2 tablespoons thinly sliced scallion greens

In a heavy skillet cook the beets and the zest in 1 tablespoon of the butter over moderately high heat, stirring, for 4 to 5 minutes, or until the beets are crisp-tender, and remove the skillet from the heat. Stir in the remaining 1 tablespoon butter, the lime juice, and salt and pepper to taste and serve the beets sprinkled with the scallion greens. Serves 2.

Beet Purée with Balsamic Vinegar

1 pound beets, trimmed, leaving the roots
   and 1 inch of the stems attached, and
   scrubbed well
1 tablespoon balsamic vinegar (available at
   specialty foods shops and some
   supermarkets), or to taste
1 tablespoon unsalted butter

In a large microwave-safe bowl combine the beets with ½ cup water and microwave them, covered tightly with microwave-safe plastic wrap, at high power (100%), turning them once, for 12 to 15 minutes depending on the size of the beets, or until they are tender. Let the mixture stand, covered, for 5 minutes, rinse the beets under cold water, and slip off and discard the skins. Chop the beets coarse and purée them in a food processor with the vinegar, the butter, and salt and pepper to taste. Makes about 1 cup, serving 2.

Sweet-and-Savory Sautéed Bell Peppers

2 garlic cloves, sliced thin
1 tablespoon unsalted butter
1 tablespoon olive oil
1 red bell pepper, cut into ¼-inch rings
1 yellow bell pepper, cut into ¼-inch rings
1 orange bell pepper, cut into ¼-inch rings
2 tablespoons golden raisins, soaked in ¼
   cup boiling water for 15 minutes
2 teaspoons drained bottled capers,
   chopped coarse
4 Kalamata or other brine-cured black olives,
   sliced thin
2 tablespoons pine nuts, toasted lightly
crusty bread as an accompaniment

In a skillet cook the garlic in the butter and the oil over moderate heat, stirring, for 1 minute, or until it is softened. Add the bell pepper rings and sauté the mixture over moderately high heat, stirring, for 1 minute. Add the raisins with the soaking liquid, the capers, and the olives, cook the mixture, covered, for 2 minutes, and stir in the pine nuts. Serve the peppers with the bread as a first course or light entrée. Serves 2.

Curried Broccoli with Hard-Boiled Egg

1 tablespoon vegetable oil
½ bunch of broccoli, separated into small
   flowerets and the stems peeled and cut into
   ⅛-inch slices
¼ teaspoon minced garlic
¾ teaspoon curry powder
1 hard-boiled large egg,
   grated coarse
1 tablespoon unsalted butter,
   softened
fresh lemon juice to taste

In a large skillet heat the oil over moderately high heat until it is hot but not smoking and in it sauté the broccoli, stirring, for 1 minute, or until it is bright green. Stir in the garlic and the curry powder and cook the mixture over moderate heat, stirring, for 30 seconds. Add ⅓ cup water, bring it to a boil, and simmer the broccoli, covered partially, for 5 minutes, or until it is just tender and the water is nearly evaporated. Stir in the hard-boiled egg, the butter, the lemon juice, and salt and pepper to taste. Serves 2.

Italian-Style Broccoli with Sunflower Seeds

½ head of broccoli, cut into ¾-inch flowerets
  and the stems, peeled if desired, cut
  crosswise into ¼-inch slices
  (about 4½ cups)
2 tablespoons olive oil
2 garlic cloves, minced
2 tablespoons shelled dry-roasted
  sunflower seeds
1 teaspoon fresh lemon juice, or to taste

In a heavy skillet sauté the broccoli in the oil over moderately high heat, stirring, for 1 minute. Add the garlic, the sunflower seeds, 3 tablespoons water, and salt and pepper to taste and cook the mixture, covered, for 3 minutes, or until the broccoli is tender and the liquid is evaporated. Remove the skillet from the heat and stir in the lemon juice. Serves 2.

Spicy Broccoli and Garlic Sauce

2 pounds broccoli
2 tablespoons minced garlic, or to taste
3 flat anchovy fillets, or to taste, chopped
¼ teaspoon dried hot red pepper flakes,
  or to taste
¾ cup olive oil
½ cup minced fresh parsley leaves

Cut the broccoli into flowerets, peel the stems, and cut them crosswise into ½-inch pieces. In a large kettle of boiling water blanch the broccoli stems and flowerets for 3 to 4 minutes, or until they are just crisp-tender, drain them in a colander, and refresh them under cold water. In a large heavy skillet cook the garlic, the anchovies, and the red pepper flakes in the oil over moderately low heat, stirring, until the garlic is golden, add the broccoli and the parsley, and cook the mixture, stirring, until it is heated through. Add salt and pepper to taste and serve the sauce immediately. Makes about 5 cups, enough for 1 pound dried pasta, cooked, such as *linguine*.

Brussels Sprouts and Carrots with Shallot Butter

2 pounds (about 2 pints) Brussels sprouts,
  trimmed and an X cut in the base of each
  sprout

1 pound baby carrots, trimmed and peeled
⅓ cup minced shallot
¾ stick (6 tablespoons) unsalted butter

In a steamer set over boiling water steam the Brussels sprouts, covered, for 7 to 8 minutes, or until they are just tender, transfer them to a bowl, and keep them warm. In the steamer steam the carrots, covered, for 4 to 5 minutes, or until they are just tender, and transfer them to the bowl. In a large skillet cook the shallot in the butter over moderately low heat until it is very soft, add the vegetables and salt and pepper to taste, and toss the mixture until the vegetables are coated with the butter and heated through. Serves 8.

PHOTO ON PAGE 78

Orange- and Ginger-Glazed Carrots

1 tablespoon unsalted butter
1 teaspoon sugar
1 tablespoon fresh orange juice
½ teaspoon orange zest
1 teaspoon grated peeled fresh gingerroot
¾ pound baby carrots, each about 5 inches
  long, trimmed

In a microwave-safe shallow baking dish combine the butter, the sugar, the orange juice, the zest, and the gingerroot and microwave the mixture at high power (100%) for 1 minute, or until the butter is melted. Add the carrots, stirring to coat them with the mixture, and microwave them, covered tightly with microwave-safe plastic wrap, for 7 minutes. Cut a 2-inch slit in the plastic wrap and let the carrots stand for 1 minute. Serves 2.

Carrots with Soy Lemon Butter

4 carrots, cut into ⅛-inch-thick slices
  (about 1½ cups)
2 teaspoons unsalted butter, cut into bits
½ teaspoon soy sauce
1 teaspoon fresh lemon juice
1 tablespoon thinly sliced scallion greens

On a steamer rack set over boiling water steam the carrots for 5 to 7 minutes, or until they are tender, and in a bowl toss them with the butter, the soy sauce, the lemon juice, the scallion greens, and salt and pepper to taste. Serves 2.

Cauliflower with Cheddar Sauce and Rye Bread Crumbs

1 slice of rye bread, ground fine in a food
    processor
1 tablespoon minced onion
½ stick (¼ cup) unsalted butter
¼ cup all-purpose flour
4 cups milk
2 cups grated sharp Cheddar
white pepper to taste
1½ heads of cauliflower with the greens
    (about 3¼ pounds), cut into 2-inch
    flowerets and the greens sliced thin

Toast the bread crumbs in a jelly-roll pan in the middle of a preheated 350° F. oven for 3 to 5 minutes, or until they are golden, and let them cool. *The bread crumbs may be made 1 week in advance and kept in an airtight container.*

In a saucepan cook the onion in 3 tablespoons of the butter over moderately low heat, stirring, until it is softened. Stir in the flour and cook the *roux* over low heat, stirring, for 3 minutes. Remove the pan from the heat and add the milk, scalded, in a stream, whisking vigorously until the mixture is thick and smooth. Simmer the sauce, stirring occasionally, for 10 minutes, add the Cheddar, and cook the sauce, stirring, until the Cheddar is melted. Season the sauce with salt and the white pepper and let it cool, its surface covered with plastic wrap. *The sauce may be made 2 days in advance and kept covered and chilled. Reheat the sauce in a saucepan over moderately low heat before continuing with the recipe.*

In a kettle of boiling salted water cook the flowerets for 5 minutes, add the greens, and cook the mixture for 3 to 4 minutes, or until the flowerets are tender. Drain the cauliflower, plunge it into a bowl of ice and cold water to stop the cooking, and drain it well. Pat the cauliflower dry with paper towels and transfer it to a buttered flameproof 2-quart baking dish. *The cauliflower may be prepared up to this point 1 day in advance and kept covered and chilled. Bring the cauliflower to room temperature before continuing with the recipe.*

In a small bowl toss the bread crumbs with the remaining 1 tablespoon butter, melted, pour the Cheddar sauce over the cauliflower, and sprinkle the cauliflower with the bread crumbs. Brown the bread crumbs under a preheated broiler about 4 inches from the heat. Serves 8.

PHOTO ON PAGES 72 AND 73

Cauliflower Purée

1 small head of cauliflower, separated into
    flowerets (about 6 cups) and the tough
    stems discarded
¼ cup heavy cream
¼ cup milk
1 tablespoon white-wine vinegar
1 shallot, minced (about 1 tablespoon)
1 garlic clove, minced
several drops of Tabasco
freshly ground white pepper to taste
1 teaspoon unsalted butter, cut into bits

In a microwave-safe casserole combine the cauliflower with 2 tablespoons water, microwave it, covered with microwave-safe plastic wrap, at high power (100%), stirring it once, for 7 minutes, and let it stand for 3 to 5 minutes, or until it is tender. In a microwave-safe bowl or glass measuring cup stir together the cream, the milk, the vinegar, the shallot, the garlic, the Tabasco, the white pepper, and salt to taste and microwave the mixture, uncovered, at high power (100%) for 1 minute. In a food processor purée the cauliflower and the liquid remaining in the casserole with the cream mixture until the mixture is smooth. Transfer the purée to a serving bowl and top it with the butter. Serves 2.

Crisp Braised Celery

1½ large bunches of celery with the leaves
2 tablespoons vegetable oil
1 tablespoon unsalted butter
½ teaspoon salt
1 teaspoon sugar
¾ teaspoon celery seeds
⅓ cup chicken broth

Trim the celery, reserving the leaves, rinsed, and cut it diagonally into ⅛-inch-thick slices. (There should be about 8 cups sliced celery.) In a large heavy skillet heat the oil and the butter over moderately high heat until the fat is hot but not smoking, add the celery, the salt, the sugar, and the celery seeds, and sauté the celery, stirring, for 1 minute. Add the broth and the reserved leaves, bring the liquid to a boil, and simmer the mixture, covered, for 3 to 5 minutes, or until the celery is crisp-tender. Serves 10.

PHOTO ON PAGE 66

Creamy Sautéed Cucumbers with Dill

1 large garlic clove, minced
1 tablespoon olive oil
2 cucumbers (about 1 pound), peeled, seeded, and cut into 2-inch strips
1 teaspoon white-wine vinegar
2 tablespoons heavy cream
1½ tablespoons snipped fresh dill

In a heavy skillet cook the garlic in the oil over low heat, stirring, until it begins to color, add the cucumbers, and cook the mixture over moderate heat, stirring, until the cucumbers are tender and wilted. Stir in the vinegar and the cream and cook the mixture, stirring, for 3 minutes, or until it is thickened slightly. Remove the skillet from the heat and stir in the dill and salt and pepper to taste. Serves 2.

Collard Greens with Bacon and Lemon

1 pound collard greens or kale, coarse stems discarded and the leaves sliced thick and washed well
5 slices of lean bacon
2 teaspoons fresh lemon juice

In a large saucepan of boiling water boil the collard greens for 15 to 20 minutes, or until they are just tender. While the collards are boiling, in a large skillet cook the bacon over moderate heat until it is crisp, transfer it to paper towels to drain, and pour off all but 1 tablespoon of the fat from the skillet. Drain the collards well, add them to the skillet with the lemon juice, the bacon, crumbled, and pepper to taste, and toss the mixture well. Serves 2.

Sautéed Eggplant with Yogurt Pomegranate Sauce

1 large eggplant (about 1 pound), peeled and cut into ⅜-inch slices
2 pomegranates (each about 8 to 10 ounces), halved and squeezed gently to yield enough seeds and juice to measure about 1⅓ cups
½ red onion, sliced thin
about ⅓ cup olive oil
1 garlic clove, minced
3 tablespoons plain yogurt
1 teaspoon fresh lemon juice
1 teaspoon finely chopped fresh parsley leaves
1 green bell pepper, roasted (procedure on page 188) and cut into thin strips

Arrange the eggplant slices in one layer on paper towels and sprinkle them with salt. Weight the eggplant with a baking sheet and several heavy objects and let it stand for 30 minutes. In a food mill fitted with the medium disk and set over a bowl purée the pomegranate seeds and juice. In a saucepan combine the pomegranate purée with the onion and cook the mixture over moderately low heat, stirring occasionally, for 12 minutes, or until it thickens to a syrup and the onion is softened.

Wipe the salt from the eggplant thoroughly with paper towels, in a large skillet heat half the oil over moderately high heat until it is hot but not smoking, and in it sauté the eggplant slices in batches, adding the remaining oil as necessary, for 3 to 4 minutes on each side, or until they are browned and cooked through, transferring them as they are browned to paper towels to drain.

In a bowl whisk together the pomegranate syrup, the garlic, the yogurt, the lemon juice, the parsley, and salt and pepper to taste. Arrange the eggplant slices on a heated serving plate, arrange the roasted bell pepper on top of them, and spoon the pomegranate mixture over the top. Serves 6 as a first course.

Confit d' Oignons et Poivre Vert (Onion and Green Peppercorn Confit)

½ pound onion, sliced thin
2 tablespoons unsalted butter
3 tablespoons white-wine vinegar
1 tablespoon sugar
1 tablespoon drained green peppercorns (available at specialty foods shops)

In a heavy skillet cook the onion in the butter, covered, over moderately low heat, stirring occasionally, until it is soft but not golden, add the vinegar, the sugar, and the peppercorns, and simmer the mixture, uncovered, stirring, until it is thickened slightly. Season the *confit* with salt. *The* confit *may be made 1 day in advance and kept covered and chilled. Reheat the* confit *in a microwave oven or in a skillet on top of the stove.* Makes about ¾ cup, serving 4.

PHOTO ON PAGE 48

Onions Stuffed with Eggplant, Tomato, and Beef

2 large onions (about ¾ pound each)
1 pound eggplant, peeled and chopped
½ teaspoon salt
2 tablespoons olive oil
¼ pound ground chuck or lamb
¼ teaspoon ground sage
¼ teaspoon dried rosemary, crumbled
1 tablespoon dry white wine
1 tomato, chopped
2 tablespoons minced fresh parsley leaves
3 tablespoons freshly grated Parmesan

Cut the top ¾ inch off each onion, discarding the tops, peel the onions, and wrap them separately in microwave-safe plastic wrap. Microwave the onions at high power (100%) for 8 to 10 minutes, or until they are tender. While the onions are cooking, in a microwave-safe bowl toss together well the eggplant with the salt and the oil. Microwave the mixture, uncovered, at high power (100%) for 10 minutes. While the eggplant is cooking scoop out the onions, leaving the shells about 3 layers thick, chop the inside of 1 of the onions, and reserve it. In a skillet cook the chuck over moderate heat, stirring and breaking up the lumps, until it is no longer pink, stir in the reserved chopped onion, the sage, the rosemary, the wine, the tomato, the eggplant mixture, and salt and pepper to taste, and cook the mixture, stirring, for 10 minutes, or until the eggplant is softened. Stir in the parsley and 2 tablespoons of the Parmesan, fill the onion shells with some of the mixture, and transfer the remaining mixture to a microwave-safe serving dish. Arrange the stuffed onions on top of the mixture, sprinkle them with the remaining 1 tablespoon Parmesan, and microwave them at high power (100%) for 1 minute. Serves 2.

Chiles Rellenos
(Cheese-and-Chorizo–Stuffed Peppers
with Tomatillo Sauce)

six 4-inch fresh *poblano* peppers*
vegetable oil for brushing the peppers
¼ pound *chorizo** (spicy Spanish sausage),
    casings discarded and the meat
    chopped fine
1½ cups grated Monterey Jack
    (about 5 ounces)
For the sauce
1½ pounds fresh *tomatillos** (Mexican green
    tomatoes), husked and rinsed, or three
    11-ounce cans, drained
½ cup chopped onion
2 garlic cloves, chopped coarse
⅓ cup fresh coriander sprigs
1 tablespoon vegetable oil
For the batter
3 large eggs, separated and the whites at
    room temperature
½ teaspoon salt
1 tablespoon all-purpose flour

vegetable oil for frying the stuffed peppers
flour for dredging the stuffed peppers
fresh coriander sprigs for garnish

*available at Hispanic or specialty produce
    markets

Brush the peppers with the oil and on a rack set on an electric burner at high heat or using a long-handled fork over an open flame roast them, turning them, for 5 minutes, or until they are evenly blistered and charred. Transfer the peppers to a bowl and cover the bowl tightly with plastic wrap. Let the peppers steam for 5 minutes, or until they are cool enough to handle, and, wearing rubber gloves, peel them, being careful not to tear the flesh. Make a lengthwise slit in the side of each pepper from the stem almost to the tip and remove the ribs and seeds carefully, leaving the stems intact. Rinse the peppers under gently running water and put them on paper towels to drain.

In a skillet cook the *chorizo* over moderate heat, stirring, for 5 to 10 minutes, or until it is cooked through, transfer it to paper towels to drain, and let it cool. In a bowl stir together the *chorizo* and the Monterey Jack. Pat the insides of the peppers dry and fill them with the *chorizo* mixture. (Be careful not to stuff the peppers too full; the slits should close when a stuffed pepper is held by the stem.)

Make the sauce: If using fresh *tomatillos*, in a large saucepan of boiling salted water boil the *tomatillos* for 10 minutes, or until they are tender, and drain them. In a blender or food processor blend the fresh or canned *tomatillos*, the onion, the garlic, and the coriander until the mixture is a slightly coarse purée. In a large skillet heat the oil over moderately high heat until it is hot but not smoking and in it cook the purée, stirring, for 5 minutes, or until it is thickened slightly. Add 1 cup water and simmer the sauce, stirring occasionally, for 15 to 20 minutes, or until it is thickened and reduced to about 2½ cups. Season the sauce with salt and black pepper and keep it warm, covered.

Make the batter: In a bowl with an electric mixer beat the whites with the salt until they barely hold stiff peaks, beat in the yolks, 1 at a time, and the flour, and beat the batter until it is just combined.

In a deep heavy skillet heat ¾ inch of the oil over high heat to 375° F. While the oil is heating pat the stuffed peppers dry, dredge them in the flour, shaking off the excess, and dip them in the batter. Fry the peppers in the oil in batches, turning them once, for 1 to 2 minutes, or until they are golden, and transfer them as they are done to paper towels to drain. Divide the sauce and the peppers among 6 plates and garnish the peppers with the coriander sprigs. Serves 6.

PHOTO ON PAGE 35

Mashed Potatoes with Scallions

2 russet (baking) potatoes
    (about ¾ pound each)
⅔ to ¾ cup milk
2 tablespoons melted unsalted butter
¼ cup chopped scallion

Scrub the potatoes and leave them wet. Prick each potato once with a fork and wrap it in a sheet of microwave-safe paper towel, tucking in the ends. Arrange the potatoes in the microwave, end to end and 1 inch apart with the tucked-in ends down, microwave them at high power (100%) for 10 to 12 minutes, or until they yield to gentle pressure, and let them stand, wrapped, for 5 minutes.

In a 1-quart microwave-safe bowl combine ⅔ cup of the milk, the butter, the scallion, and salt and pepper to taste and microwave the mixture, uncovered, at high power (100%) for 2 minutes. Peel the potatoes, while they are still hot force them through a ricer or the medium disk of a food mill into the milk mixture, and combine the mixture well, adding some of the remaining milk if necessary to reach the desired consistency. Season the potatoes with salt and pepper. Serves 2.

Pommes Pailles
(Fried Shoestring Potatoes)

1½ pounds russet (baking) potatoes
vegetable oil for deep-frying

Working with 1 potato at a time, peel the potatoes and drop them into a large bowl of ice water. With a mandoline or similar slicing device cut the potatoes lengthwise into thin (⅛-inch-thick) sticks, dropping the sticks as they are cut into the bowl of water. Stir the potatoes to help wash off the excess starch, drain them, and pat them dry between several layers of paper towels. In a deep fryer in 2 inches of 380° F. oil fry the potatoes in small batches, making sure the oil returns to 380° F. before adding each new batch, for 1½ to 2 minutes, or until they are golden, and transfer them with a skimmer or slotted spoon to brown paper bags or paper towels to drain. Season the potatoes with salt. *The potatoes may be made 8 hours in advance. Just before serving spread them in a large roasting pan and heat them in a preheated 325° F. oven for 5 to 10 minutes, or until they are crisp and hot.* Serves 4.

New Potatoes with Dill

24 small red potatoes
    (about 2 inches in diameter)
¼ cup extra-virgin olive oil
1½ tablespoons snipped fresh dill

In a kettle combine the potatoes and enough cold salted water to cover them by 2 inches, bring the water to a boil, and simmer the potatoes for 8 to 10 minutes, or until they are just tender. Drain the potatoes, return them to the kettle, and let them steam over moderately low heat for 1 minute, shaking the kettle gently. Let the potatoes cool until they can be handled. *The potatoes may be prepared up to this point 4 hours in advance and kept covered.* Cut the potatoes into ¼-inch slices, ar-range them in a shallow dish, and season them with salt and pepper. Drizzle the potatoes with the oil and sprinkle them with the dill. Serves 12.

PHOTO ON PAGE 39

Sautéed Potatoes and Celery Root

4 pounds celery root
1 lemon
4 pounds large boiling potatoes
¾ cup clarified butter (procedure on page
    219), reserved goose fat, or a combination
    of both
¼ cup minced fresh parsley leaves (preferably
    flat-leafed)

Peel the celery root, cut it into ½-inch cubes (there should be about 4 cups), and transfer it as it is cut to a bowl of water acidulated with the juice of the lemon. Peel the potatoes, cut them into ½-inch cubes (there should be about 4 cups), and transfer them as they are cut to a bowl of cold water. *The vegetables may be prepared up to this point 2 hours in advance.* Drain the celery root well and pat it dry between several layers of paper towels. In a large heavy skillet heat 6 tablespoons of the butter over moderately high heat until it is hot but not smoking and in it sauté the celery root, shaking the skillet occasionally, for 8 to 10 minutes, or until it is evenly golden and cooked through. Transfer the celery root to a bowl and keep it warm, covered. Drain the potatoes and pat them dry between several layers of paper towels. In the large heavy skillet heat the remaining 6 tablespoons butter over moderately high heat until it is hot but not smoking and in it sauté the potatoes, shaking the skillet occasionally, for 10 to 15 minutes, or until they are evenly golden and cooked through. Transfer the potatoes to the bowl and toss the mixture with the parsley and salt and pepper to taste. Serves 8.

PHOTO ON PAGE 78

Pear and Sweet Potato Gratin

2½ pounds (about 3 or 4) sweet potatoes,
    peeled and grated coarse (about 7 cups)
4 ripe Anjou or Bartlett pears (about 2
    pounds), peeled, cored, and grated coarse
    over a bowl, reserving the juice
¼ cup fresh lemon juice
3 tablespoons unsalted butter, melted
2 tablespoons firmly packed light brown sugar
1 tablespoon all-purpose flour
¼ teaspoon cinnamon
¼ teaspoon ground ginger
⅛ teaspoon ground mace
¾ cup freshly grated Parmesan
¾ cup fresh bread crumbs

In a large bowl combine well the sweet potatoes, the pears with the reserved juice, the lemon juice, 2 tablespoons of the butter, the brown sugar, the flour, the cinnamon, the ginger, the mace, and salt and pepper to taste. Divide the mixture between 2 well buttered 1½-quart gratin dishes, packing it down firmly, and bake the gratins in the middle of a preheated 400° F. oven for 45 minutes, or until the potatoes are tender and the gratins are golden brown around the edges. In a small bowl combine the Parmesan, the bread crumbs, and the remaining 1 tablespoon butter, sprinkle the mixture over the gratins, and broil the gratins under a preheated broiler about 4 inches from the heat for 30 seconds, or until the topping is crisp and golden. Makes 2 gratins, serving 8.

Sweet Potato Turnip Gratin

2 sweet potatoes (about 1¼ pounds)
2 large turnips (about 1¼ pounds)
1 tablespoon cornstarch
1 cup milk

1 cup heavy cream
white pepper to taste

Peel the potatoes, halve them lengthwise, and slice them crosswise ⅛ inch thick. On a steamer rack set over boiling water steam the potatoes, covered, for 3 to 5 minutes, or until they are barely tender. Peel the turnips, halve them, and slice them crosswise ⅛ inch thick. On the rack set over boiling water steam the turnips, covered, for 3 to 5 minutes, or until they are barely tender. Arrange the sweet potatoes and the turnips decoratively in a 2-quart buttered gratin dish.

In a bowl dissolve the cornstarch in ¼ cup of the milk, whisk in the remaining ¾ cup milk, the cream, the white pepper, and salt to taste, and pour the mixture over the potato mixture. *The gratin may be prepared up to this point 1 day in advance and kept covered and chilled. Bring the gratin to room temperature before proceeding with the recipe.* Bake the gratin in the upper third of a preheated 450° F. oven for 25 to 30 minutes, or until it is golden. Serves 8.

Sweet Potato Purée with Walnuts

2 large eggs, separated, the whites
    at room temperature
¼ cup firmly packed light brown sugar
2 teaspoons Dijon-style mustard
2½ tablespoons unsalted butter, melted
4 pounds sweet potatoes,
    cooked, peeled, and forced through a ricer
    or the coarse disk of a food mill into
    a bowl (about 4 cups)
⅓ cup walnuts, chopped coarse and toasted
    lightly, plus 8 walnut halves for garnish

In a bowl whisk together the yolks, the brown sugar, the mustard, and 2 tablespoons of the butter, add the potatoes, and combine the mixture well. In another bowl beat the whites until they hold soft peaks, fold them into the potato mixture, and transfer about 1½ cups of the mixture to a pastry bag fitted with a large decorative tip. Add the chopped walnuts to the remaining potato mixture, combine the mixture well, and spoon it into a buttered 1½-quart baking dish, smoothing the top. Pipe the potato mixture in the pastry bag into 8 mounds around the edge of the dish, brush the walnut halves with the remaining ½ tablespoon butter, and top each mound with a walnut. While the turkey is standing, bake the sweet potato purée in the upper third of a 375° F. oven for 25 minutes. Serves 8.

PHOTO ON PAGES 72 AND 73

Spinach and Feta Phyllo Rolls

2 pounds spinach, washed well and coarse
   stems discarded
1 cup minced onion
1¾ sticks (14 tablespoons) unsalted butter
½ pound Feta, crumbled (about 2 cups)
½ cup minced fresh parsley leaves
½ teaspoon freshly grated nutmeg
2 large eggs, beaten lightly
¼ cup fresh bread crumbs
sixteen 17- by 12-inch sheets of *phyllo*,
   thawed if frozen, stacked between 2 sheets
   of wax paper, and covered with a
   dampened kitchen towel

In a kettle cook the spinach in the water clinging to its leaves, covered, over moderate heat for 2 to 3 minutes, or until it is just wilted, squeeze out as much liquid as possible by handfuls, and chop the spinach fine. In a skillet cook the onion in 2 tablespoons of the butter over moderately low heat, stirring occasionally, until it is softened, add the spinach, and cook the mixture, stirring, until most of the liquid is evaporated. In a bowl combine well the spinach mixture, the Feta, the parsley, the nutmeg, the eggs, the bread crumbs, and salt and pepper to taste.

In a small saucepan melt the remaining 12 tablespoons butter over moderately low heat, stirring occasionally, and let it cool slightly. On a work surface lay enough plastic wrap to measure 2 inches larger than a sheet of *phyllo*, lay 1 sheet of *phyllo* on it with a long side facing you, and brush it with some of the butter. Layer and butter 7 more sheets of the *phyllo* in the same manner and spread half the spinach mixture on the *phyllo*, leaving a 1-inch border on all sides except the side facing you. Fold in the short sides of the *phyllo* and roll up the *phyllo* jelly-roll fashion, beginning with the side facing you and using the plastic wrap as a guide. Brush the roll with some of the butter, transfer it to a baking sheet, seam side down, and assemble another roll in the same manner using the remaining *phyllo*, butter, and spinach mixture. *The rolls may be prepared up to this point 1 day in advance and kept covered loosely and chilled.* Bake the *phyllo* rolls on the baking sheet in the middle of a preheated 375° F. oven for 40 to 50 minutes, or until they are golden, transfer them to a work surface, and cut them diagonally into ¾-inch slices. Serves 12.

PHOTO ON PAGE 39

Creamed Spinach

1 pound spinach, coarse stems discarded,
   washed well, and drained in a colander
⅓ cup sour cream
1 teaspoon cornstarch
freshly grated nutmeg to taste

Put the spinach in a large microwave-safe bowl and microwave it, covered tightly with microwave-safe plastic wrap, at high power (100%) for 3 minutes, or until it is wilted. Drain the spinach, pressing out the excess liquid, and in a food processor chop it fine. In a small bowl blend together well the sour cream and the cornstarch, add the mixture to the spinach, and purée the mixture. Transfer the mixture to a small microwave-safe bowl, microwave it, covered tightly with microwave-safe plastic wrap, at high power (100%) for 3 to 4 minutes, or until it is very hot and thickened slightly, and season it with the nutmeg and salt and pepper to taste. Serves 2.

Puffed Butternut Squash

a 1-pound butternut squash, peeled, seeds and
   strings discarded, and the flesh cut into 1-
   inch pieces
1 tablespoon unsalted butter
2 tablespoons firmly packed brown sugar
1 large egg

In a microwave-safe glass dish sprinkle the squash with 1 tablespoon water and microwave it, covered with microwave-safe plastic wrap, at high power (100%) for 7 to 10 minutes, or until it is very tender. Transfer the squash to a bowl, with an electric mixer beat it with the butter and 1 tablespoon of the brown sugar until the mixture is smooth, and beat in the egg and salt and pepper to taste. Divide the mixture between two 1¼-cup ramekins, sprinkle it with the remaining 1 tablespoon brown sugar, and microwave it, uncovered, at high power (100%) for 6 to 8 minutes, or until it is puffed and just set. Serves 2.

Squash Cups with Basil Vegetable Stuffing

two ½-pound zucchini, scrubbed
two ½-pound yellow summer squash
½ cup chopped onion
1 teaspoon minced garlic
2 tablespoons olive oil
½ cup chopped red bell pepper
½ cup chopped seeded tomato
¼ cup finely chopped fresh basil leaves
¼ cup freshly grated Parmesan

Cut two 2-inch sections from each zucchini and each yellow squash, reserving the remaining zucchini and yellow squash, cut a slice diagonally from one end of each section, and scoop out the sections from the angled ends to form eight ¼-inch-thick cups. Steam the cups on a rack set over boiling water, covered, for 3 to 4 minutes, or until they are barely tender. Invert the cups on paper towels and let them cool and drain. Cut enough of the reserved zucchini and yellow squash into ¼-inch dice to measure ¾ cup and reserve any remaining zucchini and yellow squash for another use. In a heavy skillet cook the onion and the garlic in the oil over moderately low heat, stirring, until the vegetables are softened, add the bell pepper and the diced zucchini and yellow squash, and cook the mixture over moderate heat, stirring, until the vegetables are just tender. Stir in the tomato and the basil, cook the mixture, stirring, for 1 minute, and stir in the Parmesan and salt and black pepper to taste. Divide the mixture among the squash cups. Serves 4.

PHOTO ON PAGE 42

Summer Squash, Tomato, and Dill Sauté

⅓ cup finely chopped shallot
2 tablespoons unsalted butter
2 small yellow summer squash, sliced thin
   crosswise (about 2 cups)
1 tomato, seeded and chopped
¼ cup freshly grated Parmesan
1 tablespoon snipped fresh dill,
   or to taste

In a heavy skillet cook the shallot in the butter over moderately low heat, stirring, for 10 minutes, or until it is very soft and pale golden, add the squash, the tomato, and salt and pepper to taste, and sauté the mixture over moderately high heat, stirring, for 2 minutes. Cook the mixture, covered, over moderate heat, stirring occasionally, for 3 to 5 minutes, or until the squash is tender. Sprinkle the mixture with the Parmesan and remove the skillet from the heat. Let the mixture stand, covered, for 1 minute, or until the cheese is melted, and stir in the dill. Serves 2.

Tomates Provençale
(Herbed Tomatoes)

4 tomatoes (about 1½ pounds)
3 tablespoons olive oil plus additional for
   brushing the tomatoes
⅓ cup fresh bread crumbs
1 flat anchovy fillet, rinsed, patted dry,
   and minced
1 teaspoon minced garlic
⅓ cup freshly grated Parmesan
⅓ cup minced fresh parsley leaves
3 tablespoons finely chopped fresh
   basil leaves

Cut off the top third from each tomato, discarding it, and scoop out the seeds with a small spoon. Brush the outside of the tomatoes with some of the additional oil, put the tomatoes, cut sides up, on a lightly oiled jelly-roll pan, and season the insides of the tomatoes with salt and pepper. Bake the tomatoes in a preheated 325° F. oven for 20 minutes, invert them onto paper towels, and let them drain for 15 minutes. In a small bowl toss together well the bread crumbs, the anchovy, the garlic, the Parmesan, the parsley, the basil, and salt and pepper to taste, divide the crumb mixture among the tomatoes, making sure the cavities are filled and mounding the crumb mixture on the tops, and drizzle it with the remaining 3 tablespoons oil. Broil the tomatoes on the jelly-roll pan under a preheated broiler about 4 inches from the heat for 2 to 4 minutes, or until the topping is crisp and golden brown. Serves 4.

Fried Cornmeal-Coated Green Tomatoes

¾ cup yellow cornmeal
¼ cup all-purpose flour
2 teaspoons sweet paprika
½ teaspoon sugar
½ teaspoon pepper
¼ teaspoon salt
1 large egg

1 tablespoon milk or water
6 green (unripe) tomatoes, cut into
 ½-inch-thick slices
3 to 4 tablespoons unsalted butter
3 to 4 tablespoons vegetable oil

In a shallow dish combine well the cornmeal, the flour, the paprika, the sugar, the pepper, and the salt. In a bowl whisk together the egg and the milk. Dip the tomato slices into the egg mixture, letting the excess drip off, and dredge them in the cornmeal mixture. In a large heavy skillet heat 1 tablespoon of the butter and 1 tablespoon of the oil over moderately high heat until the foam subsides, in the fat fry about one third of the tomato slices for 3 to 4 minutes on each side, or until they are golden brown, and transfer them to a heated platter. Fry the remaining tomato slices in 2 batches in the remaining butter and oil. Serve the tomatoes as a side dish with eggs or meat. Serves 6 to 8.

Sautéed Mixed Vegetables

1 tablespoon olive oil
½ zucchini (about ¼ pound), scrubbed,
 quartered lengthwise, and sliced thin
 crosswise
½ red bell pepper, cut into ½-inch dice
½ green bell pepper, cut into ½-inch dice
1 carrot, sliced thin diagonally
½ cup thinly sliced red cabbage
1 teaspoon white-wine vinegar

In a large heavy skillet heat the oil over moderately high heat until it is hot but not smoking and in it sauté the zucchini, the bell peppers, and the carrot, stirring, for 5 minutes. Add the cabbage, the vinegar, and salt and black pepper to taste and sauté the vegetables for 5 minutes, or until they are crisp-tender. Serves 2.

PHOTO ON PAGE 27

Middle Eastern–Style Vegetable Stew

½ large onion, chopped
2½ tablespoons olive oil
2 garlic cloves, minced
1 eggplant (about 14 ounces),
 cut into ½-inch cubes
½ pound mushrooms, chopped coarse
a 14-ounce can plum tomatoes including the juice

¼ cup canned tomato sauce
¼ cup dry white wine
1 tablespoon plus ¾ teaspoon ground
 coriander
½ teaspoon marjoram
¼ teaspoon allspice
¼ teaspoon ground cumin
½ teaspoon sugar
a 2-inch cinnamon stick
2 tablespoons finely chopped fresh
 parsley leaves
rice as an accompaniment

In a kettle cook the onion in the oil over moderately low heat, stirring, until it is softened, add the garlic, and cook the mixture, stirring, for 1 minute. Add the eggplant and cook the mixture, stirring, for 3 minutes. Add the mushrooms, the tomatoes with the juice, the tomato sauce, the wine, the coriander, the marjoram, the allspice, the cumin, the sugar, and the cinnamon stick, bring the mixture to a boil, and simmer it, covered, stirring occasionally, for 30 minutes, or until the vegetables are tender. Stir in the parsley, add salt and freshly ground pepper to taste, and divide the stew, discarding the cinnamon stick, between 2 bowls. Serve the stew with the rice. Serves 2.

Julienne de Courgettes et Carottes
(Zucchini and Carrot Julienne)

½ pound carrots, cut into 2-inch
 julienne strips
¾ pound zucchini, scrubbed and cut into
 2-inch julienne strips, discarding the core
1 tablespoon unsalted butter
fresh lemon juice to taste

In a steamer set over boiling water steam the carrots for 3 minutes, or until they are crisp-tender, and transfer them to a bowl. In the steamer steam the zucchini for 1 to 2 minutes, or until it is crisp-tender, and transfer it to the bowl of carrots. *The vegetables may be prepared up to this point 1 day in advance and kept covered and chilled.* In a skillet toss the vegetables in the butter over moderately low heat until they are heated through and season them with the lemon juice and salt and pepper. Serves 4.

PHOTO ON PAGE 48

SALADS AND SALAD DRESSINGS

ENTRÉE SALADS

Chicken "Club" Salad
(Chicken, Bacon, and Tomato Salad with Croutons)

3 cups ¾-inch cubes of Italian bread
  (preferably whole-wheat)
3 tablespoons olive oil
6 slices of lean bacon, chopped
3 pounds chicken breasts, poached (procedure
  follows), skin and bones discarded, and the
  meat cut into bite-size pieces (about 4 cups)
1 pint cherry tomatoes, quartered
4 scallions including the green part, minced
½ cup quick basil mayonnaise (recipe
  opposite)
basil sprigs for garnish if desired

In a bowl drizzle the bread cubes with the oil, tossing
them to coat them evenly, and season them with salt.
Spread the bread cubes in a jelly-roll pan, toast them in
the middle of a preheated 350° F. oven for 15 to 20 minutes, or until they are golden, and let them cool. In a
skillet cook the bacon over moderate heat, stirring, until
it is crisp and transfer it with a slotted spoon to paper
towels to drain. In a large bowl combine well the chick-
en, the tomatoes, the scallions, two thirds of the bacon,
the mayonnaise, and salt and pepper to taste, divide the
salad among 6 plates, and arrange the croutons around
it. Garnish each serving with some of the remaining bacon and a basil sprig. Serves 6.

To Poach Chicken Breasts

whole chicken breasts with skin and bone
  (about 1 pound each)

In a large saucepan or kettle (depending on the number of chicken breasts to be poached) combine the
chicken breasts with enough cold water to cover them
by 1 inch. Remove the chicken, bring the water to a
boil, and add salt to taste. Return the chicken to the pan
and poach it at a bare simmer for 17 minutes. Remove
the pan from the heat, let the chicken cool in the liquid
for 30 minutes, and drain it.

Quick Basil Mayonnaise

1 garlic clove
½ teaspoon salt
2 cups loosely packed fresh basil leaves
1 large egg
4 teaspoons fresh lemon juice
¾ cup vegetable oil
¼ cup olive oil

Mince and mash the garlic to a paste with the salt. In a
food processor or blender blend together the basil, the
egg, the lemon juice, and the garlic paste, with the motor running add the oils in a slow stream, and blend the
mayonnaise well. Season the mayonnaise with salt and
pepper. Makes about 1¼ cups.

Chicken Salad with Avocado, Tomato, and Olives

3 pounds chicken breasts, poached (procedure
   opposite), skin and bones discarded, and
   the meat torn into shreds (about 4 cups)
1 tablespoon white-wine vinegar
2 avocados (preferably California)
1 tablespoon fresh lemon juice
½ pint cherry tomatoes, quartered, or 1 cup
   peeled, seeded, and chopped tomato
⅔ cup Kalamata or other brine-cured black
   olives, pitted and chopped
For the dressing
2 tablespoons white-wine vinegar
1 teaspoon Dijon-style mustard
¾ teaspoon dried orégano, crumbled
¼ cup olive oil

In a large bowl toss the chicken with the vinegar.
Halve, pit, and peel the avocados, cut them into ¾-inch
pieces, and in a small bowl toss them with the lemon
juice. Add the avocado mixture to the chicken with the
tomatoes and the olives.

Make the dressing: In a small bowl whisk together the
vinegar, the mustard, the orégano, and salt and pepper
to taste, add the oil in a stream, whisking, and whisk the
dressing until it is emulsified.

Drizzle the dressing over the salad, toss the salad
gently to combine it, and season it with salt and pepper.
*The salad may be made 1 day in advance and kept cov-
ered and chilled, but if doing so do not cut up and add
the avocado until just before serving.* Serve the salad at
room temperature or chilled. Serves 6.

Chicken and Papaya Salad

2 tablespoons fresh lime juice
1 small garlic clove, minced and mashed to a
   paste with ½ teaspoon salt
3 tablespoons vegetable oil
1 to 2 drops of Tabasco
1½ cups shredded cooked chicken

1 papaya, peeled, seeded, and cut
   into ½-inch dice
3 radishes, sliced thin
2 cups watercress sprigs, rinsed and spun dry

In a small bowl whisk together the lime juice and the
garlic paste, add the oil in a stream, whisking until the
dressing is emulsified, and whisk in the Tabasco. In a
bowl toss the chicken and the papaya with the dressing
and let the mixture marinate for 15 minutes. In a salad
bowl toss together gently the radishes, the watercress,
and the chicken mixture and divide the salad between
2 plates. Serves 2.

Curried Chicken Salad with Mango and Cashews

3 pounds chicken breasts, poached (procedure
   on page 186), skin and bones discarded,
   and the meat cut into bite-size pieces
   (about 4 cups)
2 tablespoons fresh lemon juice
2 mangoes, peeled, pitted, and
   cut into ¾-inch pieces
1 cup chopped celery
4 scallions including the green part, minced
¼ cup plain yogurt
¼ cup mayonnaise
1½ teaspoons curry powder
½ teaspoon ground cumin
1 cup roasted cashew nuts, chopped
2 tablespoons chopped fresh coriander if
   desired

In a large bowl toss together the chicken, the lemon
juice, and the mangoes and add the celery and the scallions. In a small bowl whisk together the yogurt, the
mayonnaise, the curry powder, and the cumin, add the
dressing to the chicken mixture with salt and pepper to
taste, and combine the salad well. *The salad may be
made 1 day in advance and kept covered and chilled.*

Just before serving stir in the cashews and the coriander. Serve the salad at room temperature or chilled.
Serves 6.

*Grilled Chicken and Vegetable Salad
with Cumin Vinaigrette*

1½ pounds skinless boneless chicken breasts
vegetable oil for grilling
3 ears of corn, shucked and cooked
1 large zucchini, scrubbed, blanched in
    boiling water for 3 minutes, and halved
    lengthwise
¾ cup finely chopped red onion, soaked in ice
    water for 10 minutes, drained, and
    patted dry
2 red bell peppers, roasted (procedure
    follows) and cut into 1-inch squares
1 fresh or bottled pickled *jalapeño* pepper,
    or to taste, seeded and minced (wear
    rubber gloves)
For the vinaigrette
2 tablespoons white-wine vinegar
1 teaspoon Dijon-style mustard
1¼ teaspoons ground cumin,
    or to taste
¼ cup olive oil

3 tablespoons chopped fresh coriander if
    desired plus coriander sprigs for garnish
    if desired

Grill the chicken breasts, brushed with the oil and
seasoned with salt and black pepper, on a rack set over
glowing coals or, covered, in a well seasoned ridged
grill pan heated over moderately high heat until it is hot,
turning them once, for 8 to 10 minutes, or until they are
just cooked through. Transfer the chicken with tongs to
a cutting board and let it cool to room temperature.

While the chicken is cooling, grill the corn, brushed
with the oil, on the rack set over glowing coals or in the
ridged grill pan over moderately high heat, turning it
occasionally, for 10 minutes, or until it is colored lightly, and let it cool. In the same manner grill the zucchini,
brushed with the oil, for 5 to 8 minutes, or until it is colored lightly, and let it cool. Cut the chicken into bite-
size pieces, cut the corn from the cobs, and cut the
zucchini crosswise into ½-inch slices. In a bowl combine the chicken, the corn, the zucchini, the onion, the
roasted peppers, and the *jalapeño* pepper.

Make the vinaigrette: In a small bowl whisk together
the vinegar, the mustard, the cumin, and salt and pepper
to taste, add the oil in a stream, whisking, and whisk the
vinaigrette until it is emulsified.

Drizzle the vinaigrette over the salad, add the
chopped coriander, and toss the salad well. Divide the
salad among 6 plates and garnish each serving with a coriander sprig. Serves 6.

To Roast Peppers

Using a long-handled fork char the peppers over an
open flame, turning them, for 2 to 3 minutes, or until the
skins are blackened. (Or broil the peppers on the rack of
a broiler pan under a preheated broiler about 2 inches
from the heat, turning them every 5 minutes, for 15 to
25 minutes, or until the skins are blistered and charred.)
Transfer the peppers to a bowl and let them steam,

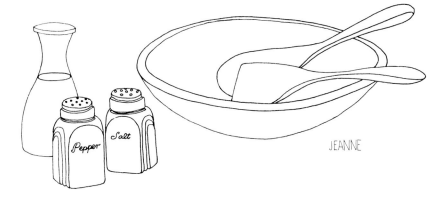

covered, until they are cool enough to handle. Keeping the peppers whole, peel them starting at the blossom end, cut off the tops, and discard the seeds and ribs. (Wear rubber gloves when handling hot peppers.)

Tarragon Chicken Salad with Walnuts

3 pounds chicken breasts, poached (procedure on page 186), skin and bones discarded, and the meat torn into shreds (about 4 cups)
2 tablespoons tarragon white-wine vinegar
1 cup finely chopped celery
⅓ cup mayonnaise
⅓ cup plain yogurt
1 tablespoon chopped fresh tarragon or 1¼ teaspoons crumbled dried, or to taste
1 cup walnuts, toasted lightly and chopped

In a large bowl toss the chicken with the vinegar and the celery. In a small bowl whisk together the mayonnaise, the yogurt, and the tarragon, add the dressing to the chicken mixture with salt and pepper to taste, and combine the salad well. *The salad may be made 1 day in advance and kept covered and chilled.*

Just before serving stir in the walnuts. Serve the salad at room temperature or chilled. Serves 6.

Thai Chicken Salad with Cellophane Noodles

4½ to 5 ounces cellophane noodles (bean threads, available at Oriental markets)
3 pounds chicken breasts, poached (procedure on page 186), skin and bones discarded, and the meat torn into thin shreds (about 4 cups)
1 cup finely grated carrot
2 cucumbers, peeled, seeded, and chopped
For the dressing
4 large garlic cloves
½ teaspoon salt
¼ cup soy sauce
½ cup fresh lime juice
1 tablespoon sugar
1 tablespoon peanut butter
1¼ teaspoons dried hot red pepper flakes
¼ cup vegetable oil

⅓ cup coarsely crushed roasted peanuts, or to taste

In a large heatproof bowl pour boiling water to cover over the noodles and let them stand for 10 minutes. Drain the noodles and arrange them on a platter or divide them among 6 plates. In a bowl combine the chicken, the carrot, and the cucumbers.

Make the dressing: Mince and mash the garlic to a paste with the salt. In a blender blend together the soy sauce, the lime juice, the sugar, the peanut butter, the red pepper flakes, and the garlic paste, with the motor running add the oil in a stream, and blend the dressing until it is emulsified.

Pour half the dressing over the chicken mixture, toss the salad well, and arrange it in the center of the noodles. *The salad may be made 1 day in advance and kept covered and chilled.*

Just before serving sprinkle the salad with the crushed peanuts. Serve the remaining dressing separately. Serve the salad at room temperature or chilled. Serves 6.

Shredded Salt Cod Salad with Lemon Yogurt Dressing

½ pound thick-cut (1 to 1½ inches) skinless boneless salt cod
1 tablespoon fresh lemon juice
2 tablespoons plain yogurt
¼ cup olive oil
½ cup grated carrot
½ cup finely chopped green bell pepper
1 hard-boiled large egg, chopped
2 tablespoons minced onion
2 tablespoons minced seeded bottled hot cherry peppers, or to taste
2 large *pita* loaves, opened to form pockets, or crackers if desired

Shred the cod into fine strands with a fork into a bowl, discarding any tough membranes, cover it with cold water, and swirl it in the water. Drain the cod in a sieve, rinse it under cold water for 1 minute, and squeeze out the excess water by handfuls. In another bowl whisk together the lemon juice and the yogurt, add the oil in a stream, whisking, and whisk the dressing until it is emulsified. Add the cod, the carrot, the bell pepper, the egg, the onion, and the cherry peppers and combine the mixture well. Serve the salad in the *pita* pockets or with the crackers. Serves 2.

Crab Meat and Couscous Salad with Mint Vinaigrette

For the vinaigrette
1 tablespoon fresh lemon juice
1 tablespoon white-wine vinegar
6 tablespoons extra-virgin olive oil
2 tablespoons minced fresh mint leaves

For the salad
¾ pound lump crab meat, picked over
1 cup couscous
2 tomatoes, diced
1 cup cooked fresh or frozen peas
2 tablespoons finely chopped fresh mint
  leaves
1 tablespoon extra-virgin olive oil
1 teaspoon fresh lemon juice

lettuce leaves for lining the plates
⅓ cup pine nuts, toasted lightly and cooled
mint sprigs for garnish

Make the vinaigrette: In a bowl whisk together the lemon juice, the vinegar, the oil, the mint, and salt and pepper to taste until the vinaigrette is combined well.

Make the salad: In a large bowl toss the crab meat with 2 tablespoons of the vinaigrette. In a saucepan bring ¾ cup water with a pinch of salt to a boil, add the couscous, and let it stand, covered tightly, for 5 minutes. Whisk the vinaigrette, drizzle 2 tablespoons of it over the couscous, and let the couscous stand, covered, for 2 minutes. Transfer the couscous to a bowl, breaking up any lumps with a fork, and let it cool. Whisk the remaining vinaigrette, drizzle it over the couscous, and toss the couscous gently. To the crab mixture add the couscous, the tomatoes, the peas, the chopped mint, and salt and pepper to taste. *The salad may be made up to this point 8 hours in advance and kept covered and chilled in the refrigerator. Let the salad come to room temperature.* Sprinkle the salad with the oil and the lemon juice and toss it gently.

Serve the salad on the lettuce, sprinkle it with the pine nuts, and garnish it with the mint sprigs. Serves 6 as a first course or 4 as a main course.

Salade Andalouse
(Rice Salad with Eggplant, Tomato, and Ham)

5½ tablespoons olive oil
1 eggplant (about 1 pound), peeled and cut
  into ½-inch dice

3 cups cooked rice
1 red bell pepper, chopped fine
¼ pound cooked smoked ham, diced
  (about ¾ cup)
1 small red onion, minced
2 tomatoes, chopped fine
1 garlic clove, minced
2 tablespoons finely chopped fresh parsley
  leaves
2 tablespoons fresh lemon juice
¼ teaspoon dried orégano, crumbled
¼ teaspoon dried tarragon, crumbled
¼ teaspoon dried chervil, crumbled, if desired
¼ teaspoon dried thyme, crumbled

In a skillet heat 3½ tablespoons of the oil over moderately high heat until it is hot but not smoking, in it sauté the eggplant for 7 minutes, or until it is tender, and let it cool. In a large bowl combine the eggplant, the rice, the bell pepper, the ham, the onion, the tomatoes, the garlic, and the parsley. In a small bowl whisk together the lemon juice, the orégano, the tarragon, the chervil, the thyme, the remaining 2 tablespoons oil, and salt and black pepper to taste and toss the salad with the dressing. Serves 6 to 8.

*Salade de Boeuf avec Sauce Vinaigrette
aux Anchois et au Raifort
(Roast Beef Salad with Anchovy
and Horseradish Vinaigrette)*

a 2-ounce can flat anchovy fillets, drained
    well, patted dry, and chopped fine
2 garlic cloves, chopped fine
¾ cup vegetable oil
¼ cup distilled white vinegar
¼ cup fresh lemon juice
3 tablespoons minced fresh parsley leaves
1 teaspoon sugar
1½ tablespoons drained bottled horseradish
2 tablespoons heavy cream
1½ pounds small red boiling potatoes
1¼ pounds cold cooked roast beef, pot roast,
    or boiled beef, trimmed well and cut into
    2- by ¼-inch strips (about 3 cups)
1 pint cherry tomatoes, halved
1 cup thinly sliced scallion
shredded romaine for lining the plate
3 hard-boiled large eggs, quartered, for
    garnish if desired

In a blender blend the anchovies and the garlic, add
the oil, the vinegar, the lemon juice, 2 tablespoons of
the parsley, the sugar, the horseradish, the cream, and
salt and pepper to taste, and blend the vinaigrette until it
is combined well. In a large saucepan combine the potatoes and salted cold water to cover, bring the water to a
boil, and simmer the potatoes for 10 to 20 minutes, or
until they are just tender. Drain the potatoes, let them
cool until they can be handled, and cut them into ½-inch
cubes. In a large bowl combine the potatoes, the beef,
the tomatoes, the scallion, and the remaining 1 tablespoon parsley, toss the mixture with the vinaigrette, and
season the salad with salt and pepper. Mound the salad
on a platter lined with the romaine and arrange the eggs
around the edge of the platter. Serves 6 to 8.

Salade Niçoise

soft-leafed lettuce leaves for lining the platter
two 6½-ounce cans tuna packed in oil,
    drained well
two 14-ounce cans artichoke hearts, drained
    well and halved lengthwise if large
1 cucumber, peeled and sliced thin crosswise
2 tomatoes, cut into eighths

2 green bell peppers, cut into thin strips
3 hard-boiled large eggs, quartered
1 small red onion, cut into rings
a 2-ounce can flat anchovy fillets if desired,
    drained well, patted dry, and halved
    lengthwise
½ cup Niçoise or other small brine-cured
    black olives
6 tablespoons olive oil
¼ cup fresh lemon juice
2 garlic cloves minced and mashed to a paste
    with ¼ teaspoon salt
2 tablespoons shredded fresh basil leaves

Line a large platter with the lettuce and in the center
mound the tuna, flaked slightly. Around the tuna arrange decoratively the artichoke hearts, the cucumber,
the tomatoes, the bell peppers, and the eggs and top the
tuna with the onion, the anchovies, and the olives. In a
small bowl whisk together the oil, the lemon juice, the
garlic paste, the basil, and salt and black pepper to taste
and pour the dressing over the salad. Serves 6.

*Salade de Nouilles aux Tomates et Maïs avec Rouille
(Pasta with Tomato, Corn, and Garlic Pepper Sauce)*

1 cup fresh French bread crumbs
¼ cup drained bottled roasted red pepper
1 garlic clove, chopped
¼ to ½ teaspoon cayenne, or to taste
¼ cup olive oil
½ pound small dried pasta such as *orecchiette*,
    macaroni, or *fusilli*
1 cup fresh corn kernels or thawed frozen
¼ cup minced scallion
¼ cup minced fresh parsley leaves
1 cup chopped seeded tomato

In a blender blend together the bread crumbs, the
roasted pepper, the garlic, the cayenne, and 2 tablespoons water, with the motor running add the oil in a
stream, and blend the *rouille* until it is smooth. Season
the *rouille* with salt. In a kettle of boiling salted water
cook the pasta for 8 to 10 minutes, or until it is *al dente*,
add the corn, and cook the mixture for 2 minutes. Drain
the mixture in a colander, rinse it under cold water, and
drain it well. In a bowl combine the pasta mixture with
the scallion, the parsley, the tomato, and the *rouille* and
toss the mixture until it is combined well. Serves 2.

Seafood Paella Salad

For the dressing
3 tablespoons fresh lemon juice
1 small garlic clove
¼ teaspoon salt
½ cup extra-virgin olive oil
For the seafood mixture
12 small hard-shelled clams
½ cup dry white wine
12 shrimp (about ½ pound), shelled, leaving
    the tail and the first joint of the shell intact
two 1¼-pound live lobsters
For the rice mixture
1 onion, chopped
3 tablespoons vegetable oil
2 cups long-grain converted rice
1 pound boneless ham steak,
    cut into ½-inch cubes
½ teaspoon crumbled saffron threads
2 cups chicken broth
½ pound green beans, cut into
    2-inch pieces
1 large red bell pepper, cut into
    julienne strips

3 scallions including the green part, cut
    diagonally into thin slices
tomato-garlic mayonnaise (recipe follows) as
    an accompaniment

Make the dressing: In a blender blend together the lemon juice, the garlic, and the salt until the garlic is puréed. With the motor running add the oil in a stream, blend the dressing until it is emulsified, and transfer it to a small bowl.

Make the seafood mixture: Scrub the clams thoroughly with a stiff brush under cold water, discarding any that have cracked shells. In a very large kettle combine the clams, the wine, and ½ cup water, bring the liquid to a boil, and steam the clams, covered, shaking the kettle occasionally, for 7 to 10 minutes, or until they are open, transferring them as they open to a bowl. Discard any unopened clams and reserve the liquid in the kettle. Drizzle the clams with 3 tablespoons of the dressing, toss them gently to coat them well. Chill the clams, covered, in the refrigerator.

To the kettle add the shrimp, bring the reserved liquid to a boil, and simmer the shrimp, covered, stirring once, for 1 minute, or until they are just firm to the touch. Transfer the shrimp with a slotted spoon to another bowl, reserving the liquid in the kettle, and toss them to coat them with 3 tablespoons of the dressing.

Add enough water to the reserved liquid in the kettle to measure 3 inches, bring the liquid to a boil, and add the lobsters. Steam the lobsters, covered, for 8 minutes, transfer them with tongs to a cutting board, discarding the liquid, and let them cool until they can be handled. Break off the claws at the body and crack them. Remove the claw meat, reserve the meat of 2 claws intact, and cut the remaining meat into ¾-inch pieces. Halve the lobsters lengthwise along the undersides, remove the meat from the tails, and cut it into ½-inch pieces. Break off the legs at the body, reserving them for garnish, remove the meat from the body cavities near the leg joints, and add the lobster meat to the shrimp, tossing the mixture gently. Chill the mixture, covered. *The clams and the seafood mixture may be made 1 day in advance and kept covered and chilled.*

Make the rice mixture: In a large heavy saucepan cook the onion in the oil over moderately low heat, stirring, until it is softened, add the rice, and cook the mixture, stirring, for 1 minute. Stir in the ham, the saffron, the broth, and 2 cups water, bring the liquid to a boil, and simmer the mixture, covered, for 18 to 20 minutes, or until the liquid is absorbed. Add the green beans and the bell pepper and fluff the rice with a fork. Remove the pan from the heat and let the rice mixture stand, covered, for 5 minutes.

Toss the rice mixture well while it is warm with the remaining dressing and let it cool. In a large shallow bowl toss the rice mixture with the seafood mixture, arrange the clams and the reserved lobster claw meat and legs around the edge, and sprinkle the salad with the scallions. Serve the salad with the tomato-garlic mayonnaise.

PHOTO ON PAGE 54

Tomato-Garlic Mayonnaise

2 garlic cloves, minced and mashed to a paste
    with ½ teaspoon salt
1 teaspoon tomato paste
2 teaspoons fresh lemon juice
1 large egg
1 cup vegetable oil

In a blender with the motor on high blend the garlic paste, the tomato paste, the lemon juice, and the egg until the mixture is smooth, add the oil in a slow stream, and add 1 to 2 tablespoons hot water to thin the mayonnaise. Makes about 1 cup.

Shrimp and White Bean Salad

two 19-ounce cans *cannellini* beans or other
   white beans, rinsed in a colander and
   drained well (about 4 cups)
1½ cups thinly sliced celery
½ cup thinly sliced red onion
1¼ pounds (about 36) shrimp, shelled and, if
   desired, deveined
1 tablespoon minced garlic
¼ teaspoon dried hot red pepper flakes
6 tablespoons olive oil
¼ cup fresh lemon juice, or to taste
¼ cup minced fresh parsley leaves, or to taste
1 tablespoon minced fresh orégano leaves or
   1 teaspoon crumbled dried plus, if desired,
   fresh orégano sprigs for garnish
8 lettuce leaves for lining the plates

In a bowl toss together gently the beans, the celery, and the onion. Reserving 8 whole shrimp, cut the remaining shrimp crosswise into thirds. In a large heavy skillet cook the garlic and the red pepper flakes in 3 tablespoons of the oil over moderate heat, stirring, for 30 seconds, or until the garlic is very fragrant, add the reserved whole shrimp and the cut shrimp, and cook the mixture, stirring, for 2 to 3 minutes, or until the shrimp are just cooked through. Transfer the whole shrimp with a slotted spoon to a small bowl and add the remaining shrimp mixture to the bean mixture. Drizzle the salad mixture with the lemon juice and the remaining 3 tablespoons oil, sprinkle it with the parsley, the minced orégano, and salt and pepper to taste, and toss it well. Arrange 2 of the lettuce leaves on each of 4 plates, divide the salad among the plates, and garnish each serving with 2 of the whole shrimp and the orégano sprigs. Serves 4.

PHOTO ON PAGE 57

Taco Salad with Salsa Vinaigrette

¾ cup finely chopped onion
1 large garlic clove, minced
2 teaspoons ground cumin
2 teaspoons chili powder
1½ tablespoons vegetable oil plus additional
   for frying the tortillas
1 pound ground chuck
2 tablespoons tomato paste
six 7-inch corn tortillas, cut into 1-inch
   triangles
8 cups shredded romaine
3 tomatoes, cut into wedges
1 cup coarsely grated extra-sharp Cheddar
⅓ cup thinly sliced scallion
For the vinaigrette
1 large garlic clove, chopped
3 tablespoons red-wine vinegar
3 tablespoons fresh lemon juice
½ teaspoon ground cumin, or to taste
½ cup plus 2 tablespoons olive oil
1 cup chopped seeded tomato
1 large *jalapeño* pepper, seeded and chopped
   (wear rubber gloves)
½ cup loosely packed fresh coriander

In a large heavy skillet cook the onion, the garlic, the cumin, and the chili powder in 1½ tablespoons of the oil over moderately low heat, stirring, until the onion is soft, add the chuck, and cook the mixture over moderate heat, stirring and breaking up any lumps, until the meat is no longer pink. Add the tomato paste and salt and pepper to taste and cook the mixture, stirring, until the meat is cooked through. Transfer the mixture to a bowl and let it cool. In the skillet, cleaned, heat ¾ inch of the additional oil to 375° F. and in it fry the tortilla chips in batches for 30 seconds to 1 minute, or until most of the bubbling subsides. Transfer the chips with a slotted spoon to paper towels to drain and sprinkle them with salt to taste. *The tortilla chips may be made 1 day in advance and kept in an airtight container.* On a large deep platter or in a large bowl arrange the romaine, spoon the beef mixture over it, and arrange the tortilla chips, the tomatoes, the Cheddar, and the scallion decoratively over the salad.

Make the vinaigrette: In a blender combine the garlic, the vinegar, the lemon juice, the cumin, and salt and black pepper to taste, with the motor running add the oil in a stream, and blend the vinaigrette until it is emulsified. Add the tomato, the *jalapeño* pepper, and the coriander and blend the vinaigrette until it is smooth.

Transfer the vinaigrette to a small bowl and serve it with the salad or pour the vinaigrette over the salad and toss the salad until it is combined well. Serves 6.

Tuna Salad with Oriental-Style Dressing

For the dressing
1½ tablespoons soy sauce
2½ tablespoons rice vinegar*
1 teaspoon Oriental sesame oil*
1 teaspoon sesame seeds, toasted lightly
¼ teaspoon sugar

a 6½-ounce can tuna packed in oil, drained well
½ cucumber, peeled, halved lengthwise,
    seeded, and sliced thin crosswise
6 cherry tomatoes, halved
½ red bell pepper, diced
2 scallions, chopped
¼ pound snow peas, trimmed, blanched for
    30 seconds, and plunged into ice water
½ cup mung bean sprouts, rinsed and
    drained well
lettuce leaves for lining the plates if desired

*available at Oriental markets and some
    supermarkets

Make the dressing: In a bowl whisk together the soy sauce, the vinegar, the oil, the sesame seeds, the sugar, and salt and freshly ground black pepper to taste.

In a large bowl combine the tuna, flaked, the cucumber, the tomatoes, the bell pepper, the scallions, the snow peas, drained well, and the bean sprouts. Toss the tuna mixture with the dressing and divide the salad between 2 plates lined with the lettuce. Serves 2.

SALADS WITH GREENS

Arugula Salad with Orange Vinaigrette

3 tablespoons white-wine vinegar
2 tablespoons fresh orange juice
½ teaspoon Dijon-style mustard
½ cup olive oil
8 cups loosely packed *arugula*, rinsed, spun
    dry, and coarse stems discarded

In a small bowl whisk together the vinegar, the orange juice, the mustard, and salt and pepper to taste, add the oil in a stream, whisking, and whisk the dressing until it is emulsified. In a salad bowl toss the *arugula* with the vinaigrette. Serves 6.

PHOTO ON PAGES 18 AND 19

Avocado and Grapefruit Salad with Spicy Honey Dressing

1 tablespoon white-wine vinegar
1 teaspoon honey
a generous pinch of cayenne, or to taste
2 tablespoons vegetable oil
1 grapefruit, the zest and pith cut away and
    the flesh cut into sections, reserving
    1 tablespoon of the juice
4 soft-leafed lettuce leaves such as Boston or
    Bibb, rinsed and spun dry
1 firm-ripe avocado (preferably California)

In a small bowl whisk together well the vinegar, the honey, the cayenne, the oil, the reserved 1 tablespoon grapefruit juice, and salt to taste. Arrange 2 of the lettuce leaves on each of 2 plates, on them arrange the grapefruit sections alternately with the avocado, pitted, peeled, and sliced lengthwise, and drizzle the salads with the dressing. Serves 2.

Bibb Lettuce with Herb Vinaigrette

1½ tablespoons tarragon vinegar
1 tablespoon dry white wine
a pinch of dried orégano, crumbled
a pinch of dried thyme, crumbled
¼ cup extra-virgin olive oil
4 cups torn Bibb lettuce or other
    soft-leafed lettuce

In a salad bowl whisk together the vinegar, the wine, the orégano, the thyme, and salt and pepper to taste, add the oil in a stream, whisking, and whisk the vinaigrette until it is emulsified. Add the lettuce and toss the salad well. Serves 2.

Chicory and Endive Salad with Roquefort and Walnuts

½ cup olive oil
2 garlic cloves, sliced thin lengthwise
½ loaf of Italian bread, cut into ½-inch cubes
    (about 3 cups)
8 cups firmly packed chicory (curly endive)
    leaves, rinsed and spun dry
3 Belgian endives, trimmed, halved
    crosswise, and cut lengthwise into thin
    strips (about 2 cups)

½ cup walnuts, toasted lightly and cooled
½ cup crumbled Roquefort (about 2 ounces)
2 tablespoons fresh lemon juice
1 tablespoon white-wine vinegar

In a bowl combine the oil and the garlic, let the mixture stand, covered, for 2 hours, and discard the garlic. On a jelly-roll pan spread the bread cubes, drizzle them with 2 tablespoons of the garlic-flavored oil, and season them with salt. Toss the bread cubes, bake them in the middle of a preheated 350° F. oven for 15 minutes, or until they are golden, and let the croutons cool. In a large bowl combine the chicory, the endives, the walnuts, and the Roquefort. To the remaining 6 tablespoons garlic-flavored oil add the lemon juice, the vinegar, and salt and pepper to taste, whisk the dressing until it is combined well, and pour it over the salad. Toss the salad lightly to coat it with the dressing and sprinkle the croutons over it. Serves 6.

PHOTO ON PAGE 21

Cucumber Mint Salad

2 tablespoons white-wine
  vinegar
1 to 2 teaspoons sugar, or to taste
½ cup spearmint or other mint leaves, rinsed,
  spun dry, and chopped
⅓ cup vegetable oil
2 unwaxed seedless cucumbers

In a small saucepan combine the vinegar, the sugar, and 2 tablespoons water and bring the mixture to a boil. Stir the spearmint leaves into the mixture and remove the pan from the heat. Transfer the mixture to a bowl and let it cool. Whisk the oil into the vinegar mixture and whisk the dressing until it is emulsified. Score the cucumbers lengthwise with a fork, halve them lengthwise, and cut them crosswise into ¼-inch slices. In a large bowl toss the cucumbers with the dressing. (The salad should be served within 30 minutes or the cucumbers will become watery.) Serves 8.

Dandelion Salad with Pine Nuts and Coppa

2 teaspoons red-wine vinegar, or to taste
3 tablespoons extra-virgin olive oil
3 cups bite-size pieces of tender dandelion
  greens, rinsed and spun dry

¼ cup pine nuts, toasted lightly
8 thin slices of sweet *coppa* (Italian-style
  pepper-coated cured ham, available at
  Italian markets and specialty foods shops)

In a small bowl whisk the vinegar with salt and pepper to taste, add the oil in a stream, whisking, and whisk the dressing until it is emulsified. In a bowl toss the dandelion greens with 1½ tablespoons of the dressing, or enough to just coat them, and divide them among 4 salad plates. Toss the pine nuts in 1 tablespoon of the remaining dressing and sprinkle all but about 2 teaspoons of the pine nuts over the salads. Brush one side of each slice of *coppa* with the remaining dressing, drape 2 slices over each salad, and sprinkle the remaining pine nuts over the slices. Serves 4.

Mesclun and Radicchio Salad

1 tablespoon rice vinegar*, or to taste
3 tablespoons extra-virgin olive oil
1 teaspoon Oriental sesame oil*
8 *radicchio* leaves, rinsed and spun dry
6 cups *mesclun* (mixed baby greens such as
  dandelion, baby romaine, baby oak leaf,
  and *mizuna*, available seasonally at
  specialty produce markets)

*available at Oriental markets, specialty foods
  shops, and many supermarkets

In a large bowl whisk together the vinegar and salt and pepper to taste, add the oils in a stream, whisking, and whisk the dressing until it is emulsified. Toss the *radicchio* in the dressing and divide it among 4 plates, letting the excess dressing drip into the bowl. Toss the *mesclun* with the remaining dressing and divide it among the plates. Serves 4.

Salade de Laitues Variées avec Rissoles de Canard
(*Mixed Green Salad with Duck Cracklings*)

about ⅓ cup duck cracklings (procedure on
    page 158)
6 cups mixed salad greens,
    torn into pieces, rinsed, and spun dry
3 tablespoons olive oil,
    or to taste
1½ to 2 teaspoons fresh lemon juice,
    or to taste

Reheat the duck cracklings in a skillet over low heat or in a microwave oven until they are warm. Put the greens in a salad bowl, drizzle them with the oil, and toss them well. Drizzle the salad with 1½ teaspoons of the lemon juice, season it with salt and pepper, and toss it well. Taste the salad, if necessary drizzle it with the remaining ½ teaspoon lemon juice, and toss it again. Divide the salad among 4 plates and sprinkle each serving with some of the cracklings. Serves 4.

Mixed Greens with Cumin Vinaigrette

1 shallot, minced
½ teaspoon Dijon-style mustard
½ teaspoon ground cumin
6 tablespoons fresh lemon juice
⅔ cup extra-virgin olive oil
6 cups assorted torn lettuce leaves such as red
    and green oak leaf lettuces, sorrel, Lollo
    rosso, and dandelion greens (available
    seasonally at specialty produce markets),
    rinsed and spun dry
2 cups watercress sprigs, coarse stems
    discarded, rinsed and spun dry

In a small bowl whisk together the shallot, the mustard, the cumin, salt to taste, and the lemon juice, add the oil in a stream, whisking, and whisk the dressing until it is emulsified. Let the dressing stand, covered and chilled, for 1 hour. In a large bowl toss together the lettuce leaves and the watercress. Whisk the dressing, drizzle it over the greens, and toss the salad until it is combined well. Serves 6.

Mixed Lettuces with Citrus Dressing

2 tablespoons fresh lemon juice
1 tablespoon fresh orange juice
⅓ cup olive oil

⅛ teaspoon Tabasco, or to taste
10 cups mixed lettuces, such as *mâche*, Lollo
    rosso, Bibb, and oak leaf, rinsed, spun dry,
    and torn into pieces
¼ cup thinly sliced *radicchio*
ornamental kale leaves for garnishing the
    plates if desired
4 Brie slices as an accompaniment

In a large bowl whisk together the lemon juice, the orange juice, and salt and pepper to taste, add the oil in a stream, whisking the dressing until it is emulsified. Whisk in the Tabasco, add the mixed lettuces and the *radicchio*, and toss the salad well. Line 4 plates with the kale, top the kale with the salad, and arrange the Brie on the plates. Serves 4.

Milanese Mixed Salad

1 large head of *radicchio*, cut into julienne
    strips (about 2 cups), rinsed, and spun dry
1 bunch of *arugula*, trimmed, cut into julienne
    strips (about 2 cups), washed well, and spun dry
3 carrots, grated coarse
2 tablespoons balsamic vinegar
6 tablespoons extra-virgin olive oil

In a large bowl toss together the *radicchio*, the *arugula*, and the carrots. In a bowl whisk together the vinegar, the oil, and salt and freshly ground pepper to taste, pour the dressing over the salad, and toss the salad well. Serves 4.

Pear, Goat Cheese, and Watercress Salad

¼ pound Montrachet or other soft mild goat
    cheese, mashed with a fork
1 tablespoon heavy cream
¼ cup finely chopped fresh watercress leaves
1 teaspoon finely chopped fresh parsley leaves
2 tablespoons finely chopped dried apricots
    (about 8 halves)
1½ tablespoons finely chopped walnuts,
    toasted lightly, plus additional for
    sprinkling over the salads
4 ripe Anjou, Comice, or Bosc pears
    (about 2 pounds)
the juice of 1 lemon
3 tablespoons white-wine vinegar

6 tablespoons extra-virgin olive oil
1 bunch of watercress, washed well, spun
   dry, and coarse stems discarded

In a bowl stir together the Montrachet, the cream, the chopped watercress. the parsley, the apricots, 1½ tablespoons of the walnuts, and salt and freshly ground black pepper to taste until the mixture is creamy. Core the pears with an apple corer, making each hollow large enough to hold a quarter of the Montrachet mixture, and rub each hollow with some of the lemon juice. Stuff the pears with the Montrachet mixture, packing the mixture in, and chill them, covered, for at least 4 hours or overnight.

In a bowl whisk together the vinegar and the oil and whisk in salt and freshly ground black pepper to taste. Halve the pears lengthwise and cut each half lengthwise into 4 wedges, being careful not to disturb the filling. Arrange the watercress in the center of 4 salad plates and arrange the pear wedges decoratively around the watercress. Sprinkle the additional walnuts over the salads and drizzle the vinaigrette over the salads. Serves 4.

Red and Green Salad with Pomegranate Seeds

8 *radicchio* leaves, rinsed and patted dry
5 cups *frisée* (French curly lettuce, available
   at specialty produce markets) or curly
   endive, rinsed, spun dry, and torn into
   pieces
1½ cups *mâche* (lamb's lettuce), rinsed and
   spun dry
2 tablespoons pomegranate seeds
3 tablespoons olive oil (preferably
   extra-virgin)
1 tablespoon walnut oil (available at specialty
   foods shops and some supermarkets)
2 tablespoons fresh lemon juice

Line a salad bowl with the *radicchio*, mound the *frisée* and the *mâche* in the center, and sprinkle the salad with the pomegranate seeds. Drizzle the salad with the oils and salt and pepper to taste and toss it to coat it with the oil. Sprinkle the salad with the lemon juice and toss it to combine it well. Serves 4.

Romaine Salad with Croutons and Blue Cheese

1 cup loosely packed ¾-inch cubes of Italian
   or French bread

1½ tablespoons unsalted butter
1 large garlic clove, halved crosswise
1 large egg
6 cups loosely packed bite-size pieces of
   romaine, rinsed and spun dry
2 tablespoons crumbled blue cheese,
   or to taste
2 tablespoons olive oil
2 teaspoons fresh lemon juice
¼ teaspoon Worcestershire sauce

In a microwave oven spread the bread cubes on a microwave-safe paper towel, microwave them at high power (100%) for 1 minute, or until they are dry and crisp but not golden, and transfer them to a bowl. In a small microwave-safe glass bowl microwave the butter at high power (100%) for 45 seconds, or until it is melted, drizzle it over the bread cubes, tossing the cubes, and season the cubes with salt. In the microwave oven spread the croutons on a sheet of wax paper and microwave them at high power (100%) for 1 minute.

Rub the cut sides of the garlic vigorously on the inside of a wooden salad bowl and discard the garlic. In a small saucepan of boiling water boil the egg in the shell for 1 minute and remove it with a slotted spoon. In the salad bowl toss together well the romaine, the blue cheese, and the oil, drizzle the mixture with the lemon juice and the Worcestershire sauce, and toss it well. Break the egg over the salad, toss the salad well, and season it with salt and pepper. Add the croutons and toss the salad lightly. Serves 2.

Spinach and Fennel Salad with Pine Nuts

¼ teaspoon Dijon-style mustard
⅛ teaspoon sugar
2 teaspoons red-wine vinegar
2 tablespoons olive oil
¾ cup sliced fennel bulb
4 cups spinach leaves, washed well, spun dry,
   and shredded
1 tablespoon pine nuts, toasted lightly

In a salad bowl whisk together the mustard, the sugar, the vinegar, and salt and pepper to taste, add the oil in a stream, whisking, and whisk the dressing until it is emulsified. Add the fennel, the spinach, the pine nuts, and pepper to taste and toss the salad to coat it with the dressing. Serves 2.

VEGETABLE SALADS AND SLAWS

Beet and Green Bean Salad with Scallion Balsamic Vinaigrette

2½ pounds beets, scrubbed
½ cup balsamic vinegar (available at specialty foods shops and many supermarkets)
¾ cup olive oil
½ cup minced scallion including the green part
2 pounds green beans (preferably *haricots verts*, thin French green beans, available at specialty produce markets), trimmed as desired

Group the beets by size and wrap each group in foil. Bake the beets in the middle of a preheated 400° F. oven for 45 minutes for the smaller beets and for 1 hour for the larger beets, or until they are tender when pierced with a knife. Open the foil packets, let the beets cool completely, and slip off the skins. In a bowl whisk ¼ cup of the vinegar with salt and pepper to taste, add ¼ cup of the oil in a stream, whisking, and whisk the dressing until it is emulsified. Stir in 2 tablespoons of the scallion, add the beets, sliced thin, and toss the mixture to combine it well. Let the beets marinate, covered and chilled, overnight. *The beets may be prepared up to this point 2 days in advance and kept covered and chilled.*

In a kettle of boiling salted water boil the green beans for 4 to 6 minutes, or until they are crisp-tender, drain them, and plunge them into a bowl of ice and cold water to stop the cooking. Drain the beans again and pat them dry. *The beans may be prepared up to this point 1 day in advance and kept wrapped in dampened paper towels in a plastic bag and chilled.*

Just before serving, in a bowl whisk together the remaining ¼ cup vinegar with salt and pepper to taste, add the remaining ½ cup oil in a stream, whisking, and whisk the dressing until it is emulsified. Stir in 3 tablespoons of the remaining scallion. Arrange the beets and the beans decoratively on a platter and brush the beans with some of the dressing. Sprinkle the salad with the remaining 3 tablespoons scallion and serve the remaining dressing separately. Serves 12.

Fattoush (Arabic Bread Salad with Pomegranate)

1 small cucumber, peeled and cubed
¼ teaspoon salt
3 small (6-inch) *pita* pocket rounds, each halved horizontally and the halves cut into 8 wedges
1 green bell pepper, cut into small dice
3 tomatoes, cut into small dice
¾ cup thinly sliced scallion (about 5)
5 inner leaves of romaine, shredded
¼ cup finely chopped fresh parsley leaves
¼ cup finely chopped fresh mint leaves
⅓ cup extra-virgin olive oil
¼ cup fresh lemon juice, or to taste
1 garlic clove, minced
1 pomegranate (about 8 to 10 ounces), halved and squeezed gently to yield enough seeds and juice to measure about ⅔ cup
1½ teaspoons ground *sumac**
(wild Mediterranean fruit) if desired

*available by mail order from Pete's Spice and Everything Nice, 174 First Avenue, New York, NY 10009

In a large colander sprinkle the cucumber with the salt, let it drain for 30 minutes, and rinse it well. Bake the *pita* wedges on a baking sheet in the middle of a preheated 300° F. oven, turning them occasionally, for 25 minutes, or until they are a deep golden brown and crisp. Let the *pita* cool.

In a large bowl combine the bell pepper, the tomatoes, the *pita*, the cucumber, patted dry, the scallion, the romaine, the parsley, and the mint. In a bowl whisk together the oil, the lemon juice, the garlic, the pomegranate seeds and juice, the *sumac*, and salt and pepper to taste. Drizzle the salad with the dressing, toss it to combine it well, and serve it immediately. Serves 6.

Green Bean, Mushroom, and Walnut Salad

6 ounces green beans, trimmed
2 mushrooms, cut into ¼-inch julienne strips
¼ cup chopped walnuts
2 tablespoons olive oil
1 tablespoon fresh lemon juice
1 teaspoon minced fresh parsley leaves

In a saucepan of boiling salted water cook the green beans for 5 to 7 minutes, or until they are *al dente*. Drain the beans in a colander, refresh them under cold water, and pat them dry. In a bowl toss the beans with the mushrooms, the walnuts, and the oil until they are coated with the oil, add the lemon juice, the parsley, and salt and pepper to taste, and toss the mixture well. Serves 2.

Minted Green Bean Salad

¾ pound green beans, trimmed
2 tablespoons white-wine vinegar
1 tablespoon fresh lemon juice
½ teaspoon minced garlic, mashed to a paste
  with ¼ teaspoon salt
2 tablespoons olive oil
1 tablespoon minced fresh mint leaves
½ tablespoon minced fresh basil leaves
¼ cup finely chopped red onion

In a kettle of boiling salted water blanch the beans for 3 to 5 minutes, or until they are crisp-tender, transfer them to a bowl of ice and cold water to stop the cooking, and drain them well. In a small bowl whisk together the vinegar, the lemon juice, the garlic paste, and salt and pepper to taste, add the oil, the mint, and the basil, and whisk the dressing until it is blended well. In a bowl toss together the beans, the onion, and the dressing and chill the salad for 20 minutes. Serves 2.

Salade aux Carottes à la Sauce Vinaigrette au Citron et à la Menthe (Julienne Carrot Salad with Lemon Mint Dressing)

2 cups julienne carrot (⅛-inch sticks)
1 tablespoon fresh lemon juice
¼ teaspoon Dijon-style mustard
2 tablespoons extra-virgin olive oil
1½ tablespoons minced fresh mint leaves
2 tablespoons thinly sliced scallion

In a saucepan of boiling salted water blanch the carrot for 1½ minutes, drain it, and refresh it under cold water. In a bowl whisk together the lemon juice, the mustard, and salt and pepper to taste, add the oil in a stream, whisking, and whisk the dressing until it is emulsified. Stir in the mint and the scallion, add the carrot, patted dry, and toss the salad until it is combined well. Serves 2.

Salade Du Barry au Roquefort (Cauliflower, Radish, Watercress, and Roquefort Salad)

a 2½-pound cauliflower, separated into
  small flowerets
16 radishes, sliced thin
1 bunch of watercress, trimmed, washed well,
  spun dry, and separated into small sprigs
¼ pound Roquefort, crumbled
2 scallions, sliced thin
1½ tablespoons finely chopped fresh
  parsley leaves
3 tablespoons fresh lemon juice
6 tablespoons olive oil
¼ teaspoon salt, or to taste
¼ teaspoon dried tarragon, crumbled
1 teaspoon minced fresh chervil leaves
  or ¼ teaspoon dried, crumbled

In a large saucepan of boiling salted water cook the cauliflower for 3 to 5 minutes, or until it is crisp-tender. Plunge the cauliflower into a bowl of ice and cold water to stop the cooking, drain it well, and pat it dry. In a large bowl combine the cauliflower, the radishes, the watercress, the Roquefort, the scallions, and the parsley. In a small bowl whisk together the lemon juice, the oil, the salt, the tarragon, the chervil, and pepper to taste and toss the salad with the dressing. Serves 6 to 8.

Salade au Céleri et au Roquefort (Julienne Celery and Roquefort Salad)

2 teaspoons white-wine vinegar
2 tablespoons extra-virgin olive oil
3 tablespoons crumbled Roquefort
2 cups julienne celery

In a small bowl whisk together the vinegar and salt and pepper to taste, add the oil in a stream, whisking, and whisk the dressing until it is emulsified. Stir in the Roquefort, add the celery, and toss the salad until it is combined well. Serves 2.

Salade de Gruyère, Celerís, et Noix avec Sauce Vinaigrette à la Moutarde (Gruyère, Celery, and Walnut Salad with Mustard Vinaigrette)

3 ribs of celery, cut into 2-inch julienne strips
½ pound Gruyère, cut into 2-inch julienne strips
½ cup coarsely chopped walnuts, toasted
1 teaspoon minced shallot
1 scallion, sliced thin
2 tablespoons Dijon-style mustard
1½ teaspoons fresh lemon juice
⅓ cup heavy cream
1 tablespoon minced fresh parsley leaves

In a large bowl combine the celery, the Gruyère, the walnuts, the shallot, the scallion, and salt and pepper to taste. In a small bowl whisk together the mustard and the lemon juice, add the cream in a stream, whisking, and whisk the vinaigrette until it is combined well. Pour the vinaigrette over the Gruyère mixture, toss the salad gently but thoroughly, and sprinkle it with the parsley. Serves 4 to 6.

Salade de Pois Chiche (Chick-Pea Salad)

1 cup (½ pound) dried chick-peas (garbanzo beans), picked over and rinsed
½ teaspoon salt
1 red onion, halved lengthwise and sliced thin crosswise
1 tomato, diced
¾ cup Niçoise or other small brine-cured black olives, pitted and chopped
1 green bell pepper, chopped
1 tablespoon finely chopped fresh parsley leaves
¼ teaspoon dried orégano, crumbled
⅛ teaspoon dried tarragon, crumbled
¼ cup shredded fresh basil leaves
2 tablespoons fresh lemon juice
1 tablespoon white-wine vinegar
3 tablespoons olive oil
2 garlic cloves, minced

In a large saucepan let the chick-peas soak in water to cover at room temperature for at least 8 hours or overnight, drain them, and rinse them well. In a large saucepan bring 8 cups water to a boil with the chick-peas and simmer the chick-peas, covered, for 1 hour. Add the salt, simmer the chick-peas for 15 minutes more, or until they are tender, and drain them well. *The chick-peas may be prepared 1 day in advance and kept covered and chilled.*

In a bowl of ice and cold water let the onion soak for 10 minutes, drain it well, and pat it dry. In a large bowl combine the chick-peas, the onion, the tomato, the olives, the bell pepper, and the parsley. In a small bowl whisk together the orégano, the tarragon, the basil, the lemon juice, the vinegar, the oil, the garlic, and salt and black pepper to taste. Pour the dressing over the chick-pea mixture and toss the salad. Serves 6 to 8.

Creamy Coleslaw

1 small cabbage (about 1½ pounds), shredded
1 small onion, minced
1 red bell pepper, minced
2 carrots, grated coarse
¾ cup mayonnise
¼ cup plain yogurt
2 tablespoons fresh lemon juice
2 teaspoons distilled white vinegar
1 tablespoon sugar
¾ teaspoon celery seeds

In a large bowl toss together the cabbage, the onion, the bell pepper, and the carrots. In a bowl whisk together the mayonnaise, the yogurt, the lemon juice, the vinegar, the sugar, and the celery seeds. Toss the vegetables with the dressing until the coleslaw is combined well and season the coleslaw with salt and freshly ground black pepper. Serves 6.

PHOTO ON PAGE 15

Corn-Salad-Stuffed Tomatoes

8 small tomatoes (about 2 pounds) plus 1 cup seeded and finely diced tomato
1½ cups cooked corn kernels (about 3 ears)
⅓ cup minced scallion
3 tablespoons snipped fresh chives
2½ tablespoons white-wine vinegar, or to taste
2 tablespoons olive oil, or to taste

Cut off the top third from each whole tomato, discarding it, and scoop out the seeds with a small spoon. Sprinkle the tomato cavities with salt, invert the tomatoes onto paper towels, and let them drain for 15 minutes. In a bowl toss together well the diced tomato, the corn, the scallion, the chives, the vinegar, the oil, and salt and pepper to taste and stuff the tomato cavities with the corn salad. *The salad may be prepared 8 hours in advance and kept covered and chilled, but do not stuff the tomatoes until just before serving.* Serves 4.

PHOTO ON PAGE 57

Mixed Vegetable Salad with Lime Vinaigrette

For the vinaigrette
1 tablespoon white-wine vinegar
2 tablespoons fresh lime juice
½ teaspoon freshly grated lime zest
6 tablespoons olive oil
2 tablespoons chopped fresh coriander, or to taste

2½ cups ½-inch-dice peeled *jícama* (available at specialty produce markets)
1 large cucumber, peeled, halved lengthwise, and sliced thin crosswise
3 carrots, sliced very thin diagonally, blanched in boiling water until just tender, and drained
¾ cup fresh or thawed frozen peas, blanched in boiling water until just tender and drained
¾ cup thinly sliced radish
lettuce leaves for lining the bowl

Make the vinaigrette: In a blender or food processor blend together the vinegar, the lime juice, the zest, and salt and pepper to taste. With the motor running add the oil in a stream and the coriander and blend the dressing until it is combined well.

In a bowl toss together the *jícama*, the cucumber, the carrots, the peas, and the radish with the dressing until the salad is combined well, line a serving bowl with the lettuce, and transfer the salad to the bowl. Makes about 7 cups, serving 6.

PHOTO ON PAGE 36

SALAD DRESSINGS

Chipotle Mayonnaise

1 large egg
5 teaspoons fresh lemon juice
1 teaspoon Dijon-style mustard
¼ teaspoon salt
¼ cup drained canned *chipotle* peppers in *adobo* sauce (available at Mexican markets and some specialty foods shops)
1¼ cups vegetable oil

In a blender with the motor on high or in a food processor blend the egg, the lemon juice, the mustard, the salt, and the *chipotle* peppers and add the oil in a slow stream. Serve the sauce with cold chicken or meats or with fried seafood. Makes about 1¼ cups.

Light Curry Mayonnaise

1 large egg
5 teaspoons fresh lemon juice
1 teaspoon Dijon-style mustard
1 tablespoon curry powder, or to taste
¼ teaspoon salt
1 cup vegetable oil
⅓ cup plain yogurt

In a blender with the motor on high or in a food processor blend the egg, the lemon juice, the mustard, the curry powder, and the salt and add the oil in a slow stream. Transfer the mayonnaise to a bowl and stir in the yogurt. Serve the sauce with poached chicken, cooked shellfish, rice salad, or *crudités*. Makes about 1⅓ cups.

Gazpacho Mayonnaise

1 large egg
7 teaspoons lemon juice
1 teaspoon Dijon-style mustard
½ teaspoon salt
¼ teaspoon Tabasco, or to taste
1 teaspoon Worcestershire sauce
1 tablespoon tomato paste
1¼ cups vegetable oil
2 tablespoons minced green bell pepper
2 tablespoons minced seeded tomato
2 tablespoons minced seedless cucumber
1 tablespoon minced red onion

In a blender with the motor on high or in a food processor blend the egg, the lemon juice, the mustard, the salt, the Tabasco, the Worcestershire sauce, and the tomato paste and add the oil in a slow stream. Transfer the mixture to a bowl and stir in the bell pepper, the tomato, the cucumber, and the onion. Serve the sauce with cold meats or cooked shellfish. Makes about 1½ cups.

Coarse Mustard Mayonnaise

1 large egg
5 teaspoons fresh lemon juice
1 tablespoon coarse-grained mustard
¼ teaspoon salt
1 cup vegetable oil

In a blender with the motor on high or in a food processor blend the egg, the lemon juice, the mustard, and the salt and add the oil in a slow stream. Serve the sauce with cold chicken or meats. Makes about 1 cup.

Saffron Mayonnaise

2 tablespoons fresh lemon juice
¼ teaspoon crumbled saffron threads
1 large egg
1 teaspoon Dijon-style mustard
¼ teaspoon salt
1 cup vegetable oil

In a small saucepan combine the lemon juice and the saffron, bring the liquid to a boil, and remove the pan from the heat. Let the mixture cool completely. In a blender with the motor on high or in a food processor blend the saffron mixture, the egg, the mustard, and the salt and add the oil in a slow stream. Serve the sauce with cooked shellfish or rice salad. Makes about 1 cup.

Quick Mayonnaise

1 large egg
5 teaspoons fresh lemon juice
1 teaspoon Dijon-style mustard
¼ teaspoon salt
¼ teaspoon white pepper
1 cup vegetable oil, olive oil, or a
    combination of both

In a blender with the motor on high or in a food processor blend the egg, the lemon juice, the mustard, the salt, and the white pepper and add the oil in a slow stream. Makes about 1 cup.

Watercress Mayonnaise

1 large egg
2 tablespoons fresh lemon juice
2 teaspoons Dijon-style mustard
¾ cup watercress leaves
¼ teaspoon salt
¼ teaspoon freshly ground black pepper
1 cup vegetable oil, olive oil, or a
    combination of both

In a blender with the motor on high or in a food processor blend the egg, the lemon juice, the mustard, the watercress, the salt, and the pepper and add the oil in a slow stream. Serve the sauce with cold poached fish or chicken. Makes about 1¼ cups.

Provençal Spiced Oil

5 cups olive oil
6 tablespoons mixed dried black, white, and
    pink peppercorns (available at specialty
    foods shops and some supermarkets)
8 fresh thyme sprigs
twelve 2- to 3-inch dried hot red chilies, 6 of
    the chilies crushed (wear rubber gloves)

In a 1½-quart jar with a tight-fitting lid combine the oil, the peppercorns, the thyme, and the chilies, stir the mixture well, and let it stand in a cool, dark place for 2 weeks. Divide the spiced oil among decorative bottles. Serve the oil drizzled over pizzas, pasta, and steamed vegetables. The oil keeps in a cool, dark place for 2 months.

Strawberry Vinegar

1 pint strawberries, hulled and sliced
2 cups white-wine vinegar
2 tablespoons sugar

In a bowl stir together the strawberries, the vinegar, and the sugar and let the mixture stand, covered, at room temperature for 2 days. Discard the strawberries with a slotted spoon and strain the vinegar through a fine sieve lined with a triple thickness of rinsed and squeezed cheesecloth into a bowl. Transfer the vinegar to a bottle with a tight-fitting lid and use it in salad dressings and marinades. The vinegar keeps in a dark, cool place indefinitely. Makes 2 cups.

SAUCES

SAVORY SAUCES

Artichoke and Olive Marinara Sauce

2 garlic cloves, minced
¾ cup finely chopped onion
1½ tablespoons minced drained bottled
  peperoncini (pickled Tuscan peppers)
¼ cup olive oil
⅓ cup dry white wine
a 28-ounce can Italian tomatoes including
  the juice, chopped
two 6-ounce jars marinated artichoke hearts,
  drained well and halved lengthwise
½ cup chopped pitted Kalamata olives
⅓ cup minced fresh parsley leaves

In a large skillet cook the garlic, the onion, and the *peperoncini* in the oil over moderately low heat, stirring, until the onion is softened, add the wine, and boil the mixture for 3 to 5 minutes, or until the wine is almost evaporated. Add the tomatoes with the juice and simmer the mixture, stirring occasionally, for 20 minutes, or until it is thickened. Stir in the artichoke hearts and the olives, simmer the sauce for 5 minutes, and stir in the parsley and salt and black pepper to taste. Makes about 4 cups, enough for 1 pound dried pasta, cooked, such as *penne*.

Cranberry Applesauce

3 pounds (about 10) McIntosh apples,
  quartered
a 12-ounce bag (about 3¼ cups) cranberries
a 3-inch cinnamon stick, halved
three 3-inch strips of lemon zest, removed
  with a vegetable peeler
1 cup firmly packed light brown sugar or
  granulated sugar plus additional to taste
ground cinnamon to taste
freshly grated nutmeg to taste

In a kettle combine the apples, the cranberries, the cinnamon stick, the zest, 1 cup of the sugar, and 1 cup water, bring the mixture to a boil, and simmer it, covered, stirring occasionally, for 30 to 35 minutes, or until the apples are very tender. Force the mixture through the medium disk of a food mill or a large sieve into a bowl and stir in the additional sugar, the ground cinnamon, and the nutmeg. Let the applesauce cool and chill it, covered. *The applesauce may be made 1 week in advance and kept covered and chilled.* Makes about 6 cups.

PHOTO ON PAGE 74

Ketchup

2½ cups sliced onion
3 garlic cloves, minced
3 tablespoons olive oil
3 pounds tomatoes (about 6),
  chopped coarse
⅓ cup distilled white vinegar
½ cup dark corn syrup
¼ teaspoon ground cloves
1 teaspoon mustard seeds
½ teaspoon ground celery seeds
2 teaspoons salt
1½ teaspoons pepper

In a kettle cook the onion and the garlic in the oil over moderate heat, stirring occasionally, until they are pale golden. Add the tomatoes, the vinegar, the corn syrup, the cloves, the mustard seeds, the celery seeds, the salt, and the pepper, bring the mixture to a boil, and cook it at a slow boil, stirring occasionally, for 1 hour. Force the mixture through the medium disk of a food mill into a bowl, return it to the kettle, and simmer it, stirring occasionally, for 45 minutes, or until it is very thick and reduced to about 3 cups. Let the ketchup cool, spoon it into sterilized jars (procedure on page 206), and seal the jars. The ketchup keeps, sealed and chilled, indefinitely. Makes about 3 cups.

Lemon Cream Sauce

1⅓ cups heavy cream
1 tablespoon freshly grated lemon rind
1 stick (½ cup) unsalted butter, cut into pieces
1½ cups freshly grated Parmesan
freshly grated nutmeg to taste

In a small heavy saucepan combine the cream and the rind, bring the mixture to a boil, and boil it for 3 minutes. Reduce the heat to moderately low and add the butter, whisking until it is melted. Add the Parmesan, the nutmeg, and salt and pepper to taste, whisking until the Parmesan is melted, and serve the sauce immediately. Makes about 2¼ cups, enough for 1 pound dried pasta, cooked, such as fettuccine.

Caramelized Onion Sauce

3 pounds onions, sliced thin (about 10 cups)
¼ cup olive oil
½ stick (¼ cup) unsalted butter
1 teaspoon sugar
2 tablespoons white-wine vinegar
¾ cup dry white wine
1 cup chicken broth
1½ cups grated Gruyère (about ¼ pound)
½ cup minced fresh parsley leaves

In a heavy kettle cook the onions in the oil and the butter, covered, over moderately low heat, stirring occasionally, for 45 minutes. Add the sugar and the vinegar and cook the mixture, uncovered, over moderately high heat, stirring, for 15 to 20 minutes, or until the onions are golden. Stir in the wine, the broth, and 1 cup water, bring the mixture to a boil, and simmer it for 5 minutes. Add the Gruyère, stirring until it is melted, stir in the parsley and salt and pepper to taste, and serve the sauce immediately. Makes about 4 cups, enough for 1 pound dried pasta, cooked, such as *fusilli*.

Tartar Sauce

1 cup quick mayonnaise (page 202)
4 tablespoons minced sweet pickle
1 hard-boiled large egg, forced through
  a coarse sieve
2 tablespoons minced shallot
2 tablespoons drained bottled capers, minced
½ teaspoon dried tarragon, crumbled

1 teaspoon Dijon-style mustard
2 tablespoons minced fresh parsley leaves
1 teaspoon fresh lemon juice, or to taste

In a bowl stir together the mayonnaise, the pickle, the egg, the shallot, the capers, the tarragon, the mustard, the parsley, and the lemon juice until the mixture is combined well. Serve the sauce with fried seafood or *crudités*. Makes about 1½ cups.

Fresh Tomato and Corn Relish

1½ pounds tomatoes (about 3), seeded
  and chopped
1¼ cups cooked fresh corn kernels (cut from
  3 ears) or thawed frozen
two 2-inch fresh *jalapeño* peppers, or to taste,
  seeded and minced (wear rubber gloves)
⅓ cup minced scallion
½ teaspoon freshly grated orange zest
3 tablespoons minced fresh parsley leaves
2 tablespoons fresh orange juice
2 tablespoons olive oil
1 teaspoon fresh lemon juice, or to taste

In a bowl combine the tomatoes, the corn, the *jalapeño* peppers, the scallion, the zest, the parsley, the orange juice, the oil, the lemon juice, and salt to taste. The relish keeps, covered and chilled, for 4 days. Serve the relish as an accompaniment to fish, poultry, or meat. Makes about 3 cups.

Winter Pesto

5 garlic cloves
1 teaspoon salt
2 cups firmly packed spinach leaves
  (stems discarded), washed well and spun dry

2 cups firmly packed fresh parsley leaves
  (preferably flat-leafed)
1 cup olive oil
1 cup walnuts, toasted lightly and cooled
1 cup freshly grated Parmesan
1 teaspoon crushed fennel seeds

Mince and mash the garlic to a paste with the salt. In a food processor or blender purée the spinach with the parsley, the oil, the walnuts, the Parmesan, the fennel seeds, and the garlic paste. The *pesto* keeps, covered and chilled, for about 2 weeks. Makes about 2½ cups, enough for 2½ pounds dried pasta, cooked, such as *fusilli*.

To use the pesto: For every pound of dried pasta cooking in a kettle of boiling salted water, stir together in a heated serving bowl 1 cup of the *pesto* and ¾ cup of the hot pasta cooking water. When the pasta is *al dente*, drain it and add it to the *pesto*, tossing it with salt and pepper to taste.

White Bean Tomato Sauce
with Sausage and Pepperoni

2 garlic cloves, sliced thin lengthwise
¼ cup olive oil
½ cup finely chopped onion
½ cup finely chopped pepperoni
  (about 2 ounces)
½ pound sweet Italian sausage, casings
  discarded
a 28-ounce can Italian tomatoes including
  the juice, chopped
a 19-ounce can white beans, rinsed and
  drained well
¼ teaspoon dried hot red pepper flakes
  if desired
⅓ cup minced fresh parsley leaves

In a heavy kettle cook the garlic in the oil over moderately low heat until it is golden, remove it with a slotted spoon, and discard it. To the kettle add the onion and the pepperoni and cook the mixture, stirring, until the onion is softened. Add the Italian sausage and cook it over moderate heat, stirring and breaking up the lumps, until it is no longer pink. Add the tomatoes with the juice, the beans, the red pepper flakes, and 1 cup water, bring the mixture to a boil, and simmer it, stirring occasionally, for 40 to 45 minutes, or until it is thickened. Stir in the

parsley and salt and pepper to taste. *The sauce may be made 1 day in advance and kept covered and chilled. When reheating the sauce thin it with water if necessary to reach the desired consistency.* Makes about 4 cups, enough for 1 pound dried pasta, cooked, such as rigatoni.

CONDIMENTS

Cranberry Citrus Relish

1 navel orange
1 lime
a 12-ounce bag (3¼ cups) cranberries, picked
  over and rinsed
¾ cup honey

In a large saucepan of boiling water blanch the orange and the lime for 5 minutes, drain them, and let them cool. Halve the orange and chop one half fine, reserving the other half for another use. Halve the lime and chop one half fine, reserving the other half for another use. Chop the cranberries coarse. In a bowl combine well the orange, the lime, the cranberries, and the honey, and let the mixture stand, covered and chilled, overnight. *The relish may be made 2 days in advance and kept covered and chilled.* Makes about 4 cups.

PHOTO ON PAGES 72 AND 73

Preserved Limes

6 to 8 limes, washed well
⅓ to ½ cup sea salt
2 to 2½ cups fresh lemon juice

Cut the limes into quarters lengthwise to within ½ inch of the stem end, leaving the stem ends intact. Sprinkle the inside of each lime with 2 teaspoons of the salt and rub the quarters together to reshape the limes. Pack the limes into a sterilized 1½-quart jar with a tight-fitting lid (sterilizing procedure on page 206), pressing them if necessary to fit, and add any remaining salt and the lemon juice. Seal the jar with the lid, shake the mixture until the salt is dissolved, and let the limes stand in a warm place for 1 month. Serve the limes, rinsed, with chicken, lamb, and fish. The limes keep, covered and chilled, in the salted lemon juice for 6 months. Makes 1 quart.

Pear Chutney

3½ pounds (about 7) firm Bartlett pears,
   peeled, cored, and cut into ½-inch dice
   (about 8 cups)
1 lemon, seeded and chopped fine,
   including the peel
1 garlic clove, minced
1 red bell pepper, chopped fine
¾ cup firmly packed light brown sugar
½ cup granulated sugar
¾ cup cider vinegar
1 cup golden raisins, chopped coarse
½ teaspoon ground ginger
¼ teaspoon allspice
a pinch of cayenne, or to taste
1 teaspoon salt
¼ teaspoon freshly ground black pepper

In a heavy kettle combine the pears, the lemon, the garlic, the bell pepper, the sugars, the vinegar, the raisins, the ginger, the allspice, the cayenne, the salt, the black pepper, and ¾ cup water and cook the mixture over moderately low heat, stirring, until the sugars are dissolved. Bring the liquid to a boil and simmer the mixture, stirring occasionally, for 1 hour, or until it is thick and a small spoonful holds its shape on a plate. The chutney keeps, chilled, for 1 week.

Alternatively, the chutney may be preserved: Spoon the chutney into sterilized Mason-type jars (sterilizing procedure follows), filling the jars to within ¼ inch of the tops, and rap the jars on a hard surface to eliminate any air bubbles. Wipe the rims with a dampened cloth and seal the jars with the sterilized lids. Put the jars in a water bath canner or on a rack set in a deep kettle, add enough hot water to the canner or kettle to cover the jars by 2 inches, and bring it to a boil. Process the jars, covered, for 10 minutes, transfer them with tongs to a rack, and let them cool completely. Store the jars in a cool dark place. Makes about 6 cups.

To Sterilize Jars and Glasses
for Pickling and Preserving

Wash the jars in hot suds and rinse them in scalding water. Put the jars in a kettle and cover them with hot water. Bring the water to a boil, covered, and boil the jars for 15 minutes from the time that steam emerges from the kettle. Turn off the heat and let the jars stand in the hot water. Just before they are to be filled invert the jars onto a kitchen towel to dry. The jars should be filled while they are still hot. Sterilize the jar lids for 5 minutes, or according to the manufacturer's instructions.

Pickled Red Onions

¾ pound red onions, cut into thin rings
½ cup white-wine vinegar
3 garlic cloves, sliced thin
½ teaspoon salt
½ teaspoon black peppercorns, crushed coarse

In a saucepan combine the onions, the vinegar, the garlic, the salt, the pepper, and 1½ cups water, bring the mixture to a boil, and simmer it for 4 minutes. Transfer the mixture to a bowl or jars, let it cool, and chill it, covered. The pickled onions keep, covered and chilled, for 1 month. Transfer the pickled onions to containers. Makes about 3 cups.

PHOTO ON PAGE 69

DESSERT SAUCES

Apricot Strawberry Sauce

½ cup sugar
1 pound (about 8) fresh apricots
2¼ cups hulled and halved strawberries
   (about 1 pint)
1 tablespoon fresh lemon juice

In a large saucepan combine the sugar with ¾ cup water, bring the mixture to a boil, stirring, and simmer it for 5 minutes. Add the apricots, pitted and quartered, and cook the mixture at a slow boil, stirring occasionally, for 15 minutes, or until the apricots are soft and fall apart. In a food processor purée the mixture and force it through a fine sieve set over a bowl. Transfer the purée to a saucepan and stir in the strawberries, the lemon juice, and a pinch of salt. Bring the mixture to a boil and simmer it for 1 minute, or until the strawberries are tender but still retain their shape. Transfer the sauce to a bowl, let it cool, and chill it, covered, for 2 hours, or until it is cold. Makes about 3 cups.

Blueberry Chambord Sauce

¼ cup sugar
2 teaspoons cornstarch
2 teaspoons fresh lemon juice
1 cup blueberries picked over, rinsed,
    and drained well
1 teaspoon grated fresh orange zest
2 tablespoons unsalted butter, cut into bits
    and softened
½ teaspoon cinnamon
1 tablespoon Chambord

In a large saucepan combine the sugar, the cornstarch, and a pinch of salt and whisk the mixture until it is combined well. Whisk in ¾ cup cold water and the lemon juice, bring the mixture to a boil, and simmer it, whisking, for 5 minutes. Add the blueberries and the zest and simmer the mixture for 2 minutes, or until half the blueberries have burst. Remove the pan from the heat, stir in the butter, the cinnamon, and the Chambord, and stir the mixture until the butter is incorporated. Makes about 2 cups.

Bitter Chocolate Custard Sauce

2 cups milk
2½ ounces unsweetened chocolate, chopped fine
2 large eggs
⅓ cup sugar
2 tablespoons Armagnac or other brandy

In a saucepan bring the milk just to a boil and remove the pan from the heat. In a metal bowl set over barely simmering water melt the chocolate, stirring, until it is smooth, remove the bowl from the heat, and add ½ cup of the scalded milk in a slow stream, whisking. In a bowl whisk together the eggs and the sugar until the mixture is combined well and add the remaining 1½ cups scalded milk in a slow stream, whisking. In a heavy saucepan whisk together the chocolate mixture and the egg mixture and cook the mixture over moderately low heat, stirring constantly with a wooden spoon, until it thickens (175° F. on a candy thermometer), but do not let it boil. Remove the pan from the heat and stir in the Armagnac. Strain the custard sauce through a fine sieve into a metal bowl set in a larger bowl of ice and cold water, let it cool, stirring, and chill it, covered, for at least 1 hour, or until it is cold. The sauce keeps, covered and chilled, for 2 days. Makes about 2 cups.

Caramel Custard Sauce

⅔ cup sugar
½ cup heavy cream
1½ cups milk
2 large eggs

In a dry small heavy skillet cook ⅓ cup of the sugar over moderate heat, stirring with a fork, until it is melted and turns a deep golden caramel, remove the skillet from the heat, and add the cream carefully. (The mixture will bubble up.) Cook the caramel mixture over moderate heat, stirring, until the caramel is dissolved and let it cool slightly. In a saucepan bring the milk just to a boil and remove the pan from the heat. In a bowl whisk together the eggs and the remaining ⅓ cup sugar until the mixture is combined well and add the scalded milk in a slow stream, whisking. In a heavy saucepan whisk together the caramel mixture and the egg mixture and cook the mixture over moderately low heat, stirring constantly with a wooden spoon, until it thickens (175° F. on a candy thermometer), but do not let it boil. Strain the custard sauce through a fine sieve into a metal bowl set in a larger bowl of ice and cold water, let it cool, stirring, and chill it, covered, for at least 1 hour, or until it is cold. The sauce keeps, covered and chilled, for 2 days. Makes about 2 cups.

Coffee Custard Sauce

2 cups half-and-half
2 large eggs
¼ cup sugar
2 tablespoons instant espresso powder
2 tablespoons coffee-flavored liqueur

In a saucepan bring the half-and-half just to a boil and remove the pan from the heat. In a bowl whisk together the eggs and the sugar until the mixture is combined well, add the scalded half-and-half in a slow stream, whisking, and whisk in the espresso powder. In a heavy saucepan cook the mixture over moderately low heat, stirring constantly with a wooden spoon, until it thickens (175° F. on a candy thermometer), but do not let it boil. Remove the pan from the heat and stir in the liqueur. Strain the custard sauce through a fine sieve into a metal bowl set in a larger bowl of ice and cold water, let it cool, stirring, and chill it, covered, for at least 1 hour, or until it is cold. The sauce keeps, covered and chilled, for 2 days. Makes about 2 cups.

Louisiana Praline Custard Sauce

½ cup heavy cream
½ cup firmly packed dark
   brown sugar
1½ cups milk
2 large eggs
2 tablespoons Sherry
½ cup pecans, toasted lightly
   and chopped

In a heavy saucepan combine the cream and the brown sugar, cook the mixture over moderately low heat, stirring until the sugar is dissolved, and boil it until it reaches the soft ball stage (240° F. on a candy thermometer). Remove the pan from the heat. In a saucepan bring the milk just to a boil and remove the pan from the heat. In a bowl whisk together the eggs and add the scalded milk in a slow stream, whisking. Whisk the egg mixture into the cream mixture and cook the mixture over moderately low heat, stirring constantly with a wooden spoon, until it thickens (175° F. on a candy thermometer), but do not let it boil. Remove the pan from the heat and stir in the Sherry. Strain the custard sauce through a fine sieve into a metal bowl set in a larger bowl of ice and cold water, stir in the pecans, and let the sauce cool, stirring. Chill the sauce, covered, for at least 1 hour, or until it is cold. The sauce keeps, covered and chilled, for 2 days. Makes about 2 cups.

Vanilla Custard Sauce

2 cups half-and-half
½ vanilla bean, split lengthwise
2 large eggs
½ cup sugar

In a saucepan combine the half-and-half and the vanilla bean, bring the mixture just to a boil, and remove the pan from the heat. In a bowl whisk together the eggs and the sugar until the mixture is combined well and add the half-and-half mixture in a slow stream, whisking. In a heavy saucepan cook the mixture over moderately low heat, stirring constantly with a wooden spoon, until it thickens (175° F. on a candy thermometer), but do not let it boil. Strain the custard sauce through a fine sieve into a metal bowl set in a larger bowl of ice and cold water, let it cool, stirring, and chill it, covered, for at least 1 hour, or until it is cold. The sauce keeps, covered and chilled, for 2 days. Makes about 2 cups.

Lemon Sauce

3 large eggs
1 cup sugar
2 teaspoons grated fresh lemon zest
½ cup fresh lemon juice

In a large bowl with an electric mixer beat the eggs until they are foamy, add the sugar in a stream, beating, and beat the mixture for 3 minutes, or until it is thick and pale. In the top of a double boiler set over boiling water whisk together the egg mixture, the zest, the lemon juice, 1 cup water, and a pinch of salt and cook the mixture, whisking, for 10 minutes, or until the sauce thickens around the edge. Transfer the sauce to a bowl and let it cool to room temperature. Makes about 3 cups.

Peach and Nectarine Sauce with Almonds

3 peaches (about 1 pound)
2 nectarines (about 1 pound)
½ cup sugar
1 tablespoon fresh lemon juice
1 tablespoon Southern Comfort, or to taste
a pinch of cinnamon
½ cup sliced blanched almonds, toasted
   lightly

In a large saucepan of boiling water blanch the peaches and the nectarines for 30 seconds, drain them, and let them cool. Peel, pit, and slice the fruit. In a large saucepan combine the sugar with ½ cup water, bring the mixture to a boil, stirring, and simmer it for 5 minutes. Add the fruit and the lemon juice and simmer the mixture for 15 to 20 minutes, or until the fruit is soft. Stir in the Southern Comfort, a pinch of salt, and the cinnamon. In a blender or food processor blend the mixture until it is smooth, transfer the purée to a bowl, and stir in the almonds. Serve the sauce warm. Makes about 3 cups.

Pineapple, Orange, and Rum Sauce

½ cup sugar
a 3½-pound pineapple, peeled, cored, and
    chopped fine (about 4 cups including the juice)
1 navel orange, peel and pith cut away, the
    fruit cut into sections and chopped fine,
    including the juice
2 whole cloves
¼ teaspoon cinnamon
1 tablespoon white rum, or to taste

In a large saucepan combine the sugar with ½ cup
water, bring the mixture to a boil, stirring, and simmer
it for 5 minutes. Add the pineapple and the orange with
the juices, the cloves, and the cinnamon and cook the
mixture over moderately high heat, stirring occasionally, for 25 minutes, or until the fruit is very soft and the
pineapple barely retains its shape. Stir in the rum and a
pinch of salt. Transfer the sauce to a bowl, let it cool,
and chill it, covered, for 2 hours, or until it is cold.
Makes about 2¼ cups.

Plum and Port Sauce

½ cup sugar
1 pound (about 5) plums, pitted and
    cut into eighths
2 teaspoons grated fresh
    orange zest
2 tablespoons Tawny Port
1 teaspoon fresh lemon juice,
    or to taste
a pinch of cinnamon

In a large saucepan combine the sugar with ½ cup
water, bring the mixture to a boil, stirring, and simmer it
for 5 minutes. Add the plums and the zest and cook the
mixture at a slow boil, adding additional water if necessary, for 10 minutes, or until the plums are soft and fall
apart. In a food processor blend the mixture until it is
smooth. Force the purée through a fine sieve set over a
bowl and stir in the Port, the lemon juice, the cinnamon,
and a pinch of salt. Let the sauce cool and chill it, covered, for 2 hours, or until it is cold. Makes about 2 cups.

DESSERTS

CAKES

Black Forest Cake

For the cherry filling

2 pounds canned or jarred sour cherries
    packed in light syrup or water (available at
    specialty foods shops and some
    supermarkets), drained, (about 3 cups),
    reserving 1 cup of the juice

¼ cup sugar

1½ tablespoons cornstarch

¼ teaspoon almond extract

2 to 3 tablespoons Cognac or kirsch,
    or to taste

For the syrup

¼ cup sugar

3 tablespoons kirsch

For the whipped cream

1 envelope of unflavored gelatin

3 tablespoons kirsch

3 cups well-chilled heavy cream

¼ cup sugar

1½ teaspoons vanilla

chocolate *génoise* (page 211), cut horizontally
    with a serrated knife into
    3 layers

about 1¼ cups bittersweet chocolate shavings
    and curls, formed with a vegetable peeler
    from a large block of chocolate

glacéed cherries for garnish

Make the cherry filling: In a small saucepan whisk together the cherry juice, the sugar, the cornstarch, and the almond extract until the mixture is smooth, bring the mixture to a boil over moderate heat, stirring, and simmer it, stirring, for 1 to 2 minutes, or until it is thickened. Stir in the cherries and the Cognac, transfer the filling to a bowl, and let it cool. *The filling may be made 1 day in advance and kept covered and chilled.*

Make the syrup: In a small saucepan stir together the sugar and ¼ cup water, bring the mixture to a boil, stirring until the sugar is dissolved, and remove the pan from the heat. Let the syrup cool and stir in the kirsch.

Make the whipped cream: In a small saucepan sprinkle the gelatin over the kirsch, let it soften for 5 minutes, and heat the mixture over low heat, stirring, until the gelatin is dissolved. In a chilled bowl with chilled beaters beat the cream until it holds soft peaks, add the sugar and the vanilla, and beat the mixture until it just holds stiff peaks. Add the gelatin mixture in a stream, beating, and beat the mixture until it holds stiff peaks.

Assemble the cake: Invert the top layer of the *génoise* onto an 8- or 9-inch cardboard round, brush it evenly with one third of the syrup, and spread half the cherry filling over it. Spread about 1½ cups of the whipped cream over the cherries, sprinkle it with ¼ cup of the chocolate shavings, and invert the middle layer of the *génoise* onto the cake. Brush the layer evenly with half the remaining syrup, spread the remaining cherry filling over it, and spread 1½ cups of the whipped cream over the cherries. Sprinkle ¼ cup of the remaining chocolate shavings over the cream, invert the third layer of the *génoise* onto the cake, and brush the top of the cake with the remaining syrup. Spread the remaining whipped cream over the top and side of the cake, reserving about ¾ cup for garnish. Working over a sheet of wax paper and holding the cake by the cardboard round in the palm of 1 hand, coat the side of the cake with some of the remaining chocolate shavings and transfer the cake to a plate. Transfer the reserved whipped cream to a pastry bag fitted with a large star tip, pipe 9 rosettes decoratively around the top edge of the cake, and top each rosette with a glacéed cherry. Sprinkle the top of the cake with the remaining chocolate shavings and let the cake stand, covered with a large inverted bowl and chilled, for at least 3 hours and up to 8 hours.

PHOTO ON PAGE 79

Chocolate Génoise

6 ounces bittersweet or semisweet
    chocolate, chopped
3 tablespoons unsalted butter, cut into bits
1 teaspoon vanilla
1 cup cake flour (not self-rising)
½ teaspoon salt
6 large eggs at room temperature
¾ cup sugar

Line the bottom of a greased 10-inch springform pan with wax paper, grease the paper, and dust the pan with flour, knocking out the excess. In a metal bowl set over a pan of barely simmering water melt the chocolate with the butter, the vanilla, and ⅓ cup water, stirring until the mixture is smooth. Remove the bowl from the heat and let the mixture cool. Into a bowl sift together the flour and the salt. In a large bowl with an electric mixer beat the eggs with the sugar on high speed for 5 to 10 minutes, or until the mixture is triple in volume and forms a ribbon when the beaters are lifted. Fold the flour mixture into the egg mixture until the batter is just combined and fold in the chocolate mixture gently but thoroughly. Pour the batter into the pan, smoothing the top, and bake the cake in the middle of a preheated 350° F. oven for 35 to 45 minutes, or until a tester comes out with crumbs adhering to it. Transfer the cake to a rack, run a sharp knife around the edge, and remove the side of the pan. Invert the cake onto another rack and remove the paper. Reinvert the cake onto the rack and let it cool completely. *The cake may be made 1 day in advance and kept wrapped in plastic wrap and chilled.*

Chocolate Coconut Almond Cupcakes

1 cup all-purpose flour
½ teaspoon baking soda
½ cup strong brewed coffee
2 tablespoons bourbon
2½ ounces unsweetened chocolate, chopped
    fine
1 stick (½ cup) unsalted butter
½ teaspoon vanilla
1 large egg, beaten lightly
1 cup sugar
¾ cup sweetened flaked coconut, toasted
    lightly and cooled
½ cup almonds, chopped, toasted lightly,
    and cooled

Into a bowl sift together the flour, the baking soda, and a pinch of salt. In another bowl set over barely simmering water combine the coffee, the bourbon, the chocolate, and the butter and heat the mixture, whisking, until the chocolate is melted. Remove the bowl from the pan and whisk in the flour mixture, the vanilla, the egg, the sugar, the coconut, and the almonds. Divide the batter among twelve ½-cup paper-lined muffin tins and bake the cupcakes in the middle of a preheated 350° F. oven for 25 to 30 minutes, or until a tester comes out clean. Transfer the cupcakes to a rack and let them cool. *The cupcakes may be made 3 days in advance and kept wrapped tightly in foil.* Makes 12 cupcakes.

Rigo Jancsi
(Glazed Chocolate Cream Cake Squares)

For the cake layers

4½ ounces fine-quality bittersweet chocolate, chopped

1 stick (½ cup) unsalted butter, softened

¾ cup granulated sugar

6 large eggs, separated, the whites at room temperature

⅔ cup all-purpose flour

¼ teaspoon salt

¼ teaspoon cream of tartar

⅔ cup apricot jam, heated and strained

For the glaze

4½ ounces fine-quality bittersweet chocolate, chopped

6 ounces sugar cubes (¾ cup crushed)

⅓ cup strong brewed coffee

1 teaspoon vegetable oil

2 envelopes of unflavored gelatin

9 ounces fine-quality bittersweet chocolate, broken into pieces

4½ cups heavy cream

2 tablespoons confectioners' sugar

2 teaspoons vanilla

Make the cake layers: Line 2 lightly buttered 15½- by 10½-inch jelly-roll pans with foil, butter the foil, and dust it with flour, shaking out the excess. In a small bowl set over barely simmering water melt the chocolate with 2 tablespoons of the butter, stirring until the mixture is smooth, and remove the bowl from the heat. In a large bowl with an electric mixer cream the remaining ¾ stick butter, add ½ cup of the granulated sugar, and beat the mixture until it is light and fluffy. Add the yolks, 1 at a time, beating well after each addition, and stir in the chocolate mixture and the flour. In another bowl with the beaters, cleaned, beat the whites with the salt until they are foamy, add the cream of tartar, and beat the whites until they hold soft peaks. Add the remaining ¼ cup granulated sugar and beat the whites until they just hold stiff peaks. Stir one fourth of the whites into the chocolate mixture and fold in the remaining whites gently but thoroughly. Divide the batter between the pans, spreading it evenly, and bake the layers in a preheated 350° F. oven for 14 to 16 minutes, or until they are springy to the touch and begin to pull away

from the foil. Let the layers cool in the pans on racks for 10 minutes, invert the racks over them, and invert the layers onto the racks. Remove the foil carefully and discard it. Brush one of the layers with the apricot jam and arrange a sheet of foil under the rack of the other layer.

Make the glaze: In a small bowl set over barely simmering water melt the chocolate and remove the bowl from the heat. In a saucepan combine the sugar cubes and the coffee, bring the mixture to a boil, stirring until the sugar is dissolved, and simmer it for 1 minute. Remove the pan from the heat and stir in the chocolate and the oil, stirring until the mixture is smooth and thickened slightly.

Pour two thirds of the glaze over the plain cake layer, spreading it with a metal spatula to form an even coating and letting it drip off the sides. Transfer the remaining glaze to a paper cone or pastry bag fitted with a very small tip and pipe the glaze in a crosshatch pattern diagonally across the glazed layer. Let the glazed layer stand in a cool place for 1 hour, or until the glaze is set.

In a small bowl sprinkle the gelatin over ½ cup cold water to soften for 5 minutes. Set the bowl over a small saucepan of simmering water and heat the mixture, stirring, until the gelatin is dissolved. Remove the pan from the heat and keep the gelatin mixture warm over it. In a food processor chop fine the chocolate. In a small saucepan bring 3 cups of the cream to a boil. With the motor running add the cream in a stream to the chocolate. Blend the *ganache* until it is smooth, transfer it to a metal bowl, and stir in half the gelatin mixture. Set the bowl in a larger bowl of ice and cold water and stir the *ganache* occasionally until it is cool to the touch. Remove the bowl from the ice water and with an electric mixer beat the *ganache* until it just holds stiff peaks. Spread it evenly over the apricot jam cake layer.

In another bowl beat the remaining 1½ cups cream with the confectioners' sugar and the vanilla until it holds soft peaks, add the remaining gelatin mixture, reheated if necessary, and beat the mixture until it just holds stiff peaks. Spread the cream mixture evenly over the *ganache*.

With a sharp knife cut the glazed layer into squares and arrange the squares on the cream, reforming the cake layer. Chill the cake, covered loosely, for 3 hours, or until it is firm, and with a sharp knife cut the cake into squares. *The cake may be made 2 days in advance and kept covered and chilled.* Serve the cake chilled or at room temperature. Makes 24 squares.

PHOTO ON PAGE 13

6 ounces fine-quality bittersweet chocolate,
  chopped

lemon leaves (available at most florists)
  for garnish

In a food processor blend the almonds, scraping the
bowl occasionally, for 5 minutes, or until they are the
consistency of a nut butter, and reserve the mixture. In a
bowl set over barely simmering water melt the chocolate and the butter, stirring occasionally, and remove
the bowl from the heat. In the large bowl of an electric
mixer beat the eggs until they are pale, add the sugar
gradually, beating, and beat the mixture until it is very
thick and pale. Beat in the chocolate mixture, the framboise, and the reserved almond butter and beat the mixture until it is combined well. Into the bowl sift together
the flour, the baking powder, and the salt, beat the mixture until it is combined well, and fold in 1 cup of the
raspberries gently. Turn the mixture into a well buttered
8½-inch springform pan, spreading it evenly and
smoothing the top, and bake the torte in the middle of a
preheated 350° F. oven for 40 to 45 minutes, or until a
skewer comes out clean. Let the torte cool on a rack and
remove the side of the pan.

Make the glaze: In a small heavy saucepan combine
the jam and the sugar, bring the mixture to a boil, stirring, and boil it, stirring, for 3 minutes. Force the mixture through a fine sieve into a small bowl, pressing hard
on the seeds, and discard the seeds.

Invert the torte onto the rack set on wax paper, remove the bottom of the pan, and spread the glaze on the
top and side of the torte. Let the torte stand at room temperature for 2 hours or chilled for 30 minutes, or until
the glaze is set. *The torte may be prepared up to this
point 1 day in advance and kept on the rack covered with
an inverted bowl at room temperature.*

Make the *ganache*: In a small heavy saucepan bring
the cream to a boil, remove the pan from the heat, and
add the chocolate. Stir the *ganache* until it is smooth and
let it cool for 3 minutes.

Pour the *ganache* over the torte, smoothing it with a
spatula and letting the excess drip down the side, and let
the torte stand for 1 hour, or until the *ganache* is set.
Transfer the torte carefully to a serving plate, garnish it
with some of the additional raspberries and some of the
lemon leaves, and serve the remaining raspberries garnished with the remaining lemon leaves separately.

PHOTO ON PAGE 43

Chocolate Raspberry Almond Torte

½ cup blanched almonds, toasted lightly
2 ounces unsweetened chocolate
2 tablespoons unsalted butter
2 large eggs
1 cup sugar
1 tablespoon framboise or raspberry brandy
¾ cup all-purpose flour
1 teaspoon double-acting baking powder
¼ teaspoon salt
1 cup raspberries plus additional for garnish
  and as an accompaniment
For the glaze
⅓ cup raspberry jam with the seeds
1 tablespoon sugar
For the ganache
¼ cup heavy cream

Deep Chocolate Torte with Coffee Buttercream

For the cake layers

14 large eggs, separated, the whites at room
  temperature
1¾ cups sugar
9 ounces fine-quality bittersweet chocolate,
  melted and cooled

For the buttercream

1 cup sugar
2 large eggs
3 sticks (1½ cups) unsalted butter, softened
3 tablespoons instant espresso powder
  dissolved in 1 tablespoon hot water

For the ganache

1½ cups heavy cream
6 ounces fine-quality bittersweet chocolate,
  chopped fine

¾ cup apricot preserves or red currant jelly,
  heated to lukewarm
chocolate coffee beans (available at specialty
  foods shops) for decoration

Make the cake layers: In a large bowl with an electric mixer beat the yolks, add slowly 1½ cups of the sugar, beating, and beat the mixture until it is thick and pale and forms a ribbon when the beaters are lifted. Add the chocolate and combine the batter well. In another large bowl with clean beaters beat the whites until they hold soft peaks, add the remaining ¼ cup sugar slowly, and beat the mixture until it just holds stiff peaks. Stir one fourth of the whites into the batter and fold in the remaining whites gently but thoroughly. Line 2 greased 15- by 10-inch jelly-roll pans with buttered and floured wax paper and pour the batter into the pans, spreading it evenly. Bake the cake layers in the middle of a preheated 375° F. oven for 18 to 20 minutes, or until a tester comes out clean. Let the cake layers cool in the pans, covered with kitchen towels, on large racks. Invert the cake layers onto the racks and remove the wax paper carefully.

Make the buttercream: In a small heavy saucepan dissolve the sugar in ⅓ cup water over moderate heat, stirring, bring the liquid to a boil, and boil it until it registers 240° F. on a candy thermometer. In a large bowl with an electric mixer beat the eggs until they are frothy, add the sugar syrup in a thin stream, beating, and beat the mixture until it is cool. Beat in the butter, 1 tablespoon at a time, the espresso mixture, and a pinch of salt, and beat the buttercream until it is combined well. If necessary, chill the buttercream, covered, until it is firm enough to spread.

Make the *ganache*: In a large heavy saucepan bring the cream just to a boil and remove the pan from the heat. Add the chocolate and stir the mixture until it is smooth. Transfer the mixture to a bowl and chill it, covered, until it is cold, but do not let it solidify. Beat the mixture until it just forms soft peaks, but do not overbeat it or it will become granular.

Assemble the torte: Transfer the cake layers to a work surface, trim the edges, and halve each cake layer lengthwise. On a serving plate arrange one of the cake layers, spread the layer with one third of the preserves,

and spread one third of the *ganache* over the preserves. Top the *ganache* with another cake layer and layer the remaining preserves, *ganache*, and cake layers in the same manner, ending with a cake layer. Spread the sides and top of the cake with a very thin layer of the buttercream and chill the torte for 30 minutes. Spread the sides and top of the torte with some of the remaining buttercream, reserving about ⅓ cup of it for making rosettes, and with a pastry comb or the tines of a fork score the buttercream lengthwise. Draw the back of a knife crosswise across the scored buttercream at intervals. Transfer the reserved buttercream to a small pastry bag fitted with a decorative tip, pipe rosettes on top of the cake along the long sides, and intersperse the rosettes with the chocolate coffee beans. *The torte may be made 2 days in advance and kept covered loosely and chilled.*

Remove the torte from the refrigerator 30 minutes before serving.

PHOTO ON PAGE 67

Toasted Coconut Cake with Lime Filling

For the cake
1 cup packed sweetened flaked coconut
2¼ cups cake flour (not self-rising)
3 teaspoons double-acting baking powder
¼ teaspoon salt
½ cup vegetable shortening at room
    temperature
1¼ cups sugar
3 large eggs, separated, the whites at room
    temperature
1 teaspoon vanilla
1 cup milk
¼ teaspoon salt
¼ teaspoon cream of tartar
For the filling
¾ cup sugar
2 tablespoons cornstarch
⅛ teaspoon salt
¼ cup fresh lime juice
2 tablespoons fresh lemon juice
1 large egg, beaten lightly
2 tablespoons unsalted butter, softened
¾ cup packed sweetened flaked coconut
For the icing
1½ cups sugar
2 tablespoons light corn syrup
3 large egg whites at room temperature
½ teaspoon cream of tartar
¾ teaspoon vanilla

1½ cups packed sweetened flaked
    coconut
lime slices for garnish

Make the cake: Line the bottoms of 2 greased 8- by 2-inch round cake pans with rounds of wax paper and grease and flour the pans, shaking out the excess flour. Spread the coconut in a jelly-roll pan, toast it in a preheated 350° F. oven, stirring once or twice, for 7 minutes, or until it is golden, and let it cool. In a bowl whisk together the flour, the baking powder, and the salt. In a large bowl with an electric mixer cream the shortening, beat in ¾ cup of the sugar, and beat the mixture until it is light and fluffy. Beat in the yolks, 1 at a time, and the vanilla and add the flour mixture alternately with the milk, beginning and ending with flour and beating until the batter is smooth. In another large bowl with the electric mixer beat the whites with the salt until they are foamy, add the cream of tartar, and beat the whites until they hold soft peaks. Beat in the remaining ½ cup sugar, a little at a time, and beat the meringue until it holds stiff glossy peaks. Stir the toasted coconut and one fourth of the meringue into the batter to lighten it and fold in the remaining meringue gently but thoroughly. Divide the batter between the prepared pans and bake the layers in the middle of the preheated 350° F. oven for 30 to 35 minutes, or until a tester comes out clean. Let the layers cool in the pans on racks for 10 minutes, invert them onto the racks, and let them cool completely.

Make the filling: In a small heavy saucepan whisk together the sugar, the cornstarch, the salt, the lime juice, the lemon juice, and the egg until the mixture is combined and bring the mixture to a rolling boil over moderately high heat, whisking constantly. (The mixture will thicken as it cooks.) Whisk in the butter and let the filling cool.

Split each cake layer in half horizontally with a long serrated knife and brush off any loose crumbs. On a cake plate arrange 1 of the cake layers, cut side up, and spread it with one third of the filling, leaving a ½-inch border. Sprinkle the filling with ¼ cup of the coconut and top the coconut with another cake layer, cut side down. Continue to layer and fill the cake in the same manner with the remaining filling and coconut.

Make the icing: In a saucepan combine the sugar, the corn syrup, and ⅓ cup water, bring the mixture to a boil, covered, over moderate heat, stirring occasionally to dissolve the sugar, and boil the syrup, uncovered, until it registers 240° F. on a candy thermometer. While the syrup is boiling, in a heatproof bowl with an electric mixer beat the whites with a pinch of salt and the cream of tartar until they are frothy. As soon as the syrup reaches 240° F. add it to the whites in a thin stream, continuing to beat the whites while the syrup is being added. Beat in the vanilla and beat the icing until the bowl is no longer hot. (If the icing is too stiff, beat in 1 to 2 tablespoons hot water, or enough to form a fluffy, spreadable icing.)

Spread the icing over the side and top of the cake and cover the cake with the coconut. Garnish the cake with the lime slices.

PHOTO ON PAGE 31

Coffee Coffeecake with Espresso Glaze

For the cake
2 cups sifted all-purpose flour
1 teaspoon double-acting baking powder
½ teaspoon baking soda
¼ teaspoon salt
1½ sticks (¾ cup) unsalted butter,
  softened
1 cup sugar
2 large eggs
2 teaspoons vanilla
1 cup sour cream
2 tablespoons instant espresso powder
  dissolved in 1 tablespoon hot water
For the glaze
2 to 3 tablespoons strong brewed coffee
1½ teaspoons instant espresso powder
¾ cup confectioners' sugar

Make the cake: Into a bowl sift together the flour, the baking powder, the baking soda, and the salt. In another bowl with an electric mixer cream the butter, add the sugar gradually, beating, and beat the mixture until it is light and fluffy. Add the eggs, 1 at a time, beating well after each addition, and beat in the vanilla. Add the flour mixture alternately with the sour cream, beginning and ending with the flour mixture and blending the batter after each addition. Transfer about one third of the batter to a small bowl and stir in the espresso mixture until the batter is combined well. Spoon half the plain batter into a well buttered 8-inch (1½-quart capacity) bundt pan, spreading it evenly, spoon the coffee batter over it, spreading it evenly, and spoon the remaining plain batter on top, spreading it evenly. Bake the cake in the middle of a preheated 350° F. oven for 55 to 60 minutes, or until it is golden and a tester comes out clean and transfer it in the pan to a rack. Let the cake cool for 30 minutes, invert it onto the rack, and let it cool completely.

Make the glaze: In a bowl stir together 2 tablespoons of the brewed coffee and the espresso powder until the powder is dissolved, add the confectioners' sugar, sifted, and stir the glaze until it is combined well. If necessary add more of the remaining 1 tablespoon coffee to obtain a pourable consistency.

Pour the glaze over the cake and let the cake stand for 10 minutes, or until the glaze is set. *The recipe may be doubled and the cake baked in a 10-inch (2½-quart capacity) bundt pan for 1 hour to 1 hour and 10 minutes, or until it is golden and a tester comes out clean.*

Glazed Cranberry Ginger Pound Cake

For the cake
2 sticks (1 cup) unsalted butter, softened
2 cups sugar
4 large eggs at room temperature
2½ cups all-purpose flour
1 teaspoon double-acting baking powder
½ teaspoon baking soda
½ teaspoon salt
2 tablespoons ground ginger
⅓ cup buttermilk
2½ cups cranberries, picked over
For the sugared cranberries
1 large egg white
sugar for coating the berries
1 cup cranberries, picked over
For the glaze
1½ cups sugar
1½ cups cranberries, picked over and rinsed

Make the cake: In a large bowl with an electric mixer cream the butter, add the sugar, a little at a time, and beat the mixture until it is light and fluffy. Add the eggs, 1 at a time, beating well after each addition. Into a bowl sift together the flour, the baking powder, the baking soda, the salt, and the ginger and add the flour mixture to the butter mixture alternately with the buttermilk, beginning and ending with the flour mixture and beating the batter after each addition. Fold in the cranberries, spoon the batter into a buttered and floured 3-quart decorative baking pan such as a bundt pan or *Kugelhupf*, smoothing the top, and bake the cake in the middle of a preheated 350° F. oven for 1¼ hours to 1 hour and 20 minutes, or until a tester comes out clean. Let the cake cool in the pan on a rack for 10 minutes, turn it out onto the rack, and let it cool completely. *The cake may be made 2 days in advance and kept wrapped tightly in a cool place.*

Make the sugared cranberries: Have ready in 2 separate bowls the egg white, beaten lightly, and the sugar. Dip the cranberries in the white, letting the excess drip off, coat them well with the sugar, and transfer them to the rack to dry. *The sugared cranberries may be made 2 days in advance and kept on the rack in a cool dry place.*

Make the glaze: In a heavy saucepan cook the sugar and 1½ cups water over moderate heat, stirring and washing down any crystals clinging to the side of the pan with a brush dipped in cold water, until the sugar is dissolved. Add the cranberries, bring the mixture to a boil, and boil it, undisturbed, until it registers 250° F. on a candy thermometer. Strain the mixture through a fine sieve into a bowl, pressing hard on the solids, and let the glaze cool slightly. *The glaze may be made 3 days in advance and kept covered and chilled. In a saucepan reheat the glaze, stirring, over moderately low heat until it is melted.*

Brush the cake with the warm cranberry glaze and garnish it with the sugared cranberries.

Rose's Legendary Honey Cake

5 large eggs, separated, the whites at room
    temperature
¾ cup sugar
2 cups all-purpose flour
½ teaspoon double-acting baking powder
½ teaspoon baking soda
½ cup strongly flavored honey (preferably
    buckwheat)
¼ cup double-strength brewed coffee
1½ teaspoons freshly grated lemon rind
2 teaspoons fresh lemon juice
1 tablespoon whiskey
3 tablespoons sliced almonds

In a large bowl with an electric mixer beat the yolks with the sugar for 5 to 7 minutes, or until the mixture is thick and pale and forms a ribbon when the beaters are lifted. Into a bowl sift together the flour, the baking powder, and the baking soda. In a small bowl whisk together the honey and the coffee, heated, whisk the mixture into the yolk mixture gradually, and whisk in the rind, the lemon juice, and the whiskey. Fold in the flour mixture until the mixture is just combined. In a bowl with the electric mixer beat the whites with a pinch of salt until they just form stiff peaks, stir about one fourth of the whites into the flour mixture, and fold in the remaining whites gently but thoroughly. Spread the almonds on the bottom of an oiled 9-inch tube pan, pour the batter over them, and bake the cake in the middle of a preheated 325° F. oven for 45 to 50 minutes, or until it

is golden and the surface springs back when pressed lightly. Let the cake cool in the pan on a rack until it is lukewarm, invert it onto the rack, and let it cool completely.

Lemon Poppy Seed Tea Cakes

⅔ cup cake flour (not self-rising)
¼ teaspoon baking soda
½ stick (¼ cup) unsalted butter, softened
⅔ cup granulated sugar
2 large eggs, separated, the whites at room
    temperature
1½ tablespoons fresh lemon juice
1 teaspoon vanilla
1½ teaspoons freshly grated lemon zest
2½ tablespoons poppy seeds
¼ cup sour cream
confectioners' sugar for dusting the cakes

Into a bowl sift together the flour, the baking soda, and a pinch of salt. In a large bowl with an electric mixer cream the butter, add ⅓ cup of the granulated sugar, a little at a time, beating, and beat the mixture until it is light and fluffy. Add the egg yolks, 1 at a time, beating well after each addition, and beat in well the lemon juice, the vanilla, the rind, and the poppy seeds. Add the flour mixture to the butter mixture alternately with the sour cream, combining the mixture well.

In another large bowl with the electric mixer beat the egg whites until they hold soft peaks, beat in the remaining ⅓ cup granulated sugar, a little at a time, and beat the meringue until it holds stiff peaks. Stir one fourth of the meringue into the cake batter and fold in the remaining meringue gently but thoroughly.

Divide the batter among 6 well buttered and floured ½-cup muffin tins and bake the tea cakes in the middle of a preheated 375° F. oven for 20 to 25 minutes, or until they are golden. Remove the tea cakes from the tins to a rack and sift the confectioners' sugar over the tops. Makes 6 tea cakes.

Gâteau de Mousse à la Nectarine
(Nectarine Mousse Cake)

For the nectarine mousse
1½ pounds nectarines
½ cup sugar
1 envelope (1 tablespoon) plus 2 teaspoons
    unflavored gelatin
¼ cup fresh lemon juice
¼ cup peach schnapps
1½ cups well chilled heavy cream

génoise cake (recipe follows), cut horizontally
    with a serrated knife into 3 layers
⅔ cup peach syrup (page 219)
¾ cup peach glaze (page 219), cooled
    to warm
1 nectarine

Make the nectarine mousse: Halve, pit, and chop the nectarines and in a heavy saucepan combine them with the sugar and ½ cup water. Bring the mixture to a boil, stirring, and cook it at a slow boil, stirring occasionally, for 15 minutes. In a food processor or blender purée the mixture and force it through a fine sieve into a large bowl, pressing hard on the solids. In a small saucepan sprinkle the gelatin over the lemon juice and the schnapps to soften for 5 minutes and heat the mixture over low heat, stirring, until the gelatin is dissolved. (The mixture will be cloudy.) Stir the gelatin mixture into the nectarine purée, blending the mixture well, and let the mixture cool to room temperature. In a chilled bowl beat the cream until it holds a soft shape (not as stiff as soft peaks) and fold it into the nectarine mixture.

Assemble the cake: Center one of the cake layers in the bottom of a 9½-inch springform pan and brush it with half the peach syrup. Pour half the mousse over the cake, and top it with one of the remaining cake layers. Brush the cake with the remaining peach syrup and pour the remaining mousse over the cake, rapping the pan on a hard surface several times to eliminate any air bubbles and smoothing the surface. Chill the mousse cake for 2 hours, or until it is set. Pour all but about 2 tablespoons of the peach glaze over the top of the mousse cake, covering it completely, and chill the cake for 2 hours, or until the glaze is set. *The cake may be prepared up to this point 2 days in advance and kept covered and chilled.*

While the cake is chilling, in a food processor grind the remaining cake layer into fine crumbs, toast the crumbs on a jelly-roll pan in a preheated 350° F. oven for 5 to 8 minutes, or until the crumbs are golden, and reserve them.

Cut half the nectarine into thin slices, reserving the remaining half for another use, and arrange the slices decoratively on the cake. If the remaining glaze has set, heat it over simmering water or in a microwave oven until it is liquid. Brush the glaze over the nectarine slices and chill the cake, covered, for 1 hour, or until the newly applied glaze is set. Run a thin knife around the edge of the pan and remove the side of the pan. Working over a sheet of wax paper coat the side of the cake with the reserved cake crumbs. Let the cake stand at room temperature for 20 minutes before serving.

PHOTO ON PAGE 49

Génoise Cake

4 large eggs
⅔ cup sugar
⅔ cup all-purpose flour
½ teaspoon salt
1 teaspoon vanilla
¼ cup clarified butter (page 219),
    melted and cooled to lukewarm

In a metal bowl whisk together the eggs and the sugar, set the bowl over a pan of simmering water, and whisk the mixture until it is warm and the sugar is dissolved. Remove the bowl from the pan and with an electric mixer beat the mixture at moderate speed for 10 to 15 minutes, or until it is triple in volume and cooled to room temperature. While the eggs are being beaten, sift the flour with the salt onto a sheet of wax paper and in a bowl combine the vanilla and the clarified butter. Sift and fold the flour mixture in batches into the egg mixture until the mixture is just combined, stir one-fourth of the mixture into the butter mixture, and fold the butter mixture quickly into the batter.

Line the bottom of a buttered 8½-inch springform pan with wax paper, butter the paper, and dust the pan with flour, knocking out the excess. Pour the batter into the pan, smoothing the top, and bake the cake in the middle of a preheated 350° F. oven for 30 to 35 minutes, or until the top is golden and a tester comes out clean. Let the cake cool in the pan on a rack for 5 minutes, remove the side of the pan, and invert the cake onto the rack. Remove the paper carefully and let the cake cool. *The génoise cake may be made 1 day in advance and kept wrapped in plastic wrap at room temperature.*

To Clarify Butter
unsalted butter, cut into 1-inch pieces

In a heavy saucepan melt the butter over low heat. Remove the pan from the heat, let the butter stand for 3 minutes, and skim the froth. Strain the butter through a sieve lined with a double thickness of rinsed and squeezed cheesecloth into a bowl, leaving the milky solids in the bottom of the pan. Pour the clarified butter into a jar or crock and store it, covered, in the refrigerator. The butter keeps indefinitely, covered and chilled. (When clarified, butter loses about one fourth of its original volume.)

Peach Syrup
¼ cup sugar
⅓ cup peach schnapps

In a small saucepan combine the sugar and ¼ cup water, bring the mixture to a boil, stirring until the sugar is dissolved, and stir in the schnapps. Let the syrup cool to room temperature. The syrup keeps, covered and chilled, indefinitely. Makes about ⅔ cup.

Peach Glaze
1¼ teaspoons unflavored gelatin
¾ cup peach preserves or jam
3 tablespoons peach schnapps

In a small bowl sprinkle the gelatin over 3 tablespoons cold water to soften for 5 minutes. In a small saucepan combine the preserves and the schnapps, bring the mixture to a boil, stirring, and simmer it for 1 minute. Remove the pan from the heat, add the gelatin mixture, stirring until the gelatin is dissolved, and strain the mixture through a fine sieve into a bowl, pressing hard on the solids. *The glaze may be made 3 days in advance and kept covered and chilled. Reheat the glaze in a bowl set over simmering water or in a microwave oven until it is liquid.* Makes about ¾ cup.

Paskha
(Russian Easter Cheese Mold)
2 large whole eggs
1 large egg yolk
¾ cup sugar
¾ cup heavy cream
1½ sticks (¾ cup) unsalted butter, softened
2 pounds packaged farmer cheese, drained between several layers of paper towels for 30 minutes and forced through a sieve
2 teaspoons vanilla
2 teaspoons freshly grated orange zest
⅓ cup finely chopped almonds
¼ cup dried currants plus additional for decoration if desired
finely diced glacéed cherries for decoration if desired
angelica for decoration if desired
kulich (page 220) as an accompaniment

In a bowl with an electric mixer beat the whole eggs and the yolk with the sugar until the mixture is thick and pale, add the cream, scalded, in a stream, beating constantly, and transfer the custard to a heavy saucepan. Cook the custard over moderately low heat, stirring constantly, until it is thickened (175° F. on a candy thermometer), being careful not to let it boil. Strain the custard through a fine sieve into a metal bowl set in a larger bowl of ice and cold water and let it cool, stirring occasionally.

While the custard is cooling, in another bowl with the electric mixer cream the butter, add the cheese gradually, beating, and beat the mixture at moderate speed for 5 minutes. Beat in the custard, the vanilla, the orange zest, the almonds, and ¼ cup of the currants. Line a 7- to 8-cup new clay flowerpot with a double layer of rinsed and squeezed cheesecloth, add the cheese mixture, packing it and smoothing the top, and fold the ends of the cheesecloth over the top. Put the flowerpot in a small bowl, weight the top of the cheese mixture with a 4-pound weight that fits just inside the pot, such as a flat-bottomed pan filled with cans, and chill the *paskha* for at least 12 hours or overnight.

Remove the weights, unfold the cheesecloth, and invert a serving plate over the flowerpot. Invert the *paskha* onto the plate, peel off the cheesecloth carefully, and decorate the *paskha* with the additional currants, the cherries, and the angelica. (The letters "XB" outlined in currants in the photo are the Cyrillic expression of "Christ is Risen" and a traditional *paskha* decoration.) Serve the *paskha* at room temperature with slices of the *kulich*.

PHOTO ON PAGE 32

Kulich
(Russian Easter Sweet Bread
with Raisins and Almonds)

a ¼-ounce package (2½ teaspoons) active
　　dry yeast
½ cup plus 1 teaspoon granulated sugar
½ cup milk
1 tablespoon dark rum
a small pinch of crumbled saffron threads
4 cups all-purpose flour
1 stick (½ cup) unsalted butter, melted
　　and cooled
2 large whole eggs
2 large egg yolks
1 teaspoon salt
⅓ cup golden raisins
⅓ cup sliced almonds, toasted lightly
For the glaze
1 cup confectioners' sugar
2 teaspoons fresh lemon juice
⅛ teaspoon almond extract

In a large bowl proof the yeast with 1 teaspoon of the granulated sugar in ¼ cup lukewarm water for 10 minutes, or until it is foamy. While the yeast is proofing, in a small saucepan scald the milk over moderate heat, stir in the rum and the saffron, and let the mixture cool to lukewarm. Add the milk mixture to the yeast mixture with the remaining ½ cup granulated sugar and 1 cup of the flour, blend the sponge well, and let it rise in a warm place, covered with plastic wrap, for 1 hour. Stir in the butter, the whole eggs, the yolks, the salt, the raisins, the almonds, and 2 cups of the remaining flour, or enough to form a dough. Turn the dough out onto a floured surface and knead it, kneading in enough of the remaining flour to keep it from sticking, for 8 to 10 minutes, or until it is smooth and elastic. Put the dough in a buttered bowl, turn it to coat it with the butter, and let it rise, covered with plastic wrap, in a warm place for 1½ hours, or until it is double in bulk.

While the dough is rising, butter the inside of a 2-pound coffee can and line the side with a sheet of wax paper. Cut the paper extending beyond the can into strips, fold the strips over the outside of the can, and butter the paper inside the can. Punch down the dough, knead it 3 or 4 times, and put it in the can. Let the dough rise, covered with a kitchen towel, in a warm place for 45 minutes to 1 hour, or until it has risen to the top of the can. Bake the *kulich* in a preheated 400° F. oven for 15 minutes, reduce the heat to 350° F., and continue to bake the *kulich* for 30 to 35 minutes, or until it sounds hollow when tapped. Turn the *kulich* out carefully onto a rack and let it cool upright. *The* kulich *may be prepared 1 day in advance and kept tightly wrapped and chilled.*

Make the glaze: In a bowl whisk together the confectioners' sugar, sifted, the lemon juice, the almond extract, and 2 teaspoons water, or enough to make a pourable glaze.

Set the *kulich* on a plate and drizzle the glaze over it, letting the glaze drip down the sides. Let the *kulich* stand until the glaze has hardened and transfer it to a serving plate.

PHOTO ON PAGE 32

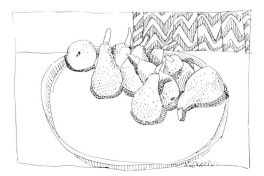

Pearsauce Cake with Caramel Pear Topping

1 cup vegetable shortening
¾ cup granulated sugar
¾ cup firmly packed light brown sugar
1 large egg
2 cups pearsauce (page 221)
3¼ cups plus 1 tablespoon all-purpose flour
2 teaspoons cinnamon
½ teaspoon ground cloves
1½ teaspoons ground ginger
½ teaspoon freshly grated nutmeg
1¼ cups raisins
2 teaspoons baking soda dissolved in ¼ cup
　　boiling water

¾ cup finely chopped walnuts
For the topping
4 firm-ripe Anjou or Bartlett pears
  (about 2 pounds)
¼ cup fresh lemon juice
2 tablespoons unsalted butter
½ cup firmly packed light brown sugar
⅛ teaspoon ground ginger

whipped cream as an accompaniment if
  desired

In a bowl with an electric mixer cream the shortening with the sugars, add the egg and the pearsauce, and beat the mixture until it is combined well. Into the bowl sift together 3¼ cups of the flour, the cinnamon, the cloves, the ginger, the nutmeg, and a pinch of salt and beat the mixture until it is just smooth. In a small bowl toss the raisins with the remaining 1 tablespoon flour and stir the raisin mixture, the baking soda mixture, and the walnuts into the batter. Spoon the batter into a well buttered baking pan, 13 by 9 by 2 inches, bake the cake in the middle of a preheated 375° F. oven for 45 to 55 minutes, or until a tester comes out clean, and let it cool in the pan on a rack for 10 minutes.

Make the topping: In a bowl toss together the pears, peeled, cored, and sliced thin, and the lemon juice. In a large skillet melt the butter over moderate heat, transfer the pears to the skillet with a slotted spoon, reserving the juices in the bowl, and cook them, stirring occasionally, for 5 minutes, or until they are just tender. Stir the brown sugar and the ginger into the reserved juices, pour the mixture over the pears in the skillet, and cook the mixture over high heat, swirling the skillet, until the sugar is caramelized and a deep golden.

Slice the cake into large squares, spoon the pear topping over it, and serve the cake with the whipped cream.

Pearsauce

6 firm-ripe Anjou or Bartlett pears (about 3
  pounds), cored and cut into chunks
¼ cup fresh lemon juice

In a kettle combine the pears and the lemon juice, cook the mixture, covered, over moderately low heat for 30 minutes, or until the pears are very tender, and force it through a food mill fitted with the medium disk into a large bowl. Transfer the purée to the kettle and cook it over low heat, stirring, for 20 minutes, or until it is thickened. Transfer the pearsauce to a bowl and let it cool. The pearsauce keeps, covered and chilled, for 1 week. Makes about 3 cups.

Strawberry Shortcake

2 pints strawberries, hulled and sliced
⅓ cup granulated sugar
½ teaspoon vanilla
For the biscuit
2 cups all-purpose flour
1 tablespoon double-acting baking powder
½ teaspoon salt
3 tablespoons firmly packed brown sugar
1 stick (½ cup) cold unsalted butter,
  cut into bits
⅔ cup plus 1 tablespoon milk
2 teaspoons granulated sugar

1 cup well chilled heavy cream
2 tablespoons confectioners' sugar
3 tablespoons sour cream

In a bowl combine three fourths of the strawberries with the granulated sugar and the vanilla, mash them lightly with a fork, and let them macerate, covered and chilled, stirring occasionally, for 1 hour.

Make the biscuit: Into a bowl sift together the flour, the baking powder, and the salt, add the brown sugar and the butter, and blend the mixture until it resembles coarse meal. Add the milk and stir the mixture until it just forms a dough. Drop the dough in 8 mounds onto a buttered baking sheet, letting the mounds touch to form an 8-inch ring, sprinkle it with the granulated sugar, and bake the biscuit in the middle of a preheated 425° F. oven for 20 to 25 minutes, or until it is golden. Transfer the biscuit to a rack carefully and let it cool. *The biscuit may be made 1 day in advance and kept wrapped well at room temperature.*

Cut the top ¼ off the entire biscuit ring with a serrated knife, transfer the bottom to a platter, and spoon the macerated strawberries and the liquid over it. In a chilled bowl beat the cream with the confectioners' sugar until it just holds soft peaks, beat in the sour cream, and beat the mixture until it is stiff. Top the macerated strawberries with the cream mixture and the remaining one fourth of the strawberries and cover the mixture with the biscuit top. Serves 8.

Tosca Cake
(Norwegian Almond Caramel Cake)

For the cake
2 cups all-purpose flour
2 teaspoons double-acting baking powder
¼ teaspoon salt
4 large eggs at room temperature
1½ cups superfine sugar
2 sticks (1 cup) unsalted butter, melted and
    cooled
1½ teaspoons vanilla
⅓ cup milk
vegetable cooking spray for coating the pan
For the topping
½ cup heavy cream
⅓ cup granulated sugar
½ stick (¼ cup) unsalted butter, cut into bits
½ cup sliced unskinned almonds, toasted
    lightly

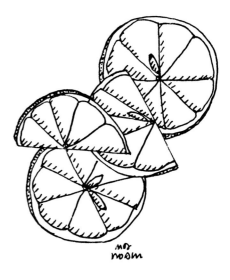

candied orange ice cream (recipe follows) as
    an accompaniment

Make the cake: In a bowl combine well the flour, the baking powder, and the salt. In the bowl of an electric mixer beat the eggs until they are foamy, beat in the sugar gradually, and beat the mixture until it is thick and pale. Beat in the butter, the vanilla, and the milk, add the flour mixture, and beat the batter until it is just combined. Pour the batter into a 2½-quart tube pan coated with the spray and bake the cake in the middle of a preheated 350° F. oven for 35 to 40 minutes, or until a tester comes out clean. Let the cake cool completely in the pan on a rack and invert it onto a plate. *The cake may be made 2 days in advance and kept covered with plastic wrap and chilled. Bring the cake to room temperature before proceeding with the recipe.*

Make the topping: In a skillet combine the cream and the sugar, cook the mixture over moderate heat, stirring, until the sugar is dissolved, and stir in the butter. Bring the mixture to a boil, boil it, stirring occasionally, until it is thickened slightly, and stir in the almonds.

Transfer the cake to a baking sheet, over it spoon the topping and put the cake under a preheated broiler about 3 inches from the heat for 30 seconds to 1 minute, or until the almonds are golden. Transfer the cake with spatulas to a cake plate and serve it warm or at room temperature with the ice cream.

PHOTO ON PAGE 25

Candied Orange Ice Cream
For the candied rind
¼ cup julienne strips of orange rind
¼ cup orange-flavored liqueur

1½ cups fresh orange juice
1 teaspoon freshly grated orange rind
2 tablespoons orange-flavored liqueur
1½ tablespoons cornstarch
¾ cup sugar
4 large egg yolks
2 cups milk
2 cups well chilled heavy cream

Make the candied rind: In a small heavy saucepan combine the julienne rind and the liqueur, bring the liqueur to a simmer, and cook the rind at a bare simmer, stirring occasionally, until the liquid is evaporated. Spread the rind on a sheet of wax paper and let it cool. *The candied rind may be made 3 days in advance and kept covered.*

In a saucepan combine the orange juice and the grated rind, bring the juice to a boil, and simmer the mixture until the juice is reduced to about ½ cup. Strain the mixture through a fine sieve into a small bowl, discarding the solids, and stir in the liqueur. In a bowl whisk together the cornstarch, the sugar, and a pinch of salt, whisk in the yolks, and add the orange juice mixture and the milk, scalded, in a slow stream, whisking. In a heavy saucepan cook the mixture over moderate heat, whisking constantly, until it comes to a boil, boil it, whisking, for 2 minutes, and pour the custard into a bowl set in a larger bowl of ice and cold water. Stir the custard until it is cold, stir in the cream, and freeze the mixture in an ice-cream freezer according to the manufacturer's instructions until it is frozen but still soft. Transfer the ice cream to an airtight container, stir in two thirds of the candied rind, and freeze the ice cream in the container until it is frozen. *The ice cream may be made 3 days in advance.* Scoop the ice cream into a bowl and sprinkle the remaining candied rind over it. Makes about 1½ quarts.

PHOTO ON PAGE 25

COOKIES

Almond and Hazelnut Biscotti

3 cups all-purpose flour
½ cup whole-wheat flour
1 teaspoon double-acting baking powder
1 teaspoon baking soda
½ teaspoon salt
¼ teaspoon allspice
1 teaspoon cinnamon
1½ cups (about ½ pound) blanched almonds, toasted lightly, chopped coarse, and cooled
¾ cup hazelnuts (about 3 ounces), toasted lightly, chopped coarse, and cooled
1¼ cups granulated sugar
¾ cup firmly packed light brown sugar
½ stick (¼ cup) unsalted butter, melted and cooled
5 large eggs, beaten
1½ teaspoons vanilla
1 teaspoon freshly grated orange rind
an egg wash made by beating 1 large egg with 1 tablespoon water

In a large bowl combine well the flours, the baking powder, the baking soda, the salt, the allspice, the cinnamon, and the nuts. In another large bowl whisk together the sugars, the butter, the eggs, the vanilla, and

the rind. Stir the dry mixture into the egg mixture and knead the dough in the bowl until it is combined well.

Turn the dough out onto a well floured board and knead it several times to distribute the nuts throughout the dough. Divide the dough into fourths, with floured hands form each fourth into a rough 9- by 2-inch rectangle, and transfer the rectangles with spatulas to 2 buttered and floured baking sheets, leaving 3 inches between the rectangles. Pat the rectangles out to lengthen them to 11 inches, brush them with the egg wash, and bake them in the upper third of a preheated 375° F. oven for 25 to 30 minutes, or until they are golden brown and a skewer inserted in the center comes out clean.

Reduce the oven temperature to 325° F., transfer the rectangles to a cutting board, and cut them crosswise into ⅓-inch-thick slices. Arrange the *biscotti* on the baking sheets, cut sides up, and bake them in the upper third of the 325° F. oven, turning them once, for 15 minutes. Transfer the *biscotti* to racks, let them cool for 2 to 3 hours, or until they are crisp, and store them in airtight containers. Makes about 84 *biscotti*.

Brown Sugar Ginger Crisps

2 sticks (1 cup) unsalted butter at room temperature
1 cup firmly packed light brown sugar
1 large egg yolk
1 teaspoon vanilla
½ cup (about 3 ounces) finely chopped crystallized ginger
¼ teaspoon ground ginger
1½ cups all-purpose flour
¾ teaspoon double-acting baking powder
½ teaspoon salt

In a bowl cream together the butter and the brown sugar and beat in the egg yolk, the vanilla, the crystallized ginger, and the ground ginger. Into the bowl sift together the flour, the baking powder, and the salt and combine the batter well. Drop the batter by teaspoons 3 inches apart onto ungreased baking sheets and bake the cookies in the middle of a preheated 350° F. oven for 10 to 12 minutes, or until they are just golden. Let the cookies cool on the baking sheets for 5 minutes, transfer them carefully with a metal spatula to racks, and let them cool completely. *The cookies may be made 1 month in advance and kept, frozen, in airtight containers.* Makes about 50 cookies.

Coconut Macaroon and Chocolate Sandwiches

2 cups sweetened flaked coconut
1 cup sugar
3 tablespoons all-purpose flour
4 large egg whites at room temperature
⅛ teaspoon salt
¼ teaspoon almond extract or vanilla
½ cup semisweet chocolate chips

In a large bowl combine well the coconut, ¼ cup of the sugar, and the flour. In another large bowl beat the whites with the salt and the almond extract until they hold soft peaks, add the remaining ¾ cup sugar gradually, beating, and beat the meringue until it is very stiff and glossy. Add the meringue to the coconut mixture, combine the mixture well, and drop it in 16 mounds onto a baking sheet lined with parchment paper. Bake the macaroons in the middle of a preheated 325° F. oven for 25 to 30 minutes, or until they are just firm to the touch and colored lightly. Let the macaroons cool on the parchment paper and peel them carefully from the paper. In a small bowl set over a saucepan of simmering water melt the chocolate and let it cool slightly. Spread the chocolate on the bottoms of half the macaroons, attach the remaining macaroons to the chocolate to form sandwiches, and chill the sandwiches for 15 minutes. *The sandwiches may be made 5 days in advance and kept chilled in an airtight container.* Makes 8 cookie sandwiches.

Hazelnut Sablés

½ cup whole hazelnuts, toasted and skinned
    (procedure follows) and cooled, plus
    chopped toasted and skinned hazelnuts
    for the topping
⅔ cup plus 2 tablespoons confectioners' sugar
1 stick (½ cup) unsalted butter, softened
½ teaspoon vanilla
1 large egg yolk
½ teaspoon cinnamon
½ teaspoon salt
1¼ cups all-purpose flour
an egg wash made by beating 1 egg white
    with 1 teaspoon water
melted bittersweet chocolate for decoration

In a food processor or an electric coffee or spice grinder grind fine the whole hazelnuts with 2 tablespoons of the confectioners' sugar and reserve the mixture. In a bowl with an electric mixer cream the butter with the remaining ⅔ cup confectioners' sugar until the mixture is light and fluffy, beat in the vanilla, the yolk, the cinnamon, and the salt, beating until the mixture is combined well, and beat in the reserved hazelnut mixture. Beat in the flour and beat the dough until it is combined well. Wrap the dough in plastic wrap and chill it for at least 6 hours or overnight. Working with one fourth of the dough at a time, roll out the dough about ¼ inch thick on a lightly floured surface, cut out shapes with a 1½-to 2-inch cutter, gathering and chilling the scraps, and transfer the shapes to baking sheets. Reroll the scraps and cut out shapes in the same manner, transferring them to baking sheets. Chill the cookies on the sheets for 30 minutes, brush half the cookies lightly with some of the egg wash, and sprinkle them with the chopped hazelnuts. Bake the cookies in batches in the middle of a preheated 350° F. oven for 15 to 20 minutes, or until they are pale golden, transfer them to racks, and let them cool. Decorate the plain cookies with the chocolate, piped through a pastry bag fitted with a very small plain tip or through a cornet made of parchment paper. Chill the chocolate cookies for 15 to 20 minutes, or until the chocolate is set. The cookies may be stored in an airtight container for up to 3 days. Makes about 50 cookies.

To Toast and Skin Hazelnuts

Toast the hazelnuts in one layer in a baking pan in a preheated 350° F. oven for 10 to 15 minutes, or until they are colored lightly and the skins blister. Wrap the nuts in a kitchen towel and let them steam for 1 minute. Rub the nuts in the towel to remove the skins and let them cool.

Lemon Almond Madeleines

4 large eggs at room temperature
⅔ cup granulated sugar
½ teaspoon almond extract
1½ teaspoons freshly grated lemon zest
1 cup all-purpose flour
½ cup almonds with the skins, toasted lightly,
    cooled, and ground coarse
1 stick (½ cup) unsalted butter, melted and
    cooled slightly
confectioners' sugar for dusting the
    madeleines

In a bowl with an electric mixer beat the eggs with the granulated sugar until the mixture is thick and pale and forms a ribbon when the beater is lifted and beat in the almond extract and the zest. Sift the flour in 4 batches over the mixture, folding it in gently after each addition, add the almonds and the butter, and fold them in gently but thoroughly. Spoon the batter into twenty-four 3- by 2-inch buttered *madeleine* molds and bake the *madeleines* in the lower third of a preheated 375° F. oven for 10 minutes, or until the edges are golden. Turn the *madeleines* out onto racks, let them cool, and sift the confectioners' sugar over them. Makes 24 *madeleines*.

PHOTO ON PAGE 50

Mexican Tea Cakes

2 sticks (1 cup) unsalted butter, softened
3 cups confectioners' sugar
1 teaspoon vanilla
¾ cup finely chopped pecans
¾ teaspoon salt
2¼ cups all-purpose flour

In a bowl with an electric mixer cream the butter with ½ cup of the sugar until the mixture is light and fluffy and beat in the vanilla, the pecans, and the salt until the mixture is combined well. Add the flour, beat the dough until it is combined well, and chill it, covered, for at least 6 hours or overnight.

Let the dough stand at room temperature until it is just pliable and form it into balls about ¾ inch in diameter. Arrange the balls of dough about 1 inch apart on lightly buttered baking sheets and flatten them slightly to form small disks. Bake the cookies in batches in the middle of a preheated 375° F. oven for 12 to 15 minutes, or until they are pale golden on the bottom. While the cookies are baking, sift the remaining 2½ cups sugar into a shallow dish and as the cookies come out of the oven roll them immediately in the sugar to coat them. Transfer the cookies to a rack, let them cool, and roll them in

the sugar again. *The cookies may be made 3 days in advance and kept in an airtight container.* Makes about 72 cookies.

PHOTO ON PAGE 37

Middle Eastern Butter Cookies

2 sticks (1 cup) unsalted butter, clarified
  (procedure on page 219)
¼ teaspoon vanilla
¼ teaspoon salt
1 cup confectioners' sugar, sifted
1⅔ cups all-purpose flour, sifted
12 blanched whole almonds, halved

Chill the clarified butter for 2 hours, or until it is solidified completely. In the bowl of an electric mixer beat the clarified butter for 4 minutes, or until it is very light and creamy, and beat in the vanilla and the salt. Beat in the confectioners' sugar, a little at a time, and beat the mixture until it is smooth. Sift in the flour, a little at a time, beating, and beat the mixture until the dough resembles coarse meal. Knead the dough on a lightly floured surface until it is smooth and pliable and chill it, wrapped in wax paper, for 1 hour.

Divide the dough into fourths and work with one piece at a time, keeping the remaining dough wrapped in wax paper and chilled. Divide the dough into 6 pieces and roll each piece into a 5-inch-long log on a lightly floured surface. Press the ends of each log together to form a ring and press an almond half onto each seam. Make cookies with the remaining dough and almonds in the same manner. Arrange the cookies 2 inches apart on ungreased baking sheets and bake them in batches in the middle of a preheated 300° F. oven for 20 to 22 minutes, or until the almonds are pale golden but the cookies are still white. (Although the bottoms will be golden the cookies should not color.) Let the cookies cool on the baking sheet for 1 minute, transfer them to a rack, and let them cool completely. The cookies keep in an airtight container for 1 week. Makes 24 cookies.

Butterscotch Oatmeal Cookies

1 stick (½ cup) unsalted butter, softened
½ cup vegetable shortening
1½ cups firmly packed light brown sugar
2 large eggs
1 teaspoon baking soda dissolved in
   2 tablespoons warm water
1 teaspoon vanilla
1⅓ cups all-purpose flour
1 teaspoon salt
3 cups old-fashioned rolled oats
1 cup walnuts, toasted lightly and chopped
1½ cups raisins or semisweet chocolate chips
   if desired

In a large bowl with an electric mixer cream the butter with the shortening, add the brown sugar, and beat the mixture until it is light and fluffy. Add the eggs, 1 at a time, beating well after each addition, and beat in the baking soda mixture and the vanilla. Stir in the flour, the salt, the oats, the walnuts, and the raisins or chocolate chips and arrange level tablespoons of the dough 2 inches apart on greased baking sheets. Bake the cookies in batches in the middle of a preheated 375° F. oven for 8 to 10 minutes, or until they are golden, transfer them with a spatula to racks, and let them cool. Makes about 48 plain cookies or about 66 with the raisins or chips.

Oatmeal Lace Cookies

1 stick (½ cup) unsalted butter
½ cup firmly packed light brown sugar
1 tablespoon light corn syrup
¼ cup all-purpose flour
¾ cup quick-cooking rolled oats (not instant)
2 tablespoons heavy cream
¼ teaspoon salt
½ teaspoon vanilla

In a heavy saucepan melt the butter over moderately low heat and stir in the brown sugar, the corn syrup, the flour, the oats, the cream, the salt, and the vanilla. Bring the mixture to a simmer, stirring, remove the pan from the heat, and let the mixture cool for 5 minutes. Arrange level teaspoons of the mixture 3 inches apart on greased baking sheets and bake the cookies in batches in the middle of a preheated 350° F. oven for 7 to 9 minutes, or until they are golden. Let the cookies cool on the baking sheet for 1 minute, or until they are just firm

enough to remove but still very pliable, and transfer them with a spatula to a rolling pin, curving them around the pin. (If the cookies become too firm, return them to the oven for a few seconds.) Let the cookies become firm enough to hold their shape, transfer them from the rolling pin to racks, and let them cool completely. Makes about 42 cookies.

Oatmeal Trail Mix Cookies

½ stick (¼ cup) unsalted butter, softened
¼ cup vegetable shortening
½ cup firmly packed light brown sugar
¼ cup granulated sugar
1 large egg
½ teaspoon baking soda dissolved in
   1 tablespoon warm water
½ cup plus 2 tablespoons all-purpose flour
½ teaspoon salt
½ teaspoon vanilla
1½ cups old-fashioned rolled oats
½ cup sweetened flaked coconut
a 6-ounce package semisweet chocolate chips
⅓ cup roasted peanuts
½ cup raisins

In a bowl cream the butter and the shortening with the sugars and beat in the egg, the baking soda mixture, the flour, the salt, and the vanilla. Stir in the oats, the coconut, the chocolate chips, the peanuts, and the raisins and combine the dough well. Spoon rounded tablespoons of the dough about 4 inches apart on greased baking sheets and with a fork dipped in cold water flatten and spread each mound into a thin round, approximately 2½ to 3 inches in diameter. Bake the cookies in batches in the middle of a preheated 375° F. oven for 8 to 10 minutes, or until they are golden, transfer them with a spatula to racks, and let them cool. The cookies keep in an airtight container at room temperature for 5 days. Makes about 30 large cookies.

PHOTO ON PAGE 68

Irish Chewy Oatmeal Squares

1 stick (½ cup) unsalted butter
¾ cup firmly packed light brown sugar
1 tablespoon light corn syrup
¾ teaspoon salt
1 teaspoon vanilla
2¼ cups quick-cooking rolled oats (not instant)

In a saucepan melt the butter over moderately low heat, stir in the sugar, the corn syrup, the salt, and the vanilla, and bring the mixture to a boil, stirring occasionally. Remove the pan from the heat and stir in the oats. Spread the mixture evenly in a greased 13- by 9-inch baking pan, smoothing the top, and bake it in the middle of a preheated 350° F. oven for 20 minutes. (The mixture will not be set.) While it is still warm, cut the confection into squares and let it cool in the pan on a rack. (The confection will harden as it cools.)

Oatmeal Date Bars

2 cups pitted dates, chopped
1 teaspoon freshly grated orange rind
½ cup fresh orange juice
2 sticks (1 cup) unsalted butter, cut into bits
    and softened
1¼ cups all-purpose flour
¾ cup firmly packed light brown sugar
¼ cup granulated sugar
2¼ cups old-fashioned rolled oats
½ teaspoon salt

In a heavy saucepan combine the dates, the rind, the orange juice, and ½ cup water, bring the mixture to a boil, mashing the dates with a fork, and simmer the mixture, stirring and mashing it with the fork, for 3 minutes. Remove the pan from the heat and let the purée cool. In a bowl combine the butter, the flour, the sugars, the oats, and the salt and blend the mixture well with your fingers. Press half the oatmeal mixture evenly in a greased 13- by 9-inch baking pan, spread the date purée over it, and top it with the remaining oatmeal mixture, spreading and pressing it to form an even layer. Bake the mixture in the middle of a preheated 375° F. oven for 40 minutes, or until it is golden, let it cool completely in the pan on a rack, and cut it into bars.

Oatmeal Shortbread

1 stick (½ cup) unsalted butter, softened
⅓ cup firmly packed light brown sugar
¾ cup plus 2 tablespoons all-purpose flour
½ teaspoon salt
¾ teaspoon cinnamon
⅔ cup old-fashioned rolled oats

In a bowl with an electric mixer cream the butter, add

the brown sugar, and beat the mixture until it is light and fluffy. In another bowl whisk together the flour, the salt, and the cinnamon, add the flour mixture to the butter mixture with the oats, and stir the mixture until it is just combined. Press the mixture evenly into an ungreased 9-inch pie pan, smoothing the top, and prick it all over with a fork. Bake the shortbread in the middle of a preheated 350° F. oven for 40 minutes, or until it is golden. While the shortbread is still warm, score it all the way through into wedges with the tines of a fork, let it cool completely in the pan on a rack, and break it into wedges.

Praline Butter Cookies

1 cup granulated sugar
1½ cups pecan halves
2 sticks (1 cup) unsalted butter, softened
⅔ cup firmly packed dark brown sugar
1 large egg
¼ teaspoon almond extract
2¼ cups all-purpose flour
1 teaspoon baking soda
1 teaspoon salt

In a heavy saucepan dissolve the granulated sugar in ⅓ cup water over moderate heat, stirring, bring the mixture to a boil, and boil it, undisturbed, until it begins to turn golden. Boil the syrup, swirling the pan, until it turns a deep caramel, stir in the pecans, and pour the mixture immediately onto a piece of foil, spreading the pecans into a single layer. Let the praline cool completely, peel off the foil, and in a food processor grind the praline coarse.

In a large bowl with an electric mixer cream together the butter and the brown sugar, add the egg and the almond extract, and beat the mixture until it is smooth. Sift the flour with the baking soda and the salt into the butter mixture, add the praline, and stir the batter until it is combined well. Drop rounded teaspoons of the batter 2 inches apart onto well-buttered baking sheets and bake the cookies in batches in the middle of a preheated 350° F. oven for 12 to 15 minutes, or until they are golden. Let the cookies cool on the baking sheets for 5 minutes, or until they can be removed easily, transfer them to racks, and let them cool completely. *The cookies may be made 1 week in advance and kept in an airtight container.* Makes about 50 cookies.

PHOTO ON PAGE 80

PIES, TARTS, AND PASTRIES

Deep-Dish Blueberry Pie

For the dough
1⅓ cups all-purpose flour
2 tablespoons sugar
¼ teaspoon salt
1 stick (½ cup) cold unsalted butter,
    cut into bits
1 large egg yolk, beaten lightly with
    1½ tablespoons ice water
For the filling
3 tablespoons cornstarch
3 tablespoons rum or water
1 tablespoon fresh lemon juice
⅔ cup sugar
¼ teaspoon cinnamon
8 cups blueberries, picked over

an egg wash made by beating 1 egg
    with 2 teaspoons water
1½ tablespoons sugar

In order to serve 12 people make 2 pies.

Make the dough: In a bowl stir together the flour, the sugar, and the salt, add the butter, and blend the mixture until it resembles coarse meal. Add the yolk mixture, toss the mixture until the liquid is incorporated, and form the dough into a ball. Dust the dough with flour and chill it, wrapped in plastic wrap, for 1 hour.

Make the filling: In a large bowl stir together the cornstarch, the rum, the lemon juice, the sugar, and the cinnamon, add the blueberries, and combine the mixture well.

Pour the filling into a 6- to 7-cup gratin dish or other shallow baking dish. Roll out the dough slightly larger than the dish on a floured surface and drape it over the filling. Fold the overhang under, pressing the dough to the edge of the dish, and crimp the edge decoratively. Make slits and holes in the crust for air vents, brush the crust with the egg wash, and sprinkle it with the sugar. Bake the pie on a baking sheet in the middle of a preheated 375° F. oven for 1 hour to 1¼ hours, or until the filling is bubbly and the crust is golden. Transfer the pie to a rack and let it cool. The pie may be made 1 day in advance and kept at room temperature.

PHOTO ON PAGE 59

Mince Pie

For the filling
5 Granny Smith apples, peeled, cored, and
    chopped
1 cup dark raisins
1 cup golden raisins
½ cup chopped mixed candied citrus peels
1 teaspoon freshly grated lemon zest
1¼ cups firmly packed dark brown sugar
2 tablespoons unsalted butter
1 tablespoon cider vinegar
½ teaspoon salt
1½ teaspoons cinnamon
1 teaspoon ground allspice
¼ teaspoon freshly grated nutmeg
¼ teaspoon freshly ground black pepper
¼ cup dark rum

2 recipes *pâte brisée* (page 94)
an egg wash made by beating 1 egg with
    1 teaspoon water
vanilla ice cream as an
    accompaniment

Make the filling: In a kettle combine the apples, the raisins, the candied peels, the zest, the brown sugar, the butter, the vinegar, the salt, the cinnamon, the allspice, the nutmeg, the pepper, and 1½ cups water, bring the mixture to a boil, stirring, and simmer it, stirring occasionally, for 40 minutes, or until the liquid is very thick. Add the rum and simmer the mixture, stirring, for 10 minutes, or until the liquid is almost evaporated. Let the filling cool, transfer it to an airtight container, and chill it for 1 day to allow the flavors to develop. *The filling may be made 1 week in advance and kept chilled.*

Roll out half the dough into a round slightly more than ⅛ inch thick on a lightly floured surface, fit it into a 9-inch (1-quart) deep-dish pie plate, and trim the edge, leaving a 1-inch overhang. Mound the filling in the shell. Roll out the remaining dough in the same manner, cover the filling with the rolled-out dough, and trim the top edge, leaving a 1-inch overhang. Fold the top overhang under the bottom overhang, crimp the edge to seal it, and cut decorative vents in the top crust. Brush the crust with the egg wash and bake the pie in the middle of a preheated 425° F. oven for 30 minutes. Reduce the heat to 375° F. and bake the pie for 25 to 30 minutes more, or until the filling is bubbly. Let the pie cool and serve it warm with the ice cream.

Strawberry Coconut Chiffon Pie

For the shell
1½ cups graham cracker crumbs
¾ cup sweetened flaked coconut
2 tablespoons sugar
¼ teaspoon salt
¾ stick (6 tablespoons) unsalted butter,
    melted

For the filling
2 pints strawberries,
    hulled and thinly sliced
⅓ cup sugar
1 tablespoon fresh lemon juice
2 tablespoons coconut-flavored rum or
    dark rum if desired
1½ envelopes (1½ tablespoons)
    unflavored gelatin
½ cup well chilled heavy cream

For garnish
½ cup well chilled heavy cream
¼ cup sweetened flaked coconut,
    toasted lightly

Make the shell: In a bowl combine well the crumbs, the coconut, the sugar, and the salt, add the butter, and with a fork combine the mixture well. Press the mixture onto the bottom and up the side of a 10-inch (1½-quart) glass pie plate, bake the shell in a preheated 375° F. oven for 10 to 12 minutes, or until the edges are just golden, and let it cool on a rack.

Make the filling: In a metal bowl with a potato masher mash the strawberries with the sugar, the lemon juice, and the rum and let the mixture stand for 30 minutes. In a small saucepan sprinkle the gelatin over ⅓ cup cold water, let it soften for 5 minutes, and heat the mixture over low heat, stirring, until it is melted. Stir the gelatin into the strawberry mixture, set the bowl in a larger bowl of ice and cold water, and stir the mixture until it has the consistency of raw egg whites. In a chilled bowl beat the cream until it just holds stiff peaks and fold it into the strawberry mixture gently but thoroughly.

Pour the filling into the shell, smooth the top decoratively, and chill the pie for 4 hours, or until it is set. *The pie may be made 1 day in advance and kept covered loosely and chilled.*

Prepare the garnish: In a chilled bowl beat the cream until it is stiff, transfer it to a pastry bag fitted with a decorative tip, and pipe it around the edge of the pie. Sprinkle the pie with the toasted coconut.

Sweet Potato Maple Pie with Pecan Crust

For the crust
1 cup pecans
2 tablespoons sugar
1¼ cups all-purpose flour
¾ stick (6 tablespoons) cold unsalted butter,
    cut into bits
½ teaspoon salt
raw rice for weighting the shell

For the filling
2½ cups sweet potato purée (page 230)
1 cup half-and-half
3 large eggs, beaten lightly
¾ cup pure maple syrup
1½ teaspoons maple extract
1 teaspoon cinnamon
1 teaspoon ground ginger
¼ teaspoon ground cloves
½ teaspoon salt

whipped cream as an accompaniment
pure maple syrup as an accompaniment

Make the crust: In a food processor grind coarse the pecans with the sugar and transfer the mixture to a bowl. In the food processor blend together the flour, the butter, and the salt until the mixture resembles meal and add it to the pecan mixture. Add 3 tablespoons ice water, toss the mixture until the water is incorporated, and press the dough onto the bottom and up the side of a 9-inch (1 quart) deep-dish pie plate, crimping the edge decoratively. Prick the crust with a fork and chill it for 30 minutes. *The crust may be made 2 weeks in advance and kept wrapped well and frozen.* Line the crust with foil, fill the foil with the rice, and bake the crust in the middle of a preheated 425° F. oven for 7 minutes. Remove the rice and foil carefully, bake the crust for 5 minutes more, and let it cool.

Make the filling: In a large bowl whisk together the sweet potato purée, the half-and-half, the eggs, the maple syrup, the maple extract, the cinnamon, the ginger, the cloves, and the salt until the filling is smooth. *The filling may be made 2 days in advance and kept covered and chilled.*

Pour the filling into the crust, bake the pie in the middle of a preheated 350° F. oven for 40 to 45 minutes, or until it is just set in the middle, and let it cool on a rack. Serve the pie sliced, topped with the whipped cream, and drizzled with the maple syrup.

Sweet Potato Purée

2 pounds sweet potatoes (about 3), peeled and
 cut into 1-inch cubes

On a steamer rack set over boiling water steam the potatoes, covered, for 20 to 25 minutes, or until they are
very tender. Force the potatoes through a ricer of in a
large bowl beat them with an electric mixer until they
are smooth. Makes about 2½ cups purée.

Red-Wine Poached Pear and Custard Tart

1½ recipes *pâte brisée* (page 94)
raw rice for weighting the shell
4 large firm-ripe Bosc or Anjou pears (about
 2 pounds), peeled, cored, and halved
 lengthwise
1½ cups dry red wine
a 2-inch cinnamon stick
3 cloves
1 cup sugar plus an additional ⅓ cup if desired
1¼ cups heavy cream
3 large eggs, beaten lightly
¼ teaspoon salt
1 teaspoon vanilla
⅛ teaspoon ground cinnamon

Roll out the *pâte brisée* ⅛ inch thick on a lightly
floured surface and fit it into a 10-inch tart pan with a
removable fluted rim. Prick the shell with a fork and
chill it for 30 minutes. Line the shell with foil, fill the
foil with the rice, and bake the shell in the lower third of
a preheated 425° F. oven for 15 minutes. Remove the
foil and the rice carefully, bake the shell for 10 minutes
more, or until it is golden, and let it cool in the pan on a
rack.

In a kettle just large enough to hold the pears in one
layer combine the wine, 1½ cups water, the cinnamon
stick, and the cloves, bring the mixture to a boil, and
add the pears. Poach the pears at a bare simmer, basting
them and turning them occasionally, for 20 minutes, or
until they are tender. Transfer the pears with a slotted
spoon to paper towels to drain. (If desired, whisk the additional ⅓ cup sugar into the wine mixture, boil the mixture until it is reduced to about ¼ cup, and serve the
syrup warm or at room temperature with the tart.)

In a bowl whisk together the remaining 1 cup sugar,
the cream, the eggs, the salt, the vanilla, and the ground
cinnamon. Arrange the pears decoratively in the tart

shell and pour the custard around them. Bake the tart on
a baking sheet in the middle of a pre-heated 350° F. oven
for 30 to 35 minutes, or until the custard is set, and let it
cool on a rack.

Apple Strudel Tartlets with Hard Sauce

two 16- by 12-inch sheets of *phyllo*, stacked
 between sheets of wax paper and covered
 with a dampened kitchen towel
3 tablespoons unsalted butter, melted
 and cooled
2 McIntosh apples
1 tablespoon golden raisins
1 tablespoon chopped pecans
1 tablespoon firmly packed light brown sugar
For the hard sauce
1 tablespoon unsalted butter, softened
4 tablespoons confectioners' sugar
½ teaspoon Calvados, rum, or bourbon

Lay 1 sheet of the *phyllo* on a work surface, brush it
lightly with some of the butter, and cut it into 8 rectangles, each approximately 6 by 4 inches. Arrange the
rectangles, overlapping them slightly, in a ¼-cup tartlet
tin or muffin tin. Repeat the procedure in another tin
with the remaining sheet of *phyllo* and some of the
remaining butter. Peel and core the apples, cut them
lengthwise into eighths, and slice them thin crosswise.
In a bowl toss the apples with the remaining butter, the
raisins, the pecans, and the brown sugar, divide the filling between the tartlets, and bake the tartlets in a jelly-
roll pan in the lower third of a preheated 400° F. oven for
20 minutes, or until the *phyllo* is crisp and golden.

Make the hard sauce while the tartlets are baking: In a
bowl whisk together the butter, the confectioners' sugar, and the Calvados until the mixture is smooth. Whisk
in ½ teaspoon hot water, whisk the sauce until it is
fluffy, and chill it.

Transfer each tartlet carefully to a plate and top the
tartlets while they are still hot with the hard sauce.
Serves 2.

PHOTO ON BACK JACKET

Chocolate Caramel Walnut Tartlets

2 recipes *pâte brisée* (page 94)
4 ounces fine-quality bittersweet chocolate,
 cut into bits

1¾ or 2½ cups walnuts, chopped coarse
    and toasted lightly
¾ cup sugar
1½ cups light corn syrup
3 tablespoons unsalted butter
4 large eggs
1½ teaspoons vanilla
lightly sweetened whipped cream
    as an accompaniment
grated bittersweet chocolate for decoration

Roll out half the dough ⅛ inch thick on a floured surface and cut out four 6-inch rounds, reserving the scraps. Fit the rounds into tart pans measuring 4 inches across the top and ¾ inch deep and using a rolling pin roll over the pan edges to trim the excess dough. Roll out the remaining dough in the same manner, cut out 4 more rounds, reserving the scraps, and repeat the procedure with the reserved scraps to cut out 4 more rounds. (Alternatively the dough may be fitted into two 9-inch tart pans with removable bottoms.) *The pastry shells may be made 5 days in advance and kept covered and frozen on a baking sheet. Let the shells stand at room temperature for 30 minutes before continuing with the recipe.* In a small bowl set over barely simmering water melt the chocolate, stirring occasionally until it is smooth, brush it onto the bottoms of the shells, and chill the shells for 15 minutes. Divide 1¾ cups of the walnuts among the shells. (If using 9-inch tart pans, divide 2½ cups walnuts between the shells.)

In a large heavy skillet cook the sugar over moderately high heat, stirring constantly with a fork, until it is melted completely and a deep golden caramel, remove the skillet from the heat, and add the corn syrup. Cook the mixture, stirring, until it is smooth and stir in the butter, stirring until it is melted. In a bowl whisk together the eggs and the vanilla, add the caramel mixture in a slow stream, whisking, and whisk the mixture until it is combined well. Divide the mixture among the shells, coating the walnuts completely, and bake the tartlets on the baking sheet in the middle of a preheated 375° F. oven for 35 to 40 minutes, or until the pastry is pale golden. Transfer the tartlets to racks and let them cool. *The tartlets may be made 1 day in advance and kept at*

room temperature. Serve the tartlets with the whipped cream and the grated chocolate. Serves 12.

PHOTO ON PAGE 38

Pumpkin Rum Raisin Tartlets

1½ recipes *pâte brisée* (page 94)
½ cup golden raisins
¼ cup dark rum
½ cup sugar
¾ teaspoon cinnamon
¼ teaspoon freshly grated nutmeg
⅛ teaspoon ground cloves
2 large eggs, beaten lightly
1 cup canned solid pack pumpkin purée
½ cup milk
⅔ cup heavy cream

Roll out the dough ⅛ inch thick on a floured surface and cut out eight 5½-inch rounds. Fit the rounds into tart pans measuring 4 inches across the top and ¾ inch deep and roll a rolling pin over the pan edges to trim the excess dough. *The pastry shells may be made 5 days in advance and kept covered and frozen on a baking sheet. Let the shells stand at room temperature for 10 minutes before continuing with the recipe.*

In a small bowl let the raisins macerate in the rum for 1 hour. Drain the raisins in a sieve set over a small bowl and divide the raisins among the shells. In a bowl whisk together the rum, the sugar, the cinnamon, the nutmeg, the cloves, the eggs, the pumpkin, the milk, and ⅓ cup of the cream, pour the mixture into the shells, and bake the tartlets on a baking sheet in the lower third of a preheated 425° F. oven for 10 minutes. Reduce the heat to 350° F. and bake the tartlets for 20 to 25 minutes more, or until a knife inserted in the center of 1 of the tartlets comes out clean. Let the tartlets cool in the pans on racks until they can be handled, turn them out onto the racks, and let them cool completely. *The tartlets may be made 1 day in advance and kept covered in a cool place.* In a bowl beat the remaining ⅓ cup cream until it just holds stiff peaks, transfer it to a pastry bag fitted with a decorative tip, and pipe rosettes around the edges of the tartlets. Makes 8 tartlets.

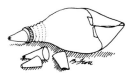

Eclairs au Moka
(Mocha Eclairs)

For the éclairs
½ stick (¼ cup) unsalted butter, cut into pieces
⅛ teaspoon salt
½ cup all-purpose flour
3 large eggs
For the glaze
2 to 3 tablespoons heavy cream, or to taste
1 ounce fine-quality bittersweet chocolate,
   chopped

mocha mousse filling (recipe follows)

Make the éclairs: In a heavy saucepan bring to a boil ½ cup water with the butter and the salt over high heat. Reduce the heat to moderate, add the flour all at once, and beat the mixture with a wooden spoon until it leaves the side of the pan and forms a ball. Transfer the mixture to a bowl and with an electric mixer beat in 2 of the eggs, 1 at a time, beating well after each addition. Beat the remaining egg lightly and add 1 to 2 tablespoonfuls of the beaten egg to the batter until the batter is stiff enough to just fall from a spoon. Spoon the batter into a large pastry bag fitted with a ¾-inch plain tip and onto 1 buttered baking sheet pipe it into eight 4½-inch lengths, each about 1 inch wide, leaving 2 inches between the lengths. Bake the éclairs in the upper third of a preheated 425° F. oven for 15 minutes, reduce the heat to 400° F., and bake the éclairs for 15 minutes more, or until they are puffed and crisp. Pierce the side of each éclair with the tip of a sharp knife and let the éclairs stand in the 400° F. oven with the door slightly ajar for 5 minutes. Transfer the éclairs to a rack and let them cool. *The éclairs may be made 1 day in advance and kept in an airtight container*.

Make the glaze: In a small saucepan bring the cream just to a boil and pour 2 tablespoons of it over the chocolate in a bowl. Stir the mixture until it is smooth and if necessary add enough of the remaining cream to form a thick but pourable mixture. Transfer the glaze to a small sealable plastic bag, forcing out the air.

Assemble the éclairs: With the end of a chopstick or similar instrument make 2 holes in the bottom of each éclair. Transfer the mocha mousse filling to a pastry bag fitted with a ⅜-inch plain tip and pipe it into the éclairs through the holes. Cut a small slice from one corner of the sealable plastic bag to form a small hole and pipe the glaze in a zigzag pattern over the tops of the éclairs.

Chill the éclairs, uncovered, for 1 hour to set the glaze. *The éclairs may be assembled 1 day in advance and kept covered and chilled*. Makes 8 or 9 éclairs.

PHOTO ON PAGE 49

Mocha Mousse Filling

¾ cup milk
2 teaspoons cornstarch
2 large egg yolks
3 tablespoons sugar
2 teaspoons instant espresso powder
1 tablespoon unsalted butter, softened
½ teaspoon vanilla
1 ounce fine-quality bittersweet chocolate,
   chopped
¼ cup well chilled heavy cream

In a bowl whisk together ¼ cup of the milk, the cornstarch, and the yolks. In a small heavy saucepan combine the remaining ½ cup milk, the sugar, and the espresso, bring the mixture just to a boil, and add it to the yolk mixture in a slow stream, whisking. Pour the mixture into the pan, bring it to a boil, whisking constantly, and simmer the pastry cream, whisking constantly, for 1 minute. Transfer the pastry cream to a bowl, stir in the butter, the vanilla, and a pinch of salt, and cover its surface with plastic wrap. In a small bowl set over a pan of simmering water melt the chocolate with 1 tablespoon water and stir the mixture into the pastry cream. Chill the pastry cream, its surface covered with plastic wrap, for 2 hours, or until it is cold. In a chilled small bowl beat the cream until it just holds stiff peaks and fold it into the pastry cream gently but thoroughly. *The filling may be made 1 day in advance and kept covered and chilled.*

Banana, Cranberry, and Walnut Turnovers

1 small banana, cut into ¼-inch-thick slices
¼ cup cranberries, halved
¼ cup finely chopped walnuts, toasted lightly
2 teaspoons fresh lemon juice
1½ tablespoons light brown sugar plus
    additional for sprinkling the turnovers
1 teaspoon cornstarch
⅛ teaspoon cinnamon
¼ teaspoon vanilla
2 teaspoons unsalted butter, cut into bits
½ sheet (about ¼ pound) frozen packaged puff
    pastry, thawed

In a bowl toss together the banana, the cranberries, the walnuts, the lemon juice, 1½ tablespoons of the brown sugar, the cornstarch, the cinnamon, the vanilla, and the butter until the mixture is combined well. On a lightly floured surface roll out the dough into a 12- by 6-inch rectangle, cut it in half crosswise into two 6-inch squares, and brush the squares very lightly with water. Divide the fruit mixture between the 2 squares, centering it on a diagonal half of each square. Spread the filling within the halves, leaving a ½-inch border. Brush a little water along the outside edge of each empty half, fold the squares diagonally in half, and press the edges together. Pierce the turnovers decoratively with a fork, brush them lightly with water, and sprinkle them with the additional brown sugar. Bake the turnovers on a baking sheet in a preheated 425° F. oven for 15 to 17 minutes, or until they are puffed and golden, and serve them warm or at room temperature. Serves 2.

CUSTARDS, MOUSSES, AND PUDDINGS

Almond Flan
with Summer Fruit

1¾ cups sugar
3 cups milk
1 cup heavy cream
5 large whole eggs
5 large egg yolks
¾ teaspoon almond extract
1 teaspoon vanilla
½ pint strawberries
½ pint blueberries, picked over
2 peaches, cut lengthwise into sixths
    and sliced crosswise
mint sprigs for garnish
    if desired

In a small heavy saucepan dissolve ¾ cup of the sugar in ¼ cup water over moderate heat, stirring, bring the syrup to a boil, covered, and boil it, uncovered and undisturbed, until it begins to turn golden. Boil the syrup, swirling the pan, until it is a deep caramel, pour it immediately into a loaf pan, 9 by 5 by 3 inches, and swirl the pan to coat the bottom and ½ inch up the sides. Let the caramel harden.

In a saucepan scald the milk and the cream. In a large bowl whisk together the whole eggs, the yolks, and the remaining 1 cup sugar, add the scalded milk mixture in a stream, whisking, and stir in the almond extract and the vanilla. Pour the custard through a fine sieve into the loaf pan, set the pan in a baking dish, and add enough hot water to the dish to reach halfway up the sides of the pan. Bake the custard, covered with a double layer of foil, in the middle of a preheated 325° F. oven for 1 hour and 15 minutes, or until a knife inserted 1 inch from the edge comes out clean. (The *flan* will continue to set as it cools.) Remove the pan from the dish and remove the foil. Let the *flan* cool on a rack and chill it, covered, for 3 hours. *The* flan *can be made 1 day in advance and kept covered and chilled.* Run a thin knife around the sides of the pan, invert a platter over the pan, and invert the *flan* onto it. Arrange the strawberries, the blueberries, and the peaches around the *flan* and garnish the *flan* with the mint sprigs. Serves 6.

PHOTO ON PAGE 55

Coeurs à la Crème with Strawberry Sauce

For the sauce
1 pint strawberries, hulled
2 tablespoons dry red wine
3 tablespoons sugar

8 ounces cream cheese
1 cup whole-milk cottage cheese
¼ cup heavy cream
1 teaspoon vanilla
¼ cup plus 1 tablespoon sugar

Make the sauce: Dice enough of the strawberries to measure ⅓ cup and reserve them, covered and chilled. In a saucepan combine the remaining strawberries, quartered, the wine, and the sugar, bring the mixture to a boil, breaking up the strawberries, and simmer it, covered partially, stirring occasionally, for 20 minutes. Force the mixture through a fine sieve into a bowl and chill the sauce, covered.

Line six ½-cup *coeur à la crème* molds with 6-inch squares of a triple thickness of rinsed and squeezed cheesecloth, letting the excess hang over the edges. In a food processor blend the cream cheese, the cottage cheese, the cream, the vanilla, and the sugar until the mixture is smooth. Fill the molds with the cheese mixture, fold the excess cheesecloth over the mixture, and chill the *coeurs à la crème*, set in a jelly-roll pan, overnight in the refrigerator.

Fold back the cheesecloth from the tops of the *coeurs à la crème*, invert each mold onto a dessert plate, and discard the cheesecloth. Spoon some of the sauce around each *coeur à la crème* and sprinkle it with some of the reserved strawberries. Serves 6.

Cappuccino Crème Brûlée

1 cup heavy cream
1 cup milk
⅓ cup granulated sugar
1 tablespoon instant espresso powder
two 2-inch cinnamon sticks
4 large egg yolks
2 tablespoons firmly packed dark
   brown sugar

In a small saucepan combine the cream and the milk with half the granulated sugar, the espresso powder, and the cinnamon sticks and heat the mixture over moderately low heat, stirring occasionally, until it is hot. In a bowl whisk together well the yolks and the remaining granulated sugar and add the milk mixture in a stream, whisking. Remove the cinnamon sticks and combine the mixture well. Divide the custard among four ⅔-cup ramekins set in a baking pan, add enough hot water to the pan to reach halfway up the sides of the ramekins, and bake the custards in the middle of a preheated 325° F. oven for 40 minutes, or until they are just set. Remove the ramekins from the pan, let the custards cool, and chill them, covered, for at least 4 hours. *The custards may be made 2 days in advance and kept covered and chilled.*

Blot dry the tops of the custards with paper towels and sprinkle them evenly with the brown sugar. Put the custards under a preheated broiler about 1 inch from the heat (if necessary, to reach the heat set the ramekins on an inverted baking pan), turning them to caramelize the sugar evenly and being careful not to let the sugar burn, for 2 minutes. Serve the *crème brûlée* immediately. Makes 4 *crèmes brûlées*.

PHOTO ON PAGE 26

Southern Coffee Parfaits

4 envelopes unflavored gelatin
½ cup Amaretto or praline-flavored liqueur
¼ cup Southern Comfort
6¼ cups hot strong freshly brewed coffee
1⅓ cups sugar
2 tablespoons instant espresso powder
¼ teaspoon salt

colored sugars for decoration if desired
3 cups well-chilled heavy cream

In a very small saucepan sprinkle the gelatin over the Amaretto and the Southern Comfort and let it soften for 5 minutes. In a large metal bowl combine the brewed coffee, 1 cup of the sugar, the espresso powder, and the salt and stir the mixture until the sugar is dissolved. Heat the gelatin mixture over low heat, stirring, until the gelatin is dissolved and stir it into the coffee mixture.

Moisten lightly the rims of 12 parfait glasses, dip the rims in the colored sugars, and spoon 2 teaspoons of the coffee mixture into each glass. Set the metal bowl in a larger bowl of ice and cold water, stir the coffee mixture until it begins to thicken, and remove the bowl from the ice water. In a large bowl with an electric mixer beat 2 cups of the cream with the remaining ⅓ cup sugar until it holds soft peaks. Return the metal bowl to the bowl of ice water and stir the coffee mixture until it is the consistency of raw egg white. With a large whisk stir the whipped cream into the coffee mixture, a little at a time, whisk the mixture until it is combined thoroughly, and divide it among the glasses. Chill the parfaits for 4 hours, or until they are set. *The parfaits may be made 1 day in advance and kept chilled.* In a chilled bowl beat the remaining 1 cup cream until it just holds soft peaks and spoon it onto the parfaits. Makes 12 parfaits.

PHOTO ON PAGE 80

Lemon and Candied Ginger Mousse with Berries
¾ teaspoon unflavored gelatin
5 tablespoons fresh lemon juice
2 large eggs, separated, the whites at
    room temperature
6 tablespoons sugar
1½ teaspoons freshly grated lemon zest
1 tablespoon unsalted butter
2 tablespoons minced candied ginger
½ cup raspberries, blueberries, or sliced
    hulled strawberries

In a small bowl sprinkle the gelatin over 1 tablespoon of the lemon juice and let it soften for 5 minutes. In a small saucepan whisk together the yolks and 4 tablespoons of the sugar, add the zest, the remaining 4 tablespoons lemon juice, and the butter, and bring the mixture to a boil, whisking. Remove the pan from the heat, add the gelatin mixture, and whisk the mixture until the gelatin is dissolved. Strain the mixture through a fine sieve into a metal bowl set in a larger bowl of ice and cold water, stir in the ginger, and stir the mixture until it is cold and the consistency of raw egg white. In a bowl with an electric mixer beat the whites with a pinch of salt until they hold soft peaks, add the remaining 2 tablespoons sugar, beating, and beat the whites until they hold stiff peaks. Stir about ½ cup of the whites into the lemon mixture to lighten it and fold in the remaining whites gently but thoroughly. Divide the mousse between 2 serving glasses, chill it for 20 minutes, and top each serving with half the berries. Serves 2.

Mocha Meringue Mousses
4 ounces fine-quality bittersweet
    chocolate, chopped
1½ tablespoons instant espresso powder
    dissolved in 1 tablespoon hot water
¼ cup dark rum
2 large egg yolks
⅔ cup sugar
4 large egg whites at room temperature
¼ teaspoon cream of tartar
whipped cream and chocolate curls
    for garnish

In a bowl set over barely simmering water melt the chocolate with the espresso mixture and the rum, whisking until the mixture is smooth, and remove the bowl from the heat. Whisk in the yolks, 1 at a time, whisk the mixture until it is combined well, and let it cool. In a small heavy saucepan combine the sugar with ⅓ cup water and bring the mixture to a boil, stirring until the sugar is dissolved. Boil the syrup until it registers 248° F. on a candy thermometer and remove the pan from the heat. While the syrup is boiling, in a bowl with an electric mixer beat the whites with a pinch of salt until they are foamy, add the cream of tartar, and beat the whites until they hold soft peaks. With the mixer running add the hot syrup in a stream and beat the meringue on medium speed until it is cool. Whisk about 1 cup of the meringue into the chocolate mixture to lighten it and fold the chocolate mixture into the remaining meringue gently but thoroughly. Divide the mousses among 6 serving glasses and chill it, covered, for at least 2 hours or overnight. Just before serving, garnish the mousses with the whipped cream and the chocolate curls. Serves 6.

Lemon Sponge Pudding

½ stick (¼ cup) unsalted butter, softened
¾ cup granulated sugar
3 large eggs, separated, the whites
   at room temperature
⅓ cup fresh lemon juice, or to taste
⅓ cup all-purpose flour
1 tablespoon freshly grated lemon rind
¼ teaspoon salt
1½ cups milk
a pinch of cream of tartar
confectioners' sugar for sifting

In a large bowl with an electric mixer cream together the butter and the granulated sugar and beat in the yolks, 1 at a time, beating well after each addition. Beat in the lemon juice, the flour, the rind, and the salt, add the milk in a stream, beating, and beat the mixture until it is combined well. In a bowl with the beaters, cleaned, beat the whites with the cream of tartar and a pinch of salt until they hold stiff peaks. Stir one fourth of the whites into the lemon mixture, fold in the remaining whites gently but thoroughly, and transfer the mixture to a buttered 8-inch-square baking pan. Set the baking pan in a deeper pan, add enough hot water to the pan to reach halfway up the sides of the baking pan, and bake the pudding in the middle of a preheated 350° F. oven for 45 to 50 minutes, or until it is puffed and the top is golden. Sift the confectioners' sugar over the top of the pudding. (The dessert will separate, forming a custard-like sauce on the bottom and a sponge layer on the top.) Serve the pudding warm or chilled. Spoon the sponge layer onto dessert plates and spoon some of the sauce over each serving. Serves 6.

Creamy Cinnamon Rice Pudding with Fresh Fruit

½ cup long-grain rice (not converted)
1 vanilla bean, split lengthwise
4 cups milk
¾ cup sugar
¾ teaspoon salt
two 3-inch cinnamon sticks, halved
3 large egg yolks
1 tablespoon cornstarch
¼ teaspoon vanilla
1 tablespoon unsalted butter
½ cup heavy cream
1 cup diced pineapple

1 cup diced papaya
1 cup raspberries
ground cinnamon for garnish

In a saucepan of boiling water blanch the rice for 5 minutes and drain it well. Scrape the seeds from the vanilla bean pod and reserve them and the pod. In a large heavy saucepan combine the rice with 3 cups of the milk, ½ cup of the sugar, the salt, the cinnamon sticks, and the reserved vanilla seeds and pod, bring the mixture to a boil, stirring, and simmer it, covered, for 55 to 60 minutes, or until the rice is very tender and most of the liquid is absorbed. Cook the mixture, uncovered, over low heat, stirring, for 3 to 5 minutes, or until all liquid is absorbed and the mixture is very thick. Transfer the mixture to a bowl, discarding the vanilla pod and the cinnamon sticks.

In a saucepan combine the remaining 1 cup milk and 2 tablespoons of the remaining sugar and bring the mixture just to a boil. In a bowl whisk together the yolks, the cornstarch, and the remaining 2 tablespoons sugar until the mixture is combined well, add the milk mixture in a stream, whisking, and pour the mixture back into the pan. Bring the mixture to a boil, whisking, and boil it, whisking, for 1 minute, or until it is very thick and smooth. Whisk in the vanilla and the butter, whisking until the butter is incorporated, and force the mixture through a sieve into the bowl containing the rice mixture. Stir the pudding until it is combined well, let it cool, covered with a buttered round of wax paper, and chill it, covered, for at least 3 hours or overnight.

Just before serving, beat the cream until it just holds stiff peaks, fold it into the pudding gently but thoroughly, and divide the pudding among 6 dishes. In a bowl toss together the pineapple, the papaya, and the raspberries, garnish the pudding with the fruit, and sprinkle it with the cinnamon. Makes about 4 cups, serving 6.

PHOTO ON PAGE 37

Tangerine and Vanilla Bavarian

For the vanilla mixture

1 envelope plus 1 teaspoon of
   unflavored gelatin
6 large egg yolks
⅓ cup sugar
1½ cups milk
1 vanilla bean, split lengthwise
1 teaspoon vanilla

For the tangerine mixture
1 envelope plus 1 teaspoon of
    unflavored gelatin
3 large egg yolks
¼ cup sugar
two 6-ounce cans frozen tangerine juice
    concentrate, thawed
1 tablespoon minced fresh tangerine peel

3 cups well chilled heavy cream
tangerine slices for garnish if desired

Make the vanilla mixture: In a bowl sprinkle the gelatin over ¼ cup cold water to soften for 5 minutes, set the bowl over a small saucepan of simmering water, and heat the mixture, stirring, until the gelatin is dissolved. Remove the pan from the heat and keep the gelatin mixture warm over it. In a bowl whisk together the yolks and the sugar, add the milk, scalded with the vanilla bean, in a slow stream, whisking, and transfer the mixture to a large heavy saucepan. Cook the mixture over moderately low heat, stirring constantly with a wooden spoon, until it is thick enough to coat the back of the spoon and a candy thermometer registers 175° F. (do not let the mixture boil). Strain the custard through a fine sieve into a bowl and stir in the gelatin mixture. Scrape the seeds from the vanilla bean and stir them into the custard with the vanilla.

Make the tangerine mixture: In a bowl sprinkle the gelatin over ¼ cup cold water to soften for 5 minutes, set the bowl over a small saucepan of simmering water, and heat the mixture, stirring, until the gelatin is dissolved. Remove the pan from the heat and keep the gelatin mixture warm over it. In a bowl whisk together the yolks and the sugar, add the tangerine concentrate, heated to a simmer with the tangerine peel, in a slow stream, whisking, and transfer the mixture to a large heavy saucepan. Cook the mixture over moderately low heat, stirring constantly with the wooden spoon, until it is thick enough to coat the back of the spoon and a candy thermometer registers 175° F. (do not let the mixture boil). Strain the custard through a fine sieve into a bowl and stir in the gelatin mixture.

Put the bowls of the vanilla mixture and the tangerine mixture into 2 larger bowls of ice and cold water, let the mixtures cool, stirring occasionally, until they are thickened very slightly (do not let them set), and remove them from the ice water. In a large bowl beat the cream until it just holds soft peaks, whisk half of it into the vanilla mixture, and whisk the remaining half into the tangerine mixture. Spoon the mixtures in alternating layers into a rinsed but not dried 1½-quart mold or divide them in layers between 2 (or more) molds whose combined volume is 1½ quarts. Chill the Bavarian, covered, for at least 6 hours or overnight. *The Bavarian may be made 2 days in advance and kept covered and chilled.* To unmold the Bavarian, dip the mold in a large bowl of hot water for 15 to 20 seconds, invert a platter over it, and invert the mold onto the platter. Garnish the mold with the tangerine slices. Serves 12 generously.

PHOTO ON PAGE 13

FROZEN DESSERTS

Coconut Caramel Granita
⅔ cup sugar
a 3½-ounce can (1 cup) sweetened flaked
    coconut, chopped coarse in a food
    processor

In a large deep heavy skillet cook the sugar over moderately high heat, stirring constantly with a fork, until it is melted completely and turns a deep golden caramel, add carefully 3 cups water (the mixture will bubble up), and cook the mixture, stirring, until the caramel is dissolved completely. In a bowl stir together the caramel mixture and the coconut and let the mixture cool. Transfer the mixture to 2 metal ice-cube trays without the dividers or a shallow metal pan and freeze it, stirring and crushing the lumps with a fork every 30 minutes, for 2 to 3 hours, or until it is firm but not frozen hard. Scrape the granita with a fork to lighten the texture and serve it in goblets. Makes about 1½ quarts.

Mocha Rum Granita

⅓ cup sugar
1 tablespoon dark rum
2 tablespoons instant espresso powder
1½ ounces fine-quality bittersweet chocolate,
  broken into bits

In a saucepan combine the sugar and 1½ cups water, bring the mixture to a boil, stirring until the sugar is dissolved, and stir in the rum. In a bowl whisk together the espresso powder and the rum syrup until the espresso powder is dissolved. Add the chocolate, whisk the mixture until the chocolate is melted, and let it cool. Transfer the mixture to 2 metal ice-cube trays without the dividers or a shallow metal pan and freeze it, stirring and crushing the lumps with a fork every 30 minutes, for 2 to 3 hours, or until it is firm but not frozen hard. Scrape the granita with a fork to lighten the texture and serve it in goblets. Makes about 1 quart.

Nectarine Ginger Granita

1 tablespoon chopped fresh gingerroot
¼ cup sugar
½ pound nectarines, pitted and chopped
  (about 1½ cups)
1½ teaspoons fresh lemon juice

In a food processor or blender chop fine the gingerroot, add 1 cup water, and blend the mixture well. In a saucepan combine the gingerroot mixture and the sugar, bring the mixture to a boil, stirring until the sugar is dissolved, and simmer it for 5 minutes. In the food processor purée the nectarines, force the purée through a fine sieve into a bowl, and force the gingerroot mixture through the sieve, pressing hard on the solids, into the bowl. Whisk in the lemon juice and let the mixture cool. Transfer the mixture to 2 metal ice-cube trays without the dividers or a shallow metal pan and freeze it, stirring and crushing the lumps with a fork every 30 minutes, for 2 to 3 hours, or until it is firm but not frozen hard. Scrape the granita with a fork to lighten the texture and serve it in goblets. Makes about 1 quart.

Papaya Lime Granita

⅓ cup sugar
1 papaya (about 1¾ pounds), halved, seeded,
  peeled, and chopped

3 tablespoons fresh lime juice
¼ teaspoon freshly grated lime zest

In a saucepan combine the sugar and 2 cups water, bring the mixture to a boil, stirring until the sugar is dissolved, and let the syrup cool. In a food processor or blender purée the papaya with the lime juice and the zest, add the syrup, and blend the mixture well. Transfer the mixture to 2 metal ice-cube trays without the dividers or a shallow metal pan and freeze it, stirring and crushing the lumps with a fork every 30 minutes, for 2 to 3 hours, or until it is firm but not frozen hard. Scrape the granita with a fork to lighten the texture and serve it in goblets. Makes about 1½ quarts.

Pineapple Grapefruit Granita

¼ cup sugar
6 ounces fresh pineapple, cut into chunks
  (about 1 cup)
½ cup grapefruit juice

In a saucepan combine the sugar and 1 cup water, bring the mixture to a boil, stirring until the sugar is dissolved, and let the syrup cool. In a food processor or blender purée the pineapple, add the syrup and the grapefruit juice, and blend the mixture well. Transfer the mixture to 2 metal ice-cube trays without the dividers or a shallow metal pan and freeze it, stirring and crushing the lumps with a fork every 30 minutes, for 2 to 3 hours, or until it is firm but not frozen hard. Scrape the granita with a fork to lighten the texture and serve it in goblets. Makes about 1 quart.

Eggnog Ice Cream

2 cups milk
2 cups heavy cream
1 vanilla bean, split lengthwise
7 large egg yolks
¾ cup sugar
½ teaspoon freshly grated nutmeg plus
  additional to taste
2 tablespoons dark rum
2 tablespoons Cognac or other brandy
½ cup finely chopped mixed glacéed fruits, or
  chopped toasted almonds, or finely

chopped bittersweet chocolate, or a combination of all three

In a large saucepan combine the milk, the cream, and the vanilla bean, bring the mixture just to a boil, and remove the pan from the heat. Let the mixture stand, covered, for 30 minutes. Scrape the seeds from the vanilla bean into the mixture and add the pod to the mixture. Return the pan to the heat and bring the mixture just to a boil. In a bowl whisk together the yolks, the sugar, and a pinch of salt, add the cream mixture in a stream, whisking, and transfer the custard to the pan. Cook the custard over moderately low heat, stirring constantly with a wooden spoon, until it coats the spoon (175° F. on a candy thermometer) and strain it through a fine sieve into a bowl. Let the custard cool, stir in ½ teaspoon of the nutmeg, the rum, and the Cognac, and chill the custard, covered, overnight. Stir in the additional nutmeg and freeze the custard in an ice-cream freezer according to the manufacturer's instructions until the ice cream is almost firm. Add the glacéed fruits and freeze the ice cream until it is firm. Makes about 1½ quarts.

PHOTO ON PAGE 79

Pignoli Ice Cream

2 large eggs
½ cup sugar
½ cup light corn syrup
1 cup heavy cream
1 cup milk
1½ tablespoons Sambuca or other anise-
    flavored liqueur
1 teaspoon fresh lemon juice, or to taste
½ teaspoon vanilla
½ cup pine nuts, toasted lightly and
    cooled

In a bowl with an electric mixer beat the eggs with the sugar and a pinch of salt until the mixture is thick and pale and beat in the corn syrup, the cream, the milk, the Sambuca, the lemon juice, and the vanilla. Freeze the mixture in an ice-cream freezer according to the manufacturer's instructions, adding the pine nuts during the last few minutes of freezing. Transfer the mixture to freezer containers and freeze it until it is firm. The ice cream is best if served within 2 days. Makes about 1 quart.

Tiramisù Ice-Cream Cake

a 10- to 12-ounce frozen pound cake, partially
    defrosted and sliced crosswise
    into ¼-inch-thick slices (about 28)
3 tablespoons dark rum
2 tablespoons Kahlúa or other
    coffee-flavored liqueur
For the mascarpone ice cream
2 large whole eggs
½ cup sugar
½ teaspoon vanilla
2 cups *mascarpone* (about 17½ ounces,
    available at most cheese shops and some
    specialty foods shops)
1 large egg white
For the espresso ice cream
2 large eggs
½ cup sugar
1 teaspoon vanilla
½ cup milk
1½ cups heavy cream
4 tablespoons instant espresso powder
    dissolved in 3 tablespoons boiling water

3 ounces fine-quality bittersweet chocolate, grated
mocha fudge sauce (recipe follows) as an
    accompaniment

On a baking sheet toast the pound cake slices in one layer in the middle of a preheated 350° F. oven for 8 to 10 minutes, or until they are colored lightly and dry. In a small bowl stir together the rum and the Kahlúa, brush the slices on both sides with the mixture, and let them cool on a rack.

Make the *mascarpone* ice cream: In a bowl with an electric mixer beat the whole eggs and the sugar until the mixture is thick and very pale and beat in the vanilla, a pinch of salt, and the *mascarpone* until the mixture is combined well. In a bowl beat the egg white until it holds soft peaks and beat it into the *mascarpone* mixture. Chill the mixture until it is cold and then freeze it in an ice-cream freezer according to the manufacturer's instructions.

Make the espresso ice cream: In a bowl with an electric mixer beat the eggs and the sugar until the mixture is thick and very pale and beat in the vanilla, the milk, the cream, and the espresso mixture, cooled. Chill the mixture until it is cold and freeze it in an ice-cream freezer according to the manufacturer's instructions.

Line a loaf pan, 9 by 5 by 3 inches, with plastic wrap, letting the plastic wrap hang over the edges by several inches. Arrange one row of cake slices, overlapping them slightly, down the middle of the pan, pack in half the *mascarpone* ice cream, smoothing it, and sprinkle the top with 3 tablespoons of the chocolate. Arrange one layer of cake slices, overlapping them slightly, to cover the chocolate completely, pack in the espresso ice cream, smoothing it, and sprinkle the top with 3 tablespoons of the remaining chocolate. Arrange another layer of cake slices in the same manner, pack in the remaining *mascarpone* ice cream, smoothing it, and arrange any remaining cake slices on top, packing the cake in firmly. Fold the plastic wrap over the top and freeze the cake overnight. Invert the cake onto a platter, discarding the plastic wrap, and sprinkle any remaining chocolate decoratively over the top. Slice the cake and serve it with the mocha fudge sauce. Serves 8.

PHOTO ON PAGE 62

Mocha Fudge Sauce

1 cup firmly packed dark brown sugar
½ cup light corn syrup
1½ tablespoons instant espresso powder,
    or to taste
3 ounces unsweetened chocolate, chopped
    coarse
½ cup heavy cream
2½ tablespoons Kahlúa, or to taste

In a small heavy saucepan combine the brown sugar, the corn syrup, and the espresso powder, bring the mixture to a boil over moderate heat, stirring, and boil it, stirring constantly, until the sugar is dissolved. Remove the pan from the heat, add the chocolate, stirring until it is melted, and stir in the cream, the Kahlúa, and a pinch of salt. Serve the sauce warm or at room temperature. Makes about 2 cups.

PHOTO ON PAGE 62

Strawberry-Amaretto Ice-Cream Cake Roll

For the ice cream
2 pints strawberries, hulled and chopped
⅓ cup Amaretto
⅓ cup plus ¼ cup sugar
4 large egg yolks
2 tablespoons cornstarch

2 cups half-and-half

For the angel food cake

1 cup egg whites (about 7 large egg whites)
   at room temperature
½ teaspoon cream of tartar
¾ cup granulated sugar
⅔ cup cake flour (not self-rising)
confectioners' sugar for dusting the cake

¾ cup well chilled heavy cream
decoratively sliced strawberries for garnish

Make the ice cream: In a bowl stir together the chopped strawberries, the Amaretto, and ⅓ cup of the sugar and let the strawberries macerate, covered, stirring occasionally, at room temperature overnight. In a blender purée half the strawberry mixture. In a small bowl whisk together well the yolks, the cornstarch, and the remaining ¼ cup sugar, whisk in the half-and-half, scalded, in a stream, and transfer the mixture to a heavy saucepan. Bring the mixture to a boil over moderate heat, whisking constantly, transfer it to a metal bowl set in a larger bowl of ice and cold water, and add the puréed strawberry mixture and the remaining strawberry mixture. Stir the custard until it is cold and freeze it in an ice-cream freezer according to the manufacturer's instructions.

Make the cake while the ice cream is freezing. Butter the bottom of a jelly-roll pan, 15½ by 10½ by 1 inches, line the bottom with wax paper, and butter the paper. (Do not butter the sides of the pan.) In a large bowl beat the whites with a pinch of salt until they are foamy, add the cream of tartar, and beat the whites until they hold soft peaks. Add ½ cup of the granulated sugar gradually, beating, and beat the meringue until it barely holds stiff peaks. Sift together the flour and the remaining ¼ cup sugar and sift the mixture in 2 batches onto the meringue, folding in each batch gently but thoroughly. Turn the batter into the jelly-roll pan, spreading it evenly, and bake it in the middle of a preheated 350° F. oven for 15 minutes, or until it is springy to the touch. Let the cake cool in the pan on a rack, run a knife around the edge, and dust the cake with the confectioners' sugar. Invert the cake onto a towel and discard the wax paper.

Line the jelly-roll pan with plastic wrap, spread the ice cream in the pan, and freeze it for 15 minutes, or until it is frozen partially but still malleable. Invert the ice cream onto the cake and discard the plastic wrap. Beginning with a long side, roll up the cake jelly-roll fash-

ion, lifting the towel underneath to aid in the rolling, wrap the cake in wax paper, and freeze it for at least 6 hours or up to 2 days. Unwrap the cake roll, trim the ends diagonally, and transfer the cake roll to a tray.

In a chilled bowl beat the cream until it is stiff, transfer it to a pastry bag fitted with a flat decorative tip, and pipe it onto the cake roll. (Alternatively, the whipped cream can be spread onto the cake roll.) Arrange the sliced strawberries decoratively on top.

Vanilla Ice Cream

2 vanilla beans
2 cups milk
4 large eggs
1 cup sugar
¼ teaspoon salt
2 tablespoons light corn syrup
2 cups heavy cream

Split the vanilla beans in half lengthwise, scrape the seeds from the pods, and in a small saucepan combine the seeds and the pods with the milk. Bring the milk just to a boil, stirring, remove the pan from the heat, and let the milk cool completely. In a large bowl with an electric mixer beat the eggs with the sugar, the salt, and the corn syrup until the mixture is very thick and pale and forms a ribbon when the beaters are lifted. Strain the milk into the bowl, pressing hard on the solids, add the cream, and combine the mixture well. Freeze the mixture in an ice-cream freezer according to the manufacturer's instructions. Makes about 2 quarts.

PHOTO ON PAGE 59

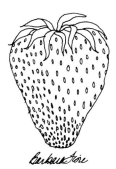

241

Blueberry Lemonade Sorbet

1½ cups blueberries
½ cup frozen lemonade concentrate
3 tablespoons honey or *crème de cassis*
For the garnish if desired
blueberries
decoratively cut lemon slices
mint sprigs

In a blender or food processor purée the blueberries with the lemonade concentrate, the honey, and 1 cup cold water and freeze the mixture in an ice-cream freezer according to the manufacturer's instructions. Transfer the *sorbet* to a freezer container and freeze it until it is firm. *The sorbet may be prepared 5 days in advance and kept tightly covered and chilled.* Arrange scoops of the *sorbet* in dessert dishes.

Garnish each *sorbet* with some of the blueberries, a lemon slice, and a mint sprig. Makes about 3 cups *sorbet*, serving 4.

PHOTO ON PAGE 56

Pomegranate and Lime Sorbet

1 cup sugar
3 pomegranates (each about 8 to 10 ounces),
    halved and squeezed gently to yield enough
    seeds and juice to measure about 2 cups
    plus additional seeds for garnish if desired
1 tablespoon plus 2 teaspoons strained fresh
    lime juice
1 large egg white

In a small saucepan combine the sugar and 1¼ cups water, bring the mixture to a boil, stirring until the sugar is dissolved, and simmer the syrup for 5 minutes. Let the syrup cool and chill it, covered, for 2 hours, or until it is cold.

In a food mill fitted with the medium disk and set over a bowl purée the pomegranate seeds and juice and strain the purée through a fine sieve into a bowl. Stir in the sugar syrup and the lime juice and freeze the mixture in an ice-cream freezer according to the manufacturer's instructions until it is almost frozen but still mushy. In a bowl beat the egg white until it is frothy, add it to the mixture, stirring, and freeze the *sorbet* in the ice-cream freezer until it is frozen. Serve the *sorbet* in scoops, sprinkled with the additional pomegranate seeds. Makes about 1 quart.

Raspberry Pineapple Sorbet

½ cup drained canned pineapple wedges plus
    additional for garnish
a 10-ounce package frozen raspberries in light
    syrup, broken into pieces
2 tablespoons white *crème de cacao*

In a blender blend ½ cup of the pineapple, the raspberries, and the *crème de cacao* until the mixture is smooth, force the mixture through a fine sieve with a rubber spatula into a bowl, and divide it between 2 metal ice-cube trays. Freeze the *sorbet* for 30 minutes, spoon it into 2 goblets, and top it with the additional pineapple. Serves 2.

Apricot Frozen Yogurt

1¼ cups sugar
½ pound dried apricots (1⅓ cups packed)
two 16-ounce containers plain yogurt
1 envelope of unflavored gelatin
2 fresh apricots for garnish
mint sprigs for garnish

In a saucepan combine the sugar and 1 cup water, bring the mixture to a boil, stirring until the sugar is dissolved, and stir in the dried apricots. Simmer the mixture, stirring occasionally, for 20 to 30 minutes, or until the apricots are softened. In a food processor purée the mixture until it is smooth and let the purée cool. (The purée will be very thick.) In a large bowl whisk the purée into the yogurt until the mixture is combined well. In a small bowl sprinkle the gelatin over ¼ cup cold water and let it soften for 3 minutes. Set the bowl in a pan of simmering water and stir the gelatin until it is dissolved. Whisk the gelatin mixture into the yogurt mixture and freeze the mixture in an ice-cream freezer according to the manufacturer's instructions. Transfer the frozen yogurt to a large pastry bag fitted with a large decorative tip and pipe it decoratively into 8 brandy snifters. Freeze the frozen yogurt, covered with plastic wrap, for at least 1 hour or overnight. Garnish the frozen yogurt with thin slivers of the fresh apricots and the mint sprigs. Serves 8.

PHOTO ON PAGE 44

ENTREMETS

Celery Aquavit Granita

2 tablespoons sugar
¾ pound celery, cut into 1-inch pieces
    (about 3 cups)
¼ cup aquavit
1 tablespoon fresh lemon juice
cayenne to taste

In a small saucepan combine the sugar and ½ cup water, bring the mixture to a boil, stirring until the sugar is dissolved, and let the syrup cool. In a food processor purée the celery, add the syrup, the aquavit, the lemon juice, the cayenne, and salt to taste, and blend the mixture well. Transfer the mixture to 2 metal ice-cube trays without the dividers or a shallow metal pan and freeze it, stirring and crushing the lumps with a fork every 30 minutes, for 2 to 3 hours, or until it is firm but not frozen hard. Scrape the granita with a fork to lighten the texture and serve it in goblets as a first course or a palate cleanser between courses. Makes about 1 quart.

FRUIT FINALES

Apple Fool

1 Golden Delicious apple
1 tablespoon firmly packed brown sugar
2 teaspoons molasses
a 1-inch strip of lemon zest removed with
    a vegetable peeler, chopped
½ cup well chilled heavy cream
⅛ teaspoon cinnamon
¼ teaspoon vanilla
2 tablespoons chopped almonds, toasted lightly

In a small saucepan combine the apple, chopped, the brown sugar, the molasses, the zest, 3 tablespoons water, and a pinch of salt, bring the liquid to a boil, and simmer the mixture, covered, for 10 minutes, or until the apple is softened. Force the mixture through the fine disk of a food mill set over a metal bowl, set the bowl in a larger bowl of ice and cold water, and stir the mixture until it is very cold. In a bowl combine the cream, the cinnamon, and the vanilla, set the bowl in the bowl of ice water, and beat the cream until it holds stiff peaks.

Fold the cream into the apple mixture until the mixture is just combined, spoon the fool into 2 stemmed glasses, and sprinkle it with the almonds. Chill the fool until ready to serve. Serves 2.

Baked Apples with Apricot and Walnut Filling

¼ cup firmly packed dried apricots, chopped
¼ cup chopped walnuts
¼ cup firmly packed light brown sugar
1 tablespoon unsalted butter, softened
2 Granny Smith apples
¼ cup fresh orange juice

In a small bowl combine well the apricots, the walnuts, the brown sugar, and the butter. Core the apples, making each opening large enough to hold half the apricot mixture, peel the top third of each apple, and fill the cavities with the apricot mixture. Arrange the apples in a deep 2½-quart microwave-safe baking dish so that they do not touch one another or the sides of the dish, pour the orange juice around them, and microwave the apples on high power (100%), covered with microwave-safe plastic wrap, for 7 minutes. Pierce the plastic wrap with the tip of a sharp knife and let the apples stand, covered, for 5 minutes, or until they are tender. Serves 2.

Apple Rings with Orange and Maple Syrup

2 tablespoons unsalted butter
a 2- by 2-inch piece of orange rind removed
    with a vegetable peeler, cut into julienne
    strips
1 cup fresh orange juice
½ cup maple syrup
¼ cup golden raisins
¼ teaspoon ground cinnamon, or to taste
2 Golden Delicious or Granny Smith apples,
    cored with an apple corer and cut crosswise
    into ⅓-inch-thick slices

In a large skillet combine the butter, the rind, the orange juice, the syrup, the raisins, and the cinnamon and bring the mixture to a boil. Add the apples and simmer the mixture, covered, stirring, for 15 to 20 minutes, or until the apples are just tender. Transfer the apples with tongs to a platter, boil the orange mixture until it is syrupy, and pour it over the apples. Serves 6.

Compote Domaine Tempier
(Fruit Compote with Rum and Pine Nuts)

a 2-inch piece of vanilla bean
¾ cup golden raisins
¾ cup golden rum
1 tablespoon dark rum
1½ cups bite-size slices of fresh pineapple
3 navel oranges, peel and pith cut away with a
    serrated knife, quartered lengthwise, and
    sliced thin crosswise
1 large Golden Delicious apple
3 large bananas
⅓ cup sugar, or to taste
¾ cup pine nuts, toasted lightly if desired

Split the vanilla bean lengthwise, scrape out the seeds, and in a bowl combine the bean and seeds with the raisins and the rums. Let the raisins macerate, covered, at room temperature for at least 8 hours or overnight. Transfer the mixture to a large shallow bowl and add the pineapple and the oranges. Cut the apple, peeled and cored, lengthwise into eighths, slice it thin crosswise, and add it to the compote with the bananas, sliced, and the sugar. Stir the mixture gently but thoroughly to dissolve the sugar and chill it, covered, for 30 minutes, or until it is cold. Just before serving, sprinkle it with the pine nuts. Serves 8.

Grape and Sour Cream Brûlée

1 cup green seedless grapes
1 cup red seedless grapes
½ cup sour cream
3 tablespoons firmly packed light brown sugar

In a small shallow flameproof casserole arrange the grapes in one layer, drop dollops of the sour cream on top of them, and spread the sour cream to cover the grapes completely. Rub the brown sugar through a sieve over the sour cream and broil the mixture under a preheated broiler about 3 inches from the heat for 2 minutes, or until the brown sugar is melted and golden. Serves 2.

Soufflés à la Noix de Coco et au Citron
(Lemon Coconut Soufflés)

5 tablespoons sugar plus additional for
    sprinkling the ramekins

2 large eggs, separated, the whites at room
    temperature
2 teaspoons cornstarch
½ teaspoon freshly grated lemon rind
3 tablespoons fresh lemon juice
½ cup sweetened flaked coconut, toasted
    lightly
crème fraîche (available at specialty foods
    shops and some supermarkets) or sour
    cream as an accompaniment

Sprinkle 2 buttered 1-cup ramekins or soufflé dishes with the additional sugar. In a bowl with an electric mixer beat the yolks with 2 tablespoons of the remaining sugar, the cornstarch, the rind, and the lemon juice for 5 minutes, or until the mixture is thick and pale, and stir in the coconut. In another bowl with clean beaters beat the whites with a pinch of salt until they hold soft peaks, add the remaining 3 tablespoons sugar gradually, beating, and beat the meringue until it just holds stiff peaks. Fold the meringue into the yolk mixture gently but thoroughly and divide the mixture between the ramekins. Bake the soufflés in the middle of a preheated 400° F. oven for 12 to 14 minutes, or until the tops are puffed and golden. Serve the soufflés with the crème fraîche. Makes 2 soufflés.

Melons with Macerated Raspberries

two ½ pints raspberries, picked over
¾ cup sweet dessert wine, such as Muscat de
    Beaumes-de-Venise
2 melons
fresh mint leaves for lining the platter

In a bowl let the raspberries macerate in the wine overnight. Cut off the top third of each melon, reserving it for another use if desired, discard the seeds, and with a sharp knife carve a decorative edge on each melon. Spoon the raspberry mixture into the melons and arrange the melons on a platter lined with the mint. Serves 6.

PHOTO ON PAGE 50

Brandied Pear and Almond Cobbler

½ cup sugar
¼ cup brandy
1 tablespoon fresh lemon juice

1 tablespoon cornstarch

5 pears (preferably Bosc, about 2½ pounds)

⅔ cup almonds

1 cup all-purpose flour

1½ teaspoons double-acting baking powder

¼ teaspoon salt

½ stick (¼ cup) cold unsalted butter,
    cut into bits

¼ cup plus 1 tablespoon milk

¼ teaspoon almond extract

vanilla ice cream as an accompaniment

In a large bowl stir together 3 tablespoons of the sugar, the brandy, the lemon juice, and the cornstarch. Peel, core, and slice the pears. Add the pears to the bowl, combine the mixture well, and transfer it to a 2-quart baking dish. In a food processor grind fine the almonds with ¼ cup of the remaining sugar, transfer the almond mixture to a bowl, and sift in the flour with the baking powder and the salt. Add the butter and blend the mixture until it resembles meal. Stir in the milk and the almond extract, stirring until the dough is just combined, drop the dough by small spoonfuls evenly onto the pear mixture (the pear mixture will not be covered completely), and sprinkle it with the remaining 1 tablespoon sugar. Bake the cobbler in the middle of a preheated 425° F. oven for 30 to 35 minutes, or until the top is browned. Serve the cobbler warm with the ice cream. Serves 6.

Pear Crumble with Cheddar and Oatmeal Topping
For the topping

½ cup all-purpose flour

⅔ cup firmly packed light brown sugar

¾ cup old-fashioned rolled oats

¼ teaspoon cinnamon

¼ teaspoon freshly grated nutmeg

1⅓ cups coarsely grated sharp Cheddar

5 tablespoons cold unsalted butter,
    cut into bits

½ cup finely chopped walnuts, toasted lightly

6 firm-ripe Anjou pears (about 3 pounds),
    peeled, cored, and cut crosswise into
    ¼-inch-thick slices

2½ tablespoons all-purpose flour

¼ cup firmly packed light brown sugar

Make the topping: In a small bowl combine well the flour, the brown sugar, the oats, the cinnamon, the nutmeg, the Cheddar, the butter, and a pinch of salt, blend the mixture until it is pebbly, and stir in the walnuts.

In a bowl combine the pears, the flour, and the brown sugar, toss the mixture to combine it well, and in a buttered baking pan, 13 by 9 by 2 inches, spread it evenly. Sprinkle the mixture with the topping and bake the crumble in the upper third of a preheated 375° F. oven for 30 minutes, or until the topping is crisp and brown. Serve the crumble warm. Serves 6 to 8.

Peach Schnapps and Vodka Plugged Watermelon

1 whole watermelon

⅔ to 1½ cups peach schnapps

⅔ to 1½ cups vodka

Stand the watermelon on end in a bowl, stem end up, and cut a 3-inch-diameter plug out around the stem like a jack-o'-lantern lid. Remove the plug, scoop out about 2 inches of the flesh, and pour out the excess liquid. With a long skewer pierce the flesh inside to the bottom and in all directions without penetrating the rind and pour out any excess liquid. Pour equal amounts of the schnapps and the vodka into the melon gradually until it cannot absorb any more and replace the plug. Chill the melon on end for at least 15 hours and up to 2 days. Serve the watermelon cut into wedges.

PHOTO ON PAGE 59

BEVERAGES

ALCOHOLIC BEVERAGES

Bourbon and Dark Rum Eggnog

9 large eggs, separated, the whites at
   room temperature
¾ cup sugar
4 cups heavy cream
1 cup bourbon (101 proof)
½ cup dark rum
1 teaspoon vanilla
2½ cups milk
¼ teaspoon salt
freshly grated nutmeg for sprinkling
cinnamon for sprinkling the eggnog

In a large bowl with an electric mixer beat the egg
yolks with the sugar until the mixture is thick and pale
and ribbons when the beaters are lifted. In another large
bowl beat two thirds of the egg whites until they hold
soft peaks. In another large bowl beat the cream until it
holds soft peaks. Fold the whites into the yolk mixture
until the mixture is combined well and fold in the
whipped cream gently but thoroughly. Pour the mixture
into a large punch bowl, whisk in the bourbon, the rum,
the vanilla, the milk, and the salt, and chill the eggnog,
covered, for at least 4 hours, or until it is cold. Just before serving, in a bowl beat the remaining 3 egg whites
until they hold soft peaks, fold them into the eggnog,
and sprinkle the eggnog with the nutmeg and the cinnamon. Makes about 18 cups.

Claret Cup

2 tablespoons sugar
2 bottles (25.4 ounces each) chilled
   dry red wine
½ cup Cointreau
½ cup crème de cassis
⅓ cup Tawny Port

⅓ cup fresh lemon juice
1 bottle (33.8 ounces) chilled club soda
thin lemon slices and thin orange slices

In a small saucepan combine the sugar with ¼ cup
water, bring the mixture to a boil, and simmer it for 5
minutes, or until the sugar is dissolved. Let the sugar
syrup cool completely. In a large punch bowl stir together the red wine, the Cointreau, the crème de cassis,
the Port, the lemon juice, and the sugar syrup. Chill the
mixture, covered, until it is cold. Just before serving
add the club soda and the lemon and orange slices.
Makes about 13 cups.

Cranberry Sunrise

¾ cup chilled fresh orange juice
1 jigger (1½ ounces) vodka or tequila
½ cup chilled cranberry juice

Pour the orange juice into a 12-ounce glass, add the
vodka, and stir the mixture well. Pour the cranberry juice
in a slow stream down the side of the glass. Makes 1 drink.

Island Iced "Tea"

1 ounce (1 pony) light Tequila
1 ounce (1 pony) light rum
1 ounce (1 pony) gin
1 ounce (1 pony) vodka
1 ounce (1 pony) triple sec
1 ounce (1 pony) fresh lemon juice
⅓ cup cola
2 lemon slices for garnish

In a cocktail shaker half-filled with ice cubes combine the Tequila, the rum, the gin, the vodka, the triple
sec, and the lemon juice, shake the mixture for 30 seconds, and strain it into 2 tall glasses filled with ice
cubes. Divide the cola between the glasses and garnish
the drinks with the lemon slices. Makes 2 drinks.

Mango Wine Cooler

½ cup chilled dry white wine
1 ounce (1 pony) Mohala (mango liqueur)
¼ pitted and peeled mango, cut into strips,
    reserving 1 strip for garnish

In a tall glass filled with ice cubes stir together the wine, the Mohala, and the mango and garnish the cooler with the reserved mango strip. Makes 1 drink.

Margaritas
(Tequila, Triple Sec, and Lime Cocktails)

1 lime wedge for coating the glasses' rims
    plus 6 lime slices for garnish
coarse salt for coating the rims
9 ounces (6 jiggers) Tequila
6 ounces (4 jiggers) triple sec
¾ cup fresh lime juice

Rub the rims of 6 cocktail glasses with the lime wedge, dip them in the salt to coat them lightly, and chill the glasses. In a pitcher stir together the Tequila, the triple sec, and the lime juice and chill the mixture for 15 minutes, or until it is cold. Fill the chilled glasses with crushed ice, divide the Margarita mixture among the glasses, and garnish each drink with a lime slice. Makes 6 drinks.

Melon Ball
(Midori and Vodka Cocktail)

1½ ounces (1 jigger) Midori
    (melon-flavored liqueur)
1½ ounces (1 jigger) vodka
⅓ cup strained fresh orange juice
a bamboo skewer threaded with
    3 melon balls for garnish

In a long-stemmed glass filled with ice cubes stir together the Midori, the vodka, and the orange juice and garnish the drink with the skewer. Makes 1 drink.

Mojito
(Rum, Lemon, and Mint Cocktail)

3 fresh mint sprigs
2 teaspoons sugar
2 tablespoons fresh lemon juice

1½ ounces (1 jigger) light rum
chilled club soda or seltzer
lemon slices for garnish

In a tall glass with the back of a spoon crush 2 of the mint sprigs with the sugar and the lemon juice until the sugar is dissolved and add the rum. Add ice cubes, top off the drink with the club soda, and stir it well. Garnish the drink with the remaining mint sprig and the lemon slices. Makes 1 drink.

Molasses, Rum, and Ginger Milk Punch

¾ cup unsulfured molasses
2 teaspoons ground ginger, or to taste
4 cups chilled milk
2 cups chilled half-and-half
1 cup light rum
½ cup brandy
freshly grated nutmeg for sprinkling the punch

In a punch bowl whisk together the molasses and the ginger, whisk in the milk, the half-and-half, the rum, and the brandy, and chill the punch, covered, for at least 4 hours, or until it is very cold. Serve the punch in punch glasses and sprinkle it with the nutmeg. Makes about 8 cups.

Orange Wine

2 pounds (about 4) oranges, each cut
    into 16 pieces
two 750-ml bottles dry white wine
1 cup sugar
¼ cup Cognac
long strips of orange zest removed with a
    vegetable peeler for garnish

In a large bowl combine the oranges and the wine and chill the mixture, covered tightly with plastic wrap, for 5 days. Discard the oranges, add the sugar and the Cognac, and stir the mixture until the sugar is dissolved. Strain the mixture through a sieve lined with a double thickness of rinsed and squeezed cheesecloth into a bowl and pour the wine into decorative bottles with corks. Insert a strip of the orange zest into each bottle and chill the wine, corked, for 1 week. The wine keeps, chilled, for 3 months. Makes about 7 cups.

Pimm's Cup

1½ ounces (1 jigger) Pimm's No. 1 Cup
1 lengthwise strip of cucumber peel
1 apple wedge
chilled club soda or seltzer
chilled ginger ale
1 lemon slice

In a tall glass filled with ice cubes combine the Pimm's No. 1 Cup, the peel, and the apple, top off the mixture with equal parts of the club soda and the ginger ale, and stir the drink well. Garnish the glass with the lemon slice. Makes 1 drink.

Planter's Punch

⅔ cup dark rum
¼ cup fresh lime juice
¼ cup triple sec
1 tablespoon grenadine
½ teaspoon Angostura bitters
½ cup fresh orange juice
4 bamboo skewers, each threaded with a lime wedge, an orange wedge, and a maraschino cherry, for garnish
lime slices for garnish

In a cocktail shaker half-filled with ice cubes combine the rum, the lime juice, the triple sec, the grenadine, the bitters, and the orange juice, shake the drink for 30 seconds, and strain it into 4 tall glasses filled with ice cubes. Garnish the drinks with the skewers and the lime slices. Makes 4 drinks.

Sea Breeze

1½ ounces (1 jigger) vodka
¼ cup chilled grapefruit juice
¼ cup chilled cranberry juice
1 small grapefruit wedge
 for garnish

In a long-stemmed glass filled with ice cubes stir together the vodka, the grapefruit juice, and the cranberry juice and garnish the drink with the grapefruit wedge. Makes 1 drink.

Shandies

caramel lemonade (page 249)
chilled beer

Fill beer glasses halfway with the lemonade and top them off with the beer.

Strawberry, Lime, and Champagne Punch

⅓ cup sugar
a 10-ounce package frozen strawberries in syrup, thawed
½ cup fresh lime juice
½ cup brandy
½ cup chilled club soda
2 bottles (25.4 ounces each) chilled Champagne
strawberries, sliced thin, for garnish if desired
thin lime slices, halved, for garnish if desired

In a small saucepan combine the sugar with ½ cup water and simmer the mixture for 5 minutes, or until the sugar is dissolved. Let the sugar syrup cool completely. In a food processor purée the strawberries with their syrup and the lime juice, transfer the mixture to a large punch bowl, forcing it through a fine sieve if desired, and stir in the sugar syrup, the brandy, and the club soda. Chill the mixture, covered, until it is cold. Add the Champagne slowly just before serving and serve the punch in punch glasses, each garnished with a slice of strawberry and lime. Makes about 10 cups.

Frozen Strawberry Daiquiris

1 pint strawberries, hulled and quartered
2 tablespoons sugar
2 tablespoons fresh lime juice
½ cup light rum
3 tablespoons triple sec

In a sturdy sealable plastic bag combine the strawberries, the sugar, and the lime juice, seal the bag, forcing out the excess air, and knead the mixture lightly until the sugar is dissolved. Freeze the mixture until it is solid. In a blender blend the frozen strawberry mixture, broken into pieces, the rum, the triple sec, and ⅓ cup water until the mixture is smooth and divide the mixture among 4 long-stemmed glasses. Serves 4.

Tomato Vegetable Bloody Mary Mix

4½ pounds tomatoes (about 8), quartered
2 cucumbers (about 1 pound), cut into pieces
2 red bell peppers, cut into pieces
4 carrots, cut into pieces
1 onion, quartered
8 ribs of celery, cut into pieces
2 teaspoons salt
½ teaspoon dried hot red pepper flakes
½ cup packed fresh parsley sprigs
⅓ to ½ cup Worcestershire sauce
½ to ¾ cup fresh lemon juice
¼ cup drained bottled horseradish
1 teaspoon Tabasco

In a food processor chop fine separately the tomatoes, the cucumbers, the bell peppers, the carrots, the onion, and the celery, transferring the vegetables as they are chopped to a kettle. Stir in the salt, the red pepper flakes, and the parsley, bring the mixture to a boil, and cook it at a slow boil, covered, for 45 minutes. Force the mixture in batches through the medium disk of a food mill into a large bowl, strain it in batches through a very fine sieve into a pitcher, pressing hard on the solids, and into the juice stir the Worcestershire sauce, the lemon juice, the horseradish, the Tabasco, and salt and black pepper to taste. The mixture keeps, covered and chilled, for 1 week or it can be frozen. Makes about 12 cups.

White Grape, Tangerine, and Asti Spumante Punch

two 24-ounce bottles chilled unsweetened
    white grape juice
a 6-ounce can frozen tangerine juice
    concentrate, thawed
1 cup chilled club soda
¼ cup strained fresh lemon juice
¼ cup brandy
1 bottle (25.4 ounces) chilled Asti Spumante
thin tangerine or orange slices, halved, for
    garnish if desired

In a punch bowl whisk together the grape juice, the tangerine concentrate, the club soda, the lemon juice, and the brandy and chill the mixture, covered, until it is cold. Add the Asti Spumante slowly just before serving and serve the punch in punch glasses, garnished with the tangerine slices. Makes about 12 cups.

NONALCOHOLIC BEVERAGES

Caramel Lemonade

1½ cups sugar
1½ cups fresh lemon juice
mint sprigs for garnish

In a heavy saucepan dissolve the sugar in ½ cup water over moderate heat, stirring, bring the syrup to a boil, and boil it, undisturbed, until it begins to turn golden. Boil the syrup, swirling the pan, until it is deep caramel, add 3 cups water carefully, stirring (the mixture will spatter and seize), and bring the mixture to a boil. Simmer the mixture, stirring, until the caramel is dissolved and let the syrup cool. In a large pitcher stir together the caramel syrup, 6 cups water, and the lemon juice. Chill the lemonade, add ice cubes, and garnish the lemonade with the mint. Makes about 10 cups.

PHOTO ON PAGES 60 AND 61

Cranberry Pineapple Punch

two 1-quart bottles chilled cranberry
    juice cocktail
a 1-quart 14-ounce can chilled unsweetened
    pineapple juice
2 cups chilled ginger ale
2 cups chilled seltzer water
fresh pineapple spears for garnish if desired

In a large punch bowl combine the cranberry juice cocktail, the pineapple juice, the ginger ale, and the seltzer water, add an ice block, and serve the punch in punch glasses, garnished with the pineapple. Makes about 20 cups.

Christmas Spice Tisane

¼ cup aniseed
three 3-inch cinnamon sticks, broken
2 vanilla beans, chopped fine
2 tablespoons dried orange peel
5 cloves, crushed lightly

In a mortar with a pestle bruise the aniseed and crush the cinnamon sticks. In a bowl combine well the aniseed, the cinnamon, the vanilla beans, the orange peel, and the cloves and divide the tisane among jars or bags. (To serve: Let 2 teaspoons of the tisane steep in ¾ cup boiling water for 10 minutes. Strain the mixture through a fine sieve into a teacup.) Makes about ¾ cup.

Sage and Mint Tisane

⅓ cup dried mint
¼ cup dried sage,
    crumbled
⅓ cup chamomile
    (from about 12 tea bags)
⅓ cup dried orange peel

In a bowl combine well the mint, the sage, the chamomile, and the orange peel and divide the tisane among decorative jars or bags. (To serve: Let 2 teaspoons of the tisane steep in ¾ cup boiling water for 5 minutes and strain the mixture through a fine sieve into a teacup.) Makes about 1¼ cups.

PART THREE

A GOURMET ADDENDUM

THE REWARDS OF NATURE:

RECIPES TO CELEBRATE SEASONAL HARVESTS

Each month *Gourmet* Magazine in its column "Gastronomie sans Argent" extols a seasonal food, provides intriguing background information on it, and then presents a dozen or so recipes, each demonstrating how this newly esteemed item—be it tomatoes or eggplant or corn—can be used to best advantage. The featured choice is always at its peak of seasonal freshness, the recipes are straightforward, and the dish is always economic in intent—no *foie gras* there! After reading "Gastronomie" and trying one or two of its recipes you will find yourself thinking differently about "common" seasonal foods; now they seem quite "uncommonly" special indeed.

This year the Gourmet Addendum appropriates the theme of "Gastronomie sans Argent," but addresses it from a seasonal vantage point. Herein we highlight the bounty of Spring, Summer, Fall, and Winter with recipes that celebrate timely fresh foods often used in surprisingly novel ways. (See Fall, for instance.) We admit that while we have studied the harvests we cannot be sure that all called-for ingredients will be stocked in your local markets. Let your curiosity, some serendipity, good sense, and gusto be your guides in making substitutions.

Each seasonal section offers nine recipes—three starters (or light entrées), three entrées, and three desserts. Menu-making is up to you. For example, our summer selection of recipes includes fresh mozzarella and tomato salad, corn chowder, and grilled vegetables with *pesto* as starters; grilled game hens, grilled tuna, and *paella al fresco* as entrées; and melon with raspberry sauce, peach and pecan crisp, and mango coupes as desserts. Imagine that it's a hot summer's day and you

have light eating in mind. Mozzarella salad with ruby-red tomatoes might be just the thing. Or, perhaps, it is a balmy summer's evening and you are having friends over for a barbecue. In this case, consider this salad as the starter, the grilled tuna as the entrée, and the melon for dessert. Menu combinations are many as you mix-and-match your way through the year with thirty-six recipes. Remember, too, that many of the recipes can be made year round. Barbecued game hens can be broiled indoors no matter the season. And simple fresh substitutions can bridge the seasonality of a particular recipe. Fiddlehead ferns, for example, are fresh for only three weeks in May. To extend the life of our sautéed chicken breasts recipe replace the fiddleheads with asparagus or artichoke hearts.

You will note that care has been taken to provide nutritional information on the kinds of foods highlighted. Sensible cooking techniques have also been used; most recipes are either grilled, braised, broiled, or baked. We have taken traditionally fried foods, such as crab cakes, and broiled them for a healthier dish with fewer calories but commensurate taste. In general, recipes are low in saturated fat, and butter has been employed sparingly. Egg yolks, too, have been kept to a minimum. Finally, ingredient substitutions or alternatives are suggested to fit personal preferences and needs.

We hope that you come to consider these Addendum recipes as the foundation of seasonal good eating, and that you will be able to shop with timely, nutritious, even delicious, ideas in mind. And as old favorites take on new meaning and new-found gems of a season become favorites, you will want to try a harvest's bounty in yet other innovative, healthful ways.

SPRING

inally, after months of waiting, it is suddenly spring. Fresh herbs pop up magically in the garden; spindly seedlings transform themselves into bright, bushy vegetables; and fishing boats come back to port brimming with the shimmering catch of the day. At roadside stands and farmer's markets we find, rediscovering them, all the specialties we have been so impatiently waiting for—aromatic basil, tarragon, and thyme; tender dandelion and other assorted greens, and sorrel; mouth-puckering rhubarb; sweet mahogany-red Bing cherries; ice-packed salmon and crab. In the recipes that follow we celebrate the rediscovered and a few of the newly discovered foods of this season.

Among the nicest of spring's surprises are wild edibles, specifically fiddlehead ferns. These small, un-furled heads of wild ferns are silver-green in color, impart a unique cinnamon-like taste, and are nutritious. We've combined them with chicken breasts, a light pairing, and add that once the fiddlehead season has come and gone, only about three weeks in May in New England and Canada—a blink, really—the dish can be made with asparagus, another spring treasure, or artichoke hearts.

Another wild edible, which you may consider almost domestic, definitely familiar, depending upon its number in your own backyard, is the dandelion green. The leaves of this perky yellow flower should be eaten young, before the dandelion blossoms and before the leaves grow big and turn bitter. We've combined them with *mâche*, lamb's lettuce, which is more and more available now at produce markets and can even be homegrown from seeds, and mild-flavored goat cheese.

Fava beans, also known as broad beans, are a cultivated taste of the season. This versatile legume is a source of vitamins A and C and potassium. We have puréed tender young beans, then paired them with a touch of tarragon to create a warming soup that can be served as either a starter or light entrée.

Since spring would not be spring without crab, we salute the feisty seasonal crustacean with a new recipe for Maryland crab cakes that boasts a feisty taste to match. Crab meat is combined with roasted garlic mayonnaise, scallions, mustard, Worcestershire sauce, and cayenne, then simply broiled to a crispy brown. This no-fuss easy entrée is notable for its no-fry finish.

If you have a notion for something a bit more fancy, the ideal entrée for the first dinner party of the season might be our salmon en papillote *printanière* that features sorrel, another spring specialty. Available from March until August, sorrel leaves should be shiny, firm, and deep green. Not only does the sorrel complement the fish with its slightly sour taste, it also provides a noteworthy dose of potassium, magnesium, and vitamin C. Carrots, leeks, and asparagus tips adorn the salmon and explain its *printanière* appellation.

Enticing combinations await you in our spring desserts, each fruit-based. Our first combines rhubarb not with strawberries, although no one would argue with that long-lasting marriage, but with Bing cherries, then tops them with the gentlest of buttermilk biscuit doughs. (Buttermilk, we hasten to mention, is low in fat, rich in flavor.) Rhubarb, a fair source of vitamin A and potassium, has a noteworthy past. Recognized as a food only some three hundred years ago, it was used for medicinal purposes in ancient China and cured tired blood in Colonial times. Bing cherries, available from the last week of May to the end of July, should be chosen for their color and size; in general, the darker the cherry, the sweeter the flavor, and the larger the size, the better the taste.

For an exotic fruit taste, you will want to try our pineapple ice. Selecting the proper pineapple is key: look for fruit that gives slightly when pressed and is fragrant. Contrary to what you may have heard, ripeness cannot be determined by plucking the top leaves.

But perhaps the most versatile dessert of the season is meringue tartlets topped with strawberries, or for that matter, with any berry that appears from late spring and throughout the summer. Meringues, arguably lighter than even the airiest of biscuits or shortcakes, can be made ahead and crowned at the last minute.

Ah . . . it's finally spring. Go ahead and enjoy each new crop. But this year, instead of just rediscovering old friends, why not let yourself discover some of the other unexpected finds that flourish in the spring?

Fresh Fava Bean and Tarragon Soup

2 tablespoons unsalted butter
the white part of 1 large leek, rinsed well
   and chopped
1 rib of celery, cut into ¼-inch pieces
3 pounds fava beans, shelled (3 cups shelled)
a cheesecloth bag containing 2 sprigs of
   tarragon or ½ teaspoon dried, 1 sprig of
   thyme or ¼ teaspoon dried, 6 parsley
   stems, and 1 bay leaf
6 cups canned chicken broth or chicken
   stock (page 117)
1 cup half-and-half
2 tablespoons minced fresh tarragon,
   or to taste

In a heavy saucepan melt the butter over moderate heat, add the leek, the celery, and salt and pepper to taste, and cook the mixture, covered, stirring occasionally, for 5 to 7 minutes, or until the vegetables are soft. Add the fava beans and cook them, stirring, for 1 minute. Add the cheesecloth bag and the broth, bring the liquid to a boil, and simmer the soup, covered, for 20 minutes, or until the beans are very tender. Discard the cheesecloth bag.

In a blender or food processor purée the mixture in batches and strain the soup through a sieve back into the saucepan. Bring the soup to a simmer, stir in the half-and-half, and season the soup with salt and pepper. Before serving, add the tarragon and simmer the soup for 5 minutes. Makes about 6 cups, serving 4.

Dandelion Greens, Mâche, and Warm Goat Cheese Salad

For the dressing
2 tablespoons fresh lemon juice
2 tablespoons Sherry vinegar or red-wine
   vinegar
3 tablespoons walnut oil
3 tablespoons olive oil

1 small bunch dandelion greens, washed,
   spun dry, and torn into bite-size pieces
2 small bunches *mâche* (lamb's lettuce),
   washed and spun dry
2 plum tomatoes, cored and cut into
   1-inch pieces
6 sun-dried tomatoes, sliced thin, or to taste
6 ounces *crottins de chèvre* or firm goat
   cheese, cut into 4 slices
3 tablespoons fresh bread crumbs
3 tablespoons chopped and skinned hazelnuts
   or blanched almonds
1 tablespoon walnut oil

Make the dressing: In a small bowl whisk together the lemon juice, the vinegar, and salt and pepper to taste, add the oils in a stream, whisking, and whisk the dressing until it is emulsified.

In a bowl toss together well the dandelion greens, the *mâche*, the tomatoes, and the sun-dried tomatoes.

Arrange the goat cheese slices in a small oiled gratin dish. In a small bowl combine well the bread crumbs and the hazelnuts. Brush the goat cheese slices with the walnut oil and coat the tops evenly with the bread crumb mixture. Bake the goat cheese slices in a preheated 425° F. oven for 4 or 5 minutes, or until they are heated through. Run the slices under a preheated broiler about 3 inches from the heat until they are golden.

Pour the dressing over the salad mixture, toss the salad until it is combined well, and divide it among 4 salad plates. Arrange a slice of goat cheese in the center of each plate. Serve immediately. Serves 4.

Artichokes Ravigote
(Artichokes with Herb, Caper, and Onion Sauce)

6 medium-size artichokes
2 lemons
3 tablespoons fresh lemon juice
2 tablespoons white-wine vinegar
1 tablespoon Dijon-style mustard
⅔ cup olive oil
1 small onion, minced fine
2 tablespoons drained capers
1 tablespoon minced fresh tarragon leaves
1 tablespoon minced fresh chervil
1 tablespoon snipped chives

Break off and discard the stems and tough outer leaves of the artichokes. Cut off the top quarter of each artichoke with a very sharp stainless steel knife, snip off the sharp tips of the leaves with scissors, and rub the cut surfaces with ½ lemon. Trim the bases, dropping the artichokes as they are trimmed into a bowl of cold water acidulated with the juice of ½ lemon. In a stainless steel or enameled kettle of boiling salted water combine the artichokes, drained, with the juice of the remaining lemon and simmer them for 30 to 35 minutes, or until their bottoms are tender and a leaf pulls away easily. Let the artichokes drain upside down on a rack until they are just cool.

Spread the leaves of the artichokes apart gently, pull out the tender center leaves in one piece, reserving them, and remove the chokes with a small spoon. Invert the center leaves and put them back in the center of the artichokes.

In a small bowl whisk together the lemon juice, the vinegar, the mustard, and salt and pepper to taste, whisk in the oil, and stir in the onion, the capers, and the herbs. Fill the inverted center leaves of each artichoke with some of the sauce and serve the remaining sauce separately. Serves 6.

Sautéed Chicken Breasts with Fiddlehead Ferns

1 pound fiddlehead ferns, washed well
   (available seasonally at specialty produce
   markets)
2 tablespoons unsalted butter, melted
2 whole skinless boneless chicken breasts,
   halved lengthwise, rinsed, and patted dry
flour seasoned with salt and pepper
   for dredging
3 tablespoons vegetable oil
¼ cup minced shallot

¼ pound white mushrooms, sliced
1 cup peeled, seeded, chopped, and
    drained tomatoes
1 garlic clove, minced
½ teaspoon dried thyme, crumbled
½ teaspoon dried rosemary, crumbled
½ cup, plus 1 tablespoon dry white wine
1½ cups beef broth
2 teaspoons arrowroot
2 tablespoons minced fresh tarragon or basil
    leaves or snipped fresh chives

Trim the fiddleheads, discarding any brown ends and cutting off any long stems. In a large saucepan of boiling salted water cook the fiddleheads for 3 to 5 minutes, or until they are just tender, drain them, and refresh them under cold water. In a bowl toss the fiddleheads with the melted butter and season them with salt and pepper to taste.

Dredge the chicken in the flour, shaking off the excess. In a large skillet heat 2 tablespoons of the oil over moderately high heat until it is hot and in it sauté the chicken for 2 minutes on each side, or until it is golden. Transfer the chicken to a buttered baking dish, surround it with the fiddleheads, and bake the mixture in a preheated 425° F. oven for 6 to 7 minutes, or until the chicken is springy to the touch. Cover the dish with foil and keep the chicken warm in a 250° F. oven.

While the chicken is cooking make the sauce: In the skillet heat the remaining oil over moderately high heat until it is hot and in it cook the shallot, stirring, until it is softened. Add the mushrooms and salt and pepper to taste and sauté them for 2 minutes. Add the tomatoes, the garlic, the thyme, and the rosemary and cook the mixture, stirring occasionally, until almost all the liquid has evaporated. Add the ½ cup wine, reduce it by half, and add the beef broth. Simmer the sauce, stirring occasionally, for 5 minutes. In a small bowl dissolve the arrowroot in the remaining 1 tablespoon wine, add it to the simmering sauce, stirring, and continue to simmer the sauce until it is lightly thickened. Stir in the fresh herb of choice.

Divide the chicken breasts and fiddleheads among 4 plates and spoon the sauce over them. Serves 4.

Maryland Crab Cakes with Roasted Garlic Mayonnaise

⅓ cup roasted garlic mayonnaise
    (recipe follows)
1 large egg white
¼ cup minced scallion
2 tablespoons minced fresh parsley leaves
1 tablespoon Dijon-style mustard
1 teaspoon Worcestershire sauce
½ teaspoon salt
½ teaspoon cayenne, or to taste
1 pound lump crab meat, picked over
½ cup fresh bread crumbs
3 tablespoons unsalted butter, melted

In a bowl whisk together the garlic mayonnaise, the egg white, the scallion, the parsley, the mustard, the Worcestershire sauce, the salt, and the cayenne. Add the crab meat and 3 tablespoons of the bread crumbs and stir the mixture gently until it is just combined. With moistened hands form the mixture into 8 cakes and coat the cakes with the remaining bread crumbs. Chill the cakes on a plate, loosely covered, for 1 hour.

Arrange the crab cakes on an oiled jelly-roll pan, drizzle them with half the butter, and broil them under a preheated broiler about 4 inches from the heat for 4 minutes, or until they are golden. Turn the cakes, drizzle them with the remaining butter, and broil them for 4 minutes more, or until they are golden. Serve the cakes with the remaining garlic mayonnaise. Serves 4.

Roasted Garlic Mayonnaise

4 medium garlic cloves, unpeeled
1 large egg
1 tablespoon fresh lemon juice
1 cup vegetable oil or olive oil or a combination
2 tablespoons snipped fresh chives

Wrap the garlic cloves in a double thickness of foil and bake them in a preheated 450° F. oven for 20 minutes. Let the garlic cool and peel it.

In a food processor or blender combine the garlic, the egg, the lemon juice, and salt and pepper to taste. With the motor running add the oil in a stream and blend the mixture until it is just emulsified. Transfer the mayonnaise to a bowl and stir in the chives. Makes about 1¼ cups.

Salmon en Papillote Printanière with Sorrel Sauce

8 baby carrots, trimmed and peeled
the white part of 2 medium-large leeks
    (about 1 inch in diameter), trimmed,
    and washed well
16 asparagus tips
3 tablespoons unsalted butter, melted
1½ pounds center-cut salmon fillet, cut
    crosswise into 4 pieces
For the sorrel sauce
¼ cup minced shallot
½ cup dry white wine
1 cup canned chicken broth or chicken
    stock (page 117)
2 teaspoons arrowroot
½ cup heavy cream
1 cup fresh sorrel leaves, cut thin crosswise

In a saucepan of boiling salted water cook the carrots for 2 minutes, add the leeks, and cook them for 3 minutes. Add the asparagus tips and cook the vegetables and refresh them under cold water. Pat the vegetables dry, halve the leeks lengthwise, and in a bowl toss them with the melted butter and salt and pepper to taste.

Cut out 4 heart shapes, each about 14 inches long through the center, from parchment paper. Butter 1 side of each heart and put a salmon fillet in the center of each buttered side. Arrange the vegetables decoratively around the salmon and season the fish with salt and pepper to taste. Beginning with the top edge of each heart fold and crimp the sides of the hearts together to seal the packets. Bake the packets on a jelly-roll pan in a preheated 425° F. oven for 15 minutes.

While the salmon is baking make the sorrel sauce. In a heavy saucepan combine the shallot with the wine and boil the liquid until it is reduced to about 1 tablespoon. Add the broth and boil the liquid until it is reduced to about ⅔ cup. In a small bowl dissolve the arrowroot in the cream. Bring the broth mixture to a boil, add the cream mixture, whisking, and simmer the mixture for 2 minutes. Stir in the sorrel and season the sauce with salt and pepper.

Transfer the packets to serving plates and cut a cross in the top of each packet. Fold back the edges. Serve the sorrel sauce separately. Serves 4.

Deep-Dish Rhubarb and Black Cherry Pie

1 pound rhubarb, cut into ½-inch slices
½ pound Bing cherries, pitted
1½ cups sugar, or to taste
4 to 5 tablespoons all-purpose flour,
    or to taste
2 teaspoons grated orange rind if desired
1 tablespoon unsalted butter, cut into bits
For the buttermilk biscuit dough
1 cup plus 2 tablespoons all-purpose flour
1 teaspoon double-acting baking powder
2 tablespoons sugar
¼ teaspoon baking soda
a pinch of salt
2 tablespoons cold vegetable shortening,
    cut into bits
½ cup plus 1 tablespoon buttermilk

In a bowl combine the rhubarb, the cherries, the sugar, the flour, and the orange rind and let the mixture stand for 30 minutes. Transfer the mixture to a saucepan and bring it to a simmer over moderate heat, stirring. Butter a 9-inch deep-dish baking dish, add the rhubarb filling, and dot the filling with the butter.

Make the buttermilk biscuit dough: Into a bowl sift together the flour, the baking powder, 1 tablespoon of the sugar, the baking soda, and the salt, add the shortening, and blend the mixture until it resembles meal. Add the ½ cup buttermilk and stir the mixture until it just forms a soft dough. On a lightly floured surface pat or roll the dough into a round ½ inch thick and transfer the dough to cover the fruit in the baking dish. Brush the top of the pie with the remaining 1 tablespoon buttermilk and sprinkle the remaining 1 tablespoon sugar over the top crust. Cut four 1-inch slits in the top for steam vents.

Bake the pie in the upper third of a preheated 425° F. oven for 20 to 25 minutes, or until the filling is bubbling and the top is golden. Serve the deep-dish pie warm. Serves 4 to 6.

Pineapple Ice

a 3½-pound ripe pineapple, peeled, cored,
    and cut into 1-inch pieces
¼ cup superfine sugar, or to taste
4 to 6 tablespoons fresh lemon juice,
    or to taste

In a food processor purée the pineapple pulp until it is smooth, blend in the sugar and the lemon juice, and transfer the pineapple mixture to 2 ice cube trays containing dividers. Freeze the ice in the freezing compartment of the refrigerator until it is frozen, transfer the cubes to the food processor, and blend them until the ice is light and fluffy. Transfer the ice to a 1-quart freezer container and freeze it until it is frozen. Makes about 1 quart.

Meringue Tartlets with Strawberries

For the tartlets
5 large egg whites at room temperature
a pinch of cream of tartar
1¼ cups granulated sugar ground to a powder
    in a food processor or blender
2 teaspoons vanilla or *eau-de-vie de framboise*
    (raspberry-flavored liqueur), or to taste,
    if desired
confectioners' sugar to taste
3 cups strawberries, or seasonal berries such
    as raspberries or blackberries
⅔ cup raspberry preserves

Make the tartlets: In a bowl with an electric mixer beat the egg whites at moderate speed until they are foamy, add the cream of tartar, and beat the whites until they hold soft peaks. Add the granulated sugar,

1 tablespoon at a time, beating, and beat the meringue until it holds stiff peaks. Beat in the vanilla and transfer the meringue to a pastry bag fitted with a medium decorative tip.

Cover 1 large baking sheet with parchment paper and using a 4-inch ring or butter plate as a guide draw 6 circles onto the paper. Invert the parchment paper onto the baking sheet and attach it by putting a dab of the meringue on the underside of each corner. Pipe the meringue inside the circles to form bases ½ inch thick and pipe a ring of the meringue around the edge of each base to form sides 1½ inches high. (Alternatively, with the back of a spoon or a metal spatula form the meringue into 6 tartlet shells by spreading a layer or meringue inside the rings, making a well in the center of each, and building up the edges to form sides.) Sift the confectioners' sugar lightly over the meringue and bake the meringues in a preheated 200° F. oven for 1½ to 2 hours, or until they are firm and dry. With the tip of a small knife loosen the meringues from the paper carefully. Store the tartlets, if necessary, in airtight containers.

Rinse, hull, and halve the strawberries if large and transfer them to a large bowl. Strain the preserves through a fine sieve over the berries and stir the mixture gently until all the berries are coated with the preserves. Chill the fruit for 30 minutes to 1 hour.

Just before serving, fill the tartlets with the strawberries and transfer them to serving plates. Serves 6.

SUMMER

As the days continue to lengthen and warm up, we rummage about attics and dark closets for shorts, sandals, and bathing suits. By the end of June, summer now official, we are happily ensconced. Life slows down, and simple meals, enjoyed languorously with family and friends, fill the calendar.

Unlike spring, when we are so grateful for the few first seasonal harbingers, summer promises bounty. A full assortment of lettuce greens packs market shelves; fresh dill, coriander, parsley, mint, and basil are there, too. Tomatoes get larger, redder, juicier, and more and more plentiful as the months progress; and summer squash, eggplant, peppers, and ears and ears of corn create potential avalanches when precariously stacked. Fresh shellfish and fish surface. Berries bloom in steady, plentiful succession. Ah, choice! Our summer recipes will avail you of this bounty.

Many of our summer dishes make use of marinades and the grill. The combination works: marinades flavor and tenderize and stave off dryness, while the grill sears in juices and imparts a wonderful flavor without adding fat. Despite renewed interest in grilling, the act of barbecuing is by no means a recent idea. Iron Age men first had the idea of cooking on spits supported by fire dogs! Centuries later, the term ''barbecue'' was invented by the British colonists in Virginia who adapted it from the French phrase ''*de barbe à queue*,'' meaning from beard to tail, overheard in Louisiana.

All of our summer entrées are designed with grilling in mind (alternate cooking instructions are given for year-round indoor cooking). Light and easy to prepare, game hens are marinated in ginger, honey, soy sauce, and coriander, then cooked over glowing coals to impart Oriental flavors. Fresh tuna is first made aromatic in an olive oil, garlic, and lemon-thyme marinade, then combined in niçoise fashion with red potatoes, olives, anchovies, fresh herbs, and both green and wax beans for a nutritious meal-in-one.

And finally, as a departure from classic *paella*, we present *paella valenciana al fresco*—made with basmati rice, a long-grain brown rice, and fresh-from-the-sea foods—that employs the grill, not the stove, as a cook top.

Summer would not be summer without fresh basil, and to many that means *pesto* on its most customary partner, pasta. We've used *pesto* instead as an accompaniment to grilled vegetables. Here is a marvelous way to use both yellow squash and zucchini when they are small and still very tender. The rule is the smaller the squash, the smaller the seeds, the better the flavor and texture.

Corn on the cob is awaited from the very onset of the season, and when it comes in we sweep it up by the dozen. While many argue the virtues of yellow versus white kernels, it's really only freshness that counts. Look for ears with green husks and firm "cool" kernels. If an ear feels hot, literally, don't buy it. All ears, regardless of summer temperatures, are cool when picked. If they are allowed to heat up a chemical change occurs and the flavor changes. We pair fiber-rich corn with vitamin A–filled red peppers, milk (or yogurt), and fresh herbs to create a low-fat light chowder.

But perhaps the crowning joy of summer is the homegrown (or almost homegrown) tomato. After a long winter of tough, tasteless orbs, the real thing finally arrives. These vitamin C–filled fruits, in fact, are featured in our watercress and fresh mozzarella salad. Start out by using plum tomatoes in early summer; then, as the season heats up, watch the intensity of redness develop before your eyes. Try all the varieties: the tiny round cherry tomatoes, long romatypes, red Marmandes (yellow, too), and large round reds, perhaps the juiciest contender of all!

Many would wager that the perfect summer dessert is a bowlful of fruit with a splash of (dare we?) heavy cream. Our desserts pay homage to the bounty of summer fruits in all of their wondrous simplicity. Melon, very rich in vitamin A, is coupled with raspberry sauce and fruit sorbet and garnished with mint. What to do with that brimming bushel of peaches? A peach and pecan crisp, bubbling and golden brown, will be sure to tempt you.

Or perhaps the mango will entice you to try our summer coupe. Sweet, spicy, and tasting somewhat like a peach, the mango, ranging in color from greenish-yellow, to orange, to red, and finally to purple, starts to peak in May and continues to be really flavorful throughout the summer. A ripe mango will feel soft to the touch, have a strong aroma, and show a few dark spots on the skin. Mangoes can be bought greenish-yellow, never green or black, and then ripened on the windowsill.

It is summer, the time to enjoy the abundance now available, all that is fresh and best. Your biggest dilemma will be what to choose.

❧

Grilled Summer Vegetables with Pesto

1 small eggplant, about 6 ounces, halved
    lengthwise
1 zucchini, about 6 ounces, halved lengthwise
1 yellow squash, about 6 ounces, halved
    lengthwise
1 red bell pepper, about 6 ounces, quartered
    lengthwise
3 tablespoons olive oil or vegetable oil
1 tablespoon balsamic or red-wine vinegar
1 garlic clove, mashed to a paste
1 tablespoon minced fresh orégano leaves
    or ½ teaspoon dried
1 teaspoon fresh thyme leaves or
    ¼ teaspoon dried

For the pesto
1 cup packed fresh basil leaves
2 small garlic cloves, chopped
¼ cup pine nuts
¼ cup freshly grated Parmesan
½ cup olive oil or vegetable oil

In a large glass or stainless steel baking dish arrange the vegetables in a single layer, cut side up, and sprinkle them with salt and pepper. In a small bowl whisk together the oil, the vinegar, the garlic, the orégano, and the thyme and pour the marinade over the vegetables. Let the vegetables marinate at room temperature for 1 to 2 hours, or chill them, covered, turning them once, overnight.

Make the *pesto*: In a food processor or blender combine the basil, the garlic, the pine nuts, and the Parmesan and purée the mixture. With the motor running, add the oil in a stream, blend the sauce until it is combined well, and add salt and pepper to taste. In a bowl chill the *pesto*, its surface covered with plastic wrap, until 30 minutes before serving.

Grill the vegetables over glowing coals about 5 inches from the heat, basting them with the marinade, for 5 to 7 minutes on each side, or until the vegetables are tender. On a platter halve the zucchini, eggplant, and squash pieces crosswise and serve them with the *pesto*. Serves 4.

Corn Chowder with Roasted Red Pepper

1 onion, minced
1 rib of celery, minced
2 tablespoons unsalted butter
3 cups fresh corn kernels (about 5 to 6 ears)
3 tablespoons all-purpose flour
5 cups canned chicken broth or chicken stock
  (page 117)
a cheesecloth bag containing 1 sprig of thyme
  or ½ teaspoon dried, 1 sprig of marjoram or
  ½ teaspoon dried, and 1 bay leaf
1 large red bell pepper
1 cup milk or plain yogurt
fresh lemon juice to taste
2 tablespoons snipped fresh dill or chives or
  minced parsley leaves

In a large saucepan cook the onion and the celery in the butter over moderate heat, stirring until the vegetables are softened. Add the corn and cook the mixture, stirring occasionally, for 3 minutes. Add the flour and cook the mixture over moderately low heat, stirring, for 2 minutes. Add the broth, the cheesecloth bag, and salt and pepper to taste, bring the liquid to a boil, stirring, and simmer the mixture, covered, for 20 minutes, or until the corn is tender. Discard the cheesecloth bag.

While the soup is cooking, prepare the red pepper. Broil the pepper under a preheated broiler about 4 inches from the heat, turning it frequently, for 10 to 12 minutes, or until it is blistered and charred. Put the pepper in a bowl and let it steam, covered, until it is cool enough to handle. Peel the pepper and dice it.

Add the diced pepper and the milk to the soup, bring the soup to a boil, and simmer it, stirring occasionally, for 5 minutes. Add the lemon juice and salt and pepper to taste and stir in the fresh herb of choice. Serves 6.

Tomato, Watercress, and Fresh Mozzarella Salad

8 small plum tomatoes, cored and cut into
  1-inch pieces
1 tablespoon minced fresh orégano or
  ¼ teaspoon dried
4 to 6 tablespoons extra-virgin olive oil
  (available at specialty foods shops and
  some supermarkets)
1 to 2 tablespoons Sherry wine vinegar or
  red-wine vinegar, or to taste
2 tablespoons minced fresh basil or
  parsley leaves
2 bunches watercress, rinsed and tough
  stems discarded
1 pound fresh mozzarella, sliced
24 oil-cured olives

In a bowl combine the tomatoes with the orégano, the oil, the vinegar, and salt and pepper to taste and let the mixture stand for 30 minutes. Add the basil and combine the mixture gently. Line 4 salad plates with the watercress leaves, mound the tomato mixture, drained, reserving the juices, in the center of each, and surround it with the mozzarella, drizzling the reserved juices over it. Garnish each plate with the olives. Serves 4.

⊸

Barbecued Game Hens with Gingered Honey Glaze

3 Rock Cornish game hens, split lengthwise
  and backbones removed
¼ cup vegetable oil or olive oil
6 tablespoons rice wine vinegar
3 garlic cloves, mashed to a paste
1½ tablespoons minced peeled fresh
  gingerroot
¼ teaspoon dried hot red pepper flakes
3 tablespoons honey, or to taste
3 tablespoons soy sauce
3 tablespoons minced fresh coriander

Pat the hens dry and arrange them in a large shallow glass or stainless steel baking dish. In a bowl combine the oil, the vinegar, the garlic, the ginger, the pepper flakes, the honey, the soy sauce, the coriander, and salt to taste, pour the marinade over the hens, and let the hens marinate, turning them once, for at least 1 hour at room temperature or chilled, overnight.

Grill the hens over glowing coals about 4 inches from the heat, basting them frequently with the marinade, for 10 minutes on each side, or until the juices run clear when the thighs are pricked. (Or broil the hens under a preheated broiler about 6 inches from the heat for 10 to 15 minutes on each side.) Serves 6.

Paella Valenciana al Fresco

1 cup minced onion

3 tablespoons olive oil or vegetable oil

1 red bell pepper, cut into 1-inch pieces

2 teaspoons fresh thyme leaves or
   1 teaspoon dried

2 tablespoons chopped fresh basil leaves or
   1 teaspoon dried

1 teaspoon cuminseed if desired

1 bay leaf

1 cup peeled, seeded, and chopped tomato

1 tablespoon minced garlic

2 cups brown basmati rice (available at health
   foods stores), or other long-grain rice

3½ to 4 cups canned chicken broth or chicken
   stock (page 117)

¼ teaspoon ground saffron or ¼ teaspoon
   ground turmeric

½ pound large shrimp, shelled and deveined

½ pound squid, cleaned, body sacks and flaps
   cut crosswise into ½-inch rings and
   tentacles cut crosswise into 1-inch pieces

6 cherrystone clams, cleaned (procedure
   follows)

6 mussels, scrubbed well, beards removed,
   and rinsed

1 cup fresh peas or frozen peas, thawed

minced fresh coriander for garnish
   if desired

lemon wedges as an accompaniment

In a paella pan (available at kitchenware specialty shops) or large deep ovenproof skillet cook the onion in the oil over moderate heat, stirring occasionally, until it is softened. Add the pepper, the thyme, the basil, the cuminseed, and the bay leaf and cook the mixture, stirring occasionally, for 3 minutes. Add the tomato, the garlic, and salt and pepper to taste and cook the mixture, stirring occasionally, until almost all the liquid has evaporated. Add the rice.

Preheat a charcoal grill. Just before assembling the paella, bring the chicken broth to a boil and stir in the saffron. Set the paella pan on the grill over glowing coals and stir in 3½ cups of the broth and salt and pepper to taste. Arrange the shrimp, the squid, the clams, the mussels, and the peas in the pan and cook the paella, without stirring, until the rice is tender, adding the remaining broth if necessary. (Cooking time will range, depending upon the intensity of the fire, from 30 minutes to 1 hour.) Discard any unopened clams and mussels. Remove the pan from the grill, cover it with a dish towel, and let the paella stand, undisturbed, for 5 minutes. (Alternatively, bake the paella on the bottom rack of a preheated 350° F. oven for 30 minutes, or until the rice is tender and the clams and mussels have opened. Let the paella stand, covered with a dish towel, for 5 minutes.)

Fluff the paella, garnish it with the coriander, and serve it with the lemon wedges. Serves 4 to 6.

To Clean Hard-Shelled Clams

Scrub the clams thoroughly with a stiff brush under cold water, discarding any that have cracked shells or that are not shut tightly.

Grilled Tuna à la Niçoise

four 6-ounce tuna steaks, each about 1-inch
    thick
2 tablespoons olive oil or vegetable oil
1 tablespoon fresh lemon juice
1 tablespoon fresh lemon thyme or thyme
    or 1 teaspoon dried thyme
1 garlic clove, minced
For the vegetable garnish
1½ pounds small red potatoes, scrubbed and
    cut into 1-inch pieces
3 tablespoons tarragon vinegar
2 tablespoons olive oil or vegetable oil
6 ounces wax beans, trimmed
6 ounces green beans, trimmed
For the dressing
1 tablespoon tarragon vinegar
2 tablespoons fresh lemon juice
1 to 2 teaspoons Dijon-style mustard,
    or to taste
⅓ to ½ cup olive oil or vegetable oil,
    or to taste

1 pint cherry tomatoes
½ cup drained Niçoise olives or similar olives
8 anchovy fillets
2 tablespoons minced fresh basil or parsley
    leaves or snipped fresh chives

Pat the tuna steaks dry and arrange them in a shallow
glass or stainless steel baking dish. In a small bowl
combine the olive oil, the lemon juice, the thyme, the
garlic, and salt and pepper to taste, pour the marinade
over the tuna, turning it to coat both sides, and marinate the tuna, covered and chilled, for 1 to 2 hours.

Prepare the vegetable garnish: Arrange the potatoes
in a steamer set over boiling water and steam them,
covered, for 17 to 20 minutes, or until they are just
tender. Transfer the potatoes to a large glass or stainless steel bowl and sprinkle them with the vinegar and
olive oil while they are still warm, tossing the mixture
gently. Let the potatoes cool and chill them, covered,
until 15 minutes before serving.

In a saucepan of boiling salted water cook the wax
beans and green beans together for 5 to 7 minutes, or
until they are just tender, drain them, and submerge
them immediately in a bowl of ice water. Drain the
beans, pat them dry, and chill them, covered, until
15 minutes before serving.

Make the dressing: In a bowl combine the vinegar,
the lemon juice, the mustard, and salt and pepper to
taste, add the oil in a stream, whisking, and whisk the
dressing until it is combined well.

Add ⅓ of the dressing to the potatoes and toss them
gently to coat them with the dressing. Transfer the
beans to a bowl, add ⅓ of the dressing, and toss them
gently to coat them with the dressing. In a bowl toss
the tomatoes gently with the remaining dressing.

Grill the tuna over glowing coals for 3 to 4 minutes
on each side for rare tuna. (Or broil the tuna under a
preheated broiler about 4 inches from the heat for 3 to
4 minutes on each side for rare tuna.) Divide the tuna
among 4 plates and arrange the vegetable garnish
around the steaks. Garnish each plate with some of the
olives and 2 anchovy fillets and sprinkle each serving
with the fresh herb of choice. Serves 4.

⊷

Summer Melon with Raspberry Sauce

1 pint fresh red raspberries or a 12-ounce
    package frozen red raspberries, thawed
3 tablespoons sugar, or to taste
1 tablespoon fresh lemon juice, or to taste
1 tablespoon *eau-de-vie de framboise*
    (raspberry-flavored liqueur), if desired
a summer melon, such as Bender, Crenshaw,
    or cantaloupe, halved, seeded, peeled, and
    sliced
assorted fresh fruit sorbet, such as lemon
    or orange
fresh mint leaves for garnish if desired

In a food processor or blender purée the raspberries
and strain the purée through a sieve into a bowl. Stir
in the sugar, the lemon juice, and the *framboise*, if
desired. Chill the sauce, covered, until ready to serve.

To serve, arrange the melon slices on dessert plates,
nap them with the sauce, and garnish each serving with
the sorbet and mint leaves. Serves 4 to 6.

Peach and Pecan Crisp

2½ pounds peaches, peeled, pitted, and sliced
¼ cup sugar, or to taste
1 tablespoon fresh lemon juice

1 tablespoon all-purpose flour
½ teaspoon cinnamon
⅛ teaspoon cloves
For the topping
¾ cup all-purpose flour
½ cup sugar
a pinch of salt
¾ stick (6 tablespoons) cold unsalted butter,
    cut into bits
½ cup chopped pecans

In a bowl combine the peaches, the sugar, the lemon juice, the flour, the cinnamon, and the cloves and transfer the mixture to a buttered 8-inch square baking pan or round pie pan.

Make the topping: In a bowl combine the flour, the sugar, and the salt, add the butter, and blend the mixture until it resembles coarse meal. Stir in the nuts. Sprinkle the topping over the peaches.

Bake the crisp in a preheated 375° F. oven for 50 minutes, or until the filling is bubbling and the top is golden. Serve the crisp warm. Serves 4.

Mango Coupes with Crystallized Ginger
2 ripe mangoes
1 to 2 tablespoons fresh lime juice, or to taste

2 to 3 tablespoons sugar,
    or to taste
1½ tablespoons minced crystallized ginger
½ cup fresh orange juice
frozen vanilla yogurt or vanilla ice cream
fresh mint leaves for garnish

Peel the mangoes and cut them lengthwise into thin slices. Reserve 12 of the largest, most attractive slices, sprinkle them with 2 teaspoons lime juice, or to taste, and chill them, covered, until ready to serve. Coarsely chop the remaining mango including the flesh on the ends and all around the pit. (There should be 1½ cups.)

In a saucepan combine the chopped mango, the remaining 4 teaspoons lime juice, the sugar, the crystallized ginger, and ⅓ cup water over moderate heat, bring the liquid to a boil, and simmer the mixture, covered, for 5 minutes, or until the mango is very soft. Transfer the mixture to a food processor or blender, add the orange juice, and purée the mixture until it is smooth. Strain the purée through a sieve into a bowl and chill the sauce, covered, until ready to serve.

Arrange the reserved mango slices in chilled coupes or dessert dishes, nap each dessert with sauce, and top each with the frozen yogurt. Garnish the coupes with the fresh mint. Serves 4.

FALL

he sun wanes a little each day until darkness descends at five. As if on cue, hearty pumpkins and winter squash color the fields. Days of clear-blue skies and crisp, dry air slowly turn colder and the threat of frost is upon us.

Inside we await comforting hearty fare made with apples and cranberries and pumpkin and, of course, turkey—the essentials of autumn. Then there are the squashes, so many of them it is hard to keep track of their names, and yes, even exotica—quince—if you are lucky enough to have that knobbly-looking fruit in your area.

Fennel, an autumn vegetable that in fact thrives when the temperatures fall, appears with its wispy fronds and pale-green whitish bulbs. Sweet and licorice in taste, fennel, also known as sweet fennel or anise, is often combined with potatoes in creamy, comforting gratins, frequent holiday fare. Here, we have paired it,

as a starter, with red peppers, very plentiful now and rich in vitamins A and C, and white beans, a member of the legume family and a well-known source of fiber.

Red bell pepper figures in another of our starters: eggplant *caponata*. For what would late summer and early fall be without mounds of those lustrous purple ovals? Similar, but not the same as that marvelous Mediterranean combination *ratatouille*, eggplant *caponata* shares many of the same ingredients, then ups the flavor quotient on its Provençale cousin by adding capers, olives, and anchovies.

If it is difficult to imagine the season without eggplant, try to imagine fall without the apple? Fall *is* apple season, and we celebrate its arrival in savory fashion with cider-braised chicken with apples. Both cider and fruit, chicken broth, and seasonal herbs create a heavenly, aromatic braising liquid for the fowl. The result is sweet in taste, tender, high in nutrition (vitamin C), and noticeably free of what might otherwise be a heavier cream-based sauce. Granny Smiths, Greenings, and Pippins are suggested, though any favorite tart apple variety may be used.

And, if it is November, it must be turkey. About those leftovers . . . let's see, there is creamed turkey, turkey hash, turkey sandwiches. This year, there *is* an alternative: our turkey tetrazzini, which is served over light and healthful spaghetti squash. Introduced in the 1970's, spaghetti squash is hard-shelled and yellow in color, with flesh that when it is cooked resembles strands of pasta in both texture and appearance. Here is an opportunity to use a low-calorie vegetable that is also priced right at this time of year as a substitute for noodles, good as they are.

Another seasonal must is broccoli, one of the single most nutritious vegetables, flush with protein, calcium, iron, and a host of vitamins. We have coupled broccoli with pasta and a very special morel sauce. The morel, with its smoky flavor and woodsy scent, is one of the tastiest varieties of wild mushrooms and considered by connoisseurs to be one of the finest. And while it will never win a beauty contest, it is well worth its hefty price. This vegetarian combination cooks the broccoli and the pasta in the same water, retaining many otherwise leached-off nutrients. The result is a low-fat, sophisticated but simple meal-in-one.

As to our fall desserts, we employ cranberries, in an icy spiced granita; pumpkin, in chewy, nutted date cookies; and the less commonly encountered quince in combination with the far more recognizable Bosc pear in a simple compote. A word about quinces, which we hope you can find in your local specialty markets: quinces peak in November but will store for months in a cool place. Resembling a short-necked pear, quinces are greenish to dark yellow in color and have a strong fragrance and a very tart taste. Like rhubarb, quinces must be cooked in sugar syrup to tone down their acerbic nature. Once cooked, the flesh turns pink or amber-hued, softens, and renders a haunting unique flavor.

And so it is with fall . . . while we struggle to hold on to the last days of summer, once we do let go, we can only embrace fall's remarkable fullness.

⋖

Roasted Red Pepper, White Bean, and Fennel Salad

1 pound small dried white beans, picked over
    and soaked in cold water to cover overnight
the white part of 1 leek, rinsed well and
    minced
1 rib of celery, minced
½ carrot, minced
1 garlic clove, minced
2 tablespoons olive oil
a cheesecloth bag containing ½ teaspoon dried
    thyme, 4 cloves, 1 bay leaf, and
    6 parsley stems
1 teaspoon salt
For the dressing
¼ cup fresh lemon juice
2 tablespoons balsamic vinegar
1 garlic clove, mashed to a paste, if desired
½ cup olive oil or vegetable oil

1 large red bell pepper, roasted (procedure on
    page 188), seeded and diced
1 cup diced fennel
½ cup minced scallion

¼ cup minced fresh basil or parsley leaves
2 tablespoons snipped fennel sprigs

Drain and rinse the beans. In a large saucepan cook the leek, the celery, the carrot, and the garlic in the oil over moderate heat, stirring until the vegetables are softened. Add the beans, the cheesecloth bag, and enough water to cover the beans by 1 inch and simmer the mixture, skimming occasionally, covered, for 15 minutes. Add the salt and cook the mixture for 10 to 15 minutes, or until the beans are tender. Drain the beans, reserving ½ cup of the liquid, discard the cheesecloth bag, and pour the reserved cooking liquid over the beans. Transfer the beans to a salad bowl.

Make the dressing: In a bowl whisk together the lemon juice, the vinegar, the garlic, and salt and pepper to taste, add the oil in a stream, and whisk the dressing until it is combined well.

Add the dressing, the roasted pepper, the diced fennel, the scallion, the basil, the fennel sprigs, and salt and pepper to taste to the beans and gently stir the mixture to combine it. Chill the salad, covered, for at least 1 hour or overnight. Let the salad stand at room temperature for 30 minutes before serving. Serves 6 to 8.

Eggplant Caponata

5 tablespoons olive oil or vegetable oil
1 pound eggplant, cut into 1-inch cubes
1 onion, minced
1 red bell pepper, cored, seeded, and diced
1 rib of celery, diced
1 pound tomatoes, peeled, seeded, and
    chopped
2 garlic cloves, minced
1 tablespoon tomato paste
½ teaspoon dried thyme
4 to 6 tablespoons red-wine vinegar,
    or to taste
2 tablespoons capers, drained
½ cup oil-cured black olives, pitted and
    chopped
¼ cup minced fresh basil or parsley leaves
4 anchovy fillets, or to taste, for garnish

In a large saucepan heat 3 tablespoons of the oil over moderately high heat until it is hot, add the eggplant, patted dry, and salt and pepper to taste, and sauté it, stirring occasionally, until it is golden. Transfer the eggplant to a bowl and add the remaining 2 tablespoons oil to the pan. Add the onion and the red pepper and cook the vegetables, stirring occasionally, until they are softened. Add the celery and cook it for 1 minute. Add the tomatoes, the garlic, the tomato paste, the thyme, and salt and pepper to taste and simmer the mixture, covered, stirring occasionally, for 15 minutes, or until almost all the liquid has evaporated. Transfer the mixture to a bowl, add the vinegar, the capers, the olives, the basil, and salt and pepper to taste and let the mixture cool. Chill the salad, covered, for at least 1 hour or overnight. Before serving, garnish the dish with the anchovies. Serves 4.

Moroccan Orange Salad with Pomegranates

4 navel oranges, peeled and pith removed
1 small red onion, sliced paper thin into rings
the seeds from 1 small pomegranate (available
    seasonally at specialty produce markets)
2 to 3 tablespoons extra-virgin olive oil, or to
    taste (available at specialty foods shops and
    some supermarkets)
1 to 2 tablespoons raspberry vinegar,
    or to taste
fresh mint leaves for garnish

Cut the oranges crosswise into ¼-inch-thick slices and arrange them in concentric circles in the center of a shallow serving dish. Scatter the onion slices around the edge of the dish and sprinkle the pomegranate seeds over the oranges. Drizzle the olive oil and the raspberry vinegar over the salad and garnish the salad with the mint. Chill the salad, loosely covered, until ready to serve. Serves 4.

❧

Cider-Braised Chicken and Apples

a 4-pound chicken, cut into serving pieces
flour for dredging the chicken
3 tablespoons vegetable oil
1 onion, minced
1 rib of celery, sliced
2 tart apples, such as Granny Smith,
    Greenings, or Pippins
3 tablespoons all-purpose flour
2 cups canned chicken broth or chicken stock
    (page 117)
1 cup apple cider
1 cheesecloth bag containing ½ teaspoon dried
    thyme, ½ teaspoon dried rosemary,
    ½ teaspoon dried sage, 1 bay leaf, and
    2 whole cloves
2 tablespoons unsalted butter
fresh lemon juice to taste
fresh sage leaves for garnish if desired

Pat the chicken dry, dredge it in the flour, shaking off the excess, and season the chicken with salt and pepper. In a casserole brown the chicken in the oil over moderate heat and transfer it to a plate. Add the onion, the celery, and 1 of the apples, peeled, cored, and cut into 1-inch pieces, to the casserole and cook the mixture, stirring occasionally, for 5 minutes, or until the onion is softened. Add the flour and cook the mixture over moderately low heat for 3 minutes. Add the broth, the cider, the cheesecloth bag, and the chicken and bring the liquid to a boil. Braise the chicken, covered, in a preheated 350° F. oven for 30 to 40 minutes, or until it is tender.

While the chicken is cooking, prepare the apple garnish. Peel, core, and cut the remaining apple into ¼-inch-thick slices. In a non-stick skillet melt the butter over moderate heat, add the apple slices, and cook them for 3 to 4 minutes on each side, or until they are golden.

Transfer the chicken to a shallow serving dish, garnish it with the apples, and keep it warm in a low oven. Discard the cheesecloth bag and skim the fat from the surface of the braising liquid. In a food processor or blender purée the braising liquid and the vegetables in batches and strain the mixture through a sieve back into the casserole. Bring the sauce to a simmer and season it with the lemon juice and salt and pepper. Pour the sauce over the chicken and apples and garnish the dish with the sage leaves. Serves 4 to 6.

Penne with Peppery Broccoli and Morel Sauce

½ ounce dried morels or similar mushrooms
  such as *cèpes* or *porcini*
½ cup olive oil
1 onion, minced
1 large garlic clove, minced
½ to 1 teaspoon dried hot red pepper flakes,
  or to taste
¼ cup minced fresh basil or parsley leaves
1 pound penne or similar tubular dried pasta
1 head of broccoli, separated into flowerets
  and stems peeled and cut into 1-inch pieces
  (about 1 pound in all)

In a bowl soak the mushrooms in 1 cup boiling water for 20 minutes, drain them, reserving the liquid, and slice them, discarding the tough stems. Strain the liquid through a fine sieve into a bowl and reserve ⅓ cup.

In a saucepan heat the oil over moderate heat until it is hot, add the onion and the mushrooms, and cook the mixture, stirring, until the onion is pale golden. Add the garlic and the red pepper flakes and cook the mixture, stirring, for 30 seconds. Add the reserved mushroom liquid and salt to taste and simmer the sauce for 1 minute. Stir in the basil.

In a large saucepan of boiling salted water cook the penne for 6 minutes, add the broccoli, and cook the mixture for 5 to 6 minutes more, or until the pasta is *al*

dente and the broccoli is just tender. Drain the mixture, transfer it to a heated bowl, and toss it with the sauce. Serve immediately. Serves 4 to 6.

Turkey Tetrazzini with Spaghetti Squash

a 3½-pound spaghetti squash
3 tablespoons unsalted butter
3 tablespoons flour
3 cups canned chicken broth or chicken stock
  (page 117)
1 bay leaf
3 cups diced cooked turkey
½ cup heavy cream or half-and-half
1 tablespoon Sercial Madeira or dry Sherry
½ cup freshly grated Parmesan
fresh lemon juice to taste
freshly grated nutmeg to taste
2 tablespoons fresh bread crumbs

Bake the spaghetti squash, pricked with a knife, on a baking sheet in a preheated 400° F. oven for 45 to 50 minutes, or until it is tender and let it cool. Halve the squash lengthwise, remove the seeds and center strings, and with a fork scrape the flesh from the skin into a buttered 13- by 9-inch baking dish. Season the squash with salt and pepper.

In a saucepan melt the butter, stir in the flour, and cook the *roux* over moderately low heat, stirring, for 3 minutes. Add the broth in a stream, whisking vigorously until the mixture is smooth. Add the bay leaf and salt and pepper to taste and simmer the sauce for 20 minutes. Stir in the turkey, the cream, and the Madeira, bring the liquid to a boil, and simmer the mixture for 5 minutes. Add ⅓ cup of the Parmesan, the lemon juice, and nutmeg and salt and pepper to taste. Discard the bay leaf.

Spoon the turkey mixture over the squash and sprinkle it with the remaining Parmesan and bread crumbs. Bake the dish in a preheated 350° F. oven for 25 to 30 minutes, or until the sauce is bubbling and the top is golden. Serves 4 to 6.

❧

Pumpkin, Date, and Nut Cookies

2 cups all-purpose flour
1 teaspoon baking soda
¼ teaspoon salt
1 teaspoon ground cinnamon
½ teaspoon freshly grated nutmeg
¼ teaspoon ginger
1 stick (½ cup) unsalted butter, softened, or
    vegetable shortening
1 cup firmly packed light brown sugar
1 large egg
1 teaspoon vanilla
1½ teaspoons grated orange rind
1 cup canned solid-pack pumpkin purée
1 cup chopped nuts, such as pecans or walnuts
½ cup finely chopped dates

Into a bowl sift the flour, the baking soda, the salt, the cinnamon, the nutmeg, and the ginger. In a bowl with an electric mixer cream the butter, add the sugar, and beat the mixture until it is light. Beat in the egg, the vanilla, and the orange rind. Add the pumpkin and stir in the nuts and the dates. Combine the flour mixture with the pumpkin mixture, drop the batter by heaping teaspoons onto greased baking sheets 1½ inches apart, and bake the cookies in a preheated 375° F. oven for 15 minutes, or until they are firm. Let the cookies cool for 3 minutes and transfer them to racks to cool completely. Makes about 4 dozen cookies.

Quince and Pear Compote

2 ripe quinces (available seasonally at
    specialty produce markets)
2 tablespoons fresh lemon juice
1 cup sugar
1 cinnamon stick, cracked
4 whole cloves
two 3-inch strips orange peel
two 2-inch strips lemon peel
2 ripe pears, such as Bosc

½ cup currants
1 teaspoon grated orange rind
½ teaspoon grated lemon rind
ice cream as an accompaniment if desired

Peel, core, and pit the quinces, reserving the peelings, cores, and pits, and cut the quinces into slices. In a bowl combine the slices with enough water just to cover them and add 1 tablespoon of the lemon juice.

In a saucepan combine the reserved quince parings with 1 quart water, bring the water to a boil, and simmer the mixture, covered, for 20 minutes. Uncover the mixture and boil the liquid until it is reduced to 2½ cups. Strain the liquid through a sieve into a saucepan, add the sugar, the cinnamon stick, the cloves, the orange peel, and the lemon peel and bring the liquid to a boil, stirring. Add the sliced quinces and poach them at a bare simmer, covered with wax paper, for 5 minutes, or until they are barely tender. Add the pears, peeled, cored, and sliced, the currants, and the remaining 1 tablespoon lemon juice and simmer the mixture, covered, for 5 to 7 minutes, or until the fruit is tender. Transfer the fruit with a slotted spoon to a serving dish and cover it loosely. Reduce the cooking liquid until it is syrupy, strain it over the fruit, and stir in the grated rinds. Let the compote cool and chill it, covered, until ready to serve. Serve the compote with ice cream. Serves 4.

Spiced Cranberry Granita

2 cups fresh cranberries, picked over
1 cup sugar
two 3-inch strips orange peel
6 whole cloves
1 cinnamon stick, cracked
1 teaspoon grated orange rind

In a saucepan combine the cranberries, 2 cups water, the sugar, the orange peel, the cloves, and the cinnamon stick over moderate heat, bring the liquid to a boil, stirring, and simmer the mixture, covered, for 15 minutes. Force the mixture through the fine disk of a food mill into a bowl, add the grated rind, and let the mixture cool. Pour the mixture into 2 freezer trays with dividers and freeze it, covered, until it is firm but not frozen hard. In a food processor purée the mixture until it is smooth, transfer it to a serving dish, and freeze it until the *granita* is firm. Serves 4.

WINTER

The first snows of winter have come, and a deep blanket of whiteness now covers the earth. Days shorten and time out-of-doors is limited. As the wind howls and radiators hiss and clang, we are drawn to the kitchen, where a variety of temptations fill the air. Here family and friends gather to sip a hot drink and chat while the chef of the house putters.

Colder temperatures call for warming, nutritious fare. Hardy traditional winter vegetables—celery, kale, collard greens, cabbage—as well as root vegetables—leeks, onions, potatoes, sweet potatoes, celery root, and carrots—are Mother Nature's ''gifts'' of nutritional goodness to warm the body and the spirit. Our recipes for this cold season put each of these vitamin-packed gifts to good use.

Winter is the natural time for soup, and we have created two different vegetable combinations. Our old-fashioned leek and potato soup, which can be used as either a starter or as a light entrée, is a simple preparation calling for only six on-hand ingredients. Thinned with buttermilk or yogurt, the soup is low in fat but

creamy in taste. A note on potatoes: generally speaking, white potatoes harvested west of the Mississippi are of the long variety and best for baking, while those grown east of that river are round and considered all-purpose. Leeks, while not as popular in this country as potatoes, contain essential vitamins, calcium, and iron. Be sure to rinse leeks thoroughly before using; they are known for stubbornly holding onto sand around their tightly wrapped leaves.

A host of other nutritious winter vegetables—cabbage, carrots, celery, green beans, and onions—are put to good use in our minestrone, almost a meal-in-one. Since all these vegetables are of the year-round variety, you could make this on any chilly day throughout the year. Either green cabbage or Savoy, both surprisingly rich in a variety of minerals, is appropriate. The greener the leaves, the fresher the cabbage. Look for solid, heavy heads, although Savoy cabbage will not be as hard as the other varieties.

Two of our winter starters highlight a legume and a root vegetable, both of which should be sampled not only for their good sense, but for their good taste as well. Lentils, a member of the Leguminosae family and a major source of vitamin C as well as soluble fiber, are most commonly used in soups; we have employed this healthful bean to star in a warm salad with garlic dressing, further enhanced, if desired, with bell peppers and smoked mozzarella. In full dress, this appetizer easily serves as a light lunch. Celery root, also known as celeriac, makes up for what it lacks in looks, rootlike, alas, in content. We have tapped this calcium-rich knob for *celeri-rave rémoulade*—a simple uncooked preparation featuring a light mustard vinaigrette.

Either of the above starters would serve as a lovely complement to the first of our winter entrées, roast duckling with chestnuts in maple syrup, a dish designed to capture the spirit of winter. We've cooked the duck very slowly to render its fat and produce a tender entrée. Chestnuts, an integral part of the sauce, were traditionally an American winter food; they no longer are grown domestically. At the turn of the century American chestnut trees were destroyed by an incurable disease called chestnut blight. Today, most chestnuts available in the United States come from Europe and the Orient.

Winter also means covered pies—a culinary tradition brought to our shores by early English settlers. Our scallop, collard green, and kale pie combines seafood and greens in a creamy sauce, then tops them with mashed potatoes and a dusting of Parmesan. Three vegetables plus seafood equal a notable meal-in-one. Collard greens and kale, both of which taste a little like green cabbage, are exceptionally nutritious year-round vegetables most flavorful during the cool months.

Speaking of pies, consider our orange sweet potato pie with gingersnap crust as a fitting finale to a dinner that features roast duckling with chestnuts in maple syrup. There are two types of sweet potatoes, those with orange skin with deep orange-colored flesh, often mistaken for yams (a completely different botanical family, in fact), and a white sweet or Jersey sweet potato with off-white or yellow flesh. Both are rich in iron and other essential minerals and vitamins. For the pie, be sure to choose orange sweet potatoes.

Winter gives us time to experiment in the kitchen and to enjoy each other's company over long and cozy meals in the comfort of our own homes. Bringing good food, essentially warming winter foods, and good friends together pleases both cook and diners alike. It is a time to reflect back, to look forward, and to cherish the time, and meals, in between.

Warm Lentil Salad

1 onion, minced
1 rib of celery, minced
1 tablespoon olive oil or vegetable oil
½ pound dried lentils, picked over
a 14½-ounce can tomatoes, puréed with
   the juice
1½ cups canned chicken broth or chicken
   stock (page 117)
2 garlic cloves, minced
½ teaspoon dried basil
½ teaspoon dried thyme
1 bay leaf
For the dressing
3 tablespoons fresh lemon juice
2 garlic cloves, minced fine, or to taste
¼ cup olive oil or vegetable oil,
   or to taste
¼ cup minced fresh parsley leaves

2 whole scallions, sliced thin

sliced bell peppers and smoked mozzarella as
   accompaniments if desired

In a saucepan cook the onion and the celery in the oil over moderate heat, stirring occasionally, until the vegetables are softened. Add the lentils, the puréed tomatoes, the broth, the garlic, the basil, the thyme, the bay leaf, and salt and pepper to taste, bring the liquid to a boil, and simmer the mixture, covered, stirring occasionally, for 45 minutes to 1 hour, or until the liquid has been absorbed and the lentils are tender. Transfer the lentils to a bowl and let them cool until they are warm.

Make the dressing: In a bowl combine the lemon juice, the garlic, and salt and pepper to taste, add the oil in a stream, whisking, and whisk the dressing until it is combined well. Stir in the parsley.

Add the scallions and the dressing to the lentils and stir the salad gently until it is combined well. Serve the salad with the sliced bell peppers and the smoked cheese. Serves 4 to 6.

Old-Fashioned Leek and Potato Soup

1½ pounds potatoes
1½ pounds (about 6 to 8 medium)
    white part of leek, well washed
    and chopped
2 ribs of celery, sliced
8 cups canned chicken broth or chicken stock
    (page 117)
1 cup buttermilk or plain yogurt
snipped fresh chives or fresh dill or minced
    fresh parsley leaves to taste

Peel and cut the potatoes into 1-inch pieces. In a large saucepan combine the potatoes, the leek, the celery, the broth, and salt and pepper to taste, bring the liquid to a boil, and simmer the mixture, covered, for 35 to 40 minutes, or until the vegetables are tender. In a food processor or blender purée the soup in batches and return it to the saucepan. (The soup may be prepared 1 day ahead to this point.) Add the buttermilk and salt and pepper to taste, bring the soup to a simmer, and cook it over low heat for 5 minutes. The soup may be served either hot or cold. Before serving, garnish the soup with the herb of choice. Makes 12 cups, serving 6 to 8.

Celeri-Rave Rémoulade
(Chilled Celery Root in Mustard Sauce)

1¼ pounds celery root, peeled and cut into
    julienne strips
1 teaspoon salt
4 tablespoons fresh lemon juice
2 tablespoons white-wine vinegar
For the dressing
3 tablespoons Dijon-style mustard
1 tablespoon fresh lemon juice
1 tablespoon white-wine vinegar
a pinch of sugar
½ cup olive oil or vegetable oil
2 tablespoons snipped fresh chives or minced
    parsley leaves

In a bowl toss the celery root with the salt, the lemon juice, and the vinegar and let the mixture marinate, covered and chilled, for 30 minutes to 1 hour. Drain the celery root and return it to the bowl.

Make the dressing: In a bowl whisk together the mustard, the lemon juice, the vinegar, the sugar, and salt and pepper to taste, add the oil in a stream, whisking, and whisk the mixture until it is combined well.

Add the dressing to the celery root and toss the salad. Sprinkle the salad with the herb of choice and chill it, covered, for at least 1 hour. Serves 4.

∽§

Roast Duckling with Chestnuts in
Maple Syrup Glaze

a 4½- to 5-pound duck, excess fat removed
    from the cavity, excess skin cut off from
    the neck end, and wings cut off at the
    second joint
2 garlic cloves, unpeeled and crushed
½ teaspoon dried thyme
½ teaspoon dried rosemary
1 bay leaf
For the glaze
¼ cup maple syrup
1 tablespoon red-wine vinegar
1 tablespoon fresh lemon juice
1 tablespoon soy sauce
1 tablespoon unsalted butter
2 teaspoons Dijon-style mustard, or to taste

1 pound chestnuts, shelled and peeled
    (procedure on page 274)

Pat the duck dry, prick it all over, and fill the cavity with the garlic, the thyme, the rosemary, the bay leaf, and salt and pepper to taste. Roast the duck on a rack set in a roasting pan in a preheated 450° F. oven for 30 minutes, reduce the heat to 275° F., and roast the duck for 1 hour and 30 minutes more. Drain the fat from the pan and chill the duck, covered, for at least 1 hour or up to 12 hours.

Make the glaze: In a small saucepan combine the maple syrup, the vinegar, the lemon juice, the soy sauce, the butter, and the mustard, bring the mixture to a boil, and simmer it, stirring, for 2 minutes.

Quarter the duck, removing the backbone and the breastbone, arrange the pieces in a baking pan, and scatter the chestnuts around them. Spoon the glaze over the duck and the chestnuts and roast the duck in a preheated 425° F. oven, basting occasionally, for 30 minutes, or until it is heated through and nicely glazed. Put the pan under a preheated broiler about 4 inches from the heat until the skin is crisp. Serves 4.

To Shell and Peel Chestnuts

With a sharp knife score each chestnut ¼ inch deep all around. In a baking pan roast the chestnuts in one layer in a preheated 450° F. oven for 10 minutes, or until the shells are just opened. Hold the chestnuts in a pot holder or thick towel and while they are still hot peel them.

Winter Vegetable Minestrone

1½ cups finely chopped onion
1 cup finely chopped carrot
1 cup finely chopped celery
2 tablespoons olive oil or vegetable oil
4 cups shredded green or Savoy cabbage
a 28-ounce can crushed tomatoes, including the liquid
8 cups canned chicken broth, chicken stock (page 117), or water
1 teaspoon dried basil
½ teaspoon dried thyme
½ teaspoon fennel seed
1 bay leaf
¼ pound green beans, trimmed and cut into 1-inch pieces
½ cup small pasta, such as small shells
1½ cups drained canned kidney beans
3 garlic cloves, minced fine
¼ cup minced fresh basil or parsley leaves
freshly grated Parmesan as an accompaniment if desired

In a large saucepan or casserole cook the onion, the carrot, and the celery in the oil over moderately low heat, covered, stirring occasionally, for 5 minutes. Add the cabbage, the crushed tomatoes, the broth, the basil, the thyme, the fennel seed, the bay leaf, and salt and pepper to taste, bring the liquid to a boil, and simmer it, covered, stirring occasionally, for 20 minutes, or until the vegetables are just tender. Add the green beans and the pasta and simmer the mixture for 10 minutes, or until the beans and pasta are tender. Add the kidney beans and the garlic and simmer the mixture, stirring occasionally, until the kidney beans are heated through. Stir in the basil. Ladle the minestrone into heated bowls and serve it with the Parmesan. Makes 12 cups, serving 6.

Scallop, Collard Green, and Kale Pie

1½ cups well washed, finely chopped leek or onion
2 tablespoons unsalted butter
¾ pound collard greens, well washed and chopped coarse
¾ pound kale, well washed and chopped coarse
1½ cups canned chicken broth, chicken stock (page 117), or water
1 bay leaf
1½ pounds Idaho or russet potatoes
¾ cup half-and-half or milk
4 teaspoons potato starch or cornstarch
1 pound sea scallops, halved, if large
½ cup freshly grated Parmesan
fresh lemon juice to taste
paprika to taste

In a large saucepan cook the leek in the butter over moderate heat, covered, stirring occasionally, until it is softened. Add the collard greens, the kale, and salt and pepper to taste and cook the mixture, covered, stirring occasionally, for 2 to 3 minutes, or until the greens have wilted. Add the chicken broth and the bay leaf, bring the liquid to a boil, and simmer the greens, covered, for 12 to 15 minutes, or until they are just tender. While the greens are cooking, prepare the potatoes. Peel the potatoes and cut them into 1-inch pieces. In a saucepan combine the potatoes with enough water to cover them by 1 inch, add salt to taste, and bring the water to a boil. Simmer the potatoes, covered, for 15 to 20 minutes, or until they are tender, drain them, and force them through a ricer into a bowl, or mash them. Beat in ¼ cup of the half-and-half and salt and pepper to taste.

In a small bowl combine the remaining half-and-half with the potato starch and stir the mixture until the starch is dissolved. Bring the collard green mixture to a boil, stir in the starch mixture, and simmer the mixture, stirring, for 1 to 2 minutes, or until it is thickened. Add the scallops and salt and pepper to taste and simmer the mixture, gently stirring, about 1 minute, or until the scallops are opaque and just firm to the touch.

Transfer the scallop mixture to a 1½-quart shallow baking dish and discard the bay leaf. Add ¼ cup of the Parmesan to the scallop mixture and salt, pepper, and lemon juice to taste and gently stir the mixture until it is combined. Spoon the potatoes over the scallop mixture, spreading them into an even layer, and sprinkle the top with the remaining ¼ cup Parmesan and paprika. (The pie may be prepared up to 6 hours in advance and be covered and chilled.) Bake the pie on a baking sheet in a preheated 375° F. oven for 20 to 25 minutes, or until the filling is gently bubbling. (The pie will take 10 to 12 minutes longer if it has been refrigerated.) Run the pie under a preheated broiler about 4 inches from the heat until it is golden. Serves 4 to 6.

✑

Orange Sweet Potato Pie
with Gingersnap Crust

For the crust

1 cup gingersnap crumbs

3 tablespoons sugar, or to taste

4 tablespoons unsalted butter, cut into bits
   and softened

2 large sweet potatoes

⅓ cup firmly packed light brown sugar

2 to 3 tablespoons honey or unsulfured
   molasses

2 large eggs, lightly beaten

2 teaspoons vanilla

2½ to 3 teaspoons grated orange rind

½ teaspoon cinnamon

¼ teaspoon freshly grated nutmeg

¼ teaspoon ground ginger

⅛ teaspoon ground clove

1 cup milk

Make the crust: In a bowl blend the gingersnap crumbs with the sugar and the butter and pat the mixture into the bottom and up the sides of a buttered 9-inch pie pan. Bake the crust in a preheated 350° F. oven for 5 minutes and let it cool on a rack.

Prick the potatoes with a fork and bake them in a preheated 400° F. oven for 45 minutes, or until they are tender. Let the potatoes cool and when they can be handled split them lengthwise. Transfer the pulp to a bowl and mash it with a potato masher. Measure 1½ cups mashed sweet potatoes and reserve the rest for another use.

In a bowl combine the mashed potatoes, the sugar, the honey, the eggs, the vanilla, the orange rind, the cinnamon, the nutmeg, the ginger, and the clove. Stir in the milk and pour the mixture into the pie shell. Bake the pie in a preheated 450° F. oven for 15 minutes. Reduce the oven temperature to 350° F. and bake the pie for 35 to 40 minutes, or until the filling is set. Let the pie cool on a rack. Serve the pie warm or at room temperature.

Banana and Walnut Tea Bread

1 cup all-purpose flour
1 cup yellow cornmeal
1 tablespoon double-acting
    baking powder
½ teaspoon baking soda
½ teaspoon salt
½ teaspoon cinnamon
¼ teaspoon allspice
½ cup vegetable shortening
1 cup sugar
2 large eggs, lightly beaten
1 cup mashed ripe bananas
    (about 2 large)
½ cup chopped walnuts

Into a bowl sift the flour, the cornmeal, the baking powder, the baking soda, the salt, the cinnamon, and the allspice.

In a bowl with an electric mixer cream the shortening with the sugar and beat the mixture until it is combined well. Add the eggs, a little at a time, and the mashed bananas and beat the mixture until it is just combined. Stir in the flour mixture and the nuts and pour the batter into a greased 9- by 5- by 3-inch loaf pan. Bake the bread in a preheated 350° F. oven for 1 hour to 1 hour and 15 minutes, or until a skewer inserted in the center comes out clean. Let the bread cool on a rack for 10 minutes and invert it onto the rack to cool completely. Makes 1 loaf.

Iced Lemon Lime Mousse

¾ to 1 cup sugar, or to taste
¼ cup fresh lime juice
¼ cup fresh lemon juice
1 teaspoon grated lime rind
1 teaspoon grated lemon rind
3 large egg whites at room temperature
½ cup chilled heavy cream
chocolate shavings for garnish if desired

In a heavy saucepan combine the sugar, the lime juice, the lemon juice, the lime rind, and the lemon rind and bring the mixture to a boil over moderately high heat, stirring and washing down any sugar crystals clinging to the sides of the pan with a brush dipped in cold water until the syrup is dissolved. Boil the syrup until it reaches the soft-ball stage, or a candy thermometer registers 238° F.

In a bowl with an electric mixer beat the egg whites until they hold soft peaks. Add the hot syrup in a stream, beating, and beat the meringue until it is stiff and cool.

In a chilled bowl with the mixer beat the heavy cream until it holds soft peaks and fold the cream gently but thoroughly into the meringue. Transfer the mousse to a 6-cup bowl or 6 individual serving dishes and freeze it, covered, in the freezing compartment of the refrigerator for at least 2 hours, or until it is frozen. Before serving, garnish the mousse with the chocolate shavings. Serves 4 to 6.

GUIDES TO THE TEXT

GENERAL INDEX

Page numbers in *italics* indicate color photographs
(M) indicates a microwave recipe

INDEX OF 45-MINUTE RECIPES

*Starred entries can be prepared in 45 minutes or less
but require additional unattended time

Page numbers in *italics* indicate color photographs

(M) indicates a microwave recipe

INDEX OF RECIPE TITLES

Page numbers in *italics* indicate color photographs
(M) indicates a microwave recipe

TABLE SETTING ACKNOWLEDGMENTS

To avoid duplication below of table setting information within the same menu, the editors have listed all such credits for silverware, plates, linen, and the like in its most complete form under "Table Setting."

Any items in the photographs not credited are privately owned.

Frontispiece

Chinese-Style Steamed Shrimp with Garlic and Scallions (page 2): Historic Charleston Reproductions "Blue Canton" porcelain plate by Mottahedeh—Bloomingdale's, 1000 Third Avenue, New York City.

The Menu Collection

Table Setting (page 8): See Table Setting credits for A New Year's Open-House Buffet below.

A New Year's Open-House Buffet

Table Setting (page 11): Puiforcat "Pompei Red" porcelain buffet plates; "Cardinal" sterling flatware—Puiforcat, 811 Madison Avenue, New York City. St. Louis "Diane" crystal wineglasses—Cardel Ltd., 621 Madison Avenue, New York City. Irish damask napkins; metal planter—J. Garvin Mecking Antiques, 72 East 11th Street, New York City. "Lion" creamware tureen and stand by Mottahedeh—Mottahedeh, Inc., 225 Fifth Avenue, New York City. Sterling ladle, circa 1780; porcelain service plate by Ron Dier; French sterling saltcellar, circa 1900; by Odiot—Thaxton & Company, 780 Madison Avenue, New York City. Sterling beaker, 1720, by John Bignell—Bulgari, 2 East 61st Street, New York City. Regency bronze mounted metal urn, circa 1815; late Empire gilt and patinated bronze candelabra, circa 1815; Louis XVI Rouge Royale marble top on nineteenth-century French steel base—Frederick P. Victoria & Son, Inc., 154 East 55th Street, New York

City. Flower arrangement—Mädderlake, 25 East 73rd Street, New York City.

Stuffed Breast of Veal with Paprika Sauce, Dilled Rice Pilaf (page 12): Robert Haviland and C. Parlon "Kakiemon" Limoges platter—The Metropolitan Museum of Art Gift Shop, Fifth Avenue at 82nd Street, New York City. Mason's ironstone tureen and stand, circa 1815; ironstone bowl, circa 1830—James II Galleries, Ltd., 15 East 57th Street, New York City. Sterling ladle, London, 1800—Thaxton & Company, 780 Madison Avenue, New York City.

Tangerine and Vanilla Bavarian, Rigo Jancsi (page 13): Glass and silver-plate compotes, circa 1910; silver-plate salver, circa 1870—James II Galleries, Ltd., 15 East 57th Street, New York City.

A Cross-Country Skiing Weekend

Creamy Polenta with Grilled Vegetables; Braised Rabbit Provençale; Garlic Bread; Arugula Salad with Orange Vinaigrette (pages 18 and 19): English stoneware plates; stainless-steel flatware—Dean & DeLuca Inc., 560 Broadway, New York City. Wineglasses; cotton napkins; wood cupboard with original paint, circa 1880—Wolfman • Gold & Good Company, 116 Greene Street, New York City. Earthenware platter—Mayhew, 507 Park Avenue, New York City. "Farm-house" antique pine tabletop on painted base; painted wood salad bowl; "Sundance" handmade stained wood chairs—Zona, 97 Greene Street, New York City. English brass candlesticks, circa 1715; eigh-

teenth-century English wood grain measures; English "bobbin" brass candlestick (one of a pair), circa 1865; English bronze preserve pot, circa 1875—Bob Pryor Antiques, 1023 Lexington Avenue, New York City.

Updated Classics

Scallop, Fennel, and Dill Gratins; Coq au Vin with Shiitake Mushrooms and Glazed Onions; Chicory and Endive Salad with Roquefort and Walnuts (page 21): Solanée "Water Lilies" faience plates; "Gascogne" hand-blown wineglasses—Solanée, 138 East 74th Street, New York City. "Spatours" silver-plate flatware—Pavillon Christofle, 680 Madison Avenue, New York City. Handmade platter by Lyn Evans—Gordon Foster, 1322 Third Avenue, New York City. Linen napkins—Cherchez, 862 Lexington Avenue, New York City. Luneville "Strasbourg Rose" faience salt and pepper shakers—Mayhew, 507 Park Avenue, New York City. "Woodrow" chintz fabric (available through decorator)—Brunschwig & Fils, 979 Third Avenue, New York City.

Easter Luncheon

Table Setting (page 23): French porcelain armorial dinner plates, circa 1820; English Ridgway porcelain dessert plates, circa 1830—Bardith Ltd., 901 Madison Avenue, New York City. Tiffany "Chrysanthemum" sterling flatware; French "Parrot" hand-painted porcelain candlesticks; French "Green Vine Nenuphal" hand-painted porcelain ginger jars (lids not shown)—Tiffany & Company, 727 Fifth Avenue, New York City. "Capri" embroidered linen place mats and napkins—Frette, 799 Madison Avenue, New York City. "Paris" crystal water goblets, wineglasses, and decanter; flat-cut crystal open salt and pepper with ivory spoons—Baccarat, Inc., 625 Madison Avenue, New York City. Flowers—Zezé, 398 East 52nd Street, New York City. Mahogany Chippendale armchairs, circa 1760—Kentshire Galleries Ltd., 37 East 12th Street, New York City. French 4-panel hand-painted screen, circa 1830; English Staffordshire 14-piece dessert service, circa 1870—Yale R. Burge Antiques, Inc., 305 East 63rd Street, New York City. "Pandora" silk fabric (available through decorator)—Clarence House, 211 East 58th Street, New York City. Mahogany dining table—Baker Furniture Company, 917 Merchandise Mart, Chicago, Illinois 60654. English Mahogany sideboard, circa 1790—Antiques Search, Louise McGill and Donna Rohs, (203) 655-6027 or (203) 655-3841. Portuguese needlepoint rug (available through decorator)—Patterson, Flynn & Martin, Inc., 950 Third Avenue, New York City.

Ham with Mustard Green Stuffing and Oat Wheat Crust, Brown Rice and Wild Rice Timbales (page 24): English Chamberlain Worcester porcelain platter, circa 1810—Bardith Ltd., 901 Madison Avenue, New York City. English "Shell" sterling carving knife and fork—James Robinson, 15 East 57th Street, New York City.

Tosca Cake, Candied Orange Ice Cream (page 25): English silver-plate salver, circa 1880; nineteenth-century English silver-plate and tortoiseshell cake knife—Thaxton & Company, 780 Madison Avenue, New York City.

Tray Meals

Sautéed Spiced Lamb Chops with Ginger Crisps, Minted Orzo with Currants, Sautéed Mixed Vegetables, Garlic Cumin Toasts (page 27): Ginori "Ercolano" porcelain dinner plate; "Lotus" wineglass designed by Andrée Putman for Sasaki; Val St. Lambert "Balmoral" crystal butter plate—Mayhew, 507 Park Avenue, New York City. English "Feather Edge" sterling

flatware—James Robinson, 15 East 57th Street, New York City. Linen napkin and tassel tie designed by Bebe Winkler—Henri Bendel, Frank McIntosh Shop, 10 West 57th Street, New York City. Victorian papier-mâché tray table, circa 1870—Kentshire Galleries Ltd., 37 East 12th Street, New York City. Victorian wool needlepoint pillow, circa 1880—Cherchez, 862 Lexington Avenue, New York City.

A Spring Luncheon

Table Setting (page 28): "Faux Bois" porcelain plates designed by Bill Goldsmith—Aventura, 463 Amsterdam Avenue, New York City. Céralene "Festivité" porcelain dessert plates—Baccarat, Inc., 625 Madison Avenue, New York City. Giraud porcelain cream soup bowls—Mayhew, 507 Park Avenue, New York City. "Old Italian" handcrafted sterling silver flatware; sterling silver salt and pepper shakers—Buccellati, Inc., 46 East 57th Street, New York City. English olive-cut wineglasses, circa 1870; English framed watercolors—Lenox Court Antiques, 972 Lexington Avenue, New York City. Linen tablecloth with crocheted lace, circa 1910; linen cutwork napkins with lace border, circa 1930—The Victorian Garden, 136-58 72nd Avenue, Flushing, New York 11367, (718) 544-1657. Victorian glass cachepot, circa 1880—James II Galleries, Ltd., 15 East 57th Street, New York City. Flower arrangement—Mädderlake, 25 East 73rd Street, New York City. Victorian walnut chairs upholstered in velvet—Newel Art Galleries, Inc., 425 East 53rd Street, New York City. English mahogany corner cabinet, circa 1880—Yale R. Burge, 305 East 63rd Street, New York City. Nineteenth-century English Staffordshire figures—Ages Past Antiques, 1030 Lexington Avenue, New York City. "Polyanthus" wallpaper (available through decorator)—Cowtan & Tout, 979 Third Avenue, New York City.

Toasted Coconut Cake with Lime Filling, Sliced Oranges (page 31): Sterling tray, Edinburgh, 1853; sterling spoons, London, 1838—F. Gorevic & Son, Inc., 635 Madison Avenue, New York City. Pressed glass compote, circa 1880—Vito Giallo Antiques, 966 Madison Avenue, New York City.

A Russian Easter Zakuska Party

Paskha and Kulich (page 32): Nicholas I "Banquet Service" porcelain plate, 1825-1855; Russian gilt bronze candlesticks, circa 1840—A La Vieille Russie, Inc., 781 Fifth Avenue, New York City. Nineteenth-century Russian enamel-on-silver plate—F. Gorevic & Son, Inc., 635 Madison Avenue, New York City. European silk brocade, circa 1860—Vito Giallo Antiques, 966 Madison Avenue, New York City. Hand-painted *faux* lapis lazuli background by Richard Pellicci, (212) 988-4365.

Smoked Salmon Canapés; Egg, Anchovy, and Caper Canapés; Radish Canapés; Creamy Mushroom Croustades; Blini with Caviar; Herring in Sour Cream Dill Sauce (page 33): Nicholas I "Banquet Service" porcelain plates; Russian silver tray with trompe l'oeil fringed cloth, Moscow, 1886; cut crystal caviar dishes mounted in silver by Fabergé, circa 1900—A La Vieille Russie, Inc., 781 Fifth Avenue, New York City. Reidel "Genova" glass bowl—Mayhew, 507 Park Avenue, New York City. Coin silver spoons, circa 1830; sterling silver spoon, circa 1890—Vito Giallo Antiques, 966 Madison Avenue, New York City. Gilded silver cream jug (ladle not shown), Moscow, 1882; Russian gilded silver and shaded enamel Easter eggs, circa 1900—A La Vieille Russie, Inc., 781 Fifth Avenue, New York City.

A Cinco De Mayo Dinner

Table Setting (page 35): Handmade ceramic dinner plates by Sara Post; Papago Indian bailing-wire basket; Beacon Mills cotton blanket, circa 1920—Zona, 97 Greene Street, New York City. Wood and steel flatware, circa 1910—Gail Lettick's Pantry & Hearth, 121 East 35th Street, New York City. Mexican hand-blown wineglasses, salad plates, and pitcher (holding flowers here); terra-cotta candlesticks; and painted metal "Tree of Life" candle holder (on wall)—Pan American Phoenix, The Market at Citicorp, 153 East 53rd Street, New York City. Guatemalan cotton place mats and napkins by Jorge Santos; Mexican pine table, circa 1900; chairs and bench, circa 1920; and hutch (far left of photo), circa 1890—Distant Origin, 153 Mercer Street, New

York City. Mexican handmade earthenware pot by Dolores Porras—Grass Roots Garden, 131 Spring Street, New York City.

Red Snapper Veracruz, Flour Tortillas, Mixed Vegetable Salad with Lime Vinaigrette (page 36): Ceramic platter; glass salad bowl—Mayhew, 507 Park Avenue, New York City. Mexican hand-blown glass sauce bowl; wooden servers—Pan American Phoenix, The Market at Citicorp, 153 East 53rd Street, New York City.

Creamy Cinnamon Rice Pudding with Fresh Fruit, Mexican Tea Cakes (page 37): Mexican hand-blown glass footed bowls and plate—Pan American Phoenix, The Market at Citicorp, 153 East 53rd Street, New York City.

A Bridal Shower

Chocolate Caramel Walnut Tartlets (page 38): Chase "Costa Azzurra" porcelain dessert plates—Chase Ltd., 19 Danbury Road, Ridgefield, Connecticut 06877.

Spinach and Feta Phyllo Rolls, Chicken Salmagundi, Coarse Mustard Vinaigrette, Russian Dressing, New Potatoes with Dill (page 39): Chase "Costa Azzurra" porcelain dinner and salad plates and serving dishes—Chase Ltd., 19 Danbury Road, Ridgefield, Connecticut 06877. Orrefors "Lisbet" wineglasses—Mayhew, 507 Park Avenue, New York City. "Fiddle, Thread & Shell" hand-forged sterling flatware and serving fork and spoon—James Robinson, 15 East 57th Street, New York City. Christofle "Spatours" and "Pompadour" silver-plate sauce ladles; "Perfection" crystal bowls—Baccarat, Inc., 625 Madison Avenue, New York City. Christofle "Perles" silver-plate tray—Pavillon Christofle, 680 Madison Avenue, New York City. Cutwork and embroidered linen place mats and napkins, circa 1900—Mark Walsh Collecting, Bergdorf Goodman, 754 Fifth Avenue, New York City. "Courtnay Strie" wallpaper (available through decorator); "Florence" cotton and linen fabric (available through decorator)— Brunschwig & Fils, Inc., 979 Third Avenue, New York City. English inlaid rosewood folding card table, circa 1815; Adams-style lyre-back armchairs, circa 1870—Kentshire Galleries Ltd., 37 East 12th Street, New York

City. English mahogany buffet-trolley—Howard Kaplan Antiques, 827 Broadway, New York City. English needlepoint rug, circa 1900—Coury Rugs, Inc., 515 Madison Avenue, New York City.

Luncheon Among the Rhododendrons

Table Setting (page 41): French faience dinner plates—Barneys New York, Seventh Avenue and 17th Street, New York City. French faience service plates—Solanée, 138 East 74th Street, New York City. Hand-forged "Feather Edge" sterling flatware—James Robinson, 15 East 57th Street, New York City. "Brummel" crystal water goblets and wineglasses; "Swirl" saltcellar and pepper cellar and ivory spoons—Baccarat, Inc., 625 Madison Avenue, New York City. Linen napkins with Italian *point de Venise* lace trim—Françoise Nunnallé Fine Arts (by appointment only, 212-246-4281). "Grapevine" cotton fabric (available through decorator)—Cowtan & Tout, 979 Third Avenue, New York City. Reproduction wicker chairs from Bielecky's original early-twentieth-century design (available through decorator)—Bielecky Bros. Inc., 306 East 61st Street, New York City.

Cold Peppered Tenderloin of Beef with Creamy Tarragon Caper Sauce; Squash Cups with Basil Vegetable Stuffing (page 42): English silver-plate tray, circa 1880—James II Galleries, Ltd., 15 East 57th Street, New York City.

Chocolate Raspberry Almond Torte; Raspberries (page 43): Silver-plate tray—F. Gorevic & Son, Inc., 635 Madison Avenue, New York City. "Vence" crystal bowl—Baccarat, Inc., 625 Madison Avenue, New York City.

A Middle Eastern-Style Dinner From the Grill

Apricot Frozen Yogurt (page 44): Brandy snifters—Mayhew, 507 Park Avenue, New York City.

Grilled Butterflied Leg of Lamb with Cumin; Grilled Marinated Eggplant and Red Onion; Pistachio, Currant, and Scallion Bulgur (page 45): Spode

Newstone platter and covered vegetable dish (one of a pair), circa 1820; English Ashworth ironstone platters, circa 1875—James II Galleries, Ltd., 15 East 57th Street, New York City. Nineteenth-century mother-of-pearl and sterling doors—Vito Giallo Antiques, 966 Madison Avenue, New York City.

Bastille Day Dinners

Table Setting (page 47): Taitu "Uno Blue" porcelain service plates; Giraud Limoges platter—Mayhew, 507 Park Avenue, New York City. Puiforcat "Cardinale" silver-plate flatware; silver-plate and enamel candlesticks— Puiforcat, 811 Madison Avenue, New York City. "Tastevin" crystal glasses; "Athena" crystal carafe—Baccarat, 625 Madison Avenue, New York City. Cotton napkins—D. Porthault & Company, 18 East 69th Street, New York City. Carafes (with flowers)—Bridge Kitchenware Corporation, 214 East 52nd Street, New York City. Wire basket—Pierre Deux, 870 Madison Avenue, New York City. Flowers—Zezé, 398 East 52nd Street, New York City. French cherry wood table, circa 1860; French side chairs, circa 1780; French table and hurricane lamps, circa 1860, with early-twentieth-century decorative finishes—Pierre Deux Antiques, 369 Bleecker Street, New York City. French doors with beveled panes, Paris, 1890 (one of 2 pairs of doors); cast-iron *bombé* balcony, Paris, 1890—Howard Kaplan Antiques, 827 Broadway, New York City. "La Villageoise" cotton fabric (available through decorator)— Brunschwig & Fils, 979 Third Avenue, New York City.

Gâteau de Mousse à la Nectarine, Eclairs au Moka (page 49): "Sceaux Fleurs" French hand-painted faience plate—The Mediterranean Shop, 876 Madison Avenue, New York City.

Un Pique-nique Sur Mer

Lemon Almond Madelaines, Melons and Macerated Raspberries (page 50): French rilsan and rattan chaise with detachable foot rest—T & K French Antiques, Inc., 120 Wooster Street, New York City.

Pan Bagnas, Marinated Black and Green Olives (page 51): Acrylic plates—Saks Fifth Avenue, New York City. Lee Bailey Shop, 611 Fifth Avenue, New York City. Cotton fabrics—Pierre Deux, 870 Madison Avenue, New York City. Plastic wineglasses—The Pottery Barn, 117 East 59th Street, New York City. Shell, ceramic crock—Bridge Kitchenware Corporation, 214 East 52nd Street, New York City.

A Poolside Spanish Luncheon

Table Setting (page 53): "The Bird" hand-thrown and hand-painted stoneware designed for Simon Pearce Pottery by Miranda Thomas; "Bell" hand-blown wineglasses and carafe—Simon Pearce Glass & Pottery, The Mill, Quechee, Vermont 05059. Italian cotton napkins—Frank McIntosh Shop at Henri Bendel, 10 West 57th Street, New York City.

Almond Flan with Summer Fruit (page 55): Ginori porcelain platter—Mayhew, 507 Park Avenue, New York City.

A Summer Supper

Blueberry Lemonade Sorbet (page 56): French sundae glasses (from a set of six)—Williams-Sonoma, Mail Order Department, P.O. Box 7456, San Francisco, CA 94120-7456.

Shrimp and White Bean Salad, Corn-Salad-Stuffed Tomatoes, Italian Toasts (page 57): Hutschenreuther "Sita" porcelain dinner plate; "Next" stainless steel flatware by Boda Nova; "Wonderful" Riedel Crystal of America wineglass—Mayhew, 507 Park Avenue, New York City. Hand-painted linen napkin by Liz Wain; rattan tray—Henri Bendel, Frank McIntosh Shop, 10 West 57th Street, New York City. "American" painted iron sofa (pillows not included) and tray on folding base designed by Hervé Baume; Chinese straw rug (available through decorator)—The Syllian Collection, 21 East 67th Street, New York City. Flowers, hanging plants, ferns, and small basket—Bridge Nurseries, 437 North Street, Greenwich, Connecticut.

Labor Day Clambake

Deep-Dish Blueberry Pie, Vanilla Ice Cream, Peach Schnapps and Vodka

Plugged Watermelon (page 59): "Louise" enamelware plates designed by Robert Steffy—Wolfman • Gold & Good Company, 116 Greene Street, New York City. White Mountain 2-quart ice-cream freezer—Williams-Sonoma, 20 East 60th Street, New York City.

Lobsters; Steamers; Sage, Lemon, and Garlic Butter; White Onions and Red Potatoes; Corn on the Cob; Tomato Butter; Parker House Rolls; Caramel Lemonade (pages 60 and 61): Enamelware serving spoons designed by Robert Steffy; galvanized pails with copper handles—Wolfman • Gold & Good Company, 116 Greene Street, New York City. Handloomed cotton throw by Turquerie—available at leading department stores.

Dinner Italian Style

Ocean Perch Fillets with Fennel, Tomato, and Fried Basil Leaves (page 63): Swid Powell "Delos" porcelain plates—Bergdorf Goodman, 754 Fifth Avenue, New York City. "Ottagonale" water and wineglasses designed by Carlo Moretti—Avventura, 463 Amsterdam Avenue, New York City. "Tiber" sterling flatware; chased sterling bud vases; "Empire" sterling open salts—Buccellati, Inc., 46 East 57th Street, New York City. "Present Mood #4" 9- by 6-foot wool rug designed by Christine Van der Hurd; "Karina" stained ashwood chairs; "Balestro" wood-and-chrome table base and glass top—Classic Age, 41 East 11th Street, New York City.

Dinner For A Special Occasion

Table Setting (page 64): Hand-painted porcelain dinner plates by Judicone exclusively for Barneys New York, Seventh Avenue and 17th Street, New York City. Giraud Limoges soup plates—Mayhew, 507 Park Avenue, New York City. "Orsay" crystal water glasses and wineglasses—Baccarat, Inc., 625 Madison Avenue, New York City. English silver flatware by Mappin & Webb—F. Gorevic & Son, Inc., 635 Madison Avenue, New York City. Reproduction eighteenth-century English sterling candlesticks; English sterling open salts by Samuel Hennell, London, 1798—Bulgari, Hotel Pierre, 2 East 61st Street, New York City. Hand-painted napkins by Liz

Wain—Tesoro Collection, 319 South Robertson Boulevard, Los Angeles, California 90048. Flowers designed by H. Robb Alverson for The Rhinelander Florist, Inc., 14 East 60th Street, New York City.

Four-Peppercorn Pork Roast, Wild Rice with Currants and Scallions, Crisp Braised Celery (page 66): Rectangular Sheffield plate tray, circa 1810—S. Wyler, Inc., 941 Lexington Avenue, New York City. Round silver-plate tray; sterling carving set and serving spoon—F. Gorevic & Son, Inc., 635 Madison Avenue, New York City. Nineteenth-century English silver-plate ladle—James II Galleries, Ltd., 15 East 57th Street, New York City. Dr. Wall Worcester gold and white porcelain dish and *sucrier*, circa 1770—Bardith Ltd., 901 Madison Avenue, New York City.

Deep Chocolate Torte with Coffee Buttercream (page 67): Hand-forged sterling platter—James Robinson, 15 East 57th Street, New York City. Paris porcelain footed basket, circa 1820—Bardith Ltd., 901 Madison Avenue, New York City.

A Picnic Under The Apple Tree

Curried Butternut Squash Soup, Assorted Sausages and Cheeses, Pickled Red Onions, Chutney, Olives, Mustard, Assorted Breads (page 69): Bennington stoneware mugs; glass jars (plastic lids not shown)—D.F. Sanders & Company, 952 Madison Avenue, New York City. Ceramic-handled cheese knife—Thaxton & Company, 780 Madison Avenue, New York City. Bread boards—Gail Lettick's Pantry & Hearth Antiques, 121 East 35th Street, New York City. Reversible denim and mattress ticking picnic cloth designed by Michael Formica for Chateau • X—Chateau • X, (212) 477-3123.

Thanksgiving Dinner

Table Setting (page 71): Mottahedeh "Tobacco Leaf" porcelain dinner plates and "pomegranate box"—Bloomingdale's, 1000 Third Avenue, New York City. "Wilton" hand-wrought sterling flatware—Old Newbury Crafters, Inc., (800) 343-1388. "English Shell" hand-forged sterling seafood forks; English wineglasses, circa 1850—James Robinson, 15 East

57th Street, New York City. Amber glass rummers, circa 1860; blown-glass carafes, circa 1790—Bardith Ltd., 901 Madison Avenue, New York City. Damask napkins from Mark Walsh Collecting—Bergdorf Goodman, 754 Fifth Avenue, New York City. George III sterling salts by William Smith, London, 1784; sterling salt spoons, circa 1840; cut-glass sugar bowl (with nuts), circa 1820; wine rinsers (with celery and olives), circa 1810; Old Sheffield plate telescopic candlesticks, circa 1785—S.J. Shrubsole Corporation, 104 East 57th Street, New York City. Tole cachepots (on table), circa 1820; *faux-marbre* tazzas (on chest between windows), circa 1800—Kentshire Gallery at Bergdorf Goodman, 754 Fifth Avenue, New York City. Marble fruit (in tazzas)—Lexington Gardens, 1008 Lexington Avenue, New York City.

Roast Turkey with Five-Rice and Chestnut Stuffing and Mushroom Giblet Gravy; Sweet Potato Purée with Walnuts; Cauliflower with Cheddar Sauce and Rye Bread Crumbs; Lima Beans with Bacon; Cranberry Citrus Relish (pages 72 and 73): Mottahedeh "Tobacco Leaf" porcelain platter; Royal Worcester "Gourmet" white porcelain casseroles—Bloomingdale's, 1000 Third Avenue, New York City. Spode pottery dishes, circa 1820—Bardith Ltd., 901 Madison Avenue, New York City. "Old Newbury" hand-wrought sterling carving knife and fork; "Windsor Shell" hand-wrought sterling serving spoon and sauce ladle—Old Newbury Crafters, Inc., (800) 343-1388.

A Holiday Weekend Breakfast

Glazed Cinnamon Buns, Cranberry Applesauce (page 74): Glass compotes—Mayhew, 507 Park Avenue, New York City.
Turkey, Ham, and Vegetable Hash with Fried Eggs; Sesame Maple Corn Sticks (page 75): Bridgewater "Brown Hen" pottery plates, cups, saucers, teapot, coffeepot, and creamer; Liberty Tree painted carved-wood chicken—Bergdorf Goodman, 754 Fifth Avenue, New

York City. "Fiddle Thread" hand-forged sterling flatware—James Robinson, 15 East 57th Street, New York City. Glasses—Mayhew, 507 Park Avenue, New York City.

Christmas Dinner

Table Setting (page 77): Minton porcelain dinner plates, 1852—James II Galleries, Ltd., 15 East 57th Street, New York City. English "Kings" hand-forged sterling flatware; sterling saltcellar and pepper shaker, 1927; "Kings" sterling salt spoon—James Robinson, 15 East 57th Street, New York City. "Empire" crystal water goblets and wine glasses—Baccarat, Inc. 625 Madison Avenue, New York City. Scottish engraved glass rummers, circa 1860; Vaseline glass nut dishes, circa 1880; Vaseline glass vases, circa 1875; Russian brass and etched-glass hurricane lamps, circa 1850; glass urns, circa 1835; cranberry glass bowl, circa 1850; Nailsea glass bells, circa 1830—James II Galleries, Ltd., 15 East 57th Street, New York City. Damask tablecloth and napkins—Frette, 799 Madison Avenue, New York City. Cranberry-over-clear-glass decanters, circa 1870—Kentshire Gallery at Bergdorf Goodman, 754 Fifth Avenue, New York City. Nineteenth-century papier-mâché side chairs—Newel Art Galleries, Inc., 425 East 53rd Street, New York City. Fireplace decoration and ornaments—Zezé, 398 East 52nd Street, New York City.
Roast Goose with Sausage, Fennel, and Currant Stuffing and Wild Mushroom Port Gravy; Sautéed Potatoes and Celery Root; Brussels Sprouts and Carrots with Shallot Butter (page 78): Mason's ironstone platter, circa 1815; Wedgwood creamware sauce tureen, circa 1810; creamware footed bowl, circa 1790; Spode creamware dish, circa 1810—Bardith Ltd., 901 Madison Avenue, New York City. Silver-plate sauce ladle, circa 1875; sterling carving set, 1903—James II Galleries, Ltd., 15 East 57th Street, New York City. English rosewood breakfast table, circa 1810—Florian Papp Inc., 962 Madison

Avenue, New York City.
Black Forest Cake, Eggnog Ice Cream (page 79): Royal Worcester porcelain dessert plates, circa 1860—Kentshire Gallery at Bergdorf Goodman, 754 Fifth Avenue, New York City.

A Southern Tree-Trimming Party

Southern Coffee Parfaits, Praline Butter Cookies (page 80): West Virginia Glass parfait glasses—Mayhew, 507 Park Avenue, New York City. Hand-painted "Ivy" cookie jar by Barbara Eigen—Carmel Bay Co., Ocean Avenue and Lincoln Street (P.O. Box 5606), Carmel, California 93921.
Lobster, Oyster, and Sausage Gumbo; Rice with Red Beans and Peas; Fried Cornmeal-Coated Okra (page 81): Handmade ceramic dinner plates, bowls, and "Ivy" serving bowl by Barbara Eigen—Carmel Bay Co., Ocean Avenue and Lincoln Street (P.O. Box 5606), Carmel, California 93921. Oneida silver-plate flatware—Oneida Silversmiths, Oneida, New York 13421. Riedel "Wonderful" wineglasses—Mayhew, 507 Park Avenue, New York City. Hand-painted linen tablecloth and napkins by Liz Wain—Gibraltar, 154 King Street, Charleston, South Carolina 29401.

A Recipe Compendium

Grilled Pork Tenderloin with Mustard Cream Sauce (page 82): Haviland "Marco Polo" porcelain dinner plate and Old Newbury Crafters "Scandia" sterling flatware from Cardel, Ltd., 621 Madison Avenue, New York City. Hem-stitched linen napkin from Cherchez, 862 Lexington Avenue, New York City. Hand-painted background by Richard Pellicci, (212) 988-4365.

Back Jacket

Apple Strudel Tartlets with Hard Sauce: Nineteenth-century Quimper earthenware dessert plates from Barneys New York, Seventh Avenue and 17th Street, New York City.

If you are not already a subscriber to *Gourmet* Magazine and would be interested in subscribing, please call *Gourmet*'s toll-free number, 1-800-365-2454.